HEARTBREAKING NEWS

On July 28, 1944, General Patton was given control of the troops of the Third Army then on the Continent of Europe.

The First Army had begun its St. Lô push on July 26. Gaining in momentum in the succeeding days, it came to a climax when General Patton exploded his Third Army onto the Brittany Peninsula on August 1.

In two weeks, troops of the Third Army had driven the fleeing Germans into the ports of Lorient and Brest and had cleared the Loire River to Angers. The drive of the Third Army to the east had by-passed Paris and had reached Reims, Verdun, and Commercy.

By the end of August, the Germans were on the run. At this point, General Patton presented his case for a rapid advance to the east for the purpose of cutting the Siegfried Line before it could be manned. Bradley was very sympathetic, but SHAEF, Supreme Headquarters, Allied Expeditionary Force, did not concur.

All supplies—both gasoline and ammunition—were to be thrown into the First Army's move north so Patton's Third Army had no gas with which to move; he was heartbroken.

"It was my opinion then that this was the momentous error of the war."

—General George S. Patton

THE BANTAM WAR BOOK SERIES

This series of books is about a world on fire.

The carefully chosen volumes in the Bantam War Book Series cover the full dramatic sweep of World War II. Many are eyewitness accounts by the men who fought in a global conflict as the world's future hung in the balance. Fighter pilots, tank commanders and infantry captains, among many others, recount exploits of individual courage. They present vivid portraits of brave men, true stories of gallantry, moving sagas of survival and stark tragedies of untimely death.

In 1933 Nazi Germany marched to become an empire that was to last a thousand years. In only twelve years that empire was destroyed, and ever since, the country has been bisected by her conquerors. Italy relinquished her colonial lands, as did Japan. These were the losers. The winners also lost the empires they had so painfully seized over the centuries. And one, Russia, lost over twenty million dead.

Those wartime 1940s were a simple, even a hopeful time. Hats came in only two colors, white and black, and after an initial battering the Allied nations started on a long and laborious march toward victory. It was a time when sane men believed the world would evolve into a decent place, but, as with all futures, there was no one then who could really forecast the world that we knew now.

There are many ways to think about that war. It has always been hard to understand the motivations and braveries of Axis soldiers fighting to enslave and dominate their neighbors. Yet it is impossible to know the hammer without the anvil, and to comprehend ourselves we must know the people we once fought against.

Through these books we can discover what it was like to take part in the war that was a final experience for nearly fifty million human beings. In so doing we may discover the strength to make a world as good as the one contained in those dreams and aspirations once believed by heroic men. We must understand our past as an honor to those dead who can no longer choose. They exchanged their lives in a hope for this future that we now inhabit. Though the fight took place many years ago, each of us remains as a living part of it.

WAR AS I KNEW IT

GEORGE S. PATTON, JR.

Annotated by Colonel Paul D. Harkins

BANTAM BOOKS

TORONTO • NEW YORK • LONDON • SYDNEY • AUCKLAND

*This low-priced Bantam Book
has been completely reset in a type face
designed for easy reading, and was printed
from new plates. It contains the complete
text of the original hard-cover edition.*
NOT ONE WORD HAS BEEN OMITTED.

WAR AS I KNEW IT

*A Bantam Book / published by arrangement with
Houghton Mifflin Company*

PRINTING HISTORY

*Houghton Mifflin edition first published November 1947
20 printings through April 1979*

*Serialized in Saturday Evening Post
November 1947 and March 1976*

Bantam edition / January 1980
2nd printing .... *April 1980*
3rd printing .... *August 1981*

*Drawings were prepared especially for this edition
by Greg Beecham.*

The selection from "The Young British Soldier," from De-
partmental Ditties and Barrack-Room Ballads, *by* Rudyard
Kipling, *copyright 1892, 1893, 1899, 1927, by Rudyard Kipling,
and the selection from "If," from* Rewards and Fairies, *by
Rudyard Kipling, copyright, 1910, by Rudyard Kipling, are
reprinted by permission of Mrs. George Bambridge and Dou-
bleday and Company, Inc.*

ISBN 0–553–20491–2

Published simultaneously in the United States and Canada

Bantam Books are published by Bantam Books, Inc. Its trademark, consisting of the words "Bantam Books" and the por-
trayal of a rooster, is Registered in U.S. Patent and Trademark
Office and in other countries. Marca Registrada. Bantam
Books, Inc., 666 Fifth Avenue, New York, New York 10103.

PRINTED IN THE UNITED STATES OF AMERICA

12 11 10 9

DEDICATION

"My sword I give to him that shall succeed me in my pilgrimage, and my courage and skill to him that can get it. My works and scars I carry with me, to be a witness for me that I have fought His battles who now will be my rewarder."

So he passed over and all the trumpets sounded for him on the other side.

PILGRIM'S PROGRESS

ACKNOWLEDGMENTS

The work of an editor is not easy, especially when that editor is also a wife, and it is with a grateful heart that I acknowledge the help of many friends in preparing this book for publication. I am especially indebted to Colonel Paul D. Harkins, my husband's deputy Chief of Staff throughout the war, for his first-hand knowledge and for the careful research embodied in his footnotes and prefaces; and to Douglas Southall Freeman, whom my husband held in honor as the greatest military biographer of our time, for his introduction to *War As I Knew It*.

BEATRICE AYER PATTON

CONTENTS

Part Three—RETROSPECT

MAPS

INTRODUCTION

General George S. Patton, Jr., kept a full diary from July, 1942, until Dec. 5, 1945, four days before his fatal accident. His entries sometimes were made while the froth and emotion of battle were still upon him. They are always candid, frequently critical, and occasionally caustic, though they never are savage in the sense that they damn everybody who did not agree with him. The spirit of the diary is that of a commander who believed that a continuous bold offensive would end the war before the snow fell on the Ardennes in the winter of 1944-45. Every obstacle to such an offensive had to be overcome; every leader who opposed it must be challenged to show why the drive would not succeed; silence or dissent appeared in Patton's eyes as overcaution or concession to Allies.

This dominant tone of General Patton's diary is so unmistakable and so clearly patriotic that it will not be misunderstood by historians; but because General Patton used words as he employed fire—to get decisive results quickly—he said many things in his diary that would hurt the feelings of individuals whose devotion and ability he would be quick to acknowledge. The diary includes more than one reference to leaders whom Patton himself criticized sharply and, as he thought, justly; but when those same individuals were treated unfairly or were blamed by others where Patton considered them correct in their action, he instantly became their defender. All this will be plain when time gives perspective. For the present, those military writers whom Mrs. Patton has consulted about the publication of the diary of 1942-45 agree with her that it should be withheld from publication.

This decision might be disservice to the study of the West-European campaign of 1944-45 if General Patton had not written *War As I Knew It.* He undertook this small book after the close of hostilities and he drew heavily from the diary for detail. Some pages of the narrative are almost verbatim the text of the diary, with personal references toned down or eliminated. Because the General himself had made extracts from the diary, the possibility of incorporating other parts of it in this volume had to be considered. This applied particularly to the account of the Battle of the Bulge, which is treated much more fully in the diary than in this text. Experiment showed that the inclusion of expurgated diary-entries might mislead the reader, and that printing those items in full would be doing what General Patton apparently had decided not to do when, with the diary on his desk, he wrote *War As I Knew It.*

The text as here printed is, then, precisely as it came from the General's swift pen with the single elimination of a criticism of one officer who, if he erred, most splendidly atoned. That incident was of no large importance in relation to the operations of the Third Army, and of none whatever in its effect on the campaign. For the rest, assurance may be given that, so far as somewhat careful comparison of the two documents has disclosed, the diary contains nothing of significance, with respect to the planning and the execution of the campaign, that is not summarized by the General in this volume. The reader loses only the strong flavor of the diary; the student may be confident that when the day-by-day is printed, it will not refute any sound conclusion based on this narrative. Something in addition may be learned from the diary by future soldiers concerning the morale of the Third Army. The vital subject of integrated command may be illustrated by other entries. Meantime, national defense loses no lesson that Patton thought America might learn from his experience. It is gratifying to be able to state this and thereby to justify withholding the diary itself at a time when Patton's forthright criticism of individuals might offend their sensibilities without contributing to military security.

General Patton had unfailing humor, soldierly-sharp powers of observation and interest that ranged from horses and yachts to archaeology and ethnology. He wrote with judgment and enthusiasm of much that he saw and he was most delightfully himself in his letters. These papers fall into two groups—those that were meant for the eyes of Mrs. Patton only, and those she quite properly had called "open letters," which she was free to show the General's friends. By good chance, some of the most charming of the "open letters" relate to the period of operations which General Patton covered lightly, or not at all in *War As I Knew It*. To introduce the man who appears in Normandy, it has seemed appropriate to publish the letters that relate to the campaign in Africa and in Sicily. These are not, strictly speaking, military papers, but they have interest in themselves besides showing what manner of man George Patton was.

Including these letters, *War As I Knew It* represents a type of early narrative—one might say of provisional narrative—that had a place in the historiography of the Second World War. The present book corresponds, for example, to the memoirs that Jubal A. Early, John B. Hodd, Richard Taylor, and Joseph E. Johnston issued a few years after the collapse of the Southern Confederacy, with the happy difference that Patton had no defeat to excuse, no grievance to vent. Those early Confederate books were undocumented and in some particulars inaccurate but they have great historical value because they were written while some of the impressions of war were fresh.

About 1960 Americans may expect more deliberate works of a character similar to the memoirs of Grant, of Sherman, and of Sheridan. Some of those future volumes will be more accurate historically than the military autobiographies issued immediately after the war. Gain in this respect may be offset by the failures of memory and by the treacherous and ineradicable impulse of a certain type of mind to read into the planning of military operations a purpose that could not have been foreseen. After 1965 or 1970 glamor will begin to envelop memoirs. Few will be valuable; most of them will deceive more than they will enlighten.

By that time, it should be possible to write measurable accurate biographies of the leading figures of the war. The official source material for those *"lives"* is so vast that if only the more important army reports of the Second World War were printed, they would fill, it is estimated, 1000 volumes of the size of the *Official Records of the Union and Confederate Armies*. As no comprehensive publication of the reports of 1941-45 is contemplated, some documents of value may be lost and not be recovered again within the next twenty-five or thirty years. In spite of this, the picture of the leaders will be clear enough in two or three decades for the biographer to undertake his task. It is to be hoped that General Patton will be among the first to attract a competent biographer and that others will leave him alone. He was a man to win, to intrigue, and sometimes to enrage his fellow-commanders. Always he fulfilled the Napoleonic mandate of supplying by picturesque conduct the *causerie de bivouac* that makes soldiers swear at their commander and then swear by him. In the larger qualities of leadership, Patton's daring reminds one of "Stonewall" Jackson. His determination to push straight to the Rhine of course recalls Sherman's march to the sea. Patton was cast in the mold of great American soldiers; his personal papers are among the fullest left by an American General. He will be an ideal subject for a great biography.

DOUGLAS SOUTHALL FREEMAN

Westbourne,
Richmond, Virginia,
July 26, 1947

PART ONE

OPEN LETTERS FROM AFRICA AND SICILY

General George S. Patton

1

OPERATION "TORCH"

Although the material that follows on the African Campaign has little to do with the actual fighting, because of the restriction imposed by censorship at the time it was written, a brief summary of the military campaign will perhaps prove useful to orient the reader.

On November 8, 1942, three task forces, of which Western Task Force was one, landed on the north coast of Africa.[1] *Its ground forces were commanded by Major General Patton and its headquarters were based on an Army table of organization, to be designated Fifth Army Headquarters after landing.*[2] *Western Task Force was composed of three task units: the northern, under Major General Lucien K. Truscott, landing at Port Lyautey; the central, under Major General Jonathan W. Anderson,*

---

[1] The following story was told me by the Public Relations Officer of the War Department, Major General A. D. Surles. On the evening of November 7, 1942, his office was invaded by the press. They begged for news; some even threatened the officer in charge. Finally, one said. "Come on, boys, let's go to the White House; they're always good to us there," and the newsmen left the office in a body.

Mr. Stephen Early, the President's secretary, met them at the door of the White House office with his usual cordiality, invited them in, and urged them to be seated. When he had done the honors, he excused himself, saying, "I'll be back in a minute." Fifteen minutes went by; then half an hour, and the press began to wonder. Someone tried the door. They were locked in.

At last, Mr. Early came in, waving a dispatch. "It's all over boys!" he shouted. "Our troops have landed. Turn on the radio." *B. A. P.*

[2] Subsequent orders changed this.

3

landing at Fedhala;[1] and the southern, under Major General Ernest A. Harmon, landing at Safi. The Army air elements were commanded by Brigadier General John K. Cannon. The task force consisted of about thirty-two thousand men. The armada was under the command of Admiral H. K. Hewitt until such time as the ground and air forces should be firmly established ashore. The Admiral zigzagged his convoy of approximately one hundred vessels across the Atlantic for fourteen days without incident, and assisted in the landings with bold support and tireless effort on the part of his entire personnel.

The landings were a complete surprise to the French, and the fighting, as evinced by the casualties, was severe. The French Navy, both at sea and on land, fought viciously and heroically to the end.

On November 11, as ground troops were alerted and the planes were over the target, the French signaled "Enough," thus missing by minutes the probable destruction of Casablanca, which was only stopped by a miracle of communication.

The peace was signed at Fedhala that afternoon, and General Patton toasted the heroic dead of both nations with the wish that they fight side by side to the destruction of the Nazis.

Rehabilitation of the harbor, roads, and railroads was started at once, and within two weeks American units were training the French in modern weapons of war.

Early in March, 1943, General Patton was ordered to Tunisia to command the II Corps, which had suffered a serious setback at Kasserine Pass. This corps was a part of the Eighteenth Army Group, under General Sir Harold Alexander. The purpose of the operation was to assist the advance of the British Eighth Army, under General Montgomery, by threatening General Rommel's rear in the vicinity of Gafsa. Late in April, Major General Omar N. Bradley took over the II Corps and General Patton returned to his interrupted work of planning the invasion of Sicily.

P.D.H.

---

[1] General Patton landed at Fedhala.

North Africa

I am sending this back by Captain Gordon Hutchins of this ship, the *Augusta*. By the time it reaches home, everything that has happened will be in the papers. We left Norfolk at 8:10 A.M. of the twenty-fourth and the sortie was remarkable for its orderly, and apparently faultless, efficiency. We moved in column through the mine fields and out the swept and buoyed channel, where we joined a line of five columns with the *Augusta* leading.

November 2

This mess is the best I have ever seen. I fear I shall get fat. I take lots of exercise each morning, including chinning myself and running in place four hundred and eighty steps (one quarter mile) in my cabin. In the morning, at battle stations, we put on rubber belts and tin hats, but as my battle station is my cabin, I don't have to hurry. Then I go up on the flag bridge till it gets light and then have breakfast. Just finished reading the Koran—a good book and interesting.

Have been giving everyone a simplified directive of war. Use steamroller strategy; that is, make up your mind on course and direction of action, and stick to it. But in tactics, do not steamroller. Attack weakness. Hold them by the nose and kick them in the pants.

November 6

In forty hours I shall be in battle, with little information, and on the spur of the moment will have to make most momentous decisions, but I believe that one's spirit enlarges with responsibility and that, with God's help, I shall make them and make them right. It seems that my whole life has been pointed to this moment. When this job is done, I presume I will be pointed to the next step in the ladder of destiny. If I do my full duty, the rest will take care of itself.

November 8

Last night I went to bed, dressed, and slept from 10:30. This was hard to do. I went on deck at 2 and saw the Fedhala and Casablanca lights burning, also shore lights. Sea dead calm—no swell. God is with us.[1]

We have had a great day so far and have been in a naval battle since eight. At 7:15, six enemy destroyers came out of Casablanca; two were on fire. All ships in range opened on them and they went back. The *Massachusetts* had been shelling the *Jean Bart* for about thirty minutes. I was going ashore at eight and my boat was on the davits with all our things, including my white pistols. I sent an orderly to get them, and at that moment a light cruiser and two big destroyers came out of Casablanca, tearing up the coast close to shore, to try and get our transports. The *Augusta* speeded up to twenty knots and opened fire. The first blast from the turret blew our landing boat to hell, and we lost everything except my pistols. At about 8:20, enemy bombers attacked the transports and the *Augusta* went to protect them. Then we went back into the fight with the French ships, and fired hard for about three hours. I was on the main deck when a shell hit so close it splashed water all over me, and later, on the bridge, one hit even closer, but I was too high to get wet. It was hazy and the enemy used smoke well. I could just see them and make out our splashes with our ships all firing like hell and going in big zigzags and curves to keep the enemy from our subs.

Admiral Hall, Chief of Staff to Admiral Hewitt, my Chief of Staff, Colonel Gay, Colonels Johnson and Ely, on the Staff of the Amphibious Landing Force, Atlantic Fleet, my Aides, Jenson and Stiller, and Sergeant Meeks and I went ashore at 12:42, and as our boat left the ship, the sailors leaned over the rail and cheered. We hit

---

[1]When Operation "Torch" was being planned, it was ascertained from local knowledge that there are only twelve days of the entire year when a landing is even possible.

the beach at 13:20, getting very wet in the surf. There was still quite a fight going on, but I had no bullets.

Harmon took Safi before dawn, though we did not get the news until noon.

Anderson had both rivers and the high ground by noon and captured eight of the German Armistice Commission. They only heard of the landing at six, so it was a complete surprise.

While we were still in Washington, Colonel W. H. Wilbur volunteered to go to Casablanca to demand the surrender. He landed in the first wave and drove to Casablanca in the dark with a white flag. He was shot at several times en route, but at Casablanca the French honored his flag, although they declined to surrender.

November 11

I decided to attack Casablanca this day with the 3rd Division and one tank battalion. It took some nerve, as both Truscott and Harmon seemed in a bad way, but I felt we should maintain the initiative. Then Admiral Hall came ashore to arrange for naval gunfire and air support and brought fine news. Truscott has taken the airfield at Port Lyautey and there are forty-two P-40's on it. Harmon is marching on Casablanca.

Anderson wanted to attack at dawn, but I made it 7:30, as I wanted no mistakes in the dark. At 4:30 this morning, a French officer came to say that the forces at Rabat had ceased firing, and all the Staff wanted to call off the attack. However, I said it must go on. I remembered 1918, when we stopped too soon. I sent the French officer to Casablanca to tell Admiral Michelier, in command at Casablanca, that if he did not want to be destroyed, he had better quit at once, as I was going to attack—I did not say when. I then sent word to Admiral Hewitt that if at the last minute the French quit, I would radio "cease firing." That was at 5:30. At 6:40 the enemy quit. It was a near thing, for the bombers were over their targets and the battleships were in position to fire. I ordered Anderson to move into the town, and if anyone stopped him, to attack. No one stopped him, but the hours from 7:30 to 11 were the longest in my life so far.

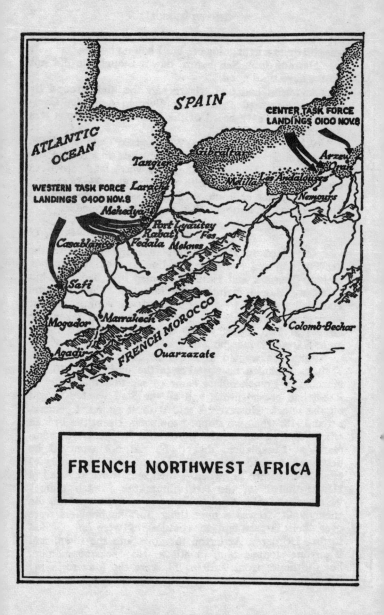

FRENCH NORTHWEST AFRICA

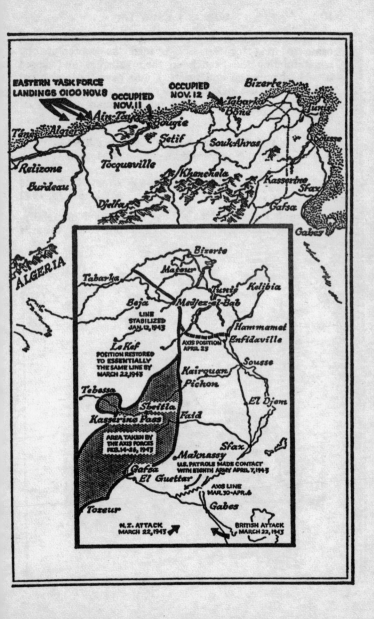

At 2 o'clock, Admiral Michelier and General Noguès came to treat for terms. I opened the conference by congratulating the French on their gallantry and closed it with champagne and toasts. I also gave them a guard of honor—no use kicking a man when he's down.

Noguès and I are calling on the Sultan in a day or two.

Visit of the Commanding General and Staff to General Noguès and the Sultan of Morocco

HEADQUARTERS WESTERN TASK FORCE
November 16, 1942

We left Casablanca, a city which combines Hollywood and the Bible, at 9:45, and proceeded towards

105 mm. Howitzer

Rabat. The country after passing Fedhala is the finest tank country I have ever seen, being rolling and open with here and there stone farms which would make infantry strongpoints, but would be useless against the 105 mm. gun.

The country in general is reminiscent of the Kona coast of Hawaii. The trees are identical, and the sea is the same startling blue. We passed large flocks of sheep and herds of cattle, all of them of nondescript breeds. All the road and railway bridges were guarded by a type of Moroccan irregular called "Goons"[1]—at least that is how it sounds. They are dressed in a black-and-white striped bathrobe, with a turban which was, some years ago, probably white, and are equipped with very ancient rifles and bayonets.

After passing Fedhala, the power of the Navy-Air arm was frequently evinced by destroyed trucks and armored cars which littered the road. On reaching Rabat, General Harmon[2] had provided an escort for me consisting of scout cars and tanks. However, I felt that to arrive at General Noguès'[3] Residency with such a force would appear boastful on my part, so I dismissed them.

Upon reaching the Residency, we were met by a battalion of Moroccan cavalry, only the officers mounted. Also, the bodyguard of the Governor General, who are Moroccans, dressed in white uniform with red leather equipment. The pistol and cartridge pouch was fastened in the middle of the stomach with cross-belts.

Both guards were very impressive, and each had its own field music, consisting of French trumpets, drums, and a brass umbrella with bells around the edge which continually rotated during the playing of the ruffles and flourishes.

We inspected both guards and complimented the French officers, commending them on their appearance, which was truly soldierly in the 1914 meaning of the word. It was rather pathetic to think that one of the

[1]Goumiers.

[2]Commanding the 2d Armored Division, part of which landed in Morocco.

[3]Général d'Armée Auguste Noguès, French Resident General of Morocco.

light tanks in the escort which I had turned down could have easily destroyed all of the splendid creatures standing at salute.

The Residency is a beautiful marble structure, built on the lines of the Alhambra, by Marshal Lyautey,[1] and I could well see why General Noguès did not want to leave it. He received us very cordially, and we talked for about twenty minutes, when it was time to proceed to the palace of the Sultan.

The palace grounds, which comprise several hundred acres, are surrounded by a wall some twenty feet high, alleged to have been built in 1300. This I seriously doubt, although it is certainly very old.

After passing through the wall, we went for about half a mile through the native huts, which apparently housed the retainers and their very numerous progeny. The palace itself is a tremendous three-story white building of Moorish architecture, which you enter through a gate just wide enough to permit the passing of an auto.

Inside, the palace guards, composed of black troops dressed in red coats, red bloomers, and white gaiters, and armed with rifles, were drawn up completely around the square. I should think at least four hundred men were present.

We dismounted, and another field music, equipped with drums, cymbals, horns, and the metal umbrella, played with great abandon.

On the left side of the gate as you entered was the green flag of the Faithful. It is made of velvet, has a gold border, and certain Arabic words in the center. Having passed through this second gate, we came into the Old Testament, a large court which was completely encircled by men dressed in white Biblical costumes. Here the Grand Vizier, or so I took him to be, met us. He was dressed in a white robe with a hood and wore underneath it a silk headdress embroidered in gold. He had the most enormous set of gold inlaid teeth I ever saw, and a scraggly beard. He told us that the Sultan had graciously consented to receive us, which, in view of the preparations, was already evident.

We mounted three flights of stairs, and on reaching

---

[1] Marshal Lyautey, 1854-1934.

the top, our guide removed his shoes. We then entered a long room with the twelve apostles and some reserves along the left side, and on the right side were a large number of gold chairs, Louis XIV model.

The floor was covered with the thickest and most beautiful rugs I have ever seen. At the end of the room on a raised platform sat the Sultan, who is a very handsome young man, extremely fragile, and with a highly sensitive face.

When you first enter, you halt and bow from the hips. You advance halfway up the room and repeat the operation. You then advance to the edge of the platform and bow a third time. The Sultan got up and shook hands with me and with General Noguès, and we all sat down.

The Sultan, talking in Arabic, although he has a perfect command of French, told the Grand Vizier to tell me in French how glad he was to see me. I then talked to him through two interpreters, expressing my contentment that his people and the French and ourselves were again reunited, and assured him that our one desire was to unite with his people and the French in making common head against the enemy. It was very amusing to see that he could understand the French conversation perfectly, but had to wait to have it translated into Arabic because his dignity did not permit him to admit that he knew a foreign language.

When the initial conversation had terminated, he informed me that, since we were in Mohammedan country, he hoped the American soldier would show proper respect for Mohammedan institutions. I told him that such an order had been issued in forceful language prior to our departure from the United States and would be enforced. I further stated that since in all armies, including the American Army, there might be some foolish persons, I hoped that he would report to me any incidents of sacrilege which some individual soldier might commit. He replied that no such incidents would happen, but that if they did, he would bring them to my attention through General Noguès.

I finished by complimenting him on the beauty of his country, the discipline of his citizens, and the splendid-looking cities. We then rose, he got off his throne and shook hands and invited me to come on Wednesday to a tea, celebrating his ascension to the throne. It had been originally intended for me to visit him on that day, but I had informed General Noguès that, since I represented the President of the United States and the Commanding General of the Allied Forces, it would be inappropriate for me to come to an audience. His inviting me to the audience indicated clearly that he appreciated my position.

When this conversation was finished, we met the twelve wise men and their reserves, about sixteen in all. They were the Pashas of the various provinces and cities of Morocco. Apparently a Pasha is a lifetime job, the senior member being ninety-two years old; the junior, I should think, was about seventy. They were all dressed in white and in their stocking feet, and were a most distinguished-looking group of men, evidently habituated to command.

We then left the palace and were again saluted by the Red Guards. We proceeded to General Noguès' Residency, where we were entertained by Madame Noguès and her niece, and treated to a most sumptuous lunch in the best taste. General Noguès impressed on me that at no time during the German occupancy had any German occupied his house or sat at his table.

After a short conversation at the end of the meal, we left, reaching Casablanca at three o'clock.

The Sultan's Anniversary

HEADQUARTERS WESTERN TASK FORCE
November 22, 1942

The second visit to the Sultan was similar to the first, except that we had an escort of a squadron of cavalry from the Residency to the palace. The men were mounted on white stallions, with white capes and blue hoods thrown back, white turbans, red coats with brass buttons and brass frogs. Three officers rode with us, one on each side and one behind the car. The mounted trumpeters played during the whole course of the ride.

On reaching the palace, a whole regiment of cavalry was drawn up. One squadron was equipped with lances. This regiment and the escort had the finest mount I ever saw. Inside the outer courtyard, we had the Black Guard, which consists of huge Senegalese, with red coats and red fezes, red leather equipment, and white spats. We also had a band similarly accoutered, which played the Moroccan national air and the *Marseillaise*.

We were met by the Grand Vizier, or Mufti, who took us into the inner court, where two very old gentlemen with staves, as in Biblical plays, preceded us. Each of these men had some sort of cartridge box tied around his stern and was also armed with a very long curved scimitar in a red leather scabbard.

The throne-room and the vestibule outside were crowded with chiefs: the farther away from the throne, the lesser the chief. The high chiefs, who were arranged on the left as one approaches the throne, were very fine-looking men, and all of them quite old and quite large.

The Sultan was accompanied by the Prince Imperial, one of his sons, about fourteen years old. The Prince Imperial sat in the first chair, Noguès in the second, and I in the third. On the previous visit, I had sat in the first and Noguès in the second, but this arrangement was quite proper. General Noguès then read a long prepared oration in French, which was translated into Arabic by the Grand Vizier, who already had a copy of it in his possession. He then very solemnly presented the Sultan with his—the Sultan's reply—neatly written in Arabic longhand, which the Sultan read and which the Grand Vizier translated into French from a paper he already held in his hand.

While this was going on, I became more and more impressed with the fact that the United States was playing too small a role, so when Noguès stopped speaking and stepped from the front of the throne, I stepped out without asking anyone's permission and spoke, as nearly as I can remember, as follows:

> Your Majesty, as a representative of the great President of the United States, and as the commander of a huge military force in Morocco, I wish to present the compliments of the United States on this occasion, the fifteenth anniversary of your ascension to the throne

of your ancestors, and I wish to assure you
that so long as Your Majesty's country, in
co-operation with the French Government of
Morocco, co-operates with us and facilitates
our efforts, we are sure, with the help of God,
to achieve certain victory against our common
enemy, the Nazis.

I am convinced that Your Majesty and the
French Government of Morocco share this
opinion. So long as we are in accord on this
point, we have only the brightest future to look
forward to. I am impelled to the belief in this
mutual accord when I remember that one of
Your Majesty's great predecessors presented to
our famous President, George Washington, the
buildings now occupied by the American Mission at Tangiers, and when I also remember
that since the days of the great Washington, the
accord and friendship with the French has been
equally profound.

I wish to take this occasion to compliment Your Majesty on the intelligent co-operation which his subjects have accorded to the
Americans and also to express again my profound appreciation of the excellent bearing and
splendid discipline of Your Majesty's soldiers.

One point of interest about the Sultan is that he
is supposed to wear a beard but prefers to go clean-
shaven, with the result that he gets by by using either
hand clippers or a razor, and has a beard not over a
thirty-second of an inch long. His mustache is equally
abbreviated. He is also not supposed to wear European
clothes, but has been seen by some of our officers and
numerous French officers riding about the country on
horseback, unattended, in English riding clothes. I am
certain he speaks French and almost certain he speaks
English. In fact, I have heard a rumor that he was
graduated from Oxford under an assumed name.

The tea on the afternoon of the ascension celebra-
tion was attended by nearly everybody of any importance. As I was unable to go, I asked General Harmon
to attend for me. During the tea some screams were

heard followed by two shots. The Sultan excused himself and walked out with great dignity and after a while returned. General Noguès asked him what happened. He said that one of the panthers in the museum had made a very beautiful leap of twenty feet and had gone through a hole and started to eat up one of the ladies of the harem, but some of the guards had shot it. The lady was only cut on the throat, and it made little difference, as she was not a wife, but a concubine. With this slight interruption the tea went on.

The old *kasbas* or forts are very interesting and really quite formidable obstacles. There are a good many of them in the country, particularly in the mountains. They have the Moorish type of crenelation, and have out-jutting towers about every two hundred yards of front. Some of the walls are ten feet thick.

Some of these forts are alleged to be of Roman origin, but as yet I have never seen one that looked that old. The fort at Port Lyautey, which held out against us for three days and was finally taken through the use of a self-propelled 105 mm. gun, blasting breaches through which the 2d Battalion, 60th Infantry,[1] assaulted with grenades and bayonets, is a very tough proposition. It had resisted six-inch naval fire, trench-mortar fire, and dive-bombers, and only yielded to the ever-victorious doughboy with the rifle and grenade. I did not go too closely into the question of who survived in the garrison, but doubt whether any of them did. In such a close fight a soldier has no time to change his mind.

Owing to the fact that there is very little you can buy in Morocco, money has ceased to have value, and it is very difficult to employ help. We are making arrangements to sell the commodities which the Arabs mostly desire, namely: sugar, tea, rice, coffee, and cloth at a low price to Arabs who work for us. We will pay the Arabs in francs, and in this way rehabilitate the value of money.

This morning General Keyes[2] and I went to the Catholic Church, which was very crowded and unques-

---

[1] Colonel F. J. de Rohan.
[2] Major General Geoffrey Keyes, Deputy Commanding General, Western Task Force.

M 7

tionably contained a large number of widows of men we had killed. Most of these people were quite young and dressed in black and were weeping, but seemed to have no animosity against us.

Madame Hardion, the wife of the Minister for Civilian Affairs, explained the situation by the fact that, after 1940, the French were so ashamed of themselves that they had no pride, and the women were more ashamed than the men; therefore, when we came they were delighted to fight with us in what she termed was a friendly manner. Seeing that they certainly lost between two and three thousand killed on shore, and at least five hundred killed at sea, while we lost better than seven hundred ashore in killed and wounded, I do not think that it was a very friendly sort of war. She insisted that it was, and that it had done a great deal to raise the morale of the French people. Particularly was this true of the French women, who formerly had been so disgusted with the men that they would not live with them. In view of the number of children on the streets, I can hardly credit this last statement.

So far I have only seen one drunken American soldier, and he was being taken care of by two of his friends in a very creditable way. Our men have had a hard time, because only on the twenty-first did we get kitchens ashore, and we have no tentage except pup tents. However, they are in very good spirits, and the health of the command remains excellent except for a little diarrhea which lasts about a day and is, I believe, attributable to the water.

It is very interesting to note the change coming over the soldiers. When they first got here, they were extremely sloppy, probably because of excessive fatigue, but within the last two days our efforts at smartening them up have borne fruit, and shortly, I believe, they will be a credit to any country.

In the fields the plowing is done with the most peculiar combinations of animals. The peasants either use a horse and a camel, a burro and a camel, a bull and a camel, or a bull and a horse. I am informed that they cannot use two camels because they fight each other. Any animal hooked up with a camel becomes disgusted and loses interest in life.

The French Army, particularly General Martin at Marrakech, has been extremely friendly. General Martin has given two parties to officers of the 47th Infantry[1] from Safi, and has invited me and any of my staff to come and stay with him for an indefinite period. I am planning to visit him shortly.

During 1940, General Martin commanded the 67th Moroccan Division, which was beaten. When General Anderson[2] called on him, he brought out the flag of the division, which he no longer commands, and asked General Anderson to remove the crepe with which it was decorated. This was to be done as a sign that the shame of the division had been removed by the fighting which General Martin had done against us. He then cut the crepe in two and gave half of it to General Anderson. It was a very touching and, I believe, significant gesture.

It is of interest to note that, on the twentieth, we unloaded thirty thousand men in thirteen hours, and

[1] Colonel E. H. Randle.
[2] Major General J. W. Anderson, 3d Infantry Division.

since that time have been unloading supplies at the rate of forty-seven tons an hour in spite of the very bad condition of the harbor. The American Navy and the French Navy have done and are doing a splendid job. This naturally also applies to our own Supply Section.

Requiem Mass, Honoring American and French Dead Held at Casablanca

HEADQUARTERS WESTERN TASK FORCE
November 23, 1942

General Keyes, Admiral Hall,[1] and I met General Noguès, Admiral Michelier,[2] and some of his Staff at the Casablanca Residency at 8:45 A.M. From there we proceeded with a police escort to the Cathedral of the Sacred Heart. The streets were lined with French and American soldiers and military police. The Cathedral was crowded to the doors.

The Bishop of Morocco, in full red robes, covered with a richly embroidered surplice and wearing a four-sided red cap, met us at the door and conducted us to the front of the Cathedral. Here there were two biers: the American on the right, covered with an American flag, and with a guard of six American soldiers, and the French on the left, with a French flag and a similar guard.

At the termination of the Mass, we followed the clergy out and entered our cars. A rather incongruous feature to me was the fact that in front of the people, when we entered and left, was a guard of Mohammedan cavalry on foot, armed with sabres.

After waiting an hour in the Residency in order to give the people time to walk to the cemetery, we proceeded to the cemetery, where there was a battalion of American infantry and a battalion of French African infantry drawn up outside of the gate, preceded by a group of people of the French Legion, a counterpart of the American Legion. We walked about half a mile

---

[1] Rear Admiral John Hall, Chief of Staff to Admiral Kent Hewitt, later in command of the ports.

[2] Admiral Michelier, in command of the French Navy at Casablanca.

through the cemetery and halted between two flagpoles, American on the right and French on the left, each with the colors at the truck.

General Noguès and I then placed a huge wreath on a tablet commemorating the heroic dead, and a red wreath was placed by the French Legion. When this ceremony was completed, the French band played our equivalent of Taps during which the flag was half-masted. Following this, they played the *Marseillaise* and the flag was run up to the truck. Our band then played Taps and the flag was half-masted. Following this, our band played the *Star-Spangled Banner* and the flag was run up to the truck.

We then inspected the graves, American and French, stopping in the middle of each group of graves to salute. We were followed by a large crowd of people—several thousand, I should think.

Each grave was properly marked with a cross, and in the case of our dead, a dogtag was on the cross. The names will be subsequently painted. We then returned to the gate, entered the automobiles, and proceeded back to the office. The whole affair was very solemn, and when I made the remark to General Noguès that I thought the intermingling of French and American blood had produced a very sacred sacrament, he seemed pleased and moved.

Lunch with General Noguès, Rabat, Morocco

HEADQUARTERS WESTERN TASK FORCE
December 8, 1942

General Noguès asked me, General Keyes, and eight other officers to lunch at his house to meet His Excellency, M. Boisson, the Governor of Dakar. General Fitzgerald, Air Corps, flew us up in his plane, as he was also invited to the luncheon.

We were received with the usual honors. In addition to ourselves, M. Boisson and the French generals, the Grand Vizier of the Sultan and the Chief of Protocol were both present. The Chief of Protocol is the man I had previously thought was the Grand Vizier. The Grand Vizier is the man who stands on the Sultan's right at the head of the twelve apostles. He is a very smart old gentleman of ninety-two, and he speaks about the same amount of French that I do.

When we first arrived, no one was paying any attention to him, so I went over and talked to him. During lunch he sat on Madame Noguès' left, and I sat on her right. Again nobody talked to him. In leaving and entering the dining room, I was supposed to precede him, but took particular pains not to do so, which seemed to have an excellent effect on the old man.

After lunch he sent the Chief of Protocol to ask if I would talk to him, which I did. One of General Noguès adherents was present and also an American naval officer who spoke French, but I talked practically directly to the old man. He said that His Majesty was very anxious for me to know that the whole life of Morocco depended upon maintaining peace. I assured him that I was a profound student of history; that since my earliest infancy my whole idea had been to maintain peace in French Morocco, and that I intended to do so by consulting the wishes of His Majesty through General Noguès. He said that when His Majesty heard these remarks from me he would be overcome with joyous emotion. I told him that I felt that whenever I could make His Majesty happy I myself was doubly glad. He then talked about the race antipathies—Jews—existing in Morocco. I told him that I fully understood those things because as a child I had been raised on a large ranch, which had the governance of twenty thousand sheep—which was not quite true, but had a good effect on the Arabs—and as a result of my acquaintance with sheep, I understood perfectly about race antipathies, and therefore I would do nothing about it because I felt that, since the Sultan's ancestors have handled such questions for thirteen hundred years, they were better fitted than I was to continue their management. He said this was completely to his way of thinking and that no racial or tribal troubles would ever stick their heads above the surface.

I then told him that it was very important for me to know what was going on in Spanish Morocco, and that I knew that he and the Sultan had better information on what went on there than anyone else. The Grand Vizier replied that there were certain natives living in Spanish Morocco, miscalled Arabs, who were always the cause of trouble, and that the Sultan would make it his special task to keep me informed of what these miscreants and their Spanish masters were planning, and that such information would be given me as if I were a member of the family.

I then told him that, in spite of my most diligent efforts, there would unquestionably be some raping, and that I should like to have the details as early as possible so that the offenders could be properly hanged. He said that this was a splendid idea, and that the hanging of such miscreants would unquestionably bring great joy to all Moroccans.

This conversation took about fifteen minutes, at the end of which time the Grand Vizier assured me that my complaisance had given him the happiest fifteen minutes of his life, to which I replied that if I had afforded happiness for fifteen minutes, I felt that I had not lived in vain.

This all sounds very funny when you write it down and must have sounded a good deal funnier when expressed in my French, but it is exactly the way the Arabs like to talk.

The Grand Vizier ended up by saying that it was necessary to converse with a great man fully to realize his greatness, and that there was an Arabic saying to the effect that those who said all men were equal were either fools or liars, and that he and the Sultan were neither.

"Fete Des Moutons" (Sheep Festival) Held at Rabat

HEADQUARTERS WESTERN TASK FORCE
December 19, 1942

The Sultan invited me, the division commanders, and forty officers to attend the ceremony at the palace. It was felt that it would be more appropriate if the escort of honor should be furnished by the Americans. To this end I informed General Noguès that I would arrive at the airport at 2:15 and inspect the escort of honor, which was a company of the 82d Reconnaissance Battalion,[1] then proceed to the Residency and pick up him and his officers.

General Noguès and I rode in a reconnaissance car with top down, and we stood up. The escort of honor had a profound effect on the populace, it being the first time I ever heard the Arabs cheer.

At the entrance to the palace enclosure, there was an escort consisting of a company of tanks, a battery of 105 mm. self-propelled guns, and a battery of 75 mm. assault guns, with the band from the 3d Division.

We halted at the front of this force, which presented arms. The band rendered the usual honors and played the national anthems of Morocco, France, and the United States in succession.

We then proceeded to the palace, leaving the escort outside. At the palace the usual ceremony with the Red Guard took place. We then paid our respects to the Sultan, who insisted on talking to me at considerable length, expressing his satisfaction that I, as a representative of the President and General Eisenhower, had been able to be present at the chief political and chief religious feast of his empire. I expressed the satisfaction which I felt the President and General Eisenhower experienced as a result of being represented, and that I felt that these fortunate instances were another illustration of the help which God had given our cause. I found that the mention of God with the Sultan is a one-hundred-percent hit.

Two new Caids were commissioned, and when this was over, we moved outside the palace to a grass plot about as long as a polo field, but only about half as wide. This was completely surrounded by a crowd of Moslems with some French. A tent was provided for the visiting officers, and I, as representative of the United States, was given the principal seat.

The Prince Imperial sat next to me, and he told me in excellent French that I was about to witness the most exciting spectacle in the world. The exciting spectacle was somewhat of a flop, but the ceremony preceding it was extremely interesting and ornate.

---

[1]Lieutenant Colonel P. A. Disney.

To our left, as we faced the arena, were the chief officials of all the large cities and tribes of the Empire of Morocco, arranged in a column of platoons, so to speak. The band of the Black Guard played continuously, and besides the palace guards there was a regiment of cavalry, half of whom were lancers.

Presently, a large number of Arabs, wearing red caps, rushed out of the palace gate and ran shouting toward us. They were followed by two men on foot, with about twenty-foot lances, held vertically; then came the Sultan dressed in Arab costume and mounted on a beautiful white stallion. The saddle and trappings were of pink silk, and a man walked behind him carrying a huge umbrella.

As he approached, the Arabs all shouted and yelled, and the foreign officers saluted. When he reached the head of the column of platoons of the city delegates, he halted and a man on each side of his horse waved a white handkerchief. This apparently was the signal for the leading platoon of citizens to bow from the hips three times and chant something in Arabic. As soon as they had done this three times, the men in red caps rushed behind them and hustled them to the side, and the process was repeated with the next group, and so on for about twenty groups.

The retinue of the Sultan was interesting. The Sultan is supposed to have seven horses, therefore he rode one and had four remounts, each caparisoned in silks of different colors, yellow, red, green, and purple. In addition to this he had a gold coach of the vintage of about 1400, I should think, with huge lamps on all four corners, and a place behind for two footmen. This was pulled by two horses, which were led by grooms. This accounted for the seven horses necessary for the Sultan's state.

Behind the coach came a cart covered with white boxes, then a camel loaded with white boxes, and then a mule similarly loaded. As far as I could see, the boxes were empty, but apparently they represented the provisions which His Majesty had normally carried with him. The significance of the ceremony is that in the old days the Sultan made a yearly progression of his realm and moved by the means indicated in this ceremonial show and was met at the gate of each city by the City

Fathers, who are now moved to the palace for this ceremonial repetition of the visit.

Upon the completion of this part of the show, the Sultan returned to the palace and then the great occasion arose of which the Prince Imperial had been telling me. It consisted of groups of from three to twenty Arabs, mounted on horses, with old-fashioned muskets. At a given signal, one of these groups would charge violently up the arena, doing a sort of manual of arms mounted, one movement of which was to hold the gun over the head in a horizontal position, muzzle to the front. This was apparently the start.

After this they would whirl the gun in various ways and finally attempt to discharge it. Since these guns are flintlocks, not over thirty per cent went off. On three or four occasions which they did, the Arab shooting it also went off, and when an Arab, usually a venerable Arab, falls—"Oh, what a fall is here, my countrymen"—his hat comes off, his shoes come off, and several bags and sacks, which he carries concealed under his robe, are scattered. The show is then halted while retainers push him onto his horse and collect his paraphernalia. In all, about three hundred Arabs passed in this way.

CASABLANCA
January 1, 1943

Early this morning we had our first air attack. The first explosion of three bombs occurred about 3:15 and woke me from a perfectly sound sleep. I lit in the middle of the floor, pulled the curtain across the window, got on some clothes, and was on the roof in about five minutes.

There was a low ceiling of some twenty-five hundred feet, with rain and wind, and all our searchlights—almost as many as George[1] has years of age—were working, probing holes in the clouds.

Presently the light anti-aircraft began going off at a great rate, with tracers looking like fireflies. This continued for about five minutes and suddenly there was a tremendous flash from which came long octopus-like

---

[1]General Patton's son.

tentacles of fire with bulbs along them. The fire from this incendiary blazed very brightly for about twenty minutes during which time nothing happened.

Then we distinctly heard airplanes, and the heavy antiaircraft began firing by the use of a device which makes it unnecessary to see the plane.

The noise continued, and pretty soon, from over the house to our back, a large four-motor enemy bomber appeared and was immediately caught in the range of two searchlights. As soon as this occurred, apparently every anti-aircraft gun in the vicinity opened fire, and the plane was literally outlined with tracer bullets and surrounded by the white bursts of high explosive, which immediately changed into a small black cloud. Although this bomber was not over two thousand feet up, and probably because of it, she passed clear through without being hit, or at least I do not think she was hit, although some others think she was.

We could hear other planes above the clouds and occasionally the explosion of bombs. Once a fragment whined by on its way down, but apparently our house was not in the line of the returning fragments.

While this was going on, I sent officers to various points to get information, and they kept telephoning in. So far as our defense was concerned, it was working correctly so there was nothing for me to do but worry.

About a quarter to five, we heard another bomber from behind us, another four-motor job. She came over still lower than the first one, and again was surrounded by tracer and high explosive. I am sure that this plane was hit at least twice and disappeared in the direction of Europe.

Just after she passed, we heard the whine of bombs, which struck near an anti-aircraft battery, about half a mile to our right. My Aide, Lieutenant A. L. Stiller, went over to ascertain the exact location and damage, but no one had been hurt.

Things then quieted down and I decided to go to bed, as the raid was apparently over. At about 5:30, firing recommenced, and I returned to the roof, as I had not undressed. There were quite a few explosions and a tremendous anti-aircraft fire from our guns and also from ships. It was better than the greatest Fourth-of-July demonstration possible to imagine.

Presently a bomber was picked up by the searchlights crossing directly in front of us at about four thousand feet, as the ceiling had lifted. The anti-aircraft shells were bursting all around her, but suddenly she fell about two thousand feet, upon which there were loud cheers from all directions. However, she straightened out and continued her course, and in about three miles again took a tumble, almost to the level of the sea. Smoke trailing from one or two of her motors could be seen distinctly, and I believe she was a dead duck, but she disappeared into the mist before hitting the water.

As soon as it was light, I went out to inspect the holes and talk to the soldiers. They were very calm, and one gun crew I talked to, who had been within fifty yards of a crater, said that it had not knocked them down, but had bruised them with mud and rocks.

The holes were about the size of an average bedroom, and there were in the craters quite a lot of bomb fragments, which we collected in order to get the numbers. In this we were fortunate, and thereby learned the type of bomb and type of fuse.

Although there were quite a number of bombs dropped, no soldiers were killed and only a very few wounded. The Arabs were less fortunate. One bomb in one town close by killed more Arabs than I am years old and wounded others. I wrote a letter of condolence to the Pasha, which may help him, but will not restore the Arabs.

About ten o'clock I had a meeting of all aviators and anti-aircraft officers to discuss the scheme of defense and to make the necessary corrections. We were of the opinion that everything had gone satisfactorily, but that a few changes were desirable. These have now been made. Material damage was zero. The bombers deliberately seemed to pick out open fields or the middle of the streets. Nothing hit the harbor.

When the last bomber flew over the house, George Meeks[1] said, "Sir, if I had my saddle, I could throw it on him and ride him."

---

[1] Technical Sergeant W. G. Meeks, General Patton's orderly.

The Sultan's Visit to Casablanca

January 12, 13, 1943

About two weeks ago, the Sultan's uncle, who lives in Casablanca, asked me if I would like to inspect the Sultan's palace here, and said that the Sultan was very anxious to be here when I visited it, but that he could not come to Casablanca without a reason; so we decided to give a demonstration of all weapons and motor vehicles in this command in his honor, and also to invite the French.

The purpose of this demonstration was twofold. Primarily, to impress the French and Arabs with our power and also, by showing our power, to take away the stigma of defeat from the French, for obviously with their weapons they could not fight such weapons as we displayed. We did not stress the fact that none of our heavy equipment was ashore when the fighting took place.

On the afternoon of January 10, I went to the Sultan's palace and was met by the Grand Protocol. Presently, the other officers, including some French, arrived and we had an audience with the Sultan, with me doing all the talking, which was indicated by the Grand Protocol, who kept looking at me to start the conversation. We still went through the rigmarole of my talking to the Protocol in French and the Protocol talking to the Sultan in Arabic, and back the same way. We had a guard of honor consisting of a company of light tanks, a number of French motorcycle infantry, and some motorcycle military police. The Sultan, his son, and the Grand Protocol got in the first car; General Keyes and I in the second car; then the twelve apostles, who were all Viziers as I have discovered. Then the rest of the American and French officers. In all, about thirty cars.

The field was very handsomely arranged by Colonel Williams.[1] The crews stood at attention with their sidearms at each vehicle, and the ammunition for all weapons stacked in front of the vehicle.

---

[1]Colonel J. J. B. Williams, Chief of Artillery, Western Task Force.

When we arrived at the grounds, I had my command car for the Sultan, and after the band had rendered the honors and played the three national airs, I helped the Sultan get into it. He indicated that I should join him. General Noguès, which had informed me that no foreigner ever rode with His Majesty, protested to the Sultan. The Sultan said that that was his business, and that I should ride with him, which I did, on his right. He then asked Noguès to come in on his left, and the Prince Imperial sat in front holding on to the handrail. This is alleged to be the first time in history that a foreigner has ever ridden with the Sultan.

We passed very slowly in front of each vehicle, and I explained it to the best of my ability, by talking in direct French to the Sultan—who speaks it better than I do. When we got to the laundry truck, I could not remember the noun in French and so I said, "I cannot remember that name." He said in perfect English, "You mean laundry truck," thereby spilling the beans that he could not speak English.

From this exposition, we drove to the airfield where Colonel Beam[1] had arranged a very fine demonstration of the various types of airplanes. These the Sultan inspected with great interest, and the Prince Imperial climbed into all of them and worked the controls.

From there we proceeded to the port and made a tour of the wharves. Then Admiral Hall took the Sultan and the senior members of the party, including the Viziers, to the destroyer *Wainwright*, where they had a battle station drill.

Most of the Viziers are around ninety, so could not climb up the ladder, and I remained with them and we got very intimate and told jokes. The theory that the Arab has no sense of humor is absurd.

We returned the Sultan to his palace and re-entered the audience chamber, and as soon as we got there, I had to speak French to the Grand Protocol and the Protocol in Arabic to the Sultan and so on. The Sultan then, with a happy smile, suggested that it would be a great honor if I would have breakfast with him the next day, the thirteenth. I said I should be delighted and

---

[1]Colonel R. Beam, on General Cannon's Staff.

asked if I might bring General Clark.[1] We then went home.

Shortly after supper, the Protocol called up and said that General Clark should not come. I was very much upset and offered not to go myself, but Clark told me to go ahead. This was very fortunate, as I found out today that the reason they had not wanted Clark was that they felt he was of too high rank to be asked so casually. I was very much gratified to learn this.

We arrived at the palace at 1:30 and were met outside by a battalion of French native infantry, with two bands and a company of the Black Guard inside.

I was conducted to the audience room alone, and I started the usual rigmarole, but the Sultan immediately cut out the interpreter and talked to me in French. After we had conversed for what seemed to me a terribly long time, the others were allowed to come in.

About this time breakfast was announced with the opening of two enormous curved wooden doors. I believe of rosewood. The breakfast room is the most beautiful room I have ever been in. It is black-and-white modeled marble to a height of about fifteen feet; above that is very fine white stucco, and above that is a curved wooden roof, gilded. The floor is black marble and the four sideboards are marble. There are white-fluted Doric half-columns all around the room. I told the Sultan it was the most beautiful room I had ever seen—and he admitted it.

I sat down between the Sultan and the Prince Imperial, and the rest of the people were separated in Arab, French, and American groups. We had a regular French breakfast of about ten courses, ending up with the Kus-Kus and ice cream. During this meal, which lasted three hours, I talked continuously in French to the Sultan and the Prince Imperial, who both understood me.

After lunch we walked through a truly beautiful garden to a pavilion made completely of mosaic, both walls and floor, inside and out, and decorated with carved

---

[1]Major General Mark W. Clark, Commanding General of the Fifth Army (just activated).

rosewood. All the banisters were of curved bronze. Having drunk some coffee here and talked some more, we proceeded through a double rank of Black Guards to a second marble building, called the Pavilion of Joy. This is entered from a sunken garden in which a fountain plays.

Inside, the Pavilion of Joy is of white marble with stucco and is divided in the middle by a raised platform with Doric columns of white marble. We sat in the right-hand half and some of the lesser people in the left-hand half where there was also a native orchestra.

In front of the Sultan and myself, there were nine different types of sweetmeats, at least a couple of hundred of each. These were in curved silver dishes or trays. The trays are raised on four legs about a foot from the ground. After we had talked some more, the servants placed these trays within our reach. No one that I saw, including the Sultan, took more than one sweetmeat. While this was going on, they served us with hot mint tea.

When we had drunk the second glass of mint tea, the sweetmeats were removed and the official photographer came in and took pictures. I was just about to leave when the Sultan got up on the steps and asked me to stand in front of him. He then decorated me with the Order of the Grand Cross of Ouissam Alaouite, on a pumpkin-colored ribbon with a white edge that goes over the right shoulder with the medal hanging over the left hip. The ribbon is about four inches wide. There is also a huge silver star which you wear normally, only using the ribbon for full dress. The Sultan stated that he was decorating me with this on account of what I had done for Morocco, and I told him in reply that nothing I had done for Morocco could compensate for the honor Morocco had done me in presenting me with the ribbon, which seemed to be the right thing to say. The Citation read, "Les lions dans leurs tanières tremblent à son approche."[1]

General Keyes, General Wilbur,[2] and General Wil-

---

[1]"The lions in their dens tremble at his approach."
[2]Brigadier General W. H. Wilbur, on General Patton's Staff.

son[1] and Admiral Hall received the same order in the next lower grade, the Grand Officer Order. Colonel Gay[2] and Colonel Conrad[3] received the next one, which is a neck ribbon, and is known as the Commander Order.

We then went to the swimming pool which is beyond the reception room. This was the finest pool I had ever seen, with red-and-green submerged lights, and a diving board in polished duraluminum. The height of the diving platform can be regulated by an electric switch, operated by the foot. There are also rowing machines and punching bags. One of the Viziers, who seems to be especially fond of me, said they had them all over Morocco, as the women could not go out and had to have exercise, and these were the only places where they could get it.

We then returned through the double rank of the Black Guard, entered the audience chamber, where the Sultan immediately lapsed into Arabic, and, after staying two minutes, I started to leave. As I got up, the Sultan said he hoped this was the beginning of a long and permanent friendship between him and me and our countries. I replied that I would do my uttermost to make the end of this friendship as fortunate and happy as the beginning.

Visit to Marrakech and Boar Hunt

CASABLANCA
February 1, 1943

The Pasha of Marrakech had been insisting for a long time that I pay him a personal visit, so on the afternoon of February 1, I, General Wilbur, Colonel Gay, Colonel Williams, Colonel Davidson,[4] and Captain Jenson[5] flew to Marrakech. We were met at the airfield

---

[1]Brigadier General Arthur Wilson, Chief of the Service of Supply supporting Western Task Force.

[2]Colonel H. R. Gay, Chief of Staff, Western Task Force, with General Patton throughout the war.

[3]Colonel A. B. Conard, on General Wilson's staff.

[4]Colonel, later Brigadier General G. H. Davidson, Assistant Engineer of Western Task Force.

[5]Captain R. N. Jenson, Aide to General Patton.

by a battalion of infantry, a French General, and the
Pasha. We first called on General Martin, the French
District Commander, and then went to the palace.

The palace of the Pasha occupies about two city
blocks and is completely walled in. To approach it, you
walk through a street where two vehicles can just pass,
and in through a very narrow gate. From this you enter
a beautiful garden, with a marble fountain and two very
beautiful white marble lions.

The Pasha has three guest houses, each one of which,
in my opinion, cost probably a million dollars. The one
assigned to General Wilbur and myself has on the first
floor a museum and the Pasha's private office. This
museum contains everything from Roman coins to the
latest type of firearms. The collection of swords is remarkable, and I am sure that one of the weapons I saw
is a Crusader's sword. It was impossible to admire any
of these, because, had I done so, they would have immediately been presented to me. However, they were
very interesting. I saw a suit of chain mail in the most
perfect condition of any suit I had ever seen, probably
due to the dry climate, which had prevented it from
rusting. There were also a backplate and a breastplate
of around 1400, which was remarkably good and very
heavy, completely chased in gold. Among other things
in the museum was a set of china presented to the
Pasha by the President of France.

On the second floor of this house was a large room
about thirty feet square, with a lot of booths around the
sides, such as we see in soda fountains, except that the
partitions were made of carved and painted wood. As you
entered the room, there was a movable bar with every
kind of liquor, but which nobody seemed to drink.

My room was on the next floor and consisted of
a bedchamber, a dressing room, and a very complete
modern bathroom. The walls were white up to about
ten feet, and above that were stucco. I had a sitting room
forty feet square with a sofa completely around it, with
the most beautiful ceiling and walls I have ever beheld.
The entire wall above six feet was made of Arabian
stucco work, as fine as lace. The Pasha told me it took
a year to make, and I believe he was not exaggerating.

The lower part of the wall was a mosaic of white, red, and yellow tiles.

At the end of the hall leading to the apartment and bedroom was an Arab whom the Pasha referred to as a slave. He was very amiable and armed with a dagger, and spent his time trying to find out how he could do something for me.

The house occupied by the other officers was similar to mine, but had more bedrooms, four, I believe. The beds were covered with velvet, over which were laid real lace counterpanes. Each bedroom had a modern bathroom.

After we had washed for half an hour, which apparently was the rule, we went into the third house, built on similar lines, where we drank tea. When this was finished, the Cadi, who is the Pasha's son, took us on a tour of the city and surrounding country, all of which belongs to the Pasha.

They have several very large concrete tanks, I should think about two hundred yards on a side and about ten feet deep. At one of these tanks the guide informed me a Sultan had been drowned, although he personally thought he had been murdered; and he showed me the boat in which the accident had occurred. It was a large steam launch with a steam engine, dated about 1880. The boat was about thirty feet long, in a fairly dilapidated state, but once had been painted yellow and green, with a gold design laid on.

The "diffa," at which only about twelve people were present, was along the usual lines except that everything was more elegant. In fact, General Martin, who has served in Morocco for forty years, said he had never seen such a banquet. After dinner we went to a room and had two sets of dancers entertain us for about an hour. These women would seem to be about thirty, and are, I understand, very highly trained. Each one wears a pastel-colored dress and over it a sort of surplice of lace. There are six women in each group with one male fiddler playing the single stringed instrument which always accompanies these dances. Four of the women beat time and squeal, while two go out and do a sort of duet. They waltz around for a little while, then kick the front of their dresses about three times, stamping their feet in time to the music, and then do one minute of a violent hula. They then return to their place in the line and two other girls do the same thing. This continues without alteration until the end of the show.

We were called at six on the morning of the third for a light breakfast. The light breakfast, which Wilbur and I ate, took five men to serve, and consisted of coffee, toast, three kinds of preserves, tea, four kinds of candy, and some cakes that looked like scones, only not so well cooked. Afterward I found the five men eating what was left, which was ample for about fifteen.

We left the palace in the pitch dark about seven o'clock. I rode with the Pasha and his personal body-guard in a Rolls-Royce. The others followed in two other cars accompanied by the son of the Pasha. We drove for about two hundred miles through desert gradually changing into the foothills of the Atlas Mountains. This was the country in which as a young man the Pasha had fought, and it was very interesting to hear him describe the fights which had taken place. He is a Berber, and for three hundred years his family has ruled this part of the country as absolute chiefs. I have never met a man in whom the hereditary qualities of leadership are so apparent. The idea of his superiority is so inbred that he does not have to show it. Wherever he passes, the Arabs bow and give a modified Hitler salute. So far as he is concerned they do not exist, and yet at the table he will help clear off a course and pick up the crumbs. In profile he looks very much like an Egyptian mummy with a café-au-lait complexion on the dark side. His hands are beautiful.

He said that Arabs would never fight against Berbers except in buildings; and in his early days they had very few weapons except muskets, so the only way he could kill Arabs—of whom he had destroyed many hundreds—was by sneaking up to a defended house at night and putting a bomb under it. In this operation they would make a fuse out of hairs from their whiskers and threads from their coats, impregnating them with powder; and when the sun came up, they would tell the Arabs they would blow up the house if they did not come out. If they came out, they shot them, which the Pasha described with appropriate gestures. If they refused to come out, they blew a hole in the wall and stormed it and killed them with swords. He described one fight in which he had attacked with two platoons for about twelve hours against a thousand Arabs.

The road we drove along was the one where he had had this fight. Apparently this time the Arabs were not in the houses. He had one platoon attack by fire, and he led the other one in a mounted charge from the flank. He said it was very gay, and that nearly all his men were killed as well as the Arabs. He also showed me an olive grove where he said there were so many dead Arabs that the jackals got sick eating them.

The country is full of almond trees, which are really beautiful. Viewed from the air, they look like ghost bouquets or like bits of cobweb covered with dew. When you get close, they look very much like cherry trees, only more beautiful, and more numerous than any cherry trees I have ever seen. There is an Arab custom that when a man is married or has a birthday, all his friends come and each brings five almond seeds which they plant. This account for the large number of trees.

After driving one hundred and twenty miles we came to a tent where a second breakfast of cake, wine, and coffee was served and where we were met by six French officers. There were a number of Goums present, armed with carbines, and riding one horse and leading another. I drew a very nice Arab stallion. He was about fifteen-two and probably weighed a thousand pounds. The saddle was an exact copy of the military saddle I bought of Jannin at Saumur in 1912. The Pasha rode a mule, large and black, with a red saddle shaped something like a bathtub. When we were all mounted, we proceeded up the mountains for about an hour. In addition to the mounted grooms, there were an equal number of footmen, who carried shotguns for the mounted men, or simply went along for the fun. We were moving at a good hound trot and these men kept up with perfect ease, barefooted, over sharp rocks and a few cactus.

When we reached the place for the drive, the Pasha personally placed the important guests. I was on the left in unquestionably the best place. Wilbur was next beyond me, and on the Pasha's right were Colonels Gay and Williams. Each post was in a blind made of cut brush about three feet high. I could see to the front about forty feet.

When everyone was in position, the beaters, of whom there were about a thousand, started to work. First, jackals and foxes came running very fast through the trees, and I missed three shots, but so did everyone else. Then a very large boar charged immediately in front of the Pasha, who missed him, and then turned with his Männlicher rifle and opened fire at the boar and the retainers, who were all getting out of his way. Fortunately, no one, including the boar, was hit.

About this time the largest and blackest boar I have ever seen came straight at me over rocks, and downhill. I hit him in the left eye with a slug at about fifteen feet, and his momentum carried him so that he fell close enough to splash blood on me. It was really quite exciting, because, had I failed to stop him, he would probably have hit me, and he had very fine teeth.

Another boar came whom the Pasha shot through the body, but failed to stop until he had pursued a number of Arabs. Everybody except me turned and shot at this one, and again no one was hit except the boar.

At the completion of this beat, we moved downhill, about five hundred yards, and had what they called a "contrebattu," which means that they drive the game back over the ground they have just passed. This time I shot a jackal, but did not have a shot at a boar. The Pasha killed two more boars, still with his rifle. In all, we killed fourteen boars, five jackals, three foxes, and two rabbits.

We drove back to the tent where the cars were waiting, had some more food, and were informed that the local chief was holding a diffa for us. We got to his place, which was a one-building village like Ouarzazate, only smaller, with about three hundred inhabitants, all of whom lined the courtyard, dancing and singing during the entire meal.

Owing to the fact that I had to get a plane back before five o'clock, this was a short affair lasting only an hour and a half, but not during one moment of this time did the inhabitants stop singing and dancing.

Flying back in the evening, I was struck by the fact that the whole country is pockmarked with old Arab tent emplacements. They give one the impression of leech bites on horses. The number of these indicates that this country has been tremendously inhabited for a very long time.

It has always been my ambition to meet a robber chief in his own country, and also to have an exciting hunt with little danger. The Pasha and my wild boar, which was the largest killed, satisfied my two ambitions.

Victory Parade Held at Tunis, May 20, 1943[1]

HEADQUARTERS I ARMOURED CORPS
May 20, 1943

On the night of the eighteenth, General Eisenhower phoned and asked General Bradley[2] and myself to be present at the parade, probably feeling that we had something to do with its existence.

B-25 Mitchell

We secured a B-25 from General Cannon and flying at better than two hundred and forty miles an hour, with a tail wind, reached Tunis at 9:45 A.M. The flight up was particularly interesting to us, as we passed over most of Bradley's battlefields. We also passed over the ruins of Carthage, which are only visible on the map— on the ground there is nothing to see. However, the

---

[1]This has already been covered in the newspapers and news-reels; what I am saying is simply my impression. *Author's note.*

[2]At that time Major General O. N. Bradley commanded the II Corps.

mountains back of it, of which I read a description in some old book, were perfectly familiar.

Our bombing of Tunis had been extremely accurate, because, while the waterfront was largely obliterated, the other portions of the city were hardly hit at all. All the airfields were covered with destroyed German planes, probably several hundred.

When we reached the field, General Eisenhower had just arrived, driven by Kay.[1] We both shook hands with him and congratulated him, but he was so busy meeting high ranking officers of the French and British Armies that we had no time to talk to him.

Shortly after we arrived, General Giraud[2] came and was warmly greeted by everyone. After a while the "sacred families" got into automobiles, escorted by British armored cars, and we followed behind the escort with General Catroux[3] as our companion. He speaks the clearest and most beautiful French I have ever heard, and we had quite a nice conversation.

Bradley and I were put on the right of the reviewing stand, which was largely occupied by French civilians and minor military officers.

Immediately in front of us was the line of French Colonial Infantry, of a very dark color, although I do not believe they were Senegalese. Just across from us was a battalion from one of the British Guard Regiments, who put up an exceedingly fine appearance.

On my immediate left was a very large French ecclesiastic with a purple sash around his middle, which acted as a background for a tremendous cross with an amethyst in it. I do not know who this man was, but he was apparently much beloved, as many French officers and enlisted men came up and shook hands with him and called him General. I think he spoke English, as he apparently understood what I said to Bradley.

Presently, there was a great fanfare of trumpets and much saluting, followed by what the French call "A fire of joy." It was very amusing to notice the change

---

[1]Captain Kay Summerby, W.A.C., Army of the U.S.
[2]General Henri Honoré Giraud.
[3]General Georges Catroux, Deputy for General de Gaulle in Africa.

in people's expressions—practically all of whom had been bombed—when they found out that it wasn't an air attack.

All this noise heralded the arrival of General Giraud and General Eisenhower, accompanied by Admiral Sir Andrew Cunningham,[1] General Sir Harold Alexander,[2] General Anderson,[3] Chief Air Marshal Tedder,[4] Air Marshal Conyngham,[5] Mr. Macmillan,[6] the British political officer, and Mr. Murphy,[7] the American. Mr. Murphy and General Eisenhower were the only two Americans on the stand.

The next event was a march-past by a band of Highland pipers, I think from the 42d Regiment. They came by in the traditional half-step, counter-marched, and re-passed. It was a very splendid sight.

When they had cleared the front, the band of the Foreign Legion, with the traditional white caps and red epaulets, numbering at least one hundred instruments, marched by leading the French contingent.

Then, for nearly an hour, the French troops, who had participated in the battle, marched by. As usual, they marched magnificently. They have an innate capacity for ceremonial marching, and, as far as that goes, for any other kind of marching. They consisted of French white troops, French Senegalese, Goums, and the Foreign Legion. The Foreign Legion was very resplendent, with enormous whiskers, many of which were red or blond. In fact, it seems to me that the French Foreign Legion is largely composed of Germans and Swedes. They are very fine-looking troops.

One impressive thing was that these troops, who had participated in a victorious campaign, were armed with Model 1914 equipment, in spite of which fact they had done well. Of course, now, they will be immediately

---

[1]Commander of the Mediterranean British naval forces.

[2]Commander of the British 18th Army Group, composed of First and Eighth British Armies.

[3]Major General A. N. Anderson, Commander of the British First Army in Tunisia.

[4]Air Marshall Sir Arthur Tedder, Air Commander under General Eisenhower.

[5]Vice Air Marshal Sir Arthur Conyngham.

[6]Representative of the British Foreign Office in Algiers.

[7]Political and civil affairs adviser to General Eisenhower.

re-equipped with American Lend-Lease matériel. However, during the fighting, the only American equipment they had were some Thompson sub-machine guns and some Bazookas.

Thompson

Each French regiment and separate battalion carried the Tri-Color, with the battalion honors written on it. This caused almost continual saluting on the part of the spectators.

After the French had passed, a battalion of the

34th Infantry Division came by. Our men were magnificent physical specimens, very well turned out, but there were no flags, not even company guidons; and regimental commanders marched on the right of the file closers of the leading company.

In spite of their magnificent appearance, our men do not put up a good show in reviews. I think that we still lack pride in being soldiers, and must develop it.

Following the Americans came the British contingents with a representation from every division in the First Army, each led by its division or corps commander. The Guard units were big men; the others were very small. All of them were dressed in shorts, except the Gurkhas, who are very small, and, in addition to their bayonets, carry a huge knife something like the Philippine bolo.

The British also understand the art of ceremonial marching and really put on a splendid show. There was one sergeant major who should be immortalized in a painting. He typified all that is great in the British noncommissioned officer, and he certainly knew it. I have never seen a man strut more.

Following the British infantry came the American tanks manned by British, and the British Churchill tanks, also a number of field guns.

The whole march-past lasted about two and one-half hours. When it was over, about thirty of us were asked to a lunch at the French Residency, given by General Giraud. It was a very formal affair, but there were no toasts. Afterward, most of us had to leave at once in order to get back to our stations before dark.

I hope this is only the first of many such triumphal processions in which I shall participate.

The flight back was very fast because the wind had changed, and again we had about a thirty-mile tail wind, with the result that we got in half an hour before we were expected and had to wait.

At the lunch I met my friend General Briggs, who commands the British 1st Armored Division, and had a chance to introduce him to General Harmon, who is commanding our 1st Armored Division. They are very much alike and both very successful.

General Giraud remembered me at once and was

extremely complimentary in his remarks. He is a very impressive man and looks exactly like a modernized Vercingetorix.

Bazooka

Notes on the Arab

CASABLANCA
June 9, 1943

It took me a long time to realize how much a student of medieval history can gain from observing the Arabs.

All members of our oil-daubed civilization think of roads as long slabs of concrete or black-top, or at least as dragged and graded thoroughfares full of wheel ruts. As a matter of fact, roads, or perhaps it is better to call them trails, existed thousands of years before the earth-shaking invention of the wheel was even dreamed of, and it was along such roads that our sandaled or barefoot progenitors moved from place to place just as the Arabs do today.

Viewed from the air, the Arab road is a gently meandering tracery of individual footpaths. Where the going is good, this collection of paths may spread to a width of twenty to forty yards, while, where rocky out-croppings must be circumvented or defiles pass through the wandering tendrils, they come into focus and form a single path, only again to spread out when the going improves. Nowhere is a wheel track or a heelmark, because the Arabs wear heelless slippers or go bare-footed; their animals are unshod—there are no vehicles.

In the waterless districts, the roads are generally straight, but not in the brutal mathematical meaning of the term. They are straight only as a man would walk from one point to another, or as the dried slime path where a snail has crossed the sidewalk.

In the coastal lands where there is rain, we have alternative roads. The principal track follows the ridges for the same reason that, in our West, the Indian trails and buffalo paths, and even the highways made by the pioneers, stick to the high ground. In the dry season, the meanderings of the crestlined road are short-cir-cuited at times by trails leading across low ground which would be useless in the rainy season.

In the forest, the roads are even more sinuous. The men who made them could not see very far, so the trail wanders largely and keeps only a general direction.

It takes little imagination to translate the Arab on his white stallion and the men and women on donkeys into the Canterbury pilgrims, while the footman, equipped with a large staff and poniard, can easily be mistaken for Friar Tuck, Little John, or Robin Hood. This similarity not only applies to their dress, save the turban, but also to their whiskers, filth, and probably to their morals; and they are all talking, always talking. They have no other recourse. Few can read, there are no books, no newspapers, no radios, to distract them. Only the spoken word, and truly they are "winged words" with a daily rate of from forty to sixty miles, as we learned during the battles in Tunisia by checking the known origin of a rumor against the time we heard it.

Of course rumors were not factual, but were in general little less garbled in transmission than some of those received by radio. In the rumors, tanks often were reported as trucks and trucks as tanks, and always the number attained astronomical proportions; but that is natural. Once I asked a farmer in Virginia how many soldiers had passed him, and he replied, "Ah don't know for sure, but Ah reckon about a million"—and he could read and write and had a radio.

For a long time I was greatly intrigued by constantly seeing groups of Arabs squatting in the dust or mud—how they avoid piles is a mystery—gossiping. Then I got the answer from a chance remark by a soldier who referred to such a group as "the morning edition of the daily news."

The agricultural habits of the Arab are a strange mixture of old and new. Mowing machines and combines work side by side with Ruth and Naomi—many Ruths and Naomis—cutting wheat with a sickle and carefully tying each bundle with a wisp of straw. But even when using modern machinery, the influence of the trail road is apparent because the Arab has never learned to hitch animals abreast; therefore, we see a mowing machine or a header being pulled, not by a span or two of horses, but by four horses in tandem, each horse personally conducted by an Arab, while one, or, more often, two, handle the machine. They actually also have gleaners as in Biblical times.

The threshing is done on a dirt floor by horses walking or trotting in a circle and spreading manure as they go. Sometimes the animals simply move at liberty. At other times they pull a small roller. After some days of this operation, men armed with three-pronged wooden forks throw the chaff into the air and the wind blows it away. Finally, women, using large tray-like baskets, throw the remaining grain and manure into the air in the final stage of winnowing and get rid of at least half of the droppings and some of the dirt.

The burial customs too are strange. In many places, usually on hilltops, there are small, square, white buildings with a dome-shaped roof which contains the remains of a holy man. These graves of Marabouts are not churches nor even shrines, simply tombs, but it is the custom to plant the dead near them without any markers or even mounds. In fact, our men have unwittingly walked on these graves with resulting unpleasantness.

From the air, the graves can be easily seen clustered around the Marabout tomb or simply grouped on some low hill. Apparently the Arabs are as much afraid of water in death as they are in life.

One day I saw a funeral which, for its rugged simplicity, was outstanding. In the leading cart were several elderly men sitting on the floor, while between their feet was the body, wrapped in white cloth, with half of its length sticking out of the tail of the cart and dangling in the wind. Behind this came other carts and one four-wheeled wagon, some bicyclists, and then men and women on foot, perhaps thirty in all.

The Arab influence on Spain and Latin America is again emphasized as summer weather approaches. There is a regular epidemic of sombreros made of particolored straw, exactly like those we know at home, except that, since they are worn superimposed on the turbans, they are much larger.

I have never had a satisfactory explanation for the turban—the one usually given that it is a tropical head-dress does not hold, in view of the fact that many Arabs, particularly in the army, wear turbans which consist simply of a rag wrapped around the head, leaving the whole shaven crown bare.

Another similarity between the Arab and the Mexican is the utter callousness with which both treat animals. Neither an Arab nor a Mexican would think of unpacking an animal during a prolonged halt. If the beast is chafed raw, the Arab does not even bother to treat the wound with lard, which is the invariable panacea with the Mexican. He just lets it bleed and trusts to Allah. Because a horse is dead lame is no reason for not working him.

All the animals are head-shy and many are blind as a result of the cheerful custom of beating them on the head with a stick.

The method of castrating sheep and cattle is unspeakably cruel. I think that the reason that the horse and donkey are not altered is due to their architecture, which forbids the employment of the Arab method.

One cannot but ponder the question: What if the Arabs had been Christians? To me it seems certain that the fatalistic teachings of Mohammed and the utter degradation of women is the outstanding cause for the arrested development of the Arab. He is exactly as he was around the year 700, while we have kept on developing. Here, I think, is a text for some eloquent sermon on the virtues of Christianity.

Ceremony Held at Headquarters I Armored Corps

June 19, 1943

Colonel Chauvin informed me that he would like to confer upon me and two other officers designated by me, who had served with me in the Tunisian Campaign, an honorary membership in the 2ème Régiment de Marche de Tirailleurs Algériens, together with the regiment's Fourragère of the Legion of Honor.

I named General Bradley and General Gaffey,[1] and then asked if it would be possible to confer the same honor posthumously upon Major R. N. Jenson,[2] which request was granted.

The ceremony was as follows. The 1st Company of the 1st Battalion of the 2ème Régiment de Marche de Tirailleurs Algériens, preceded by the French colors and the French band, arrived at the courtyard of our Headquarters at 4:35 in the afternoon. Inside the court was one of our platoons and the band of the 36th Engineers.

When the French were in position, our platoon came to present arms and the band played, "To the Colors," in honor of the French flag.

Colonel Chauvin then accompanied General Bradley, General Gaffey, and myself to inspect the French company. When we arrived in front of the colors, which were posted on the left, the French band played the *Marseillaise*. At the termination of this, Colonel Chauvin, accompanied by his Chief of Staff, Commandant Gerrier, took a position in front of us and in a loud voice said, "Lieutenant General G. S. Patton, Jr., is hereby made an honorary member of the Deuxième Régiment de Marche de Tirailleurs Algériens and is presented with the Fourragère of the Legion of Honor." He repeated this announcement in front of Bradley and Gaffey.

---

[1]Brigadier General, later Major General Hugh J. Gaffey, at that time commanded the 2d Armored Division.

[2]General Patton's Aide de Camp, killed in action in Tunisia.

He then stated, "Major R. N. Jenson, dead on the field of honor, April 1, 1943, is hereby made an honorary member of the Deuxième Régiment de Marche de Tiralleurs Algériens and is presented with the Fourragère of the Legion of Honor."

Colonel Chauvin then took a position on my right, and the regular American Retreat was played, the flag lowered, and then our band played first the *Marseillaise* and then the *Star-Spangled Banner*. This terminated the ceremony.

The French Color Guard consisted of Lieutenant Biard, who carried the flag, and four tirailleurs. Each of these four men was decorated with the Military Medal, which is the highest award a French soldier can receive, it being restricted to enlisted men and army commanders. The Lieutenant had the Grand Cross of the Legion of Honor, and the Croix de Guerre with a number of palms.

The officers in the French company were all Frenchmen. The men were all Berbers and were extremely fine-looking.

It is always amazing to note the difference between a Berber dressed in his normal costume of a bathrobe and a Berber dressed in uniform. Their appearance changes for the better.

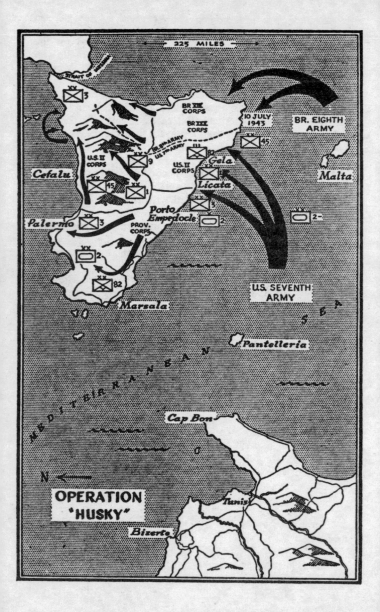

OPERATION "HUSKY"

2

OPERATION "HUSKY"

The I Armored Corps, which planned the Sicilian Campaign, was what remained of Western Task Force Headquarters after furnishing men and officers for the newly created Fifth Army. Corps Headquarters was reinforced for the invasion, and upon landing in Sicily, was renamed United States Seventh Army Headquarters.

The Allied Ground Forces were commanded by General Sir Harold Alexander and comprised the British Eighth Army, under General Montgomery, and the United States Seventh Army, under General Patton. The American and British naval forces were commanded by Admiral Sir Andrew Cunningham, and the air forces by Air Chief Marshal Sir Arthur Tedder.

The armies were landed on July 10, 1943,[1] with the British Eighth Army taking the southeast side of the island and the American Seventh, the southwest.

Troops of the 7th Infantry Regiment, 3d Division, Colonel H. B. Sherman commanding, entered Messina on the night of August 16. On the morning of the seventeenth, General Patton entered the city, and Sicily fell. The campaign had lasted thirty-eight days.

P.D.H.

---

[1]General Patton was lying in his bunk the night before the Sicilian landing when he heard two doughboys talking outside his window. "Well," said one, "when we go ashore in the morning, I reckon we'll hear that the marines have landed."

B. A. P.

51

The Invasion of Sicily

July 11, 1943

General Gay, Captain Stiller, and I, and some soldiers left the *Monrovia* in the Admiral's barge at 0900 and reached the beach at Gela at 0930.

Dukw

Standing on the beach, I noticed two Dukws,[1] destroyed by personnel mines, and about seven small landing craft beached. While I was making these observations, the enemy opened fire with what was probably an 88 mm. or a 105 mm. gun. The shells hit the water about thirty yards from the beach, but could not get into the beach on account of the defilade afforded by the town.

After our scout car was de-waterproofed, I intended to go to the Headquarters of the 1st Division, about three miles to the southeast along the coast road. As we got into Gela, we noticed a flag on the left and decided to call on Colonel W. O. Darby, commanding the Rangers. This was

---

[1] Amphibious two-and-a-half-ton trucks.

very fortunate, because, had we proceeded down the road, we should have run into seven German tanks, which at that moment were advancing along it toward the town.

As we arrived at the Rangers Command Post, Colonel Darby and the town of Gela were being attacked from the northeast by quite a number of Germans and Italians. Darby had a battery of captured German 77's, "K" Company of the 3d Battalion of the 26th Infantry, two Ranger battalions, a company of 4.2 chemical mortars, and a battalion of the 39th Engineers.

4.2 Chemical Mortars

He was cut off from the 1st Division on his right by the seven tanks, which now closed in to one thousand yards of the right side of the town.

We went up to an Observation Post, about a hundred yards behind the front line, where we could plainly see the enemy moving across the field, perhaps eight hundred yards away.

Darby had the roads patrolled by groups of three

half-tracks. These half-tracks, intended, not for combat, but to carry engineers' equipment, worked very well, greatly annoying the Italians, who apparently had no mobile artillery with them.

The Italian advance seemed to stick at about 1150, and we went back to Darby's Headquarters to find out what was taking place on the right, which we could see from the town of Gela.

About the time we got there, two Hurricane Bombers dropped bombs in the town. Then German artillery, apparently 88 mm. all-purpose guns, opened fire. They hit the building we were in twice, and also made a hole in the roof of the building across the street, but no one was hurt except some civilians. I have never heard so much screaming.

About that time an officer from the 3d Division came in with ten tanks, having made the trip by the shore road from Licata[1] to Gela. Two tanks of Combat Command "B" also arrived.[2]

I told Gaffey to close the gap between Gela and the 1st Division and to send a company of tanks to help Darby. This was done. Darby counter-attacked at once to his left and took five hundred prisoners. We also destroyed the seven tanks east of Gela.

After I got the situation of the 3d Division from the officer who had made the trip, General Roosevelt[3] arrived and I talked to him about the failure of the 1st Division to carry its objective last night. The chief reason, as far as I can see, is that the division attacked without anti-tank guns and without moving up their artillery. When they were counter-attacked by the German tanks, they did very well and accounted for quite a few of them.

The bag of enemy tanks for the day is, I think, about fourteen. I have seen eleven.

I then decided to go down and see General Allen[4]

[1]The 3d Division and Combat Command "A," 2d Armored Division, landed at Licata.

[2]Combat Command "B," 2d Armored Division, landed at Gela on D + 1.

[3]Brigadier General Theodore Roosevelt, Assistant Division Commander.

[4]Major General Terry de la M. Allen, commanding the 1st Division.

and General Gaffey. While we were driving down the
road, we met Allen coming in and halted on a hill. This
was about 1530. While we were there, fourteen German
bombers came over and were attacked by the anti-aircraft. We got off the road, but as it was parallel to the line
of flight of the enemy airplanes, quite a number of fragments from the anti-aircraft hit along the road. One piece
struck within, I should think, five to ten yards of General
Gay and myself. During this attack, we saw two bombers
and one other plane shot down.

After this, we mounted our cars and drove to the
Headquarters of the 2d Armored Division. While we were
there, a German battery kept shelling us, but not very ac-
curately, or else the hill behind was too high to clear, as
nearly all of the shots were overs. We arranged for Allen
and Gaffey to take Ponte Olivo Airfield in the morning.

We then drove back to Gela without incident except
that I think it is quite unusual for an Army Commander
and his Chief of Staff to travel some six miles on a road
parallel to the fronts of two armies and about equally
distant from the two.

On the way back to Gela, I happened to be looking
out to sea. From a Liberty freight ship, which the Germans had bombed about a half-hour earlier, smoke was
issuing. Before our eyes a tremendous explosion threw
white and black clouds several thousand feet into the air.
The ship was literally blown in two, but at the present
writing, some six hours later, the rear half is still afloat.
Most, if not all, of the army personnel on board, who
numbered only one hundred and fifteen, were saved.

While we were on the beach at Gela, waiting for a
boat to take us out to the *Monrovia*, I saw the most stupid
thing I have ever seen soldiers do. There were about three
hundred 500-pound bombs and seven tons of 20 mm.
high-explosive shell piled on the sand, and, in between the
bombs and boxes of ammunition, these soldiers were
digging foxholes. I told them that if they wanted to save
the Graves Registration burials that was a fine thing to do,
but otherwise they'd better dig somewhere else.

About the time we got through explaining this to
them, two Hurricane Bombers came over and strafed the
beach, and all the soldiers jumped right back into the same

holes they had dug. I continued to walk up and down and soon shamed them into getting up.

We got back to the *Monrovia* at 1900, completely wet. This is the first day in this campaign that I think I earned my pay.

July 18, 1943

Since the initial successful assault on the beaches before daylight on the tenth, we have continued to push along several days ahead of our assumed schedule. This has been due to the fact that having once got the enemy started, we have not let him stop, but have, so to speak, kept on his heels.

It is also due to the fact that the Italians and Germans spent tremendous effort in time, labor, and money, building defensive positions. I am sure that, just as in the case of the Walls of Troy and the Roman walls across Europe, the fact that they trusted to defensive positions reduced their power to fight. Had they spent one-third as much effort in fighting as they did in building, we never could have taken the positions.

On the other hand, the Italian troops, most of whom are from Northern Italy, have fought very desperately. The German troops have not fought as well as those we destroyed in Tunisia. This is particularly true of their tanks. They have shown gallantry, but bad judgment.

The tally of prisoners, guns, etc., speak more forcefully than words as to the success of the operation. While comparisons are odious, I believe that up to yesterday the Eighth Army had not taken over five thousand prisoners.

The enemy has been booby-trapping his dead, firing on us from the rear after we have passed through him, and using dum-dum bullets. This has caused us some casualties, but has caused him a great deal more.

On the field south of Biscari Airport, where we had quite a fight, I could smell dead enemy while driving for at least six miles along the road.

The Germans have, on several occasions, put mines in behind the Italians, so that when the Italians attempt to run, they get blown up. This naturally does not make the Italians love the Germans.

There have been several very gallant instances. On the tenth, some Italian tanks entered the town of Gela, which was defended by Colonel Darby and two battalions of Rangers. Darby personally engaged one of the tanks at fifty yards with a light machine gun from his peep. When he found that these bullets would not penetrate, he hurried down to the beach, under fire of three tanks, got hold of a 37 mm. gun just unloaded, split the box of ammunition with an axe, hurried back up the hill, and went into position with his gun less than a hundred yards in front of a tank coming down on him. The first round failed to stop the tank, but the second did stop it. However, the enemy crew did not get out until Darby put a thermite grenade on top of the tank and roasted them out.

The other day this same officer was offered the command of a regiment with an increase of one grade in rank, but he refused to take it because he wished to stay with the men he had trained. On the same day, General Wedemeyer[1] requested to be reduced to a Colonel so that he could take command of a regiment. I consider these two acts outstanding.

During the landing, an artillery lieutenant flew his Piper Cub off a landing boat with a run of about fifty feet of chicken wire. During the rest of the day, he circled the town under continuous fire. His plane was hit several times, but he kept the Commanding General of the 3d Division informed of the situation.

A naval officer bringing in an LCT 175-foot landing craft, found the water too shallow to get his bow in, so he broached it to the beach and engaged the enemy machine guns with his two 20 mm. cannon and silenced them, thereby permitting the troops to get ashore.

The naval gunfire support—that is, naval fire put on the beaches from vessels at sea—has been outstanding. We have even called for this support at night and got it on the target on the third salvo.

The people of this country are the most destitute and God-forgotten people I have ever seen. One day, when I was in the town and the enemy nearly took it, some shells and bombs killed a few civilians, and everyone in the town screamed like coyotes for about twenty minutes.

The animals are much better cared for and fatter,

---

[1] Brigadier General Albert C. Wedemeyer.

and also larger, than the animals in Africa; otherwise, everything here is much worse than in Africa.

The carts are very peculiar. They are in the form of a box about four feet square with things that look like bed-posts at the corners and along the sides. The panels between these bedposts are painted with pictures. Under the cart there is a scrollwork built up between the axle and the bottom of the box, just like the porches of houses built around 1880.

The collar of the cart animal has a spike projecting upwards about two feet, and many of the horses wear plumes on the crown piece of the bridle.

During the first two or three days, when we were having fighting close to the towns, the inhabitants were, to say the least, not friendly; but since we have demon-strated that we can destroy either the Germans or Italians, they have become quite Americanized and spend their time asking for cigarettes.

The Capture of Palermo

July 23, 1943

On the afternoon of the twenty-first, we secured a position northeast of Castelvetrano from which to launch the 2d Armored Division,[1] which heretofore had been held back near the middle of the island so that the enemy could not tell which way it was going.

The troops moved into position, beginning at 4 P.M., and were all set by dark. In the morning they started their relentless advance.

The first act was to break through the enemy on his immediate front. This was done by the 41st Infantry,[2] supported by a battalion of medium tanks from the 66th,[3] This started the enemy rolling back. From then on, it was a question of attacking him with converging tanks whenever he tried to stop us, which he attempted on three occasions.

---

[1]Commanding, Major General Hugh J. Gaffey.

[2]Commanding Officer, Colonel, later Brigadier General S. R. Hinds.

[3]Commanding Officer, Colonel, later Brigadier General J. H. Collier.

In one case a 75 mm. assault howitzer in a half-track engaged a German 105 at five hundred yards and destroyed him. This act was as lucky as it was heroic.

The last stand was made in the mountains southwest of Palermo, which was a most difficult nut to crack, but was finally done with artillery fire and tanks.

We met some of the most ingenious tank traps I have ever seen. The Germans would dig a hole about eighteen feet long and ten feet deep halfway across the right side of the road and cover it with chicken wire and dust to make it look like the road. Then, about thirty feet beyond, on the lefthand side of the road they would make a similar pit. In front of each pit they would put a wire entanglement with the hope that our tanks would disregard the wire and crash into the holes. Fortunately we did not do so. In other places they dug traps about twenty feet wide and fifteen feet deep for distances of several miles, but by sticking to the roads and blasting our way through, we had no trouble with them.

I drove up through the column and received a very warm reception from the 2d Armored, all of whom seemed to know me, and all of whom first saluted and then waved.

As we neared the city, it was dark, so I picked up Colonel R. F. Perry, Chief of Staff of the division, to act as a guide. He stated he believed the town had fallen, and we therefore decided to go in and see.

As we approached, the hills on each side were burning. We then started down a long road cut out of the side of a cliff which went through an almost continuous village. The street was full of people shouting, "Down with Mussolini!" and "Long Live America!"

When we got into the town, the same thing went on. Those who arrived before dark, among them General Keyes,[1] had flowers thrown on the road in front of them, and lemons and watermelons given them in such profusion that they almost became lethal weapons.

The Governor had left, but we captured the two Generals, both of whom said that they were glad to be

---

[1]Major General Geoffrey Keyes was Deputy Commanding General of Seventh Army and also Commanding General of a Provisional Corps in Sicily.

captured because the Sicilians were not human beings, but animals. The bag in prisoners for the day must have been close to ten thousand. On the morning of the twenty-third, when I was inspecting the harbor, I passed a group of prisoners, all of whom stood up, saluted, and then cheered.

The harbor is not too badly damaged, but the destruction around the lip is really appalling. For about two blocks in depth practically every house is a pile of rocks. Some ships, small fishing steamers, were apparently blown completely out of the water and landed on the dock; at least I can account for their being there in no other way. A good many of the small craft in the harbor are sunk, several of them being cut completely in two.

We took over the so-called Royal Palace for a Headquarters and had it cleaned by prisoners for the first time since the Greek Occupation. We are also having the prisoners remove the rubbish from the streets and plug the holes in the dock.

The Italians here are much better-looking than the ones we took in the rest of Sicily, being bigger and older.

The Cardinal's Vicar came to call on me, and I assured him that I was amazed at the stupidity and gallantry of the Italian Army: stupid, because they were fighting for a lost cause, and gallant, because they were Italians. I asked him to tell them that and to spread the rumor. I further said that we had demonstrated our ability to destroy them, and that if they failed to take the hint and surrender, we would certainly do so. As a matter of fact, I called off the air and naval bombardment we had arranged, because I felt enough people had been killed, and felt that with the drive of the 2d Armored Division we could take the place without inflicting unproductive losses on the enemy.

I believe that this operation will go down in history, certainly at Leavenworth,[1] as a classic example of the proper use of armor, and I also believe that historical research will reveal that General Keyes' Corps moved faster against heavier resistance and over worse roads than did the Germans during their famous Blitz.

---

[1] The Command and General Staff College.

We did not waste any time, however, and started this morning, capturing the north road and also moving artillery to support the final effort of the II Corps which will begin in a few days.

HEADQUARTERS SEVENTH ARMY
APO 758   U.S. ARMY
August 1, 1943

GENERAL ORDER ⎫
NUMBER   10 ⎬
        TO BE READ TO TROOPS

Soldiers of the Seventh Army and XII Air Support Command:

Landed and supported by the navy and air force, you have, during twenty-one days of ceaseless battle and unremitting toil, killed and captured more than 87,000 enemy soldiers, you have captured or destroyed 361 cannon, 172, tanks, 928 trucks, and 190 airplanes—you are magnificent soldiers! General Eisenhower, the Commander-in-Chief, and General Alexander, the Army Group Commander, have both expressed pride and satisfaction in your efforts.

Now in conjunction with the British Eighth Army you are closing in for the kill. Your relentless offensive will continue to be irresistible. The end is certain and is very near. Messina is our next stop!

G. S. PATTON, JR.,
Lieut. General, U.S. Army,
DISTRIBUTION: "D"   Commanding

HEADQUARTERS SEVENTH ARMY
APO 758   U.S. ARMY
August 22, 1943

GENERAL ORDER ⎫
NUMBER   18 ⎬
Soldiers of the Seventh Army:

Born at sea, baptized in blood, and crowned with victory, in the course of thirty-eight days of incessant battle and unceasing labor, you have added a glorious chapter to the history of war.

Pitted against the best the Germans and Italians could offer, you have been unfailingly successful. The rapidity of your dash, which culminated in the capture of Palermo, was equalled by the dogged tenacity with which you stormed Troina and captured Messina.

Every man in the Army deserves equal credit. The enduring valor of the Infantry and the impetuous ferocity of the tanks were matched by the tireless clamor of our destroying guns.

The Engineers performed prodigies in the construction and maintenance of impossible roads over impassable country. The Services of Maintenance and Supply performed a miracle. The Signal Corps laid over 10,000 miles of wire, and the Medical Department evacuated and cared for our sick and wounded.

On all occasions the Navy has given generous and gallant support. Throughout the operation, our Air has kept the sky clear and tirelessly supported the operation of the ground troops.

As a result of this combined effort, you have killed or captured 113,350 enemy troops. You have destroyed 265 of his tanks, 2324 vehicles, and 1162 large guns, and, in addition, have collected a mass of military booty running into hundreds of tons.

But your victory has a significance above and beyond its physical aspect—you have destroyed the prestige of the enemy.

The President of the United States, the Secretary of War, the Chief of Staff, General Eisenhower, General Alexander, General Montgomery, have all congratulated you.

Your fame shall never die.

G. S. PATTON, JR.,
Lieut. General, U.S. Army,
Commanding.

Sidelights on the Sicilian Campaign

October, 1943

Now that sufficient time has elapsed, it is permissible for me to give you a general idea of the lighter side of the Sicilian Campaign and subsequent incidents.

The first intimation I had that we were in the transport area was when the davit for a landing boat gave way and the boat crashed into my porthole. For a moment we thought that a bomb had hit. As we were sleeping in full pack, we went on deck. The whole coastline as far as we could see was a mass of flames. In some places they looked like burning mountains; in other places, simply like a line of fire.

At intervals along the flaming shore, searchlights would suddenly flare and sweep the water. This was very interesting, because, while the lights made it so bright on deck that we could read a paper, the enemy was apparently unable to see us from the land. I think this had something to do with refraction and the haze caused by the fires.

Whenever one of these searchlights flickered on, innumerable tracer bullets from our destroyers and patrol boats hurried toward it like bees returning to a hive. That searchlight immediately went out.

The fires along the shore, we discovered, were caused by our high explosives igniting the wheatfields. Fortunately for the Sicilians, the wheat had been harvested, but the stubble was still there and that is what burned.

The southern Sicilian is, if possible, the dirtiest of all Sicilians. There were actually cases in which they lived with corpses in their houses for several days because they were too lazy to remove them. Yet, when we used posthole diggers to bury them, they were very angry and said the dead should be buried horizontally and not vertically. We gave them the opportunity of horizontal burial by "permitting" the civilians to dig the graves.

In the courtyard back of the house I occupied, I once counted eight children, eleven goats, three dogs, a flock of chickens, and a horse, all picking up filthy scraps from the pavement. None of them seemed to die. I suppose people that have been raised on tomato sauce made after the Sicilian manner are immune. Their method of preparing this sauce is to collect tomatoes, many of them overripe, and squeeze them out with their hands onto old sheets, or pieces of paper, or doors, or anything else they can find. They leave this bloody-looking mess for several days, and then put it on trays, usually lying on the sidewalks, to dry. Since the streets are never cleaned, there is plenty of germ-laden dust to mix with the sauce. This is the thing with which they eat their macaroni.

The Italians, under German tutelage, were extremely clever in the construction of pillboxes. In fact, in many cases they were too clever, because they camouflaged them with hay or bushes and our first phosphorous shells set them on fire.

In other cases they went to the trouble of building stucco houses outside of the pillboxes. In order to put the latter into action, they simply gave the wall a kick and there was the pillbox. In spite of the tremendous number of these things, we had practically no trouble in destroying them. One battalion alone got thirty-nine in one day.

Owing to the lack of water and other causes, we decided to drink champagne while at Gela and secured a case, which would seem ample, but owing to the large number of visiting firemen, it disappeared in about two days. It was then necessary to secure more champagne. In order to do this, the dealer, who was a bootlegger, had to be got out of jail through the interposition of the Bishop. After he was removed from jail long enough to sell us more champagne, he obligingly returned to his cell.

Agrigento was one of the earliest Greek cities, as later it was to be one of the earliest Carthaginian cities. At Agrigento there are three very beautiful Greek temples —one to Juno, one to Concordia, and one to Hercules. There is also a sacred way connecting these temples, bordered on each side by rock-hewn tombs, now all pilfered.

The Mayor of the town, who was by way of being an archeologist, took me to look at these temples. When we came to the temple of Hercules, which was the biggest but in the worst state of repair, I asked him had it been destroyed by an earthquake. He said, "No, General, it was an unfortunate incident of the other war." When I asked which was the other war, he said that this temple was destroyed in the Second Punic War.[1]

The emergence of the Carthaginians at Agrigento, in 470 B.C. is of interest as showing that global war is not new. At that time Carthage owed a sort of lip-service alliance, or in fact vassalage, to Xerxes, King of Kings. This was the time when Xerxes was planning to cross the Hellespont and attack Greece. In order to prevent the Greeks from Syracuse and the cities in the heel of Italy from sending reinforcements to the mother country, Xerxes ordered the Carthaginians to land in Sicily and in the heel of Italy for the purpose of keeping the colonial Greeks at home.

When one thinks of the staff work and prevision necessary to arrange such an operation, when it probably took the courier a year to get from Sardis to Carthage, we can give ourselves, with our instantaneous means of communication, less credit for good planning. On the other hand, the Carthaginian Army, which landed at Agrigento and points west, and which numbered some three hundred thousand men, took five years to get to Syracuse, and having got there suffered complete defeat and total annihilation.

At a small road junction called Segesta, Hugh Gaffey and I saw the most beautiful Greek temple and theatre that I have yet encountered. With the exception of the fact that the roof of this temple no longer exists, it is in a perfect state of preservation and has been very little repaired. Since the Greeks were driven from this part of Sicily in 470 B.C.—that is, some twenty-five hundred years ago—the temple must have been built at an earlier date.

There is one rather peculiar thing about this temple. The columns are not monolithic, or composed of two or three blocks, as is usually the case, but are built up of a number of small stones. It is further noteworthy that, after the lapse of two and one-half millenniums, you cannot get a sharp knife edge between the joints and the stones.

When I was about eight years old, a minister named Mr. Bliss told me that when he visited the Parthenon he had put his silk hat on one end of the steps, and having gone to the other end had sighted across and could not

---

[1] 218-201 B.C.

see the top of his silk hat, indicating that, in order to secure agreeable lines, the straight lines of the Greek temples were actually curves. Gaffey and I tried the same thing at Segesta with two steel helmets, one on top of the other, and were unable to see them over the curve of the steps.

The theatre, capable of seating perhaps two thousand people, is on top of a very high hill, so that in addition to the view of the actors, the spectators also had ever before them a magnificent seascape. Apparently, the Greeks who built this theatre had lived in a village back of it, but owing to the inevitable cannibalism of all ancient things by succeeding generations, the town no longer exists and can be traced only by the fact that nearly all the stones lying over the hill show traces of having been worked. Speaking of cannibalism, I read that a great deal of Pisa is constructed with stone taken from Carthage.

The city and harbor of Syracuse are to me of particular interest because this place probably has been the scene of more amphibious operations than any other harbor in the world. When looking over its water I could almost see the Greek triremes, the Roman galleys, the Vandals, the Arabs, the Crusaders, the French, the English, and the Americans, who, to mention only a few, have successively stormed, or attempted to storm, that harbor.

When we first came to Sicily—and the same thing is true of Sardinia and Corsica—we were surprised at the large number of small towers dotting the coastline. These towers were apparently built between 1500 and 1600 under the influence of Genoa. The system consisted of a man picking out for himself a good spot for a tower and building it. He would then go to the government and offer to garrison the tower, usually with himself and family, if he were paid. The pay was not excessive—in our money, about fifty dollars a year. Apparently that, and not the Arab pirates, is the origin of the towers.

Another very striking characteristic, particularly of Sicily, is the fact that nearly all the towns cling like limpets to the tops of the precipitous peaks. On closer examination you will find that the highest building on these peaks is the ruin of a Norman castle.

The Normans captured Sicily between 900 and 970,

and then apparently each Norman gentleman built himself a tower—for that is what most of them are—on the highest peak he could find. In the course of time, as his riches increased, he sometimes added an inner and then an outer bailey, but this is not the general rule. The town then grew from the descendants of his soldiers and from the local people who came close to the castle in order to secure protection.

The Palais Royal at Palmero ("The Paleopolis" of Polybius) had such an origin. Its site was a volcanic outcropping, surrounded by two streams on which the Arabs erected a castle called a "ksar." This outcropping, much manicured, still exists and the original ksar, built by the Arabs around A.D. 700, still forms part of the central keep of the palace. Unfortunately the palace also has been overmanicured, and only in the basements and inner walls can one see the original building.

In the basement of the old keep we found the Norman treasury. It consisted of two stone rooms based on bedrock, one room completely within the other. In order to get into the inner room, it was necessary to open two doors and pass through a short vestibule. These doors were constructed so that when the outer door was opened giving entrance to the hallway, the inner automatically shut. When the inner door was opened, the outer door was shut. Inside, there is a pit about ten feet deep and twenty feet square with a monolithic block in the bottom. On this block was piled the largest treasure, such as vases, dishes, and the like.

In the four corners of the room are huge wine jars, which are suspended from the ceiling so that a sentinel going down through a door could see that nobody had cut into the bottom of them. It was in these wine jars that the money was kept.

When we were storming these towns or driving past them, I could almost picture in my mind's eye the small groups of knights and men-at-arms who, by virtue of occupying these strong points, ruled the world as they knew it, and how pitifully weak in numbers and armor they were in comparison with our guns, tanks, and infantry, which rolled by them in endless streams.

However, there were some things which the ancient knights and their ill-smelling companions would have understood and have laughed at—that was our improvised mule cavalry. In order to move over the terrific country through which we had to fight, we had to improvise mounted units. These men rode whatever they could find —mules, burros, and occasionally bullocks. The saddles were either of local construction, captured Italian equipment, or simply mattresses.

Once I met a young soldier with a captured Italian saddle which he had casually placed on the horse's neck in front of the withers. When I stopped him to question his ideas in so placing the saddle, the horse lowered his neck and the soldier rolled off. He said that he thought that was the place to put a saddle. I suppose that the only time he had ever been on a quadruped was at a circus when he rode on an elephant's head.

Nevertheless, this improvised horse cavalry was a tremendous advantage. In fact, we could not have won the war without it. We all regretted that we did not have a complete American cavalry division with pack artillery. Had we possessed such a unit, not a German would have escaped.

The home life of the natives is very peculiar. Apparently they have never decided to cook in any special place, so that all cooking is done in the streets. The cooking equipment has improved considerably since we came, as they now use our discarded five-gallon oil cans. Not only do they cook in the street, but sit in the street, and, what is more distressing, sing in the streets at all hours of the day and night. Owing to the fact that they live primarily on garlic, which is sold by old men carrying garlands of garlic over their shoulders, the singing not only impresses the ear, but also the nose.

The Sicilian takes much better care of his animals than does the Arab, and he practically never uses a bit, all the horses and mules being controlled by a hackamore. Also the Sicilian animals, being house-raised, are the most docile creatures I have ever seen. This also applies to the mules. To encourage these animals to pull or move forward, the Sicilian emits a noise between a belch and a groan. He has no verbal means of checking the horse because, whenever he stops groaning at it, the horse automatically halts.

One very funny thing happened in connection with the Moroccan troops. A Sicilian came to me and said he had a complaint to make about the conduct of the Moroccans, or Goums, as they are called. He said that he well

Goum

knew that all Goums were thieves, also that they were murderers, and sometimes indulged in rape—these things he could understand and make allowances for, but when they came to his house, killed his rabbits, and then skinned them in the parlor, it was going too far.

Since the greater portion of the Sicilian life is spent in sitting, it would naturally seem that after thousands of years he would have thought of making comfortable seats, but no, he sits on rocks, mud, boxes, or anything but chairs. However, they are a very cheerful people and seemingly contented with their filth, and it would be a mistake in my opinion to try to raise them to our standards, which they would neither appreciate nor enjoy.

Corsica looks exactly as if you had taken the worst part of the Rocky Mountains and submerged it in the ocean. It is nothing but a succession of high, absolutely barren hilltops, composed of polished granite in the majority of cases. However, it has two striking characteristics; it is wholly French, and it has not suffered from the air. It is a distinct shock to arrive in a city which has not been blown up. Ajaccio is just as it was.

Naples, on the other hand, has been very badly raided, but, owing to the absolutely marvelous performance of our people, the docks are in fair working order.

Pompeii comes up to the highest ideals of what a ruin should be. It also gives you the highest idea of the type of men who built it. It is very unfortunate that during our attacks it became necessary to bomb the ruins. Luckily, no very great damage was done.

"The Flight into Egypt"

Since it has been announced over the radio and also in the press that I have been to Cairo, I can now write about it.

Colonel Codman,[1] myself, and eight other members of the Staff of the Seventh Army took off from Palermo at 0715 December 12 and flew first to Benghazi, where we stopped to re-gas and to lunch.

The airfield is about fifteen miles from the town and is covered with small bomb and shell fragments, but otherwise is in fine condition. The country, while devoid of

---

[1] Colonel Charles R. Codman, Aide de Camp to General Patton and with him throughout the war.

landmarks of any sort and practically without vegetation
so that it requires navigational methods, is nevertheless
quite rolling, and I believe there are few places where at a
distance of fifteen hundred yards troops would not be in-
visible. It occurred to me that had it been possible to use
them, observation balloons, or even the old battery commanders' ladders, would have been very useful. The surface is a sort of hard-baked mud of a brownish color and
is much easier to traverse than is the sand around Indio.[1]
However, after several vehicles have gone on any one
track, the surface breaks up. This accounts for the fact
that we were informed that in desert movement vehicles
should not follow in trace. However, in Indio, we found
that it was much better to have them follow in trace.
Certainly the country seems to me very much easier to
operate in, particularly with armor, than is our own desert.

From Benghazi we flew straight across the desert to
Tobruk, which is a very small and badly banged-up town
with an artificial harbor full of wrecks.

From Tobruk we flew along the railway to El Alamein, and, although we came close to the ground, we
could see very few wrecked vehicles or guns, and practically no wire.

From El Alamein we flew along the coast to Alexandria and then up the Nile Delta to Cairo. There is a very
striking demarcation between the green of the Nile Valley and the brown of the desert. I was informed that, except for the Delta, which is about one hundred and fifty
miles wide; the rest of Egypt is less than thirty miles
wide and some twenty-five hundred miles long.

It was quite a thrill, as we approached Cairo, to see
the pyramids. We were met at the airfield by General Sir
Henry Maitland-Wilson's Aide de Camp, Major H. Chapman Walker. The Aide took Codman and myself to the
General's house, where we stayed during our entire visit.
The General himself was absent when we arrived, but his
former chief of staff and several officers lived at the house,
which, while very unpretentious, is quite comfortable. It
is situated about a twenty minutes' drive south of the city

---

[1]Indio, California, United States Desert Training Center.

in a section called Madi. Major Chapman Walker had arranged a very complete program, which, after inspection, we approved.

December 13, 1943

Codman, myself, and Major Chapman Walker, accompanied by Lady Ranforly, secretary to General Wilson, went on a shopping trip in the morning.

Cairo is really a disgusting place. It looks, and the people act, exactly as they did in New York in 1928. Both sides of the street are solid with automobiles and there are other automobiles parked in the middle of the streets. All the stores are running full blast and seem to have plenty of goods to sell, but at terrific prices. For example, I priced a pair of silk stockings which cost four pounds.

The Egyptian peasant, who abounds in large numbers, is distinctly lower than the Sicilian, whom I had previously considered at the bottom of the human curve. When the Assouan Dam was constructed, it gave a certain type of fresh-water snail a chance to develop in large numbers. This snail is the host for a sort of hookworm, which, since the construction of the dam, has become a menace. As a result of this hookworm, the Egyptian peasant constantly suffers from the bellyache and has his sexual vigor reduced. In order to relieve his pain and restore his vigor, he has taken to smoking hashish. This has the desired results for a few months and then becomes impotent, and the peasant even more susceptible to the attack of the hookworm, so that he is in a vicious circle. Prior to the war, the traffic in hashish was well under control, with the result that the natives were quite discontented; but since the war they have been able to get all the hashish they want and are now very happy. They are unspeakably dirty in their habits and in their dress. On the fresh-water canal I saw a man defecating in the water, while below him, at a distance of not more than ten yards, women were washing clothes; and a short distance farther downstream a village was drawing drinking water.

Of the whole population of Egypt, some twelve hundred own practically all the land except for a few million peasants who own approximately four-fifths of an acre apiece, while the rest own nothing. The average pay of a peasant is fifty dollars a year from which he has to rent his drinking water.

The sailboats on the Nile have the same lines they had in the days of the ancient Egyptians, but since A.D. 762 they have adopted the Arab lateen sail in place of the square sail which they formerly used. In spite of their awkward appearance, these boats sail very well, and it is said that, when an English company brought out some specially constructed sailing barges which they thought would beat the native craft, the natives sailed circles around them. As far as I could determine, the native boats have no keel, but a huge rudder which, in a sense, acts as a centerboard as well as a rudder.

After we got through shopping, we had cocktails at the famous Shepheard's Hotel. The cocktails were good, but cost about a dollar and a half apiece.

In the afternoon we visited the British Tank School, which is interesting but not anywhere as well arranged as our schools at Knox or Benning.

The Holy Land

December 14, 1943

We took off by plane for Jerusalem at 0700 and crossed the canal just south of Lake Tenes, which is near where the children of Israel crossed.

It never occurred to me until this flight that, at the time the Jews crossed, it was unnecessary for them to ford anything, because there is a stretch of desert from Bitter Lake to the Mediterranean which had no water on it. However, they did get across and Napoleon crossed at about the same place and also lost his baggage when the wind shifted.

From the canal we flew along the line of Allenby's advance and crossed at Wadi El Arish at the spot where the battle occurred. It is a much less formidable obstacle than I had gathered from the books.

Beersheba and the surrounding country do not look too difficult, but certainly away from the wells the country is an absolute sand sea, and it is difficult to understand how Allenby ever moved a cavalry corps across it.

From Beersheba we flew over Hebron and Bethelehem and turned westward just south of Jerusalem, finally landing at Aqir, near the coast, where we were met with some cars and driven thirty miles to Jerusalem.

The only reason for calling Palestine a "land of milk and honey" is by comparison with the desert immediately surrounding it. It consists of nothing but barren stony hills on which a few olive trees eke out a precarious existence. We did not see a single beehive, although there were quite a number of mimosa trees.

On reaching Jerusalem, we were met by Major General D. F. McConnell, who commands the district. He gave us a British priest, who had lived a long time in Jerusalem, as a guide to see the sights.

We entered the city through the gate which Tancred stormed when the city was first taken (A.D. 1099). The Church of the Holy Sepulchre covers both the Tomb of Christ and also the place where the Cross stood. It is run by a composite group consisting of Catholics, Greeks, and Copts, and by a strange freak of chance, or British political insight, the doorkeeper is a Mohammedan.

It struck me as an anomaly that, during my entire visit to Jerusalem, I was guarded by four secret service men, and the oddest part of it was that, when I entered the Tomb, the secret service men came in with me. People must have very little confidence to fear assassination in such a place.

From the Tomb we went to the Crusaders' Chapel where those who became Knights of Jerusalem were knighted. In this chapel is the sword which is supposed to have been used on these occasions. In my opinion it is a fake, since the pummel is not of the correct shape, nor has it sufficient weight. The pummels of Crusaders' swords were usually carved in the form of a stone or a piece of lead, which in an earlier date had actually been tied there. This pummel was in the shape of a blunt acorn. The crossguard and the shape of the blade were correct.

From here we went to the place where the Cross had stood. Most of the mountain was cut away during the Roman occupation, when they filled up the Tomb and erected a Temple of Venus over both the Mount and the Tomb. However, there is an altar which is supposed to be on the exact spot where the Cross was erected.

While I was in this chapel, I secured a rosary for Mary Scally[1] and had it blessed on the altar.

After we left the church, we followed the Way of the Cross, which is a dirty street, to the point where the Roman Forum had stood. I should think the distance is less than half a mile. In addition to the Stations of the Cross used by the Catholics, the Greeks have a number of extra ones, so that it is practically a day's trip for a Greek priest to walk down the street, as they have to stop in front of each station.

From the Forum we got into the cars and drove to the Garden of Gethsemane, where there are still olive trees which just possibly may have been in existence at the time of the Crucifixion.

After lunching with the Commanding General, we drove back to the airfield and flew back to Cairo along the coast, passing over Gaza. Although I looked very carefully, I could see no indication of the fighting, but I did recognize the cactus hedge where the tanks got stuck. We reached Cairo just at dark, having completed in one day the trip which took the Children of Israel forty years to accomplish.

On the fifteenth, it had been arranged for an eminent scholar to show us the sights, which we presumed were the pyramids. We went to Shepheard's Hotel to pick up this genius, but when I told him I wanted to go to the pyramids, he was shocked, and said that, though he had lived in Cairo for forty years, he had been there only once, and that the only things worth seeing in Cairo were the mosques. I told him I had seen all the mosques I wanted to and would have to dispense with his services.

We drove to the pyramids and picked up a fairly fluent but very ignorant native guide. To me the pyramids were quite disappointing. They are not as big nor as impressive as those around Mexico City. The Sphinx is in a poor state of preservation and rather smaller than I had expected. However, the rock temple at the foot of the Sphinx is a remarkable construction. Apparently they piled up the rocks and then cut the chapels or tombs out of them.

One of the tombs has a slab roof about twenty feet

---

[1]General Patton's nurse, ninety-six years old.

long by six feet wide by two feet thick which has been slipped into notches and upright walls and is very highly polished. This polishing and chipping was all done with bronze chisels, the Egyptians having some method of tempering bronze which has now been lost.

At 5:30 I made a talk on landing operations to all the officers of the Middle East Command, some five hundred in all. I believe that the talk went off quite well as, contrary to the British custom, they applauded and several of them wrote me letters, one of them saying that in all his previous military career he had not learned as much as in my thirty-minute lecture.

December 16, 1943

Major General Beaumont Nesbitt, in charge of visiting firemen, took me to Shepheard's Hotel, where we picked up the rest of the Staff and drove for two and one-half hours along the fresh-water canal to the Combined Operations Training Center which is on the shores of the small Bitter Lake. Apparently the British were so interested in the talk I had given yesterday evening that they asked me to repeat it to some two hundred student officers and Lieutenant General R. M. Scobie, who commands the British training there.

The Training Center, while not nearly as large or as good as the one we had at Mostaganum, had one or two improvements over our methods. They had mock-ups of the sides of ships built out into the water so that actual landing boats could come alongside, and the men could have the practice of going down the nettings into moving boats.

On the way back we had a regular dust storm, and it was quite hard to see.

General Sir Henry Maitland-Wilson had returned and was at dinner. He is a very large man and quite jovial. I was more impressed with him than with almost any other British officer I have met. All of them, including the General, were very much interested in my reaction to General Montgomery, but I was very careful in what I said and refused to be drawn out.

On the seventeenth, General Nesbitt took me to meet

General Anders, who commands the Polish II Corps. Accompanied by General Anders and the rest of our Staff, we drove to the Polish camp near Faqus, which is on the eastern side of the Delta. We had a guard of honor of a very fine-looking group of soldiers. We then had lunch. At lunch, General Anders pinned on me the insignia of a Polish Lieutenant General and the shoulder patch of the II Polish Corps. Not to be outdone, I gave him one of my United States insignia and the shoulder patch of the Seventh Army.

He struck me as very much of a man. He was Chief of Staff of a Russian division in World War I. He has been hit seven times and won the Polish decoration for valor twice. His troops are the best-looking troops, including British and American, that I have ever seen. He told me, laughing, that if his corps got in between a German and Russian army, they would have difficulty in deciding which they wanted to fight the most.

After we had inspected the II Polish Corps, Colonel Cummings[1] and I drove to Alexandria where we had been invited by the Commanding officer of the Levant, Vice Admiral Sir Arthur Willis. We crossed the whole of the Delta to get to Alexandria, but unfortunately most of the trip was in the dark so that we did not see a great deal.

December 18, 1943

At ten o'clock, Colonel Mosely, who has ridden in the Grand National four times, called for us and took us to the Yacht Club, where we were met by an Admiral and taken in a barge to inspect the harbor.

We then visited the British Tank Repair Works, which is very imposing in size and uninspiring in organization and maintenance. Among other things, we found gaskets were made by hand.

We drove back to Cairo across the desert, a distance of about one hundred and fifty miles.

---

[1]Colonel R. E. Cummings, Adjutant General for General Patton during entire service overseas.

December 19, 1943

We left Cairo at 0700 and flew up the Nile to Karnak. General Wilson had provided us with a Major Emory, who is a very distinguished Egyptologist in civil life and was number two in the Carter Expedition which dug up Tut's grave.

Karnak is on the east bank. Here we took some dilapidated Fords from the airfield to the river and then crossed in a native boat. We then took three other Fords and drove first to the Valley of the Kings. This was most interesting, as Major Emory had made many of the excavations there himself.

We first entered King Tut's tomb, which, according to Major Emory, is very small. There were originally three sarcophagi beside a stone casket. At the present time only the number two sarcophagus is in place, and in it are the remains of King Tut. The number one sarcophagus, which was of solid gold, the bullion value of which is seven thousand pounds, is in the Museum at Cairo. The one in which the King reposes is of wood, but covered with gold plating. The third outside wooden one is also in the Museum at Cairo.

Major Emory stated that the tomb of the King is built more or less as a replica of his house, and that in each room of the tomb there were the implements appropriate to that room in the house. He pointed out that, whereas an enormous amount of valuable objects were taken from King Tut's tomb, there must have been a vastly greater number in some tombs through which he led us, because, in comparison to the tomb of some of the Rameses, King Tut's was just a cubbyhole.

From the Valley of the Kings we drove to Thebes and inspected the tomb of a Prime Minister who lived in the next reign following King Tut. This was a most interesting tomb for two reasons: first, it had been discovered and opened by Major Emory; and second, it is one of the few places in Egypt where the stereotyped form of bas-relief does not exist. On one side of the entrance to the tomb the bas-relief is of the old type. On the other side it is quite modernized. The reason for this was that during the tour of office of the Prime Minister the reform religion came in, so that, while half of his tomb was cut before he was reformed, the other half was cut afterwards.

Another point which is very interesting was to see how the Egyptians worked. On the wall of this tomb, which had never been completed, you could see the line drawings of the artists who drew the sculptures, next you could see where they had been roughly chiseled out, and finally as they were completed.

We then drove to the temple and dwelling of Rameses II. There is a very interesting thing there. During his fighting in Syria, Rameses had come across crenelated battlements and had crenelations on the battlements of his palace.

We crossed the river, had lunch, and then visited the Temple of Luxor and that of Karnak. These two temples are about half a mile apart. Certainly, anyone who is interested in ruins should see all the non-Egyptian ones first because the Egyptian ruins make others look like nothing.

In the courtyard of Karnak there is a Roman Forum, which if viewed by itself would be quite impressive, but to which you have to have your attention called in order to see it, on account of its being so much overshadowed by the Egyptian monuments.

There is still in one part of Karnak the inclined plane which the Egyptians used to move stones for the erection of their buildings.

There are several obelisks in the temple. Major Emory called our attention to the fact that in the obelisks in New York, London, Paris, and Madrid, when our skilled engineers tried to erect them, they always chipped the base by not having them land perfectly perpendicularly on the pediment, but these obelisks at Karnak, which weigh at least seventy-five tons apiece, are in perfect position and alignment on the bases with no chipping.

We returned to Cairo, landing after dark. The next day, the twentieth, we flew to Palermo.

MALTA

Field Marshal Lord Gort invited me to visit him at Malta, so after a trip to Algiers, Colonel Codman, Captain Stiller, and I took off on the morning of January 4, 1944. As we were not to reach Malta until three o'clock, we had time to fly over the battlefields where the II Corps fought last spring.

When we were about sixty miles northwest of Constantine, the pilot, Captain Hetzer, told me that he had once seen a Roman ruin in that vicinity, so we hunted for it and presently found it. It is quite a large city with a big temple in a good state of preservation and a fine theatre, and yet its name is not shown on any map which I have been able to find.

As we approached Tebessa, we flew over the places where I had first taken command of the II Corps. In my mind's eye I could still see the fields covered with tanks, guns, and tents, but even in so short a time every trace of those troops had been obliterated.

The great dumps at Tebessa, which were the object of the German thrust through the Kasserine Pass, have now been completely cleared up and there is no indication that they ever existed. The same is true at Feriana where we had a Command Post, and also at Gafsa.

Looking over the country where we fought during the battle of El Guettar gives one a definite idea of the greatness of the American soldier. The mountains are impossibly difficult. I am glad that when I fought this battle I did not know how hard the country was, since we could not get an airplane from which to look at it and we had to make our decisions from the map. Had I known how difficult it was, I might have been less bold—but it is always well to remember that the country is just as hard on the enemy as it is on you.

On the other hand, the gum-tree road which penetrated our position, and over which I spent many anxious hours, is not anywhere as dangerous an avenue as it shows on the map, and had I been able to look at it from the air, I might have slept better.

After leaving El Guettar, we flew over Maknassy, where, too, all the wreckage and tanks we lost there have been completely removed.

Malta, which we reached at three o'clock, is quite different from the way I had pictured it. It is almost completely covered with villages and the areas between them are crowded with tiny fields. The only place where this crowding does not exist is on the airfields.

The island is made out of a soft porous stone which works as easily as wood when in a quarry, but which hardens when exposed to air.

In order to protect themselves against the German bombardments, a great many of the vital installations at Malta have, as the world knows, been buried in caves, but I do not believe the world knows how big these caves are, nor how relatively easy it is to construct them. Certainly, the clean-up job which the British have done since the Blitz is worthy of the greatest praise.

All the Air Corps installations, including the caves, were shown us by my friend. Air Marshal Park, who had commanded the RAF in Malta during the fighting there and had done a very wonderful job. The RAF in Malta is the best-dressed and best-disciplined Air Force that I have ever seen, whether it be American or English.

On the next day, Captain Holland, Lord Gort's Aide, took us on a sightseeing trip around the island during which we visited forts, the harbors, several churches, and other points of interest.

The forts are of a different type from any I have ever examined, being pre-Vauban, but nevertheless artillery-proof. This means that the walls are from eight to sixteen feet thick and the crenelations are for artillery rather than for small arms.

During the Siege of 1528, the three forts, one on the island and the others on the two peninsulas, were held by about four hundred knights and some eight hundred mercenaries against some forty thousand Turks.

In the construction of these forts, the nature of the island is again of advantage and has been exploited, as it is simply necessary to cut away the rock to produce a wall, while the rock thus cut away is utilized to project the wall farther up.

The most interesting thing I saw is the library of the Knights of Malta. We were taken through this by the librarian. He speaks and reads in script nine languages, so he is perfectly capable of translating the valuable collection of manuscripts in the library.

One codex, dating from 1420 and depicting the life

of Saint Anthony, who spent his time being pursued by devils in the form of beautiful women, was particularly interesting to me because in one of the pictures it showed an armorer's shop in which suits of armor, varying in date from early 1100 to 1400, were hung up for sale just as one hangs up clothes now in a pawnship. The point of interest is that most historians are prone to classify armor by dates, whereas here we have visual proof that as late as 1400 all types of armor, both mail and plate, were still being used.

Another codex which was interesting was one of the original printings of the Bible, using wood type. In this case all the capitals were omitted and subsequently illuminated by hand.

In order to be a Knight of Malta, it was necessary to have sixteen crosses of nobility, so that when anyone came up to be a knight, he had to present his genealogy, which was then studied by a college of heralds, and, if proven correct, permitted him to join. Since all these genealogies, covering the knights from sometime in 1100 to date, are preserved in the library, it gives the greatest historical family tree in the world.

In addition to the requirement of sixteen crosses of nobility, a knight had to spend eighteen months at sea on the galleys as a fighter, and then work in a hospital.

The knight also had to take four vows—Poverty, Chastity, Humility, and Obedience. The vow of Poverty required him to give four-fifths of his then estate to the Order. However, if he was a successful knight, he received from the Order more than a hundredfold over what he gave, so that most of them died very rich. This was particularly true before 1800 when the knights had a sort of stranglehold on the privateering business in the Mediterranean and used their hatred for the Turks as a means of veiling their personally conducted piracy against Turks and against anyone else whom they could catch.

The vow of Chastity was not enforced except by one Grand Master, who, in order to discourage the amorous activities of his dependents, required that all the girls live across the harbor from the forts, so that when a knight wanted to see his lady-love, he had to row across and thereby bring discredit upon himself. Apparently the discredit consisted of the other knights cheering him.

The vow of Humility was got around by the simple expedient of washing a poor man's feet three times. The vow of Obedience was rigidly enforced.

It is interesting to remember that the average Maltese has never seen a mountain, a river, a lake, a forest, or a railway train, and, according to my friends, he has no desire to meet any of them.

PART TWO
OPERATION
"OVERLORD"

This brief account of the actions of the Third Army and the XIX Tactical Air Command, commanded by Brigadier General, later Major General, O. P. Weyland, in the conflict just terminated, is a hastily written personal narrative for the benefit of my family and a few old and intimate friends.

I apologize for the frequent appearance of the first personal pronoun, and since I have criticized numerous individuals without knowing their side of the question, I must add that the story is as factual as it is possible for me to make it from my personal notes and at the time it is written.

G.S.P., Jr.

July-August, 1945

1

THE CAMPAIGN OF FRANCE, AVRANCHES, BREST TO THE MOSELLE

1 August to 24 September, 1944

On July 28, 1944, General Patton was given control of the troops of the Third Army then on the Continent of Europe.

The First Army had begun its St. Lô push on July 26. Gaining in momentum in the succeeding days, it came to a climax when General Patton exploded his Third Army onto the Brittany Peninsula on August 1.

In two weeks, troops of the Third Army had driven the fleeing Germans on the peninsula into the ports of Lorient and Brest; had cleared the Loire River to Angers; and had moved beyond Le Mans and Alençon in its drive east. (See Map, pages 102-103.) By the end of August, the Germans were still contained in the Brittany ports, and the drive of the Third Army to the east, gaining in momentum, had by-passed Paris and had reached Reims, Verdun, and Commercy. (See Map, pages 118–119.)

As early as the fifth of September, Third Army elements were in Metz and Pont-à-Mousson, and by September 15 (see Map, page 138), elements of the XII and XX Corps were along the Moselle, and, in some places, across the river. Plans from above anchored the Third Army progress to the east and lack of gas and other essential supplies brought the all-out advance to a standstill.

As the campaign ended on September 25, the Third Army had cleared the enemy from the west bank of the

Moselle, north of Metz, and had gained substantial bridge-heads east of the Moselle, south of Metz. Lunéville and Rambervillers were well within the Third Army's front lines.

During the period covered in this chapter, the American Seventh Army landed successfully in Southern France and moved north with speed and daring, contacting elements of the Third Army on September 11, north of Dijon.

The First American Army and Second British Army made parallel drives across Northern France, reaching the Belgian border, and in early September captured Antwerp and Namur. The Russians and Rumanians crossed Bulgaria, and the Russians opened a new offensive south of East Prussia. The American Ninth Army was formed on the Continent and took over from the Third Army the reduction of the ports on the Brittany Peninsula.

The American and British Air Forces continued their support of the ground forces and their bombing of the inner Reich.

As the period ended, the British had made their ill-fated paratroop drop at Arnhem; the First Army was breaching the Siegfried Line in and around Aachen; the Ninth Army completed operations on the Brittany Peninsula, except for Lorient and St. Nazaire; the Seventh Army, after clearing Epinal, was approaching the Belfort Gap.

P. D. H.

Touring France with an Army

When I was at Peover Hall, the initial Headquarters of the Third United States Army in England, in March, April, and May, 1944, it became evident that the Third Army would land either on the Cherbourg Peninsula or in the vicinity of Calais. Personally, I favored the latter place, because, while the landing would have been expensive, the subsequent price would probably have been less. In amphibious operations we should land as near the objective as possible. Calais was nearer this objective[1] than was Cherbourg.

Thinking over the probable course of events, I picked out certain points which I felt sure would be the scenes of battles or else be very critical in the operation. In fact, I told Mr. J. J. McCloy, the Assistant Secretary of War, when he visited Peover, that the first big battle of the Third Army would be at Rennes. Actually it was the second big battle.

I also picked Laval, Châteaubriant, Nantes, Angers, Tours, Orléans, and Bourges and Nevers, because at that time I felt we should go south of the bend of the Loire. I am still not sure that we should not have done so.

Many other points, at most of which we subsequently fought, were selected; but since I have not my map here, I cannot name them all. I do remember that Chartres and Troyes and, strange to say, Worms and Mainz, were marked. It is of interest to note that this study was made on a road map of France, scale 1:1,000,000, and if "The greatest study of mankind is man," surely the greatest study of war is the road net.

It is my opinion that, in the High Command, small-scale maps are best because from that level one has to decide on general policies and determine the places, usually road centers or river lines, the capture of which will hurt the enemy most. How these places are to be captured is a matter for the lower echelons to determine from the study of large-scale maps or, better still, from the ground.

I also read *The Norman Conquest* by Freeman, paying particular attention to the roads William the Conqueror used in his operations in Normandy and Brittany. The roads used in those days had to be on ground which was always practicable. Therefore, using these roads, even in modern times, permits easy by-passing when the enemy resorts, as he always does, to demolition.

We[2] left the United Kingdom on July 6, taking off by

---

[1]The heart of Germany and the destruction of the Reich.

[2]"We"—General Patton was accompanied by Major General H. J. Gaffey, then Chief of Staff of Third Army, his Aides, Lieutenant Colonel C. R. Codman and Major Alexander Stiller, Sergeant Meeks, his orderly, and "Willie," the General's dog.

plane at exactly 1025. That was a year to the minute from the date on which we left Algiers on the road to Sicily. As we flew down the east coast of the Cherbourg Peninsula, there was a tremendous mass of shipping lying off shore. After we landed and drove along the beach, the sight of the destruction of vessels was appalling. Some of this had been done by enemy action, but a great deal of it was due to the storm which raged for several days just after the initial landing. The beach defenses, particularly the pillboxes, were impressive. The fact that the Allies made a successful landing demonstrates that good troops can land anywhere.

Leaving Omaha Beach, we drove to General Bradley's Headquarters south of Isigny, where I spent the first night in the midst of the most infernal artillery preparation I have ever heard. Bradley's Headquarters was well in front of the corps artillery and right amongst the batteries of the divisional units.

Next day we drove to our first Command Post on the Continent at Nehou, southeast of Bricquebec. This château, Bricquebec, is supposed to have belonged to one of Caesar's lieutenants, and is interesting in that the principal tower is eleven-sided and shows the transition from the early square tower to the round tower. In driving to the Command Post, we had to cross the bridge at Carentan, which was supposed to be under fire and had to be crossed at high speed with big distances between vehicles. When I went over, I saw four of our soldiers sitting on it, fishing. However, every visiting fireman whom I subsequently met told me of the dangers he had encountered crossing the bridge.

Our Command Post had been very well laid out by General Gay[1] in an old apple orchard.

While there I took occasion to examine the German defenses around Cherbourg both from the ground and from the air. I also had the Army Engineer, Colonel Conklin, make drawings of them, as I felt that the Germans,

---

[1]Brigadier General, later Major General, Hobart R. Gay was General Patton's Chief of Staff throughout the war with the exception of a brief period in England and the initial months on the Continent. See Appendix F.

being a methodical people, would probably use the same form of defenses wherever we should meet them. In my opinion, these defenses were not too formidable and the results proved me correct.

The whole northern tip of the Cherbourg Peninsula

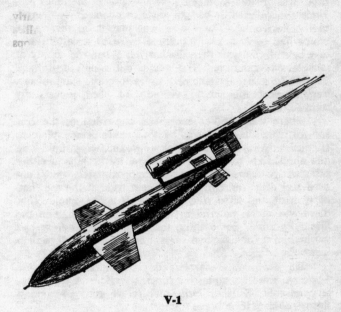

V-1

was covered with launching sites for V-1 bombs. These were very interesting. Usually a small concrete road, camouflaged to look like dirt, led off from a main road and eventually came to a concrete slab about the size of two tennis courts. On the edges of this slab were semicircular points where trucks could be left. Down the center of the slab were a number of holes. At some of the sites were caves or dugouts in which rockets could be stored. In others these were absent. The method of procedure was that, during the night, a convoy containing a certain number of rockets and a knocked-down ramp moved up. The ramp was erected by placing the uprights in the holes previously mentioned. It had an angle of about thirty degrees to the horizontal. The rocket was placed on this ramp, which had been carefully pointed to reach a certain area of England, and was then discharged. When the supply of rockets was exhausted, the whole outfit picked up and left, while a detail remained to restore the camouflage. Very few of the sites I visited had been successfully bombed.

There was another enormous construction, the reason for which has, so far as I know, never been explained. It consisted of a concrete block approximately a mile long and about sixty to eighty feet square. In the hills at either side, wedge-shaped excavations, approximately one hundred feet deep and two hundred feet wide at the top, had been made and filled with concrete. It is my opinion that there was more material in this construction than in the Great Pyramid. Some three thousand slave laborers had worked on it for over two years, and it was not more than half-completed.

On July 12 General Teddy Roosevelt[1] died, and while we were attending his funeral services at the cemetery near St. Sauveur our anti-aircraft guns sounded a fitting requiem for a brave soldier.

Secretary of War Stimson, accompanied by Mr. Bundy[2] and General Surles,[3] visited us on the seventeenth.

On the twenty-fourth, Colonel Flint[4] was killed, and

---

[1]Brigadier General Theodore Roosevelt, Assistant Division Commander of the 1st U.S. Infantry Division at the time of his death.

[2]Mr. Harvey H. Bundy, Special Assistant to the Secretary of War.

[3]Major General Alexander D. Surles, Chief of War Department Public Relations Branch.

[4]Colonel Harry A. (Paddy) Flint, Commanding Officer of the 39th Infantry Regiment of the 9th Division at the time of his death.

he and General McNair[1] were buried on the twenty-sixth. Paddy would have been pleased with his funeral. We had a special coffin made for him and he was carried to his grave in a mechanized cavalry half-track. He had an Army Commander, three Corps Commanders, an Army Chief of Staff, and a Deputy Chief of Staff, and all the cavalry-men around Headquarters for his pallbearers.

General McNair's funeral, on the other hand, was, for security reasons, a small affair. Only Bradley, Hodges, myself, Quesada,[2] and his personal aide were present.

On the twenty-fourth, General Henry[3] spent the night and we had a very pleasant time examining the launching sites and spoke to the 6th Armored Division.

The first Sunday I spent in Normandy was quite impressive. I went to a Catholic Field Mass where all of us were armed. As we knelt in the mud in the slight drizzle, we could distinctly hear the roar of the guns, and the whole sky was filled with airplanes on their missions of destruction . . . quite at variance with the teachings of the religion we were practicing.

I shall always remember very unpleasantly the time spent in the apple orchard, because I was obsessed with the belief that the war would end before I got into it. I was also certain that, by pushing harder, we could advance faster. I stated at the time, and still believe, that two armored divisions, preceded by a heavy artillery concentration using air bursts, and followed by two infantry divisions, could have cut straight down the west coast to Avranches without the necessity of waiting for an air blitz.

My belief in the practicability of this operation was greatly strengthened when the 3d Armored Division invented the hedge-spade for tanks, which was subsequently improved by Colonel Nixon.[4] All the Cherbourg Peninsula

---

[1]Lieutenant General Lesley J. McNair, Chief of the Army Ground Forces.

[2]Lieutenant General, later General, Omar Bradley, Commanding General of the Twelfth U.S. Army Group in Europe. Lieutenant General C. H. Hodges, Commanding General, First U.S. Army. Major General E. R. (Pete) Quesada, Commanding General, Ninth Tactical Air Command.

[3]Major General Guy V. Henry, War Department Staff.

[4]Colonel Thomas F. Nixon, Chief Ordnance Officer for General Patton throughout the war.

"Bocage" country—that is, it is composed of innumerable and a great deal of eastern Brittany is what is called small fields separated by banks of earth from four to six feet high surmounted by hedges. These form ideal delaying positions for infantry. The tank spade, however, cut through them like a spoon through warm butter.

An arresting sight were the crucifixes at road intersections; these were used by Signal personnel as supplementary telephone posts. While the crosses were in no way injured, I could not help thinking of the incongruity of the lethal messages passing over the wires.

While the Third Army did not become operational until 1200 on the first of August, General Bradley appointed me to command it by word of mouth on the twenty-eighth of July and explained the plans for the initial use of two corps, the VIII (Middleton) on the right and the XV (Haislip) on the left.[1]

In conformity with this plan, I visited the troops near Coutances on the twenty-ninth and found an armored division sitting on a road, while its Headquarters, secreted behind an old church, was deeply engrossed in the study of maps. I asked why they had not crossed the Sienne. They told me they were making a study of it at the moment, but could not find a place where it could be forded. I asked what effort they had made to find such a place and was informed that they were studying the map to that end. I then told them I had just waded across it, that it was not over two feet deep, and that the only defense I knew about was one machine gun which had fired very inaccurately at me. I repeated the Japanese proverb: "One look is worth one hundred reports," and asked them why in hell they had not gone down to the river personally. They learned the lesson and from then on were a very great division.

The morning of July 31, we moved our Command

---

[1]*VIII Corps* (Middleton)	*XV Corps* (Haislip)
4th Armored Division	5th Infantry Division
6th Armored Division	83d Infantry Division
8th Infantry Division	90th Infantry Division
79th Infantry Division	

The remainder of the Third Army, consisting of the XII Corps (80th Division) and XX Corps (2d French Armored Division), was not ready for action at this time.

Post to a point north of the Granville—St. Sever—Lende-lin road. It was here that Willie contracted a violent love affair with a French lady dog and also exhumed a recently buried German, to the shame and disgrace of the military service.

Gaffey, Gay, and I stayed in the old Command Post until 1545, but were not idle, because during that time we succeeded in talking the Communications Zone out of three cavalry groups which we badly needed. After supper, Gaffey and I drove to the Command Post of the VIII Corps at Brehal. Middleton was very glad to see us, as he had reached his objective, which was the Sélune River, and did not know what to do next. I told him that, throughout history, wars had been lost by not crossing rivers, and that he should get over at once. While we were talking about how to bridge it in the vicinity of Pontau-boult, the telephone rang and we were told that the bridge, though damaged, was still usable. At the time I considered this an omen of the future success of the Third Army. We also heard that the 4th Armored Division had just captured the dams east of the bridge, which also served as crossings and that they had taken four thousand prisoners. As a result of this news, I told Middleton to head for Brest and Rennes, with the 6th Armored Division and the 79th Infantry Division on Brest, and the 8th Infantry Division and 4th Armored Division on Rennes and also to create a task force under General H. L. Earnest[1] to go along the north coast of the Peninsula.

Returning to Headquarters, we passed one of the deadest Germans I have ever seen. He was half-lying, half-sitting, under a hedge in full uniform with his helmet on his chin strap in place, and was perfectly black. I had never before seen this happen to a corpse.

On the morning of August 1, everyone was busy at our camp except Harkins[2] and myself, so at high noon he and I decided to celebrate the birthday of the Third Army with a drink. The only thing we could find was a bottle of alleged brandy given Harkins by Campanole.[1] We tried to drink this, but gagged.

---

[1] See Appendix H.
[2] Colonel Paul D. Harkins, Deputy Chief of Staff for General Patton throughout the war. See Appendix F.

The passage of the two Army Corps (VIII and XV) through Avranches is one of those things which cannot be done, but was. It was only made possible by extremely effective use of veteran staff officers and by the active part taken in it by corps and division commanders who, on occasion, personally directed traffic. It was very evident that if a jam occurred, our losses, particularly with truck-borne infantry, would be terrific, and I had to say to myself, "Do not take counsel of your fears."

The immediate mission of the Third Army was to secure and maintain a bridgehead over the Sélune River between Avranches and St. Hilaire-de-Harcouet. I conceived this had best be done by the immediate capture of Brest and Lorient and proceeded on that assumption.

By evening of August 1, the 6th Armored Division had taken Pontorson where Beatrice[2] and I spent a night in 1913, when we visited Mont St. Michel. In this operation the 6th lost a battery of self-propelled guns, due to stupidity. The guns were too far to the front, too close together, and had no security detachment. The officer responsible for this was killed in the action. On the same day the 4th Armored Division was near Rennes. Here a very amusing thing happened. About an hour before sundown we received a report that an armored column was fifteen kilometers southwest of Rennes, moving in rapidly. I asked General Weyland, commanding the XIX Tactical Air Command, to send some fighter bombers to stop it. The bombers were unable to find the column, because it actually was the 4th Armored Division moving in from the northeast. However, the planes did do some very effective work knocking out enemy resistance ahead of the 4th Armored Division and this was the precursor of many other such jobs. It was love at first sight between the XIX Tactical Air Command and the Third Army.

On the second of August, Stiller and I joined the column of the 90th Division marching east from Avranches, and walked in ranks with them for some hours. At that time the efficiency of this division was extremely

---

[1]Colonel N. W. Campanole, Chief Civil Affairs Officer, Third Army. See Appendix F.

[2]Mrs. Patton.

dubious, but had just secured the services of General McLain[1] and General Weaver.[1] When we got to a point where the road turned south to St. Hilaire, I met McLain and Haislip, and was informed that the fighting down the road was caused by Weaver personally leading an assault over a bridge. This was the beginning of the making of one of the greatest divisions that ever fought, and was due largely to these two men. The division subsequently had a series of great commanders.[1]

Driving back to Army Headquarters with Haislip, I saw a young officer leap wildly out of a peep and into a ditch. I went up to find out what was the matter and they said an enemy plane was overhead. That was true, but it was so high it was practically innocuous; just another instance of the nervousness of a first fight. They got back into the car even faster than they got out.

Coming back from Avranches, sometime around the second of August, I saw one of the worst accidents I have ever witnessed. One of our engineers had fallen off a bulldozer and been run over lengthwise, so that he was practically split in two. He was still alive, and I stayed with him and gave him morphine until an ambulance came.

During this period we had a great deal of enemy air over us, although in comparison with what we gave them it was probably quite paltry. I remember one night distinctly hearing a hundred different explosions in about an hour. Of course, the fact that I could hear them showed that they were scattered.

Another night the enemy deliberately bombed and strafed their own prisoners in one of our cages. The Provost Marshal in command there turned them loose, and out of several thousand, all but fifty came back. Those who returned were extremely mad with the Germans and talked very freely.

On the fourth, Codman, Stiller, and I decided to find the 6th Armored Division. Stiller rode in the armored car to lead the way and Codman and I followed in the peep, moving via Avranches, Pontorson, Combourg, and Merdrignac. We met a very excited laison officer who told

---

[1]See Third Army Organization, Appendix H.

us that the road was under fire. Afterward we found out that the poor boy was slightly touched in the head. However, proceeding down a road for over fifteen kilometers in country known to be occupied by the enemy, and not seeing one of our soldiers, was rather exciting. Finally we caught up with the Command Post of the division.

Next day, at the briefing, I learned with considerable perturbation that I had driven right through a German division. I did not wish to chagrin our G-2 by telling him I had not been able to find it.

As we advanced into the Breton Peninsula, the attitude of the people became much more friendly. I think this is because there had been less fighting there and less bombing. The Normans in the Cherbourg Peninsula were certainly not particularly sympathetic. However, since both we and the Germans had had to bomb their towns, perhaps they should not be criticized.

On account of the great distances I had to cover, most of my travel was done in an L-5 Liaison plane and I saw hundreds of crashed planes. Around each one of these wrecks there was a path beaten by curious ghouls. The sight reminded me of dead birds partly eaten by beetles. The gliders with their big heads and wings far forward were reminiscent of dragonflies.

One day, on visiting Twelfth Army Group, General Bradley's Headquarters, I passed through St. Lô, where Beatrice and I spent a night in 1913 and bought some furniture. Up to that time it was the most completely ruined city I had ever seen. Since then my education has been improved.

The seventh of August was the heaviest air bombardment we received. I think they were light bombs, probably about two hundred pounds, and some personnel bombs. During this operation they got one of our ammunition dumps to the tune of about one thousand tons. It was still going off three days later.

As of the seventh—that is, the beginning of the second week—the 83d Division of the VIII Corps was in the outskirts of St. Malo. The 6th Armored Division was close to, but not in, Brest. Dinan had been captured by an infantry combat team of the 8th Division, which then moved on up the Peninsula west of St. Malo to attack Dinard. The 4th Armored Division was in Vannes and was approaching Lorient. The 79th Division was across the river at Laval and the 90th across at Mayenne, while the 5th Armored was near Château Gontier and reconnaissance elements of another part of the 8th Division were in Châteaubriant.

At 0830 an American Air Corps officer, who had been shot down near Angers and rescued by a member of the French Forces of the Interior, came in and told us that he had driven from Angers to Châteaubriant on the back roads and found no large formed bodies of Germans —only a few Signal Corps men taking up wire and moving east. He stated that the bridge at Angers was intact. I sent General Gaffey, the Frenchman, and Colonel Carter[1] of the Staff to Vitry to pick up a combat team of the 5th Infantry Division with some tanks and a reconnaissance troop, and attack Angers. It was a slightly risky operation, but so is war. In this case it was successful, except that the bridge was blown up in their faces just as they reached it.

Late on this day we got a rumor that the Germans had several Panzer Divisions and would attack west from the line Mortain-Barenton on Avranches. Personally I thought this a German bluff to cover a withdrawal. However, I stopped the 80th and 35th Infantry Divisions and the 2d French Armored Division in the vicinity of St. Hilaire in case something should happen.

On the eighth, Hughes[2] and I drove to Dol, which is supposed to contain the largest phallic symbol in the world, although I could not find it; then to see the VIII Corps. Next on to near St. Malo, which the 83d Division was attacking. I found Macon, who commanded the division, well up in front. When he saw General Hughes in the car with me, he turned white, and I realized he thought I was about to relieve him, so I called out, "Fine work." As a matter of fact, the division was doing well, but not too well. They had already lost eight hundred men and had taken thirteen hundred prisoners.[3]

---

[1] Lieutenant Colonel B. S. Carter, Assistant G-2, Third U.S. Army.

[2] Major General E. S. Hughes of General Eisenhower's Staff.

[3] At the time General Patton visited General Macon and the 83rd Division in St. Malo, the fighting had degenerated to a sniping

This was the day we ordered the XV Corps to attack on the line Alençon-Sées. On the eighth, St. Malo fell to the 83d and the last resistance to the 5th Division in Angers ceased.

General Spaatz,[1] Tedder, and Bradley came to Headquarters. This was the first time we had all been together since GAFSA,[2] the day the Germans bombed the main street in broad daylight just after Spaatz had told me that the British had complete mastery of the air. Tedder laughingly said, "I'll bet Patton laid that on as a wheeze." I told him I had not, but if I could find the German who did the bombing, I would certainly decorate him. As a result of this bombing, we also had the unique experience of seeing Arabs and camels run.

I became worried because there was a big hole in the American flank from St. Hilaire to Mayenne; also a second gap southwest of Alençon. The only thing I could do to safeguard these gaps was to assemble the 8th Armored at Fougères.

On the eleventh, Codman and I visited Headquarters of the XV Corps northeast of Le Mans, then the 79th and 90th Infantry Divisions and the 5th Armored Division. I could not find General LeClerc of the 2d French Armored, as he was running around up in front, although I followed him farther than caution dictated. The 2d French Armored and the 5th Armored had had quite a fight the day before in which they lost between them some forty tanks.

An amusing incident occurred on this trip. I have always insisted that anti-tank guns be placed where they can see without being seen. I came to a crucifix in the middle of a three-way road junction, and sitting exactly under the crucifix was an anti-tank gun completely unconcealed. I gave the non-commissioned officer in charge the

---

contest. Though there wasn't much noise, it was dangerous to stick one's neck out. Because of the quietude, General Patton suggested that General Macon take General Hughes and himself closer to the front. General Macon is reported to have replied, "General, if you just move up there forty yards, you'll be in the enemy front line." Nothing else was said.

[1] Lieutenant General Carl Spaatz, Commanding General, American Air Forces, under General Eisenhower.

[2] GAFSA—General Patton's Headquarters in Tunisia.

devil for not having carried out my instructions. When I got through he said, "Yes, sir, but yesterday we got two tanks from this position." So I had to apologize. Perhaps the sanctity of the location saved the gun?

We made plans for the 7th Armored Division to cross the Mayenne River at Mayenne and move on Alençon, while the 80th Division moved north to join them on the Laval-Le Mans road. Whenever the 35th Division was relieved by the First Army, it was to close up on these divisions to form the XX Corps, which then would go in on the left of the XV Corps. The 5th Infantry Division, less a combat team which was still at Angers, assembled at Le Mans and was to be joined by the 4th Armored as soon as it was relieved. These two divisions were to form the XIII Corps, prepared to move northeast—that is, on the south of the XV Corps and on the right flank of the army.

The islands off St. Malo were still giving trouble, firing at our troops on shore with their long-range guns, but so far I had had no success in persuading the British Navy to do anything about it. We also decided to ask for the air on Dinard, because we were having too many casualties trying to avoid bombing towns.

In driving to our new Command Post, six miles northwest of Le Mans, Codman and I stopped at the Château Fougères. This is the best château from a military point of view, I have ever seen, because the dwelling part of it was destroyed by Richelieu and no people have lived in it and improved it since this day. It has been taken only twice, once about A.D. 1100 and once when we took it.

On the thirteenth, it became evident that the XX Corps was hitting nothing, so we moved it northeast of Le Mans, using the 7th Armored Division and the 5th Infantry Division and sending a combat team of the 80th to Angers. This permitted us to make the XII Corps out of the 4th Armored and 35th Infantry, which was now assembled. The XV Corps, consisting as before of the 5th Armored, 2d French Armored, 90th and 79th Divisions, had taken the Alençon—Sées—Argentan line. It could easily have entered Falaise and completely closed the gap, but we were ordered not to do this, allegedly because the British had sown the area with a large number of time bombs. This halt was a great mistake, as I

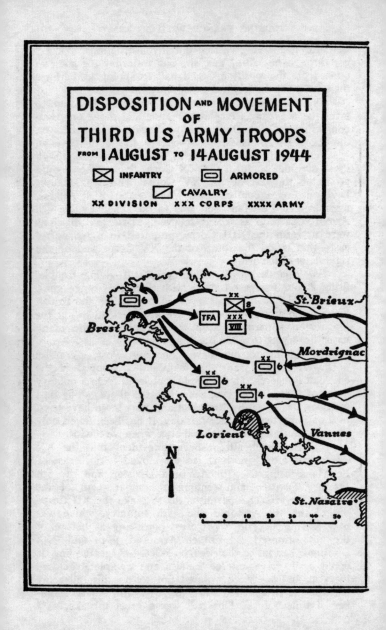

DISPOSITION AND MOVEMENT
OF
THIRD US ARMY TROOPS
FROM 1 AUGUST TO 14 AUGUST 1944

INFANTRY   ARMORED

CAVALRY

XX DIVISION   XXX CORPS   XXXX ARMY

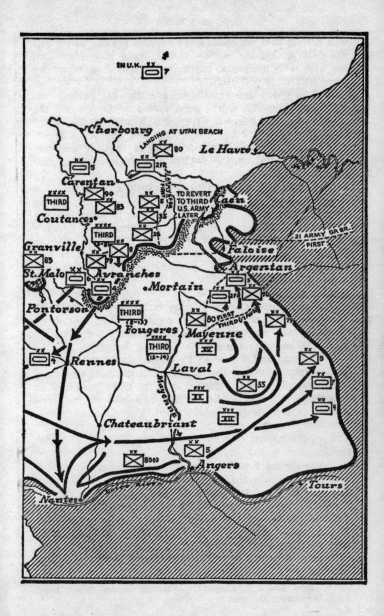

was certain that we could have entered Falaise and I was
not certain that the British would. As a matter of fact,
we had reconnaissance parties near the town when we
were ordered to pull back.

Owing to the resulting necessity of halting the
XV Corps, the XX Corps now moved on Dreux and the
XII Corps on Chartres. From this formation the army,
consisting of four corps (VII, XII, XV, and XX Corps),
could attack in any direction without crossing columns
and, in fact, did on the twelfth and thirteenth and also
later.

Thanks to the foresight of Colonel Cummings,[1] the
Adjutant General, the system of administration in the
Third Army passed direct from divisions to army, leaving
the corps in its proper sphere as a tactical unit. Because
of this arrangement we had perfect facility in shifting
divisions without losing a moment's time. We never had
to regroup, which seemed to be the chief form of amuse-
ment in the British armies.

As of August 14 the Third Army had advanced
farther and faster than any army in history. The night of
the fourteenth was the first night we had not been
bombed since starting, but in the morning we were attacked by an American plane which had got lost.

Codman and I flew to Le Mans, and I never recall
getting into a plane with more reluctance, because I had
been assured by all the Staff that, if the Germans failed to
shoot me from above, the Americans would get me from
below, as they were trigger happy, due to considerable
bombing. It was one of the few days, in fact, that I have
had a premonition of impending death. It failed to materialize.

We landed beside a road and immediately secured a
medical peep which happened to be passing. Before get-
ting into it, I had them take down the Red Cross flag, as
I did not wish to travel under false colors. After seeing
McLain of the 90th, we went to the XV Corps to orient
Haislip on what was going on. He agreed with me that,
with two divisions, he could move on Dreux and hold the
Falaise Gap with the other two. Later, I saw Bradley,

---

[1]Colonel Robert E. Cummings, Adjutant General of the Third
Army throughout the war.

who approved the plan, so we started the XV Corps on Dreux, the XX on Chartres, and the XII on Orléans. He also let me keep the 80th Division for the eastern march, replacing it in the VIII Corps with a division from the First Army which had been pinched out. To sum up, at the close of this day the arrangements were that three corps would attack east at 2030 and the VIII Corps would continue mopping up in Brittany.

Just east of Le Mans was one of the best examples of armor and air co-operation I have ever seen. For about two miles the road was full of enemy motor transport and armor, many of which bore the unmistakable calling card of a P-47 fighter-bomber—namely, a group of fifty-caliber holes in the concrete. Whenever armor and air can work together in this way, the results are sure to be excellent. Armor can move fast enough to prevent the enemy having time to deploy off the roads, and so long as he stays on the roads the fighter-bomber is one of his most deadly opponents. To accomplish this happy teamwork two things are necessary: first, intimate confidence and friendship between air and ground; second, incessant and apparently ruthless driving on the part of the ground commander. A pint of sweat saves a gallon of blood.

The spirit of the men in the Evacuation Hospitals was improving and the incidence of "battle fatigue" and of self-inflicted wounds had dropped materially. Soldiers like to play on a winning team.

General LeClerc came to see me, quite upset because he and the 90th Division were standing fast, while the 5th Armored and the 79th Infantry Divisions were moving on Dreux. I explained to him that that was the quickest way to shuffle the troops, and that I was not interested in the political repercussions of who got to the Seine first. In spite of a little rough talk, we parted friends.

There was another scare about five Panzer Divisions at Argentan, so I was ordered to halt on the line Dreux-Châteaudun. However, I talked my way out of this and started again in the morning.

On the fifteenth, Prince Felix of Luxembourg joined us.

On the sixteenth, Stiller, Codman, and I drove to Chartres, which had just been taken by Walker whom we met at the bridge, still under some fire. The bridge had been partly destroyed by a German hiding in a fox hole who pulled the detonator and blew the bridge, killing some Americans, after the leading elements had passed. He then put up his hands and surrendered. The Americans took him prisoner, which I considered the height of folly.

From there, we visited the Headquarters of the XV Corps at Châteauneuf-en-Thymérais. General Haislip had a very bad eye, due to an accident with a French truck, but he and the troops were in good spirits.

At 1830 on the sixteenth of August, Bradley called and told me to attack and capture Trun, in the Falaise Gap, with the 2d French Armored and the 90th and 80th Divisions. He also said that General Gerow, whose V Corps in the First Army had been pinched out, and whose divisions had been sent to my VIII Corps in the attack on Brest, would take over these troops (2d French Armored and 90th and 80th Divisions) as a corps, Bradley also intimated that Gerow would take over the new attack on Trun.

In the meantime, I sent Gaffey to Alençon to carry out Bradley's order and start the war; and as Bradley had sent for me, I arranged with Gay that if Gaffey was to be replaced by Gerow, I would telephone Gay the words "change horses" and add the time of attack.

Next morning I learned that Gerow and Staff had arrived at Third Army Headquarters. I called Gay, and gave what I believe was the shortest attack order ever issued to an army corps: "Change Horses 0600."[1]

In place of the three divisions we lost, we got two pinched out from the First Army and also two Ranger Battalions.

In the meantime I told Haislip to attack and take Mantes-Gassicourt with the 5th Armored and 79th Infantry Divisions. In this way we would control the German barge traffic on the Seine.

On the seventeenth of August a very sad thing happened. Major General Gilbert Cook, who commanded the XII Corps and had been Deputy Army Commander during the movement of the army from England to the Continent, became so ill from circulatory disorders that he could no longer retain command. This was a great blow to

---

[1] Gerow's arrival actually delayed the attack twenty-four hours.

both of us, and I acceded to medical opinion only after a very soul-searching time. Cook was, and is, a fine soldier and an audacious leader. He had hung onto command longer than a proper regard for his health justified. On the nineteenth, I secured Major General Manton C. Eddy to replace him. Eddy had commanded the 9th Division in Tunisia and Sicily and in the cross-Channel landing.

Colonel Odom[1] was wounded by a sniper while passing through the same woods I drove through on the sixteenth. He was standing up in his peep, having just remounted, when he felt a blow over his heart and heard a shot. He put his hand up and it came away covered with blood. When the driver saw it he said, "We will get the hell out of here," and turned so fast that Odom was almost thrown out. The bullet followed a rib and did not go into the lung cavity. Had it done so, it would have killed him. Disregarding his own medical education, he returned to duty three days after being hit.

The Sicilian Campaign had ended a year before, on the seventeenth.

On the nineteenth, in company with General Wyche of the 79th Division, we went to Mantes and saw the Seine River. I was strongly tempted to order the 79th across, but did not do so until I had seen General Bradley. When I did see him that evening, after a long flight in which we twice had to turn back on account of bad weather, he not only approved the crossing of the 79th, but ordered the 5th Armored Division of the same corps to attack north along the western bank of the Seine, while the XIX Corps (Major General C. H. Corlett) of the First Army came up on its left rear. Furthermore, he sanctioned my plan to cross the XX Corps at Melun and Fontainebleau and the XII Corps at Sens. It was evident that when these crossings were effected, the Seine and Yonne became useless to the Germans as military barriers. The Melun crossing is the same as that used by Labienus with his Tenth Legion about 55 B.C.

Colonel Codman went to Vannes and brought back my old friend, General Koechlin-Schwartz of the French Army. In World War I he was one of the leading instruc-

---

[1]Lieutenant Colonel Charles Odom, on Medical Staff of Third Army Headquarters.

tors at the Army General Staff School at Langres. We had
a very pleasant evening talking over old times and he said,
among other things, that had he thought, much less taught,
at Langres what I had been doing, he would have been
put in the madhouse. He also stated that when he heard
an armored division was heading for Brest, he knew I was
in command. I asked him why the French Army had done
so badly in 1940. He replied at once that for ten years
prior to that time the French Army had thought, taught,
and practiced defense—never attack.

On the twentieth, one combat team of the 79th
Division, XV Corps, forced a crossing at Mantes. At the
same time the 5th Armored Division, same corps, started
north on Louviers. Just as it was clearing Evreux, it was
struck in the left rear by some German armor. The 7th
Armored, which was at Evreux at the time, joined in the
fight and the Germans lost ten tanks and withdrew. However, this fight delayed the move of the 5th Armored.

In consonance with the plans I had already made on
the twentieth, I fixed the time of attack for the XX and
XII Corps on Melun, Montereau, and Sens respectively
as of daylight Monday, the twenty-first of August, so that
no one would be up in time to halt me. However, to play
safe, I gave them the code word "Proset" which, if it
came over the radio, would mean "Halt in place."

I always had a very funny feeling at such times. The
plans, when they came into my mind, seemed simple, but
after I had issued the orders and everything was moving
and I knew that I had no reserve, I had a feeling of worry
and, as usual, had to say to myself, "Do not take counsel
of your fears." The sensation is very much like that I used
to have steeplechasing. I was always very anxious to ride
the race, but when the saddling bell rang I felt scared.
When the flag dropped and the race was on, my fear left
me.

When this move started, Eddy of the XII Corps
asked me how much he should worry about his right flank.
I said that that depended on how nervous he was by nature. Of course, there was nothing to cover his right flank,
but by advancing in depth—that is, one division following
the other—this lack of defense was immaterial. If I had
worried about flanks, I could never have fought the war.
Also, I was convinced that our Air Service could locate

any groups of enemy large enough to be a serious threat, and then I could always pull something out of the hat to drive them back while the Air Force in the meantime delayed their further advance.

Having completed these instructions, we moved the Army Command Post to Brou, fifteen miles northwest of Châteaudun. It was in these woods that Willie was attacked by a large number of ferocious hornets. It took the Commanding General, the Chief of Staff, the Deputy Chief of Staff, several soldiers, and about five gallons of gasoline to burn out the hornets. Willie was very sorry for himself, and we put soda and water on his wounds.

About this time Colonel Nixon secured three complete fuses for the V–1 bombs from matériel we captured at the airdrome northwest of Orléans.

As of August 21, the end of the first three weeks, casualties for the Third Army were:

Killed	1,713
Wounded	7,928
Missing	1,702
Non-battle casualties	4,286
Total	15,629 [1]

Our replacements during the same period had amounted only to 10,622. This was the beginning of our constant dwindling in strength, caused by lack of replacements, which did not terminate until about halfway through the Bastogne fight.

During this same three weeks' period we estimated that the enemy had lost:

Killed	11,000
Prisoners of war	49,000
Wounded	48,000
Total	108,000 [1]

From our experience in Tunisia and Sicily our estimates were very accurate. Matériel losses were as follows:

---

[1] These and other sets of figures in following chapters are taken from figures posted daily on the "situation map" kept at Third Army Headquarters. They were as accurate as the reports at the time could indicate.

Third Army		*Enemy*	
Light tanks	70	Medium tanks	269
Medium tanks	157	Panther or	
Guns	64	Tiger tanks	174
		Guns	680

Tiger Tank

While we were at this camp, Judge Robert P. Patterson, Under-Secretary of War, and General Brehon E. Somervell, Chief of the Army Service Forces, visited us.

The crossings over the Seine and Yonne Rivers were successful at Montereau and Sens. The XX Corps had not yet got across at Melun, owing to the fact that there had been a very severe fight between our 2d Infantry (Colonel A. W. Roffe) of the 5th Division and several thousand Germans at Bauillet. I felt at this time that the great chance of winning the war would be to let the Third Army move with three corps, two up and one back, to the line Metz—Nancy—Epinal. It was my belief then, and still is, that by doing this we could have crossed the German border in ten days. The roads and railways were adequate to sustain us.

Elements of the 5th Infantry Division ran into some Gestapo in Orléans, who, unfortunately, attempted to escape. They also captured a very fine Cadillac car, which they presented to Third Army Headquarters.

I flew to Bradley's Headquarters to sell the above plan to him, but found that he had already gone to see Generals Eisenhower and Montgomery on a similar plan, the only difference being that he proposed to use two armies, the First and Third, whereas I proposed to use simply the Third.

The citadel at St. Malo fell to the 83d Division on the twenty-first, allegedly because an American-born German, who had been captured, was put on cook police in the citadel and had persuaded the two German cooks on duty there, who were also from Brooklyn, that the best way to end the war was to punch a hole in the water tank. This was done, and the garrison was forced to surrender because of lack of water. Whether true or not, this is a good story.

On the morning of the twenty-third, we had great excitement when it was reported that a group of Frenchmen were in camp with a proposition. I immediately thought they were asking for surrender and so had the conversation taken down. However, it turned out they simply wanted to get a suspension of hostilities in order to save Paris, and probably save the Germans. I sent them to General Bradley, who arrested them.

Just after they departed, my friend, General Juin,[1] came to see me. He was extremely complimentary and said that my daring was Napoleonic. He also said, and this was more to the point, that the easiest way through the Siegfried Line was the Nancy Gap. I had come to this same conclusion from a study of the map, because, if you find a large number of big roads leading through a place, this is the place to go regardless of enemy resistance. It is useless to capture an easy place that you can't move from. In order to make my plan for the movement on the Nancy Gap more workable, it was desirable to secure two extra divisions. Neither the 90th nor the 80th would get up in time, so I tried to persuade

---

[1]Lieutenant General A. Juin, Chief of Staff of the National Defense of France.

General Bradley to let me have two divisions from the VII Corps (Major General J. L. Collins) of the First Army, which I thought had closed on Chartres. When I talked to Bradley, I found out that this was not the case, so I had to proceed east without them.

Colonel Muller[1] and I then flew to Laval to see Bradley on the question of supply. He was at the airport waiting for me, as he had to go to see Generals Eisenhower and Montgomery. Bradley was very much worried, as he felt that Montgomery was overinfluencing General Eisenhower and would cause all or part of the American armies to turn north. Air Marshal Sir Leigh-Mallory[2] had been talking to Bradley all day trying to sell the idea. After Bradley left and in the short period of time, about ten minutes, which was necessary to ride from the airport to the Headquarters, I had what I believe was my greatest tactical idea—namely, for the Third Army to turn north, the XX Corps from Melun and Montereau, the XII Corps from Sens. This could be done faster than anything else. We would head initially on Beauvais, and could have picked up the 4th Infantry Division, First Army, which was closing in on Paris, the 79th Division, also First Army, from Mantes, and possibly the 5th Armored Division. After reaching Beauvais, we could have paralleled the Seine River and opened it to the British and Canadians, and thereafter have taken our supplies across at Mantes, saving at least fifty per cent of the haul necessary to take them via Montereau. General Leven C. Allen, Bradley's Chief of Staff, was enthusiastic, so we decided that when Bradley returned, if he telegraphed me "Plan A," I would turn north and if "Plan B," I would continue east.

If the doings of the Third Army and its General are subject to inquiry by future historians, the two points just mentioned should be a warning. In the space of two days I had evolved two plans, wholly distinct, both of which were equally feasible. The point I am trying to

---

[1]Colonel, later Brigadier General, Walter J. Muller, G-4, Chief of Supply for General Patton throughout the war.

[2]Air Marshal Sir Leigh-Mallory, Commander in Chief, Allied Expeditionary Air Forces.

bring out is that one does not plan and then try to make circumstances fit those plan. One tries to make plans fit the circumstances. I think the difference between success and failure in high command depends upon the ability, or lack of it, to do just that.

The French 2d Armored and the 4th Infantry Division entered Paris on the twenty-third. On the twenty-fourth, the British Broadcasting Company announced that Patton's Third Army had taken Paris. This seemed to me poetic justice, as I could have taken it had I not been told not to. Later, I found that when the French 2d Armored entered Paris, they told everyone they belonged to the Third Army and not to the First.

On the twenty-fifth of August, we moved the Third Army Command Post to a point between Orléans and Pithiviers. Just before starting for this point, Bradley wired me to come to Chartres. The Cathedral, from which all the glass had been removed, was not hurt in any way, and, to my mind, was more beautiful than ever, because there was enough light inside to appreciate its architecture.

Monty had won again, and the weight of the operation was to be turned north rather than east. The First Army with nine divisions was to cross the Seine at Melun and Mantes, both of which places had been captured and bridged by the Third Army. Upon crossing, the First Army would move on Lille. The Third Army, with seven divisions—namely, XII Corps, 4th Armored, 35th and 80th; XX Corps, 7th Armored and 5th Infantry; and XV Corps, 2d French Armored and 90th Infantry—was to advance alone in the direction of the line Metz-Strasbourg. So far things were not too bad, as we still had seven good divisions going in the direction in which Bradley and I always wanted to go.

Returning from this conference, I reached the new Command Post rather late and decided to fly to the XX Corps, which I had not seen for a few days. My regular pilot (Major W. W. Bennett, Commanding Officer, 14th Air Liaison Squadron, Third Army) was not there, so a sergeant pilot flew me. Presently it became very clear that we were lost, but we kept wandering around until we flew right over a German field hospital in a woods. This convinced me that we were at least fifteen miles in the rear of the German lines, so we climbed and got out as fast as we could.

On the twenty-sixth, the Signal Corps sent people around to take "A Day with General Patton." We first drove to the XX Corps, which was at Fontainebleau, then via Nemours to beyond Montereau and found the 5th Infantry Division. I complimented General Irwin on the splendid work which his division had done and had the good luck to be able to decorate several of his men with Distinguished Service Crosses.

When, early in the campaign, I had issued orders that at least one regimental combat team of infantry should ride on the tanks of an armored division, the 5th Infantry Division complained most bitterly, stating, among other things, that there was nothing for the men to hold on to. I told them that was the men's hard luck, but I was sure soldiers would rather ride on anything for twenty-five miles than walk fifteen miles. I remember that on this day Irwin was loud in his praise of tank-borne infantry. The professional soldier is certainly conservative.

We retraced our steps and crossed the Seine at Melun in company with elements of the 3d Armored Division, First Army. When they recognized me, all these men stood up in their tanks and cheered.

After leaving them, I found the Headquarters of the 7th Armored Division and told the Commanding General in very incisive language that I was not satisfied with him nor his division as to appearance or progress. This is important, because it was later necessary to relieve this officer.

I then returned to Fontainebleau and flew to the XII Corps, which was situated on the Sens—Troyes road. While there, General Wood came in to state that the 4th Armored had just captured Troyes. This capture was a very magnificent feat of arms. Colonel, later General, Bruce Clark brought his combat command up north of the town, where a gully or depression gave him cover, at about three thousand yards from the town. The edge of the town was full of German guns and Germans. Clark lined up one medium tank company, backed it with two armored infantry companies, all mounted, and charged with all guns blazing. He took the town without losing a man or a vehicle. Later, it was necessary to re-attack to get him out, because the Germans closed in behind his small force.

In reading over the account in the preceding pages of the places I went in one day, I am impressed with my own agility. Perhaps some day I shall figure out the number of miles I drove and flew trying to direct the campaigns of the Third Army. I'll bet it was about a million.

On the twenty-seventh, the XX Corps took Nogent and continued to move on Reims, while the XII Corps moved out on Châlons via Vitry. Higher authority compelled me to leave the 35th Division east of Orléans covering my right flank, although personally I did not believe you could have persuaded a German to cross the Loire in a northerly direction. I flew to Orléans, which was being shelled from across the river in a very moderate manner. The airport northwest of the town was doing a roaring business. The day before it had dispatched six hundred airplanes and was doing about the same this day. These airplanes carried gasoline and ammunition for our troops.

On the twenty-eighth, we took Château-Thierry and closed in on Vitry-le-François, Châlons, and Reims. General Bradley came about 1030. I had considerable difficulty in persuading him to let me continue the attack to the Meuse. He finally assented.

The twenty-ninth of August was, in my opinion, one of the critical days in this war, and hereafter many pages will be written on it—or, rather, on the events which produced it. It was evident at this time that there was no real threat against us as long as we did not allow ourselves to be stopped by imaginary enemies. I therefore told Eddy of the XII Corps to move on Commercy and directed Walker of the XX to do the same on Verdun. Everything seemed rosy, when suddenly it was reported to me that the 140,000 gallons of gas we were to get that day had not arrived. At first, I thought it was a backhanded way of slowing up the Third Army. I later found that this was not the case, but that the delay was due to a change of plan by the High Command, implemented, in my opinion, by General Montgomery.

I saw Bradley, General H. R. Bull (General Eisenhower's G-3), and Allen, Bradley's Chief of Staff, at Chartres on the thirtieth. I presented my case for a rapid advance to the east for the purpose of cutting the Siegfried Line before it could be manned. Bradley was very sympathetic, but Bull and, I gather, the rest of SHAEF's[1] Staff, did not concur.

It was my opinion then that this was the momentous error of the war. So far as the Third Army was concerned, we not only failed to get the back gas due us, but got practically no more, because, in consonance with the decision to move north, in which two corps of the First Army also participated, all supplies—both gasoline and ammunition—had to be thrown in that direction.

In addition to this, the air lift, on which we had previously counted for a good proportion of our supplies, was being diverted to feed the Parisians; while other transport planes were being assembled, unknown to me at the time, for an air drop in front of the Twenty-First Army Group. Finally, as a last straw, Com Z[2] used several truck companies to move their Headquarters from Cherbourg to Paris at this very date.

After receiving the above heartbreaking news, I went to our new Command Post at La Chaume, near Sens. There I found that Eddy had obtained permission from Gaffey to halt at St. Dizier, because he said that to continue beyond that point would find his tanks without any gasoline. I immediately called him and told him to continue until the tanks stopped, and then get out and walk, because it was mandatory to get crossings over the Meuse. In the last war, I drained three-quarters of my tanks in order to advance the other quarter, and I felt Eddy could do the same. I was sure it was a terrible mistake to halt even at the Meuse, because we could continue to the Rhine in the vicinity of Worms. It was a good time to quote Kipling's poem. "If." "If you can fill the unforgiving minute with sixty seconds' worth of distance run . . ."

To add to our troubles, General DeGaulle attempted to detach the 2d French Armored, which was badly needed to relieve the 35th Division, then guarding our right flank.

---

[1]Supreme Headquarters, Allied Expeditionary Force.
[2]Communications Zone, commanded by Lieutenant General J. C. H. Lee.

On the thirty-first of August, I flew with General Bradley to Morlaix on the northwestern end of the Brittany Peninsula. From there we drove to the Headquarters of the VIII Corps and then on to Plougastel—Daoulas Peninsula, which is just southeast of Brest, and met Middleton. He was not sanguine about the capture of Brest, and was full of complaints about the lack of daring on the part of the infantry. Also the Com Z had failed to bring up the amount of ammunition they had promised. I told him the explanation concerning the infantry was that they were tired out from having fought so long. On the way back, I told Bradley I could not fight on four fronts indefinitely and would like the VIII Corps turned over to someone else, Bradley, as usual, had been thinking the same thing. It was quite remarkable during this war how often the same ideas struck both of us. Spent the night with Bradley and Simpson.[1] Simpson was to take over command of the troops in the Peninsula, with the idea of using the 94th Division, when it arrived, to relieve the 6th Armored Division.

On the second of September, at Chartres, General Eisenhower gave Bradley, Hodges, and myself his plan, which was to support Montgomery in clearing the Pas de Calais area. We told him that the Third Army already had patrols on the Moselle in the vicinity of Nancy, and that patrols of the 3d Cavalry had entered Metz.

We finally persuaded General Eisenhower to let the V Corps of the First Army and the Third Army go on and attack the Siegfried Line as soon as the Calais area was stabilized. Until that time we would be able to get very little gas or ammunition. He was impressed with the thought of a great battle of Germany. Personally I did not believe, and so stated, that there would be a great battle if we pushed right on. It finally ended up with permission to secure crossings over the Moselle and prepare to attack the Siegfried Line whenever I could get the fuel to move.

On the third of September, I visited the XII Corps at Ligny-en-Barrois and explained our new plan to Eddy. I was delighted to learn he had captured one hundred

---

[1] Lieutenant General W. H. Simpson, Commanding General, Ninth Army.

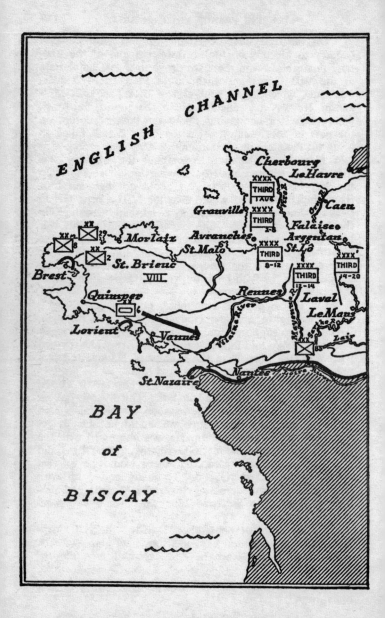

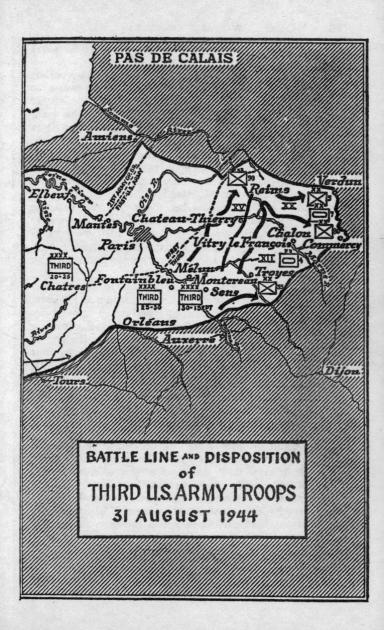

PAS DE CALAIS

Amiens

Elbeuf

Mantes

Chateau-Thierry

Paris

Reims

Verdun

Châlon

Commercy

Vitry le François

XII

Fontainbleu

Mélun

Montereau

Troyes

Chatres

THIRD
20-25

THIRD
25-30

THIRD
30-15 SEPT

Sens

Orléans

Auxerre

Dijon

Tours

BATTLE LINE AND DISPOSITION
of
THIRD U.S. ARMY TROOPS
31 AUGUST 1944

thousand gallons of aviation gasoline and so could move on; also six hundred thousand pounds of meat.

We then drove via Commercy to the Headquarters of the 80th Division at Gironville. Many of the towns we passed were pretty well smashed up. General McBride seemed to be in good form and the Colonel of his leading regiment, Davidson,[1] had the situation very well in hand. From this Regimental Command Post, Montsec stood well out to our left front, while Apremont, Pannes, and Essey were all round and very reminiscent of the time—twenty-six years, less nine days before—when we attacked in this region. Montsec has a huge monument to our dead. I could not help but think that our delay in pushing forward would probably result, after due course of time, in the erection of many other such monuments for men who, had we gone faster, would not have died. Some weeks afterward, I went over this same ground with Mr. Byrnes, later Secretary of State.

On the way back, we stopped off to see Colonel Clark, Combat Commander of the 4th Armored Division, and learned that at Vitry he had performed another remarkable feat of arms. As they approached the town, a French civilian told him that the bridge was at the end of a certain street and was covered on the far side by four German 88's, placed hub to hub on a causeway leading from the bridge. Clark charged into the town with a company of light tanks, firing in all directions and throwing hand grenades, rushed across the bridge, smothering the gunners with fire, and actually knocked the 88's off the causeway without receiving any vehicular casualties.

Since our progress from now on had to be along the lines of what General Allen calls the "rock soup" method, I will describe it. A tramp once went to a house and asked for some boiling water to make rock soup. The lady was interested and gave him the water, in which he placed two polished white stones. He then asked if he might have some potatoes and carrots to put in the soup to flavor it a little, and finally ended up with some meat. In other words, in order to attack, we had first to pretend to re-

---

[1] Colonel O. L. Davidson, Commanding Officer of the 319th Infantry Regiment, 80th Infantry Division.

M5A1

connoiter, then reinforce the reconnaissance, and finally put on an attack—all depending on what gasoline and ammunition we could secure.

There was a rumor, which, officially, I hoped was not true, that some of our Ordnance people passed themselves off as members of the First Army and secured quite a bit of gasoline from one of the dumps of that unit. To reverse the statement made about the Light Brigade, this is not war but is magnificent.

As of the end of the fourth week, casualties for the Third Army were:

Killed	2,678
Wounded	12,756
Missing	2,474
Total battle casualties	17,908
Non-battle casualties	6,912
Grand Total	24,820

Replacements numbered 19,506 and were already 5000 short.

Our estimate of the German losses was:

Killed	19,000
Wounded	62,000
Prisoners of war	73,000
Total	154,000

Matériel losses were:

Third Army		Enemy	
Light tanks	94	Medium tanks	402
Medium tanks	223	Panther and	
Artillery	83	Tiger tanks	247
		Artillery	1236

When we moved our Command Post to a point southeast of Châlons, we were visited by Mrs. Anna Rosenberg of the War Mobilization and Reconversion Office. Apparently Willie was much outraged at her appearance in a very tight pair of slacks, so gently but firmly inserted his teeth into her leg. She took it in good part.

On the fourth of September, we learned from Bradley that, the situation in the north having been stabilized, we would now get our half of the available supplies, and could cross the Moselle and force the Siegfried Line. Also that we were to get the 2d French Armored and 79th Infantry at once, and the 6th Armored and 83d Infantry as soon as they were relieved by elements of the Ninth Army. The return of the 2d French and 79th gave back to the Third Army the XV Corps which we had lost with great regret after crossing the Seine. General Haislip, the Corps Commander, came and was as delighted to be back as we were to have him.

Pending the arrival of the XV Corps east of Troyes, I had to hold the shoulder from Neufchâteau to Nancy with the XII Corps and at the same time secure a crossing over the Moselle at Toul and Pont-à-Mousson. As soon as the XV Corps was operational, the XII Corps was to advance along the line Nancy—Château Salins, the XV Corps attacking in echelon to its right rear, crossing the Moselle south of Nancy, probably in the vicinity of Charmes. The XX Corps would attack and force crossings in the vicinity of Metz.

I drove to the front, passing through Verdun and Etain, where we turned north and came to Headquarters of the 90th Division. However, we got there before the division arived. We then returned to Etain and drove to Conflans, which is famous as the birthplace of the imaginary Brigadier Gerard's Hussars. Conflans was on the front line and was being held by elements of the 2d Infantry of the 5th Division. On the eastern edge of the town, I found a combat command of the 7th Armored, which had been held up for over an hour by machine-gun and mortar fire. Of course it was absurd for an armored unit to make such a statement. I ordered it to advance, and then went back to the Division Headquarters to express my opinion to the Commander. This was the second occasion it had been my personal duty to demand more combat activity from him. General Walker had first noted his lack of pugnacity when we were at Chartres and at that time recommended that I relieve him. In spite of my reputation as a head-cutter, I really am very long-suffering.

On reaching Headquarters, I found that we were having some trouble with the First Army over gasoline. We also heard that the XII Corps had got a bloody nose at Pont-à-Mousson where one of the battalions of the 5th Division had been thrown back for a loss.

On the eighth, I drove to Ligney-en-Barrois to see Eddy, and then on to the line south of Toul, where it appeared possible that quite a battle was building up. Eddy and I went up to Wood's Headquarters, which was too close to the front, as we could actually see the fighting, and shells were dropping across the road from where we sat. It was very refreshing to find a man who got up that close.

On the ninth, General Bradley agreed to let the 83d Infantry and 6th Armored Division go up, after which we had quite a conversation about the Brest operation. We both felt that the taking of Brest at that time was useless, because it was too far away and the harbor was too badly destroyed. On the other hand, we agreed that, when the American Army had once put its hand to the plow, it should not let go. Therefore, it was necessary to take Brest.

On this same day I saw Madame de Vaux and her

son in Paris, my first visit. I had known them in Bourg[1] twenty-seven years before. After lunch she took me to see General Sérigny, Pétain's old Chief of Staff, who had broken with Pétain as a result of the latter's actions, Sérigny, whom I had known in the old war, was very gushing and said that, while he admired General Pershing, my tactics were a thousand times better. Of course, this was more French than fact. Also the mobility of the present armies is greater than anything General Pershing had. Had he possessed our mobility, I am sure he would have gone as fast or faster.

On the night of the ninth of September, the Command Post of the 90th Division was attacked by the Germans and General McLain awoke to find an enemy tank firing at a distance of about twenty feet. Fortunately, the tank was not firing at him; it apparently belonged to a group that was lost. They went back and rejoined the rest of the division and attacked at dawn. However, McLain, a great fighter, had not wasted his time and as a result of the second attack the Germans lost forty tanks and nine hundred men killed. One of the few tanks to escape was a Panther. I saw the tracks where it had gone straight into our line, oblivious of what we could do to stop it, and then turned sharply to the left on a road leading to Germany. It disappeared in a cloud of dust and sparks where our tracers were hitting it.

We learned that the XV Corps would attack along the line Chaumont—Neufchâteau—Lunéville at 0800 on the eleventh. While the XII Corps had a hard fight east of the river and south of Nancy, it continued to progress. A strange thing about this river crossing was that one regiment received heavy resistance and consequent casualties and the next regiment on its right received no resistance and no casualties. In the books, we would have stopped the attack where the resistance was and pushed the attack where the going was easy, but the books don't consider the difficulty of communication and the difficulty, or danger, of stopping a night attack once it has been launched.

The XX Corps got some infantry across south of Metz, and the 90th Division was pushing up toward the river from Metz to Thionville. Elements of the 2d French

---

[1]Headquarters, 1st U.S. Tank Brigade, 1918.

Armored Division, XV Corps, made contacts with elements of the 1st French Infantry Division, Seventh Army, in the vicinity of Sombernon on the tenth.

While flying over France, I was continually struck with the amount of human effort that had been spent in the construction of trenches and other lethal agents during both this and World War I. A pacifist could get a splendid text for a sermon on human frailty from such monuments to the evil of war. But he could get even better arguments against himself by looking at the cemeteries, where each little white cross attests to the human folly which has invariably resulted in more wars.

The twenty thousand Germans who surrendered to the Ninth Army on the eleventh stated that they wished it specifically understood that they surrendered to the Third Army and XIX Tactical Air Command and not to the Ninth Army.

On the twelfth, we had a meeting at Twelfth Army Group Headquarters on the question of supply. As Colonel R. W. Wilson, G-4 of First Army, was there, I watched my step very carefully. He had been my G-4 in the II Corps. We learned that Montgomery had told Eisenhower that the delay in the advance of the American VII Corps had been due to lack of gasoline. This was not the case; it was simply another instance of Monty trying to force everything to the north to attack the Low Countries and the Ruhr. If the High Command yielded to his blandishment, there would be nothing left for the Third Army to do but hold the west bank of the Moselle defensively, and even move the XX Corps into Luxembourg. However, I felt that could we force a crossing, this unfortunate situation could be prevented, and Bradley gave me until the night of the fourteenth to do it. Had I not secured a good bridgehead by that time, I was to stop arguing and assume the mournful role of a defender.

General Hughes brought me a new pearl-handled .38 pistol and a new issue winter coat, which was very thoughtful of him. He and I tried to visit the XV Corps, but, owing to a mistake, only got to its rear echelon. Bennett, with two planes, picked us up there on a sloping hill covered with cows. Eventually we got off. The next day Hughes and I went to the XII Corps, only to find that Eddy had gone at daylight to the 80th Division, which was heavily counter-attacked south of Pont-à-Mousson. In fact, the Germans actually got to the bridge, but the ubiquitous Colonel Bruce Clark of the 4th Armored was coming that way with his combat command and drove the Germans back. The 2d Infantry of the 5th Division and one combat command of the 7th Armored were also driven off a hill northwest of Metz by a German counterattack. However, the 35th Division and Dager's (Brigadier General H. E. Dager) combat command of the 4th Armored were well over the river south of Metz and advancing on Lunéville. The 5th Infantry, less the 2d Infantry, got across south of Metz.

While making this tour, Hughes and I saw a very nice tank fight at a range from one thousand to fifteen hundred yards. We were in a plum orchard, so could combine business with pleasure. In the foreground were two German tanks burning brightly, while beyond them three of our tanks were going up against a line of woods. We could see the gun flashes and could tell the difference between the American and German machine guns. The rate of fire of the latter is much higher than ours. We then drove to the Headquarters of the XV Corps, which we had failed to find on our last attempt. They had done an excellent job taking Neufchâteau and by-passing Chaumont. Also, they secured a crossing over the Moselle at Charmes. Archbishop Spellman visited us that evening.

By the evening of the fourteenth I had made good my promise to Bradley and had secured, in both his opinion and mine, a good bridgehead across the Moselle and felt that I could still, with luck, keep edging toward the east.

We moved to a new Command Post five miles south of Etain, which had been the German railhead for the Verdun operation in World War I; therefore, the town and the surrounding country had been very heavily shelled. In fact, the town had been completely rebuilt in 1921 with American money. On the way there I stopped for lunch at Verdun with General Bradley and General Bull. Bradley was quite depressed, because apparently Montgomery had again succeeded in persuading the High Command to move all the supplies to the First Army, leaving the Third Army to hold; but Bradley thought that the Third Army could push on. Even more depressing was the news that one corps of two divisions from the Twelfth Army Group was to go to the Seventh Army which at the moment had but one corps. Then Simpson of the Ninth Army was to get seven divisions and the First and Third Armies were to be raised to nine infantry and three armored divisions. At that time, being optimistic, I felt that the war would be over before we got the troops. Actually, during the Bulge I commanded seventeen divisions and, in April-May, 1945, eighteen.

While all this discussion was going on, we received a very welcome message that Nancy had fallen and that the XV Corps had destroyed the 16th German Infantry Division (General Lieutenant Ernst Haeckel), including sixty tanks while these tanks were in the act of attacking the right flank of the XII Corps. The XV Corps had gone over the Moselle at Charmes for the purpose of stopping this attack, and had arrived in time.

While the Command Post was at Etain, I visited the Verdun battlefields of World War I, particularly Fort Douaumont. This is a magnificent, though futile, monument to heroism. You can see all over the ruinous fragments where brave men died to maintain something they could have saved much more easily by attacking. To me Douaumont epitomizes the folly of defensive warfare.

At this time it appeared that there was a possibility of the XII Corps breaking through, and I planned that, in such an event, I would give it the 7th Armored Division and let the XX Corps, with the 83d, 90th, and 5th, contain Metz while the XII Corps, with 7th, 6th, and 4th Armored and the 35th and 80th Infantry Divisions, would drive through to the Rhine.

Next day we had a visitation of Russians, whom I avoided by going to the front, but I retaliated for their treatment of our observers by fixing them a G-2 map which showed exactly nothing. On visiting the XII Corps, I found General Eddy quite nervous. I told him to go to bed early and take a large drink, as I wished him to be in position to rush the Siegfried Line.

I was certainly very full of hopes that day and saw myself crossing the Rhine. I even advised Eddy that, in the advance, he should form a column of divisions and, after securing the gap in the Siegfried Line, he should send some armor, backed by a mounted combat team, straight on with the hope of securing a bridge at Worms, while, with the remainder of his command, he pushed back the shoulders of the hole and mopped up the area between the Saar and the Moselle. "The best-laid plans of mice and men gang aft agley."

In driving to the XII Corps via Toul, Pannes, and Essey, I went over the same places I had lived in and attacked twenty-six years and four days before. Some of the landmarks were very clear, but a wall behind which I had lain while directing an attack was made of cement, whereas in my memory it had been stone. Possibly they had built a new one. In any event, I must have walked a terribly long way on that twelfth of September, 1918.

At this same time the French were again trying to gain control of the 2d French Armored Division, which was kicking vigorously through its Corps Commander, Haislip.

Casualties for the seventeenth:

Third Army		Enemy	
Killed	3,841	Killed	26,000
Wounded	18,441	Wounded	73,000
Missing	4,120	Prisoners of war ..	87,000
Total	26,402	Total	186,000

Matériel Losses			
Light guns	121	Medium tanks	542
Medium tanks	264	Panther and	
Guns	99	Tiger tanks	307
		Guns	1596

Bradley called to say that Monty wanted all the American troops to stop so that he, Monty, could make a "dagger thrust with the Twenty-First Army Group at the heart of Germany." Bradley said he thought it would be more like a "butter-knife thrust." In order to avoid such an eventuality, it was evident that the Third Army should get deeply involved at once, so I asked Bradley not to call me until after dark on the nineteenth.

On the eighteenth, I decorated General LeClerc with the Silver Star and also gave him six Silver Stars and twenty-five bronze Stars to spread among the soldiers of

his divisions. At this time Colonel Vennard Wilson's 106th
Cavalry Group reported two columns of German infantry
attacking Lunéville from the direction of Baccarat. I told
Haislip to attack at once. He issued the orders most ex-
peditiously, and since Wyche happened to be there, everything started at once.

I then went to see Eddy at Nancy and found him
unworried. He was sending Combat Command "B" of the
6th Armored, which had closed at Toul, on Lunéville to
stop the counter-attack. I was determined that the attack
of the XII Corps on the Siegfried Line should go on in
spite of what happened at Lunéville. I was also glad to
find that the XII and XX Corps had made physical contact
north of Pont-à-Mousson.

When going over an Engineer and G-2 study of the
Siegfried Line, I found that the two places already picked
for a probably break-through by a study of the road map
exactly accorded with what a meticulous study of con-
toured maps had developed.

The nineteenth, instead of being the day I hoped it
would be, was bad. The 35th Division had been pushed off
a hill northeast of Nancy, so the enemy had observation
and could fire into the town. The 4th Armored was being
heavily attacked and the XV Corps had not yet reached
Lunéville. To cheer Eddy up, I told him two stories: first,
that Grant once said, "In every battle there comes a time
when both sides consider themselves beaten; then he who
continues the attack wins"; second, what Lee is supposed
to have said at Chancellorsville, "I was too weak to defend, so I attacked." As a result, Eddy retook the hill at
once.

He and I then drove out to see Wood. We met him
right up with Bruce Clark's Combat Command, which
had just destroyed twenty tanks. Since crossing the Moselle, Clark had killed seven hundred, taken fourteen
hundred prisoners, and destroyed seventy tanks and
twenty-seven guns. It was very apparent that Wood's
division was spread pretty thin, but I still believed we
should continue the attack. This I felt was particularly
true against Germans, because as long as you attack them
they cannot find the time to plan how to attack you.

On the twentieth, at Bradley's Headquarters, I saw a
map study which completely confirmed the line of advance

which Bradley and I had favored since the beginning, namely, to drive through with two corps abreast and the third one echeloned to the right rear on the general axis, Nancy—Château Salins—Saarguemines—Mainz or Worms, then northeast through Frankfurt. It was evident that the Third Army should have an increase of at least two infantry divisions and retain four armored divisions. I was convinced then, and have since discovered I was right, there were no Germans ahead of us except those we were actually fighting. In other words, they had no depth. It was on this day that I definitely decided not to waste capturing Metz, but to contain it with as few troops as possible and drive for the Rhine.

On the twenty-first, things picked up so far as fighting was concerned, but one of my staff, who had been with General Devers' Sixth Army Group, had heard Devers remark that he was going to take a lot of troops from the Third Army, so I flew to Paris to argue against it with General Eisenhower. Events proved my trip useless, but at the time I thought I had done something.

The next day Codman, Stiller, and I visited the 90th Division and the 358th Infantry, commanded by Lieutenant Colonel Christian Clark, who had been General Drum's Aide in 1936. We then picked up Colonel Polk of the 3d Cavalry Group and went to the far left of our line, where we were the only thing between the flank and the Germans. During this drive we passed some alleged French soldiers who were undisciplined and unarmed and solely interested in eating American rations. I decided to get rid of them.

The twenty-third was one of the bad days of my military career. Bradley called me to say that higher authority had decided that I would have to give up the 6th Armored and also assume a defensive attitude, owing to lack of supplies. General Devers had told General Eisenhower that he could supply the XV Corps via Dijon by October 1, and therefore demanded it. But Bradley and I felt that he would eventually get it, which he did. When I told my sorrows to General Gay, he said, "What price glory?" meaning that after the Moroccan victory, the Tunisian victory, the Sicilian victory, and finally now in France, we had always been whittled down. However, I had the optimism to remember that all through my life, every time I had been bitterly disappointed, it worked for the best. It did in this case, although at the time I didn't know it.

On the twenty-fourth, Gaffey, Maddox,[1] and I met the three Corps Commanders, Eddy, Haislip, and Walker, at Nancy (Headquarters, Third Army), and arranged a definite defensive front east of the Moselle. We also selected successive points along this front at which we would attack on the "rock soup" plan, ostensibly for the purpose of securing a jump-off line—actually hoping for a break-through. General Haislip was depressed at the prospect of leaving the Third Army and we were depressed at the thought of losing him.

A very fine feat of air co-operation occurred on the twenty-fourth. Five tanks of the 4th Armored were being attacked by some twenty-five German tanks, and the only thing we could send to their help was air. The weather was unflyable according to all standards, but General Weyland ordered two squadrons to attack. This they did, being vectored in by radar at a height of not over fifteen feet from the ground. Having located the enemy, they skip-bombed and also strafed him. While this fighting was going on, the pilots had no idea that they could ever land and yet carried out their job magnificently. Actually they did land successfully far back in France, where they found a hole in the clouds. One of the officers who led this attack was named Cole, and I subsequently heard that he had received the Medal of Honor. He deserved it.

The casualty report as of September 24 was:

Third Army		*Enemy*	
Killed	4,541	Killed	30,900
Wounded	22,718	Wounded	89,600
Missing	4,548	Prisoners of war	95,600
Total	31,807	Total	216,100
Non-battle casualties	13,323		
Grand Total	45,130		
Replacements	43,566		

---

[1] Colonel H. G. Maddox, G-3, Third Army, with General Patton throughout the war.

Matériel Losses

Light tanks	140	Medium tanks	708
Medium tanks	342	Panther or	
Guns	103	Tiger tanks	415
		Guns	1718

2

FORCING THE LINE OF THE MOSELLE
25 September to 7 November, 1944

The period of Third Army activities covered within the dates of this campaign was the most unproductive and uncompensatory in its history. Weather and restraining directives seemed to join hands in impeding the progress of its troops. After two months of rapid advances and offensive warfare, units were called upon to take limited objectives and to fight the elements.

In spite of the above, and with the future in mind, the front improved from the insecure bridgeheads of September 25 to secure bridgeheads, well established, with sufficient area taken, and from which successful attacks could be launched. (See Map, 138.)

During this period, German resistance increased on other European fronts. General Montgomery's Twenty-First Army Group spent the period clearing enemy troops from the port of Antwerp and the Walcheren Islands. The First Army, after clearing Aachen, continued to buck increasing resistance in the Siegfried Line. In the Vosges Mountains, the going was rugged and slow for General Devers' Sixth Army Group (American Seventh and French First Armies). The Russians entered Czechoslovakia and cleared Budapest. In Italy, the advance to the Po Valley proceeded slowly. The air forces continued to pound German airfields and industrial centers.

P.D.H.

The Flood

The period from September 25 to November 7, was a difficult one for the Third Army. For the first time in our experience we were not advancing rapidly, if at all. We were fighting, with inadequate means, against equal or superior forces in excellent defensive positions, and the weather was against us. On September 25, I received from General Bradley a Top Secret document reiterating the fact that we were to assume the defensive. It was nothing but a written restatement of the information I had received some days before. In order to make it a matter of record, I drew up and gave to General Bradley my plan for occupying a defensive position and enlarging the bridgehead over the Moselle River. The whole plan was based, as stated in the last chapter, on maintaining the offensive spirit of the troops by attacking at various points whenever my means permitted it.

On the twenty-sixth, Colonel Codman, Colonel Campanole, and I drove to Gondrécourt for the purpose of locating a Madame Jouatte, who had been General Marshall's landlady in 1917. Gondrécourt had not changed at all since I had last seen it, but the family we were in search of had gone to Southern France. However, the mayor, who had two charming daughters, gave us some wine, and one of the girls played the piano.

From Gondrécourt we drove, via Neufchâteau, to Chaumont and had lunch at the Hôtel de France, where General Pershing, General Harbord, de Chambrun,[1] and I lunched in the fall of 1917 when we visited Chaumont for the first time and selected it as Headquarters for the AEF. The same people were running the hotel—only one generation younger. They offered us some of the same kind of meat we had had in 1917. After lunch we visited General

---

[1] Colonel Jacques de Chambrun, a French officer who acted as General Pershing's personal liaison officer in World War I.

Pershing's house in town and also the barracks which had housed our Headquarters for two years.

Some fifteen days before, the XV Corps, Third Army, recaptured Chaumont, our Air Force had attacked and ruined the barracks. However, my little office by the gate was intact. I rather like it, as it was the seat of my first considerable command as Commandant of General Pershing's Headquarters, American Expeditionary Force.

While at the barracks, Colonel Campanole received a horrible shock. All the way down he had been telling us of a beautiful French girl he had known, in 1917 and 1918, and whom he had high hopes of again meeting. This lady was connected with the police in some manner, so at the barracks I asked a policeman if he knew her, explaining that she was a great friend of Colonel Campanole's. The policeman, with more candor than politeness, turned to Campy and said, "Oh, yes, I know her well, but she is too old even for you."

After receiving this shock, we drove to Val des Ecoliers, where General Pershing lived during the latter part of the war and where I was Aide to the Prince of Wales, danced with him and taught him to shoot craps. Unfortunately, the place had been very much looted.

We then drove through Langres, where we had no time to stop, and on to Bourg, my Tank Brigade Headquarters in 1918. The first man I saw in the street was standing on the same manure pile whereon I am sure he had perched in 1918. I asked if he had been there during the last war, to which he replied, "Oh, yes, General Patton, and you were here then as a Colonel." He then formed a triumphal procession of all the village armed with pitchforks, scythes, and rakes, and we proceeded to rediscover my old haunts, including my office, and my billet in the château of Madame de Vaux.

The grave of that national hero, "Abandoned Rear," was still maintained by the natives. It originated in this manner. In 1917, the mayor, who lived in the "new house" at Bourg, bearing the date 1760, came to me, weeping copiously, to say that we had failed to tell him of the death of one of my soldiers. Being unaware of this sad fact and not liking to admit it to a stranger, I stalled until I found out that no one was dead. However, he in-

sisted that we visit the "grave," so we went together and
found a newly closed latrine pit with the earth properly
banked and a stick at one end to which was affixed cross-
wise a sign saying, "Abandoned Rear." This the French
had taken for a cross. I never told them the truth.

On the way back to Etain, we passed the airfield
from which Codman had done a great deal of his flying
in World War I, and from which they operated to bomb
Conflans.

The twenty-seventh was a big day for visiting firemen. We had ten generals altogether, of whom Generals
Hughes and Spaatz were very pleasant. We also got
definite news that we would lose the XV Corps, consisting
of the 2d French Armored and the 79th Division. However, we were promised the infantry elements of the 26th
Division, Major General Willard S. Paul, and as much
more of it as we could move. I could always move any
troops given me, but I had difficulty in moving those taken
away.

This shortage of troops lasted for some time and
was scandalous. We apparently had to provide eleven infantry battalions to act as stevedores, and we also had to
use the motor transport of all newly arrived divisions to
haul supplies.

I planned to relieve elements of the 80th and all of
the 4th Armored with the 26th when it came up. The two
former divisions had had very hard fighting, and the 80th
had been occupying particularly difficult terrain. The 4th
Armored Division repelled three attacks, but a regiment
of the 35th Infantry Division was kicked off a hill north of
Château Salins. I used to get disgusted with, and still dep-
recate, the way our troops had of being kicked off places.

Stiller and I drove to Pont-à-Mousson via St. Benoit
and Thiaucourt, at which latter place is a huge United
States Cemetery—a monument to the pacifists who produced the last war. We visited a forward Observation
Post of the 80th Division in company with General
McBride. They certainly were not holding a secure bridgehead, as there were three hills looking straight down the
valley to the bridge. It was down this valley, as mentioned
in the last chapter, that the 80th received a violent counter-attack. In order to take the hills, we would have to let
one combat team of the 80th rest. I planned to do this

by relieving it with a combat team of the 26th when it arrived.

On the way back, I decorated several soldiers at a Regimental Headquarters, and also had the chance of making three battlefield promotions from Sergeant to Lieutenant.

I then picked up General Irwin of the 5th Division and we drove to visit a forward battalion of the 2d Infantry. To reach this, there was a choice of going over a high mountain in the mud on foot, or driving down a road which was under direct enemy observation and fire for about a mile. I selected the road. On the way down, they missed us quite widely, but shelled the Battalion Headquarters while I was there. They must have practiced on the road, because driving back they dropped a salvo of four 150 mm. shells; the first was well beyond us, the second near enough to be uncomfortable, the third threw mud and rocks all over us, and the fourth lit about two feet from the left-hand runningboard of my peep—it was a dud.

On the twenty-ninth of September, east of Nancy, I was present when the 35th Division was attacked by portions of one or two German divisions and lost more ground. The 4th Armored Division was also being attacked. I told Eddy to use the rest of the 6th Armored to help out the 35th. He demurred, saying if it failed, he would have nothing left. I told him that was a very good reason why it should not fail, and reminded him that Cortez burned his ships. We sent for Combat Command "B" (Colonel, later Brigadier General G. W. Read) of the 6th Armored, which was with the XX Corps. It moved in fifteen minutes.

General Eisenhower and General Bradley came to lunch and we had a new drink we called the 170. It was half brandy and half champagne. Most people thought it was all champagne, so the results were exceptionally good.

General Eisenhower explained the situation in a very lucid and convincing manner. He stated that the Sixth Army Group (Lieutenant General Jacob L. Devers' Headquarters) was not to exceed sixteen divisions and that the Twenty-First Army Group (Field Marshal Montgomery's Headquarters) was limited to seventeen divisions, owing to shortage of manpower. It actually dwindled much below this before the end of the war. Therefore, all the re-

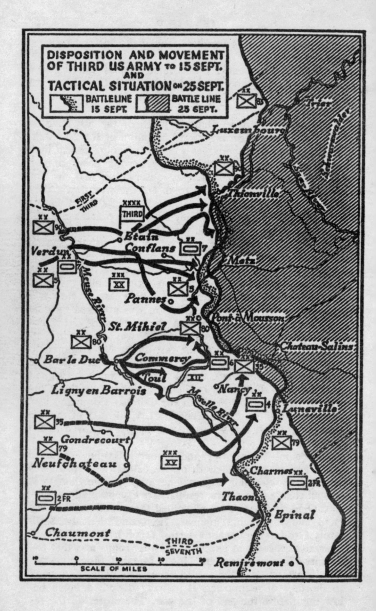

DISPOSITION AND MOVEMENT
OF THIRD US ARMY TO 15 SEPT.
AND
TACTICAL SITUATION ON 25 SEPT.

BATTLE LINE 15 SEPT.   BATTLE LINE 25 SEPT.

Trier

Luxembourg

Thionville

FIRST
THIRD

XXXX
THIRD

Etain
Conflans

90

Verdun

7

5

Metz

XX
XX
Pannes

5

St. Mihiel

80

Pont-à-Mousson

80

Commercy

Chateau-Salins

Bar le Duc

Toul

6

12

Nancy

Ligny en Barrois

Moselle River

4

Luneville

35

Gondrecourt

XV

19

Neufchateau

Charmes

2n

2 FR

Thaon

Epinal

Chaumont

THIRD
SEVENTH

Remiremont

SCALE OF MILES

maining divisions arriving in France would come to the First, Third, and Ninth Armies. At that time it was his plan to have the Ninth Army come in between the First and Third Armies, and take over Metz when we resumed our drive to the east.

After he had finished, I made the suggestion that somebody, either himself or a very high ranking officer, be designated to arbitrate between the Twelfth Army Group (General Bradley's Headquarters), the Com Z, and the Air Corps on the question of supplies. At that time the Com Z provided the supplies and also said where they were to go. Furthermore, I stated that they were too inflexible in their methods. If fighting troops had been equally inflexible, the war would have been already lost.

I also persuaded General Eisenhower to release the names of officers to the press to include regimental commanders. The names of junior officers had already been released.

As I visualized it at that time, the Germans wanted both Metz and Nancy, but, since they possessed Metz and we were not bothering them, they would be quiet there and expend all their efforts on the recapture of Nancy, because it was very apparent that Nancy, and more particularly Château Salins, was the doorway to the invasion of Germany. I explained this in my Letter of Instruction Number 4.[1]

On the thirtieth of September, I decided to take a rest, but sent General Gaffey to the XII Corps. At 1500 he called me on the radio-telephone to say I had best come to Nancy at once. When I got there, I found that the 35th Division had been permitted to withdraw from the woods west of Château Salins, and that the 6th Armored had not been put into the fight as I had directed. Apparently the 15th and 539th German Divisions were attacking the 35th. As a result of a somewhat heated conference, the 6th Armored went in and, attacking at dawn the next day, recaptured the hill and killed a large number of Germans. This could have been done the day before had my instructions been carried out. It was very fortunate that General Gaffey arrived in Nancy when he did.

---

[1] See Appendix D.

The situation, however, did not look well, and I had one combat command of the 90th Division, XX Corps, assemble with trucks ready to move on half an hour's notice. I think one explanation for the failure of the troops to stay on the hill was that three of the generals concerned had escaped death by nothing flat that same day. They were standing in a gateway when a shell came through killing two MP's and fatally wounding three others not two feet from them.

Once, in Sicily, I told a general, who was somewhat reluctant to attack, that I had perfect confidence in him, and that, to show it, I was going home. I tried the same thing that day, and it worked again.

Flying back to Headquarters, we just made it, and we actually landed in blackness. This was not too remarkable, because Major Bennett was a skillful flier.

I called the Chief of Staff of the XII Corps (Brigadier General Ralph J. Canine) at midnight and on being informed that he was asleep, I too went to bed, as I knew the situation must be all right.

Casualties for October 1:

Third Army		Enemy	
Killed	4,849	Killed	32,900
Wounded	24,585	Wounded	99,300
Missing	5,092	Prisoners of war	96,500
Total	34,526	Total	228,700
Non-battle			
casualties	14,637		
Grand Total	49,163		

Matériel Losses

Light tanks	143	Medium tanks	808
Medium tanks	363	Panther and Tiger	
Guns	103	tanks	439
		Guns	1751

On the second of October I decorated the Commanding Officers of two regiments which had retaken the hill, and then had a look over the country the 4th Armored, Major General J. S. Wood, was defending. As usual with that division the dispositions were excellent. I then visited Baade, who commanded the 35th Division and had been wounded in the fight the day before. He is the quietest man under fire I have ever seen.

For about ten days, we had been contemplating trying out the defensive qualities of the German forts covering Metz west of the Moselle. The 5th Division believed that Driant, one of these forts, could be taken with a battalion. On the third of October, they put their plan into execution and had considerable initial success. However, after about seven days of it we decided to quit, as the operation was too costly.

The 83d Division closed in on the city of Luxembourg on the fourth of October. I drove up to inspect it, and was amazed that the whole duchy was untouched by war, save for the railroad yards in the city itself. There must be something peculiar about the status of the country, because nobody bombed it.

This was the anniversary of the day I first started my efforts with the Ordnance to secure two co-axial machine guns in the mantles of all tanks. Up to the present I have had no success.

On the fifth, it was necessary to add a second battalion to the Driant attack.

Eddy came to see me about one of his division commanders, who had the pernicious habit of commanding battalions instead of combat teams. We discussed relieving him, but finally decided we didn't know anyone any better, so it would be necessary to educate him. Subsequently, he became one of the finest Division Commanders in the Third Army.

This habit of commanding too far down, I believe, is inculcated at schools and at maneuvers. Actually, a General should command one echelon down, and know the position of units two echelons down. For example, an Army Commander should command corps, and show on his battle map the locations of corps and divisions, but he should not command the division. A Corps Commander should command divisions and show on his map the location of combat teams. A Division Commander should command combat teams and show on his map the location of battalions. The Regimental Commander should command battalions and show on his map the location of companies; similarly, with the Battalion and Company Commanders.

It has been my observation that any general officer who violates this rule and at, let us say, the Army level, shows the location of battalions, starts commanding them and loses his efficiency. In Tunisia, the British G-3 to General Alexander, began telling me where to put battalions and it was necessary for me to refuse flatly to receive such orders. Alexander backed me up.

The 26th Division closed in, taking over the sector held by the 4th Armored, and one combat team relieved the northern combat team of the 80th Division.

The Germans bombarded the Headquarters of the XX Corps near Conflans with a 280 mm. gun. From the thickness of the wall of the shell and the size of the fragments, this was apparently a naval gun, probably fired from a railroad car concealed in a tunnel.

The plans for the XII Corps attack on the eighth of October were completed and approved at this time. The operation was as follows: The 80th Division to attack straight east, with its rested combat team taking the three hills in its front; one battalion of the 35th, with a tank company attached, was to attack northwest to clear the woods on the division sector, while two combat commands of the 6th Armored Division attacked north between the left of the 35th Division and the right of the 80th Division. The operation was planned as an inexpensive method of straightening the line and maintaining the offensive spirit of the troops.

On the seventh of October, General Marshall and General Bradley came, and after lunch the whole Staff was assembled and we went over the plans for taking Fort Driant, and also for the XII Corps attack. As usual, General Marshall asked very incisive questions, but I believe we were able to answer him. He was very disappointed that, owing to a promise to see Montgomery, he would not be able to be present on the eighth of October to watch our attack.

On the eighth, I decided to fly to Nancy, which was a mistake, because, owing to the weather, I could not take off until too late to see the opening phase of the battle. When I did get to the Observation Post of the XII Corps, four towns in our immediate foreground were blazing brightly and from one of them there was a column of smoke at least four thousand feet high. The tanks of the

German Railway Gun

6th Armored were moving forward against the southern flank of two villages, from which they were receiving considerable fire, while in the background the P-47's of the XIX Tactical Air Command were doing a wonderful job of bombing. Immediately in front of us, several hundred prisoners were grouped in a field awaiting further disposition. It was unfortunate that General Marshall could not have seen the fight.

After watching this for some hours. I visited General Paul, who commanded the 26th Division. He had been Adjutant of the 27th Infantry at Schofield Barracks in 1925 and 1926, where I had formed a very high opinion of him,

which was subsequently amply justified. From his Headquarters we drove to the Observation Post of the 80th Division. The southernmost of the two hills in its front had
been taken, but the northern hill, which was heavily
wooded, was apparently still occupied by the Germans.
When I arrived, they seemed content to let the Germans
stay there until morning. I conceived this to be dangerous
and directed the hill to be taken that night; this was done.

On the tenth, the three Army Commanders (Hodges,
Patton, and Simpson), with their G-4's (Chiefs of Supply),
assembled at Army Group Headquarters. When we arrived, General Bradley explained that Montgomery
claimed that the capture of the Ruhr was a two-army job
under one commander, and that he, Montgomery, should
be that commander, using his own Army and the First
United States Army. General Eisenhower agreed that it
was a two-army job, but felt that it should be two
American armies. Therefore, the Ninth Army, instead of
remaining between the First and Third Armies and using
as its initial corps the VIII Corps which was then closing
in from Brest, would move north of the First Army and
take over its XIX Corps, while the VIII Corps would
join the First Army with a Command Post in the vicinity
of Bitburg. The Third Army would lose the 83d Division
to the VIII Corps, but would eventually receive the 95th
Division and 10th Armored Division. The First and Ninth
Armies were to start the attack on the Ruhr as soon
as ammunition was available, which at that time was supposed to be October 23.

This business being settled, as Caesar says, we then
discussed the supply situation, pending the arrival of Major General Walter B. Smith, Chief of Staff to General
Eisenhower. When Smith arrived, he stated that my suggestion of having a senior officer umpire the decisions of
the Communications Zone, as to supplies, had been put
into effect, and that General R. C. Crawford, G-4 of
SHAEF, would be the officer. At this meeting, I emphasized the fact that too much attention was paid to
tonnage and not enough to requisitions. For instance, it is
perfectly useless to get a thousand tons of gasoline when
you need five hundred tons of gasoline, two hundred tons
of ammunition, and three hundred tons of bridging material. Yet the Communications Zone told you they had

moved so much tonnage. We also succeeded in putting over the point that ammunition should be issued in kind, and that we should not be told what to shoot, but what we would get, and allowed to use our own judgment on how to make the savings. It was further determined that, from this date forward, ammunition would be listed in rounds per gun per day and not in units of fire, because nobody knew what a unit of fire was. We believed at this time that sixty rounds per gun per day for 105's and forty rounds for the larger caliber were the minimum. This meant that if the supply people could average that number of rounds, an army could make a saving, so that on days of battle we could fire up to three hundred and fifty or four hundred rounds of 105's.

Casualties for October 8:

Third Army		Enemy	
Killed	5,131	Killed	36,800
Wounded	25,977	Wounded	103,000
Missing	5,096	Prisoners of war..	98,900
Total	36,204	Total	238,700
Non-battle			
casualties	16,494		
Grand Total	52,698		

Matériel Losses			
Light tanks	154	Medium tanks	822
Medium tanks	368	Panther and	
Guns	103	Tiger tanks	444
		Guns	1754

On the morning of the tenth, I drove to Nancy in time to have breakfast with General Marshall, who had spent the night with Eddy. Eddy had arranged an excellent itinerary which we followed, and saw all the divisions in his corps. During the drive, I had an opportunity of arguing for stars for Colonels Bruce Clark (later Brigadier General, Combat Command Commander, 4th Armored Division) and George W. Read (later Brigadier General, Combat Command Commander, 6th Armored Division). On the way back from the 35th Division, two salvos of enemy shell hit on the mountain above us, about three hundred yards away. This was the third time I had been shelled on that road and it seems probable that the enemy had good observation, or else a radio.

After leaving the XII Corps, we inspected the divisions of the XX Corps, accompanied by General Walker. When we visited the 90th Division, I was very emphatic in praising General McLain. After we left, General Marshall stated he had hopes of being able to give McLain a corps. During the course of the day I had several opportunities to talk at length to General Handy,[1] which was always a pleasure to me.

On the eleventh, we decided to abandon the attack on Driant. The ammunition supply at this time was extremely precarious, averaging about seven rounds per day for the 155's and not much more than twice that for the 105's.

On the twelfth, at General Bradley's invitation, I went to Verdun to meet Mr. J. F. Byrnes, Secretary of State, and, as Bradley had to go to see General Eisenhower, I spent the rest of the day taking Mr. Byrnes over the battlefields of the St. Mihiel and Meuse—Argonne. I found him one of the most interesting and well-informed men I have ever met, and enjoyed his company and comments.

On the thirteenth, we moved the Command Post to Nancy, where we were very well established in a German barracks. This was one of six barracks originally built by the French, which had been bombed at our request when we were taking Nancy. Fortunately for us, the bombing had not been very effective; when Spaatz saw it he said he hoped I would never tell anyone the Americans had done it.

On the fourteenth, General Eisenhower invited all Corps and Army Commanders to come to the Headquarters of the First Army, east of Liége, and lunch with King George of England. After the departure of His Majesty, General Eisenhower gave us a pep talk on keeping up the spirit of the offensive and also on not criticizing the Communications Zone. Under the circumstances, both of these things were easier said than done.

On the fifteenth, accompanied by General Eddy and General Wood, I gave the officers, and as many non-

---

[1] Lieutenant General T. T. Handy, Deptuy Chief of Staff, United States Army.

commissioned officers and privates of the 26th Division as we could collect, my usual pep talk. I particularly emphasized marching fire. This division was one of the first to adopt the doctrines I advocate, and throughout its fighting secured good results with small casualties.

Casualties for October 15:

Third Army		Enemy	
Killed	5,438	Killed	40,100
Wounded	27,111	Wounded	110,500
Missing	5,457	Prisoners of war	100,600
Total	38,006	Total	251,200
Non-battle casualties	18,537		

Matériel Losses			
Light tanks	156	Medium tanks	834
Medium tanks	374	Panther and	
Guns	104	Tiger tanks	445
		Guns	1766

Shortly after this, McLain was relieved to get the XIX Corps whose former commander, Major General C. H. Corlett, had gone home sick, and Major General J. A. Van Fleet took over the 90th Division. General Van Fleet, who made a wonderful Division and Corps Commander, had landed in Normandy commanding a regiment of the 4th Division, and had been among the first officers to be recommended for temporary promotion. He terminated the war commanding the III Corps.

I also visited the 95th Division which had just come in under Major General H. L. Twaddle, and gave my usual talk to the field and company officers. We drove about eight hours in the rain that day, in an open car, and got extremely wet.

On the seventeenth, Generals Gaffey and Gay and Colonels Harkins, Maddox,[1] Muller,[1] Koch,[1] and I went over the plans for the next operation. The plan was to initiate the assault with the three infantry divisions of the

---

[1]Colonel H. G. Maddox, G-3, Third Army, Colonel Walter J. Muller, G-4, Third Army, and Colonel Oscar W. Koch, G-2, Third Army, were with General Patton throughout the war.

XII Corps for the purpose of getting a bridgehead over the Seille River. When this had been accomplished, the 4th and 6th Armored Divisions were to move through the infantry. The 6th Armored Division was to secure the high ground east of Metz while the 4th Armored Division was to go on directly to the Saar River and secure a crossing south of Saargemund. One day later, the XX Corps was to attack, the 5th Division south of Metz following the 80th. The 95th Division was to contain—keep the defenders occupied—Metz and make a feint crossing north of the city, while the 90th Division was to cross north of Thionville and be followed immediately by the 10th Armored. As soon as the high ground east of Metz had been secured, the 10th Armored was to turn north and attack Saarburg, which, prior to the arrival of the 90th Division, was to be attacked by a task force under Colonel J. K. Polk, 3d Cavalry Group. It was hoped that the operation would eventuate in the capture of Metz and in the release of two armored divisions, the 4th and 6th, for a rupture of the Siegfried Line and subsequent assault on the Rhine River.

It will be noted that both the plans for the operation for the capture of Metz and the Saar campaign were worked out with much greater detail than were our operations while going across France. The reason for this is evident. Touring France was a catch-as-catch-can performance where we had to keep going to maintain our initial advantage. In this operation we had to start moving from an initial disadvantage.

On the nineteenth, Harkins took the plans to Bradley for approval. Brigadier General R. E. Jenkins (G-3, Sixth Army Group) and Colonel J. S. Guthrie (G-3, Seventh Army) called to arrange a boundary between the Seventh and Third Armies. They also wanted to procure the railroad from Toul to Nancy. There was no trouble about the boundary, since they took the one we proposed, and there was no trouble about the railroad, since I refused to share it—not from any ungenerous attitude, but simply because it was being used to the utmost to supply the Third Army.

This same evening an alleged sixty enemy planes flew over Nancy and our anti-aircraft got three certains and three probables. I have never found out what these planes were doing, as they did not drop any bombs.

On the twentieth, General Patch[1] of the Seventh Army asked me for a treadway bridge company for an operation he proposed for November 1. I arranged to give it to him.

On the twentieth, General Spaatz and I visited General Wood and saw a very interesting demonstration of tanks with and without ducks' feet.[2]

General Spaatz stayed on with Wood, and I went to visit the regiments of the 26th Division, as they were each shortly going to put on an initial show. Everything was in excellent shape, except for the lack of ingenuity in taking care of men. I showed them how to make drying rooms, and cautioned them particularly about keeping the men's feet dry. This is of interest because, shortly afterward, this division had over three thousand cases of trenchfoot.

On the twenty-first, Major General John Millikin, Commanding General, III Corps, now part of the Third Army, reported. I was opposed to having Millikin because I believed it wrong to put an officer in command of a corps who had never commanded a division in battle, while all the Division Commanders were veterans. Aside from this, I considered Millikin an excellent general.

I told Millikin to send up all the senior officers of his Corps Staff to do duty with their opposite numbers on the Army Staff, so that, when he became operational, he would know what to expect.

Eddy brought in his plan for the offensive, which was approved.

That same night the only V-1 bomb to enter the territory of the Third Army hit a hill east of the city, doing no harm.

The first attack of the 26th Division was successful, and the casualties whom I visited in the hospital were in good spirits and much elated over their triumph.

---

[1] Lieutenant General A. M. Patch, Command General, Seventh Army.

[2] Ducks' feet was a name given to extensions put on the outer edge of tracks of tanks to give more flotation in mud. They were manufactured in France and Luxembourg specifically for Third Army tanks.

Casualties as of October 22 were:

Third Army		Enemy	
Killed	5,511	Killed	40,900
Wounded	27,405	Wounded	113,100
Missing	5,407	Prisoners of war	101,300
Total	38,323	Total	255,300
Non-battle casualties	20,221		
Grand Total	58,544		

Matériel Losses

Light tanks	156	Medium tanks	834
Medium tanks	374	Panther and	
Guns	106	Tiger tanks	445
		Guns	1766

On the twenty-second, Bradley and Allen, his Chief of Staff, came and we went over the plans for the impending attack. General Bradley's contention was that if all the armies—that is, the two British, three American in the Twelfth Army Group, and Seventh Army in the Sixth Army Group—attacked simultaneously, it might well end the war. I contended, as I had set forth to him in the letter of October 19, that we were fighting three enemies. One was the German, the second was the weather, and the third was time. Of these three I conceived the weather to be the most important, because, at that moment, our sick rate for the first time equaled our battle casualty rate, and the weather was not improving. As to time, every day's delay meant more defenses to attack. I further stated there was not enough ammunition to supply all the armies, but there was enough to supply one army, and that the Third Army could attack twenty-four hours after getting the signal from then on. After considerable argument, I was given a minimum date of November 5, the attack to take place any time on or after that date that air bombardment would be available.

On the twenty-third, Walker and Eddy had a meeting under my supervision to arrange the details for their attack. General Millikin, commanding the III Corps, which was not then operational, was also present. After the meeting, I made an inspection of the supply installations in the vicinity of Toul, using for the first time a special railway car, captured from the Germans, that Muller had provided for Army Headquarters. The car was reputed to be Hindenburg's, and later Goering's, special car.

On the early morning of October 24, the Germans opened fire on Nancy with a 280 mm. gun or howitzer, continuing to fire until 0445. Three of the shells hit in the immediate vicinity of our quarters; none, I should say, more than thirty-five yards from my house. One struck the house exactly across the street from us, and the angle of fall was such that it could not have missed the roof of General Gaffey's room by more than a few inches. Nearly all the glass in our house was broken.

I heard quite a lot of screaming in the ruins and, taking my flashlight, went across the street, where I encountered a Frenchman pulling vigorously at the leg of a man who seemed to be stuck in the ruin. Taking the other leg, I joined in the good deed, with the result that the man began to scream and eventually to choke and finally ceased all noise. On investigation, we found that his head was stuck under a table and we had almost pulled it off. Aside from a sore neck, he was uninjured.

While this was going on, an old lady, caught in the ruins farther back, kept screaming, and my French friend kept reassuring her in this fashion: "I implore you, Madame, do not derange yourself; be calm, be tranquil. Try to realize that the great General Patton is himself occupying himself with the removal of the bricks so that you, too, may be saved. He has further had the humanity to send for a doctor and an ambulance. I again urge you to be tranquil." While we were getting the untranquil lady, the third near-miss arrived and threw quite a lot of rocks on us. I really believe that I was more frightened that night than at any time in my career.

The supply situation, particularly as to rations, gasoline, and ammunition, was exceptionally bad; so much so that, as of October 25, General Lee and his adherents paid us a personal visit and, I believe, made every effort to ameliorate the situation.

On the twenty-fifth, Colonel D. T. Colley's 104th Infantry Regiment, of the 26th Division, made an attack. They were about three-quarters successful, as a portion of the hill remained still in enemy possession. However, General Paul thought that they had had sufficient practice and directed another regiment to take over the assault, as of 1800. Colley got wind of this at about 1300, went up to his leading battalion and told them that the honor of the regiment did not permit them to turn over an incomplete job. He stated he would lead the assault himself, which he did with great gallantry. The position was taken, but Colley was shot in the right shoulder, the bullet progressing diagonally through both lungs and emerging from the lower part of his left lung, miraculously missing heart and blood vessels on the way. I gave him an Oak-Leaf Cluster to the Distinguished Service Cross which he had won in World War I. He made a complete recovery and returned, at his own urgent request, to command a regiment.

I visited the three combat teams of the 95th Division and made them a speech on combat.

About this time we thought we had figured out the observation posts from which the person directing the 280 mm. gun operated, and a very complicated plan was made for their capture, as they were supposed to be within our lines. Actually they were not. The P-47 dive-bombers probably accounted for the gun, because we had very little more trouble from it.

The ammunition supply was still bad, and the gasoline was not sufficient to replace the daily expenditure.

The 761st Tank Battalion (colored, commanded by Lieutenant Colonel P. T. Bates) reported to the Army on the twenty-eighth of October. This was the first of such battalions to report.

On the twenty-eighth, I directed General Walker to stop fooling around with Maizières-le-Metz, which the 357th Regiment of the 90th Division had been attacking for some days, and go in and take it. This was done successfully on the twenty-ninth, but in the action Colonel G. B. Barth, the Regimental Commander, received a wound which at the time was considered fatal. However, he recovered.

On the twenty-ninth, Weyland and I visited the Twelfth Army Group for the purpose of securing the assistance of the 83d Infantry Division in our impending attack. The idea was to have the 83d cross the bridge secured by the 90th and advance rapidly, covered by

Polk's cavalry group, to take Saarburg and possibly Trier, then revert to First Army. After considerable discussion, Bradley consented to give me operational control of the 83d Division, provided I would not use more than two regimental combat teams.

Another point of discussion was whether or not we would have to reduce our units to T/O[1] strength prior to the anticipated assault, as, during the lull, we had secured sufficient replacements to be over strength for the first time. General Bradley was very cute about this. He said, "You will notice that the order for reduction of over strength takes effect after the fifteenth of November, by which time the action of the enemy will probably have done it." General Weyland, with my assistance, argued for the retention of one of the fighter groups of the XIX Tactical Air Command, which was being sent to the Ninth Army, but we were unsuccessful.

On the thirty-first, I inspected and made a talk to the 761st Tank Battalion. A good many of the lieutenants and some of the captains had been my sergeants in the 9th and 10th Cavalry. Individually they were good soldiers, but I expressed my belief at that time, and have never found the necessity of changing it, that a colored soldier cannot think fast enough to fight in armor.

Before we left England, Bradley and I evolved the idea of having one extra colonel in each division, so that in the event of a casualty we would have a man immediately available. This was necessary, because the difference in age between the regimental and battalion commanders was such that the latter did not have the necessary experience to take over a regiment. One of the colonels I secured for this job was my classmate, Bob Sears, who is three years older than myself. He took command of a regiment of the 35th Division about the third of August and commanded it through all its fighting until the thirty-first of October, when, in spite of his great heart and meticulous personal care, it became evident that he would have to be relieved, or die at his post. He had made a great reputation for himself and had

---

[1]Tables of Organization, the controlling documents for the strength of Army units.

actually killed seven Germans with his own hands. I believe
this is a record for a regimental commander in any war.

When General Spaatz visited General Wood, as already recounted, he was distressed at the fact that Wood
lived in a very wet and muddy tent, so he sent him his
own trailer. We had a presentation of this trailer to
General Wood. It was a huge affair and most luxurious.
I have never seen a man more pleased than Wood, and
yet more determined not to use the trailer.

On November 2 at 1400, we had a conference of
Corps Commanders, General Weyland, myself, and the
Army General Staff, and representatives of the 8th and
9th Air Forces to make a definite arrangement as to when
and where the Air would strike in the impending attack.
As the result of this meeting, the priorities on targets,
notably the Metz forts and the woods in front of the 80th
Division, were established, and it was decided that the
date of the First Army's attack would be called D-Day;
that the XII Corps would launch its infantry attack on D
plus 1 and its armor on D plus 2, unless the situation permitted a more rapid engagement of armor; that the XX
Corps would launch a demonstration by the 95th Division to the north and west of Metz on D plus 1 and the
90th Division would launch its attack north of Thionville
on D plus 2. After much discussion, the boundary between
the XX and XII Corps was also established.

On November 2, General Bradley and General A.
Franklin Kibler (his G-3), came to Nancy and stated it
was evident that the British would not be ready to jump
off prior to November 10, and probably not before the
first of December. He further stated that the First Army
could not jump off until at least two of the American
divisions, then attached to the British, were released and
returned to the First or Ninth Armies. He wanted to know
when I could jump off. I told him that, as already stated,
I could jump off the day after a successful air attack, or
not later than the eighth in the event that weather prevented an air attack. General Bradley said he was very
glad to find somebody who wanted to attack.

On November 3, I addressed the assembled officers
and non-commissioned officers and a few selected privates
of the three infantry divisions of the XII Corps; namely,
the 26th, 35th, and 80th. I impressed upon them the honor

which had been given the Third Army of being permitted to attack alone. I also reiterated my insistence on the use of marching fire and of all supporting weapons.

Final arrangements were made through Weyland that, in the event the Air could not bomb prior to darkness on November 7, the XII Corps would jump off on November 8 without air support. I had a telephone conversation with Bradley, at this time, on the use of 83d Division. I requested that some of the corps artillery with it be authorized to cross the Moselle River and support the two combat teams in their attack. We did not get to a definite decision on this subject.

Due to bad weather the tentative air bombardment of Metz set for the fifth was impossible, and the bombers went deep into Germany to release their loads.

Devers visited me that day and promised that the Seventh Army would support my right flank.

On the fifth, I addressed the officers of the 10th Armored 90th Infantry, 95th Infantry Divisions and Headquarters of the XX Corps. Each of these addresses took place in the rain. They were my usual pre-battle pep talks.

General Hughes came to visit me on the fifth. On the sixth, he and I made talks to the 4th and 6th Armored Divisions at their request. I had not originally included them in my schedule, because I felt they were such veteran and experienced divisions that it was painting the lily to talk to them; but they seemed to feel quite hurt, so I talked to them. In talking to the 4th, I said, making a joke of the fact that the First Army was not coming in as originally planned, "the First shall be last and the 4th shall be first."

On the sixth, I told the press that the attack would come off on or before the morning of the eighth of November. I gave them full details and asked them to keep the thing a secret. I further asked a radio representative to announce on the air that the attack was a limited objective attack for the purpose of straightening the line for winter occupation and told him I would inform him when he could change this statement. He did exactly as asked, and I believe the broadcast had some effect in deceiving the Germans.

It was strange to think that two years ago on the seventh of November we were approaching Africa aboard the *Augusta*. It blew hard all afternoon, but at 1600 the wind stopped and we made a perfect landing on the Moroccan coast. At 1430 on the afternoon of the seventh this year, it was raining hard as it had been for some time. At 1900, Generals Eddy and Grow came to the house and argued with me to hold off the attack on account of bad weather and swollen rivers. I asked them whom they wished to name as their successors because the attack was to go off as scheduled. They immediately assented and, as usual, did great work.

The casualty report as of November 7 was:

Third Army		Enemy	
Killed	5,734	Killed	42,500
Wounded	28,273	Wounded	117,000
Missing	5,421	Prisoners of war	103,000
Total	39,428	Total	262,500
Non-battle casualties	24,386		
Grand Total	63,814		
Less total casualties (battle and non-battle) as of September 24	45,130		
Total casualties for period September 24 to November 7 inclusive	18,684		

It is interesting to note that the necessity of halting on the Moselle resulted in the above losses, which, had we been able to continue our advance on September 24 might not have occurred and certainly not in such numbers.

Matériel losses as of November 7 were:

Third Army		Enemy	
Light tanks	157	Medium tanks	834
Medium tanks	374	Panther or Tiger tanks	445
Guns	109	Guns	1173

3

THE CAPTURE OF METZ AND THE SAAR CAMPAIGN
8 November to 8 December, 1944

It was not difficult to get the troops of the Third Army out of the lethargy produced by the inactivity of October. They were never defensive-minded, and were ready at the drop of a hat to take off in any direction.

The hat dropped with the beginning of the November 8 offensive. Though the elements were against them, through October, Third Army units had nudged farther forward into the German lines in order to gain the use of better springboards.

From September 25 to November 7, they had pushed forward an average of four thousand kilometers to the east, south of Metz, and north of that city they were strong enough to cross the Moselle at any place.

The new offensive to the east began early on the morning of November 8. One thousand thundering guns opened the attack, which jumped off despite floods, rain, and fog. Slow, tedious, and costly though the advance, by mid-December operations had progressed sufficiently to call for a new set of plans—a new co-ordinated effort —a break-through to the Rhine. Metz fell to the Third Army on December 13, the first time it had been taken by assault A.D. 641. (*See Map pages 160–161.*)

This new offensive was planned, with the help of General Spaatz and his Eighth Air Force, for the nineteenth of December. The air-blitz was to be the greatest of its kind yet attempted. One thousand heavy bombers of the Eighth Air Force were to pound enemy positions for

*three consecutive days. Orders were issued, commanders
informed, replacements promised, troop movements begun, prayers offered: everything was in readiness. One
thing only was amiss—the German High Command had
not been consulted. The result—"The Bulge." (See Map,
page 190.)*

*On other fronts the Twenty-First Army Group
moved slowly against strong resistance. The First Army
consolidated its gains. The Russians advanced to Budapest.
In Italy, Ravenna was taken. The Sixth Army Group swept
through the Vosges Mountains and reached the Rhine at
Strasbourg Colmar, and beyond Hagenau. The Air Force
continued its heavy offensive strikes. In the Pacific, Tokyo
began to feel the full weight of the American offensive,
while the Navy supported the ground troops in taking
Leyte.*

P. D. H.

Stuck in the Mud

I woke up at 0300 on the morning of November 8,
1944, and it was raining very hard. I tried to go to sleep,
but finding it impossible, got up and started to read Rommel's book, *Infantry Attacks*. By chance I turned to a
chapter describing a fight in the rain in September, 1914.
This was very reassuring because I felt that if the Germans
could do it I could, so went to sleep and was awakened
at 0515 by the artillery preparation. The rain had stopped
and the stars were out. The discharge of over seven hundred guns sounded like the slamming of so many heavy
doors in an empty house, while the whole eastern sky
glowed and trembled with the flashes. I even had a slight
feeling of sympathy for the Germans, who must now have
known that the attack they had been fearing had at last
arrived. I complacently remembered that I had always
"Demanded the impossible," that I had "Dared extreme
occasion," and that I had "Not taken counsel of my fears."

At 0745, Bradley called up to see if we were attacking. I had not let him know for fear I might get a stop order. He seemed delighted that we were going ahead. Then General Eisenhower came on the phone and said, "I expect you to carry the ball all the way." Codman, Stiller, and I immediately drove to the Observation Post of the XII Corps, but there was so much artificial fog and smoke from the pots covering the bridges that we could see little. At about 1000, fighter-bombers appeared in force and attacked the known enemy command posts. The day was the brightest and best we had had for two months.

I visited the Headquarters of the 80th, 35th, and 26th Divisions and also saw General Wood. By dark that night every unit was on its assigned objective for the day; unfortunately it started to rain.

Visiting the front on the ninth was very disheartening. Many of the bridges were out; trucks, airplanes, and one hospital platoon were marooned by the flood waters, and things looked bad. However, when I got to the 5th Division, General Irwin, Division Commander, and Colonel A. W. Roffe, Commander of the 2d Infantry, and myself went up on a hill and saw 1476 planes of the Eighth Air Force come over and bomb the targets at Metz. It was a great sight. At first we saw smoke corkscrews in the air, and some of us thought they were German anti-aircraft rockets. Actually they were markers from our lead planes. We were close enough so that the roar of the motors was very distinct, and the ground where we were shook constantly.

On the way back, we found that every bridge on the Moselle River, except one at Pont-à-Mousson, was out, and that the Seille River had increased in width from two hundred to five hundred feet. On the other hand, I ran into Combat Command "B" of the 10th Armored Division, Brigadier General E. W. Piburn, near Mars la Tour, the scene of the great cavalry battle in 1870, and they were looking fine and moving right into action with beautiful discipline. Five battalions of the 90th Division were over the Moselle River that night.

Generals Spaatz, Doolittle,[1] and Curtis,[1] and Profes-

---

[1]Lieutenant General James H. Doolittle, Commanding General, Eighth United States Air Force, and Brigadier General E. F. Curtis, Chief of Staff for General Spaatz.

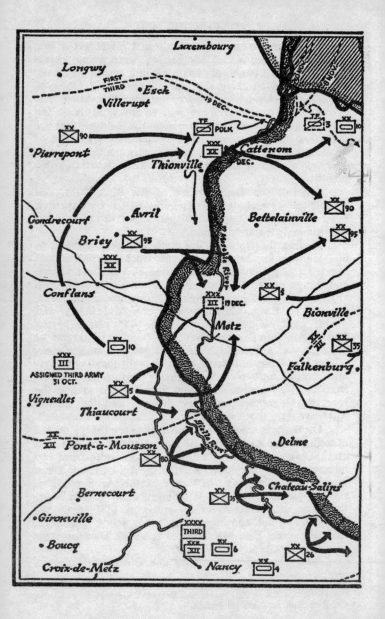

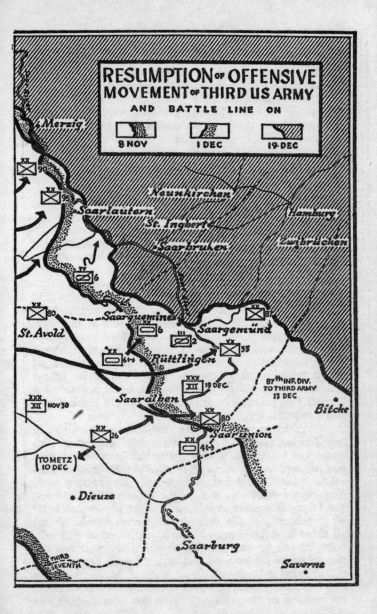

RESUMPTION OF OFFENSIVE MOVEMENT OF THIRD US ARMY

AND BATTLE LINE ON

8 NOV   1 DEC   19 DEC

Merzig

Neunkirchen

Saarlautern

St. Ingbert

Hamburg

Saarbruken

Zweibrücken

Saarguemines

Saargemünd

St. Avold

Rüttlingen

Saaralben

87th INF. DIV.
TO THIRD ARMY
13 DEC

Bitche

XXX XII NOV 30

(TO METZ
10 DEC)

Saarunion

Dieuze

Saar River

Saarburg

THIRD
SEVENTH

Saverne

sor Bruce Hopper, historian for the Air Force, spent the night. I was very grateful to them, because I am quite sure that the wonderful air support we had received that day was due largely to the friendship of these men.

On the tenth, the river had gone down a little and the bridge at Pont-à-Mousson, which went out on the night of the ninth, was again usable. This was very satisfactory, as, prior to that time, I had seven divisions across an unfordable river, and no bridges. The 4th Armored Division went well and the 6th Armored Division, moving northeast, caught a column of Germans between it and the 5th Infantry Division and had a big killing. Haislip of the XV Corps came in to assure me that the XV Corps would cover the right flank of the Third Army. The XV Corps was at this time assigned to the Seventh Army.

I had hoped to win this battle by the eleventh, as it was my birthday and my lucky day in West Africa. However, I did not win it.

Bradley called up at 1710 and, in my opinion, crawfished quite flagrantly in forbidding me to use the 83d Division. I believe he had been overtalked, either by Middleton or Hodges, or both. I was very sore at the time, and still regard it as a great mistake. Had two combat teams of the 83d been used to attack Saarburg, that town would have fallen on the twelfth or thirteenth, and we would probably have captured Trier. With Trier in our hands, Von Rundstedt's break-through could not have occurred. This probably is another case of "On account of a nail a shoe was lost," etc.

Trenchfoot was becoming very acute at this time. In one division alone there were three thousand cases. This could not have been wholly prevented, because the men had to ford rivers more than waist-deep, so that even rubber boots would not have helped. However, a good deal of the fault was due to the officers and non-coms not taking corrective measures. I wrote a personal letter on trenchfoot and the situation improved. I ordered that all shoes be dubbed prior to issue, and directed that prisoners of war be used for this purpose. Also that one dry pair of socks per man be sent forward each day with the rations. Owing to the efforts of Colonel Muller, we were now practically equipped with overshoes for the infantry, but in some of the regiments the unfortunate mistake was made of thinking that the overshoes tired the men too much, and they did not wear them when they should have. Because of the difficulty with trenchfoot, it became more and more evident that it was desirable to get both corps into column of divisions so that some divisions could rest and dry out while others went on.

The heads of the Staff sections gave me a birthday party in Colonel Koch's quarters, where we had Armored Diesels[1] to drink, field expedient type—"field expedient" meaning that the adequate liquors for making the old 2d Armored Diesel were not available.

On the twelfth, the 90th Division received a violent counter-attack by the equivalent of a German infantry division. This they repelled in a very gallant manner, although they had no tanks and no tank-destroyer guns on the east side of the Moselle River, and the bridge behind them was out. However, the corps artillery, to the extent of some thirty battalions, came in effectively.

The ammunition situation had improved, except in the case of 240 mm. howitzers and eight-inch guns.

General Eisenhower called to tell me he had removed General Silvester, Commander of the 7th Armored Division, from his command, and that Silvester had stated I had a personal animus against him. This was not true, because I had kept corps commanders from reducing him as early as August.

On the thirteenth, the Seventh Army jumped off. Bradley and Bonesteel[2] visited me and we drove to the Headquarters of the XII Corps at Château Salins. We also visited the 4th Armored Division, and Bradley had an opportunity of seeing how really bad the mud conditions were. Tanks actually bellied down when off the roads.

We were promised the infantry of the 75th Division[3] on December 10 and the whole of the division by December 15. Also, that we would get the 11th Armored Division, which was then embarking in the United Kingdom.

---

[1] Ingredients of the original: Juice of one lemon, sugar to taste, one and one-half ounces of rye or bourbon, one teacup of shaved ice; whirl in a mixer.

[2] Major General Charles H. Bonesteel, of General Eisenhower's staff.

[3] Commanded by Major General Fay B. Prickett. This division did not become assigned to the Third Army at this time.

At that time Bradley had the idea that, when the Fifteenth United States Army was organized, he would use it to take over the area back of the Third and First Armies so as to give us a smaller army area to look after.

Later in the evening, we visited the wounded in the hospital, and found them in excellent spirits. The attitude of the wounded throughout this operation was magnificent.

On the fourteenth, I had to dissuade General Eddy from by-passing Falkenberg.

I visited Walker and we inspected the 95th Division. The losses of this division since November 8 had been 80 killed and 482 wounded. This was too many casualties for the little ground gained, and I so told Twaddle.

At Thionville we saw the longest Bailey bridge in the world. It had just been completed by the Engineers, and was built under fire. Some fire was then falling in the vicinity, but the bridge was not hit while we were on it. We then drove to Cattenom and crossed a treadway bridge under a smoke screen, and visited the 90th Division. The crossing of the 90th Division over the Moselle was an epic river crossing done under terrific difficulties. After they got two battalions over, the bridge went out and everything else had to come across in assault boats.

General Van Fleet took us to see the battlefield of the twelfth, and I have never seen so many dead Germans[1] in one place in my life. They extended for a distance of about a mile, practically shoulder to shoulder.

The 10th Armored Division started crossing at this date, so we were really making progress.

On the fifteenth, General Eisenhower came, and we visited the XII Corps and the 26th and 35th Divisions. He was very well pleased with what was going on and was photographed walking in the mud, of which there was an ample supply.

That night we had a very amusing incident. I wanted to have a good fire for General Eisenhower in his room, and we had such a good one that the hotel caught fire and

---

[1] The dead Germans were the result of a concentration of twenty-seven battalions brought down on their heads by the XX Corps. The American Graves Registration Service, in policing the battlefield, had carried many to the roadside for further disposal.

we had considerable difficulty in putting it out. In fact, Colonel Jimmy Gault, his British Aide, and myself got in quite a sweat.

As of November 15, the operation was quite satisfactory, except that the 4th Amored had been set back a little bit and the Seventh Army had not done as much as we hoped. The XII Corps started to shift divisions with the idea of getting the 6th Armored Division ready to exploit, should they get a break-through.

Casualties as of November 15 were:

Third Army		*Enemy*	
Killed	6,778	Killed	48,000
Wounded	35,296	Wounded	131,000
Missing	7,700	Prisoners of war..	111,000
Total	49,844	Total	290,000
Non-battle casualties	29,857		
Grand Total	79,701		

Matériel Losses			
Light tanks	182	Medium tanks	857
Medium tanks	410	Panther or	
Guns	114	Tiger tanks	454
		Guns	1836

On the sixteenth, General Eisenhower left, after visiting the Ordnance and Quartermaster installations, and also a hospital.

I heard from Marlene Dietrich,[1] who was in Germany during the First World War, that the Germans used tetanus antitoxin, or serum, as a treatment for trenchfoot, so we started trying it on a few volunteers in the hospital; it had no results.

At Falkenberg, on the seventeenth, we learned from prisoners that there were a number of delayed bombs with as much as twenty-one days' delay fuses buried throughout the town. Subsequently, about fifteen of these went off.

Eddy called me to state that his allowance of shells

---

[1] On the U.S.O. Show Circuit.

for the eighteenth was nine thousand, but I told him to go ahead and shoot twenty thousand, because I could see no reason for hoarding ammunition. You either use it or you don't. I would lose more men by shooting nine thousand rounds a day for three days than I would by shooting twenty thousand in one day—and probably not get as far. I believe in fighting until lack of supplies forces you to stop—then digging in.

The eighteenth was a great day for the Air. The XIX Tactical Air Command started flying at dawn and flew until well after dark; then they sent out their night fighters which attacked some fifteen convoys in the darkness.

The XX Corps made good progress. The 90th and 95th Divisions both advanced long distances and were practically within contact of the 5th Division east of Metz. The 10th Armored Division was on its objective. Things looked so good that I could almost picture myself going through the Siegfried Line any day. I was slightly overoptimistic.

I visited the Headquarters of the 5th Division at Fort Leisne in the vicinity of Verny. The 10th Infantry (commanded by Colonel Robert P. Bell) in that division made a night attack and advanced six kilometers to cut the last enemy escape route from Metz. While I was at the fort, this unit made physical contact with elements of the 90th Division, and elements of both the 5th and 90th started fighting in the streets of Metz by 1100 that day. The night attack was interesting, because they had to advance through a mine field. They chose to do it in the dark and, as a result, lost about thirty-five men. Had they advanced in the daytime, they would probably have lost the same thirty-five men to mines; and, in addition, several hundred men to machine gun and rifle fire.

At Verny we saw a very good example of heavy bombing. When a direct hit with a big bomb was made on one of the forts, the bombs crippled it, but not to the extent one would imagine. However, the shock effect due to the detonation is probably very great.

The last German column to attempt to get out of Metz was caught on the road by a company of medium tanks from the 6th Armored Division, who opened fire on them at a range of about one hundred and fifty yards.

on their way to the Sixth Army Group and I tried to sell the idea of using the XV Corps, basing my demand for it on the fact that between Lunéville and Thionville there was room for only one army, and there was just one natural corridor. While this was a sound argument, it did not succeed.

The short days and tremendous distances made it very desirable to move the Command Post forward, but, with the exception of St. Avold, there was no road net from which one could command, and at that time St. Avold was occupied by the XII Corps. In picking a Command Post, you must always have a road net from which you can move forward to any portion of your line. A Command Post situated at a spot where it is necessary to move to the rear is disadvantageous. In this connection it is always best, where practicable, to drive to the front, so that the soldiers can see you going in that direction, and to save time, fly back by Cub so that you are never seen going to the rear.

Speaking of flying reminds me that, when we first began moving across France, I used to notice from the air innumerable fox holes on each side of the main roads. On inquiry it turned out that, in order to make the

Piper Cub

German truckdrivers stick to their jobs, such protection had to be provided, so that when our bombers came down on them they could jump into a hole. The local inhabitants were required to dig and maintain these places and they very promptly filled them up once we had passed.

Another thing which impressed me was the number of shell craters in open fields, where they had apparently done no harm at all. Unquestionably this was often the case, but when one thinks how seldom bullets from either guns or rifles find their billets, one should not be too critical of the air bombing. On the other hand, practically all the German airfields looked as if they had had a recent case of erysipelas, they were so full of craters.

On the twenty-fifth, I visited the 95th Division. The morale of the men was good, but their method of attack seemed to me wanting in push. Several 88's or 105's struck near us on this drive. We then passed through Metz, and it was a very pleasant feeling to enter a city which had not been captured for thirteen hundred years.

We received a number of replacement captains. I initially assigned them to companies under lieutenants until they had learned the ropes. While this is not authorized in Regulations, I did it in both this and the First World War, and it works.

The Seventh Army sent a proposed boundary between themselves and the Third Army which would have pinched us completely out, but we finally persuaded them to accept the boundary which we would have used between the XII and XV Corps had we secured the XV Corps; namely, north boundary: Lorentzen—Rahlingen —Boulin—Waltholben—Kaiserslautern—Bobenheim. I called General Haislip to congratulate him on his breakthrough, which had really been a fine piece of work.

Averell Harriman, Ambassador to Russia, visited us, and I took him to the 4th Armored Division to show him that the Russians were not the only people who had to contend against mud. On this drive we traversed four old and two new tank ditches, varying from twelve to fifteen feet deep and from twenty-five to thirty-five feet in width. Also innumerable lines of trenches, all of which had been passed by our men, because, almost invariably, they had not been adequately defended. The amount of man-hours used in digging these futile defenses is appalling. When we were with the 4th Armored, we crossed the Saar River and spat on the far bank.

I decorated a lieutenant, who, in command of one of our M-4 Shermans had put out five German Panther tanks. I then searched out the location of this great exploit and found all the destroyed vehicles still smoking. The tracks in the mud showed what had happened. Our tank had been coming down the road, hugging a high bank, and suddenly saw slightly ahead, in a hollow to its right, two Panther tanks at a range of about two hundred and fifty yards. These it engaged and put out of action; then, apparently, charged to finish them, and, by so doing, uncovered three more tanks, which it engaged at a range of not more than forty yards. All the German tanks were put out and so was ours.

Harriman told me that Stalin, in the presence of the Chief of Staff of the Russian Army, had paid the Third Army a very high compliment when he stated, "The Red Army could not have conceived and certainly could not have executed the advance made by the Third Army across France."

On the twenty-eighth, Generals Brereton[1] and Ridgway[2] called at Third Army Headquarters looking for a job for the Airborne Army. I showed them an area between Worms and Mainz which, from a ground standpoint, was the most desirable crossing place. They stated that it looked all right to them and that they would make a study.

The trouble with the Airborne Army is that it is too ponderous in its methods. At the present stage in airborne development, it is my belief that one airborne regiment per army, available on twelve hours' notice, would be more useful than several airborne divisions which usually take several weeks to get moving. Three times in our crossing over France, plans were made to use the airborne divisions, but we always got to the place they were to drop before they could get ready to drop.

General Walker stated that he could attack Saar-

---

[1] Major General L. H. Brereton, Commanding General, First Allied Airborne Army.

[2] Major General M. B. Ridgway, Commanding General XVIII Corps, First Army.

lautern any time after the morning of the twenty-ninth of
November, and that, while he would like air support, he
did not have to have it. Bradley called to say that the First
and Ninth Armies seemed stalled, and that, if we got a
breakthrough, we would get the support which would
otherwise have been sent to them.

On the twenty-ninth of November, I went over with
the XII Corps plans to secure a crossing over the Saar
River by using the 26th Division northwest of the 4th
Armored, with the idea of working down the east bank of
the river to facilitate the crossing of the 35th Division at
Saar-Union which, in turn, would probably permit the
6th Armored to cross at the same point.

In driving from Château Salins to St. Avold, we
crossed the Maginot Line and were impressed by its lack
of impressiveness. In fact, elements of the 80th Division
fought their way through this part of the line without
knowing it.

The shortage of replacements had now reached nine
thousand, and I took five per cent of the Corps and Army
Headquarters troops to train as infantry. This produced
loud wails from all the Section Chiefs, who declared they
could not run their offices if any cut were effected. As
matter of fact, even the ten per'cent cut which we subsequently made had no adverse effect.

Among the other shortages experienced at this time
was that of liquor. The good old days when we captured
twenty-six thousand cases of champagne at one town and
fourteen thousand cases of cognac at another (all the
property of the German Army and so marked) had gone
forever.

General Weyland and I, with our Staffs, went over
the use of medium bombers on Saarlautern and decided
that, if they could not bomb visually before the first or
second of December, they would have to bomb on OBO;[1]
and that if they could not bomb prior to the second of
December, the 90th and 95th would attack anyway. Late
that evening, Weyland called up to say he feared that, if
we did not attack on the first of December, the bombers
might not get off at all, so I directed Walker to follow

---

[1] Air Corps expression for bombing by instruments when visi-
bility is poor.

them in on that date. This was probably a mistake on my part, as the 95th Division would have been better set with an additional day's delay.

When the medium bombers attacked Saarlautern on the first of December, only four of the eight groups succeeded in dropping their bombs on the target, and the 95th Division found a great deal more trouble getting to the river than they had anticipated. On the second, ten groups of medium bombers did get in their attack on Saarlautern with fine effects, one of the most significant being that they put out the city electric plant. The Germans were using electricity from this plant as the power to detonate the bridges across the river. As the result of this bombing, the bridges were taken intact.

I then visited the 90th Division and the Command Post of the 359th Infantry under Colonel Raymond E. Bell. I asked him to take me to an Observation Post north of Saarlautern. We drove part way and, descending from the cars in a wood, started down a long road. Across the river, enfilading the road, I saw a German pillbox with a gun of some description sticking out of it. I asked Bell if the pillbox was manned, and he said he thought it was. The range was less than two hundred yards. Fortunately, they did not shoot, but when we got to the Observation Post, which was in a house, they dropped quite a heavy concentration around us without getting a hit. I have always hated OP's in houses because I feel so conspicuous in the upper floors—especially when being shelled.

On the second, it became evident that General Wood had to be sent home for a rest. This was arranged through General Eisenhower, and I sent General Gaffey, then Army Chief of Staff, to take over the division. It was quite a favor to ask of a man, but there was no one else available, and the necessities of war demanded that the 4th Armored have a good commander. The subsequent exploits of this division showed that my choice was correct.

The situation as to replacements was now extremely bad. In an army of six infantry and three armored divisions we were eleven thousand men short, which, being translated into terms of riflemen—and they are the people who get hurt—meant that the rifle companies were at only fifty-five per cent of their strength. We issued orders to take a second five per cent of corps and army troops and also for the divisions to cannibalize[1] their non-essential units, such as anti-tank companies, to provide riflemen.

On the fifth of December, the day after Gaffey assumed command, the 4th Armored Division advanced seven miles, with General Earnest leading the attack. The 90th Division crossed the Saar above Saarlautern and the 95th Division succeeded in getting a second regiment across south of the town. While enemy artillery fire was heavy, our losses were not excessive.

On the sixth, Members of Congress Luce and Merrick, while being conducted around the front of the Third Army, pulled the lanyards on two guns firing at Fort Driant. I was very much put out over this, because, in World War I, one of our Congressmen did a similar thing and aroused great public indignation.

That night Generals Spaatz, Doolittle, and Vandenberg[2] came, and we arranged for a heavy bombing attack on the Siegfried Line in the vicinity of Kaiserslautern. This was probably the most ambitious air blitz ever conceived. It was to consist of three successive days of attack, each one in considerable depth, and each day to consist of one thousand heavy bombers. In order to reduce the possibility of our men being hit, we planned to pull the infantry back four thousand yards from their most forward position, so that the bomb line could be put on our former front line. In order to prevent the enemy reoccupying the four-thousand-yard strip thus evacuated, we planned to scatter tanks through the area immediately behind the bomb line. The chance of a direct hit on tanks was small and fragmentation has practically no effect against them.

In the Saarlautern fight, the 90th Division was unable to maintain its bridge, owing to direct enemy fire, but maintained its position with great gallantry through the use of ferries at night.

The capture of Metz and the Saar campaign of the

---

[1]Cannibalize: to reduce the number of men in the gun crews to provide needed riflemen.

[2]Major General H. S. Vandenberg, Commander of 9th United States Air Force.

Third Army began on November 8, 1944. On December 8—that is, after one month's fighting—we had liberated 873 towns and 1600 square miles of ground. We had taken 30,000 prisoners and had killed or wounded about 88,000. We had also accounted for 137 tanks and 400 guns. Our battle losses during the same month aggregated 23,000 killed, wounded, and missing, our non-battle 18,000, for a total of something over 41,000. Our replacements were only 30,000 making us 11,000 short. To delve further into figures, during the 130 days of fighting from August 1 to date, the average losses of the Third Army from all causes had been 812 a day; the average daily losses of the Germans in front of us had been 2,700.

In order to make our date with the Air Force for the Third Army break-through to the Rhine, which was initially set at December 19, we had to get to the Siegfried Line prior to that date, so from then on the operations on the front of the XII Corps became a horse-race against time. To win this race, it was necessary to bring in the leading combat team (346th Infantry, commanded by Colonel N. A. Costello) of the 87th Division (Brigadier General Frank L. Culin, Jr.) as soon as the combat team arrived, and also to be prepared to re-employ the 4th Armored and the 80th Divisions which had been resting for a few days.

The weather was so bad that I directed all Army chaplains to pray for dry weather. I also published a prayer with a Christmas greeting on the back and sent it to all members of the Command. The prayer was for dry weather for battle.[1]

---

[1] On or about the fourteenth of December, 1944, General Patton called Chaplain O'Neill, Third Army Chaplain, and myself into his office in Third Headquarters at Nancy. The conversation went something like this:

General Patton: "Chaplain, I want you to publish a prayer for good weather. I'm tired of these soldiers having to fight mud and floods as well as Germans. See if we can't get God to work on our side."

Chaplain O'Neill: "Sir, it's going to take a pretty thick rug for that kind of praying."

General Patton: "I don't care if it takes the flying carpet. I want the praying done."

Chaplain O'Neil: "Yes, sir. May I say, General, that it usually isn't a customary thing among men of my profession to pray for clear weather to kill fellow men."

General Patton: "Chaplain, are you teaching me theology or are you the Chaplain of the Third Army? I want a prayer."

Chaplain O'Neill: "Yes, sir."

Outside, the chaplain said, "Whew, that's a tough one! What do you think he wants?"

It was perfectly clear to me. The General wanted a prayer— he wanted one right now—and he wanted it published to the Command.

The Army Engineer was called in, and we finally decided that our field topographical company could print the prayer on a small-sized card, making enough copies for distribution to the army.

It being near Christmas, we also decided to ask General Patton to include a Christmas greeting to the troops on the same card with the prayer. The General agreed, wrote a short greeting, and the card was made up, published, and distributed to the troops on the twenty-second of December.

Actually, the prayer was offered in order to bring clear weather for the planned Third Army break-through to the Rhine in the Saarguemines area, then scheduled for December 21.

The Bulge put a crimp in these plans. As it happened, the Third Army had moved north to attack the south flank of the Bulge when the prayer was actually issued.

PRAYER

Almighty and most merciful Father, we humbly beseech Thee, of Thy great goodness, to restrain these immoderate rains with which we have had to contend. Grant us fair weather for Battle. Graciously hearken to us as soldiers who call upon Thee that, armed with Thy power, we may advance from victory to victory, and crush the oppression and wickedness of our enemies, and establish Thy justice among men and nations. Amen.

REVERSE SIDE

To each officer and soldier in the Third United States Army, I wish a Merry Christmas. I have full confidence in your courage, devotion to duty, and skill in battle. We march in our might to complete victory. May God's blessing rest upon each of you on this Christmas Day.

G. S. PATTON, JR.
Lieutenant General
Commanding, Third United States Army

Whether it was the help of the Divine guidance asked for in the prayer or just the normal course of human events, we never knew; at any rate, on the twenty-third, the day after the prayer was issued, the weather cleared and remained perfect for about six days. Enough to allow the Allies to break the backbone of the Von Rundstedt offensive and turn a temporary setback into a crushing defeat for the enemy.

We had moved our advanced Headquarters to Luxembourg at this time to be closer to the battle area. The bulk of the Army

On the twelfth, Stiller and I visited the Command Posts of the 4th Armored, the 26th and the 87th. The 87th was taking over from the 26th and one combat command was in fighting, and apparently doing well. Later it turned out that it had not, in fact, done as well as was first thought; however, it was a good division.

We next visited the 35th Division, which was fighting along stubbornly, although very tired and very short of men. Its mission was to secure the high ground on the left of the XII Corps at Saarguemines. I decided definitely to place the 6th Armored and the 26th Division in the III Corps near Saarbrücken, because, if the enemy attacked the VIII Corps of the First Army, as was probable,[1] I could use the III Corps to help by attacking straight north, west of the Moselle River. If, on the other hand, the XX Corps got jumped from the north, where the enemy was certainly concentrating in the vicinity of Trier, it could face to the left and hold off the attacks, while the III Corps could advance to the east at Saarbrücken, in conformity with the advance of the XII Corps. I talked this thing over with General Eddy and he agreed that the solution was correct.

On December 13, we definitely set the nineteenth as the date for the air blitz. It was planned to get the XII Corps through the enemy positions by the night of the twenty-second. If, at that time, the VI Corps (commanded

---

Staff, including the Chaplain, was still in Nancy. General Patton again called me to his office. He wore a smile from ear to ear. He said, "God damn! look at the weather. That O'Neill sure did some potent praying. Get him up here. I want to pin a medal on him."

The Chaplain came up next day. The weather was still clear when we walked into General Patton's office. The General rose, came from behind his desk with hand outstretched and said, "Chaplain, you're the most popular man in this Headquarters. You sure stand in good with the Lord and soldiers." The General then pinned a Bronze Star Medal on Chaplain O'Neill.

Everyone offered congratulations and thanks and we got back to the business of killing Germans—with clear weather for battle.

P. D. H.

---

[1] It should be noted that General Patton saw possibilities of an enemy break-through in the First Army zone on this date, December 12. He had his Staff make a study of what the Third Army would do if called upon to counter-attack such a break-through.

by Major General E. H. Brooks) of the Seventh Army on our right had not broken through, we would still have time to move the air blitz down for a second operation in front of this corps.

The fighting at Saarlautern was very tedious, as we were fighting from one house to the next, but, on the other hand, the casualties had been remarkably low.

The 80th and 5th Divisions were now at full strength, owing to the first five per cent cut in the overhead of the army and corps, and we had four thousand additional men gleaned from corps and army troops training at Metz. This would fill the 26th Division and leave some over for the 90th and 95th. If the Communications Zone had done the same thing, we would have had enough soldiers to end the war. All that would have been necessary to attain this result was for General Eisenhower to issue an order that the troops of Com Z be cut ten per cent for the production of riflemen.

On the fourteenth, at Saarlautern, Codman and I crossed the bridge over the river under alleged fire. It was purely a motion on my part to show the soldiers that generals could get shot at. I was not shot at very much. Nearly all the houses I inspected in Saarlautern on either side of the river were actually forts. The ground floor of each house was made of reinforced concrete about twelve inches thick, and there were machine-gun openings fitted just above sidewalk level in practically every cellar. The Germans are certainly a thoroughgoing race.

The 90th Division had been doing a magnificent job moving on east of the river, in spite of the lack of a bridge. Also their rifle strength was extremely low, but they were cheerful and were killing an enormous number of Germans.

We then drove through Thionville to Luxembourg to see Bradley. Apparently Montgomery, with the assistance of the Prime Minister, had secured the services of the Ninth Army. Montgomery was bitterly opposed to the operations of both Patch and myself. He still wanted all available forces massed on the north and wanted to command them himself, maintaining that the Rhine could be crossed only in the vicinity of Cologne and that it must be done under him. All this was very distressing to me, because, while my attack was going forward by short leaps, it was not very brilliant, and I felt that, if I failed to break through after the air blitz, I would have to go on the defensive and lose several divisions.

On the sixteenth, Eddy was very depressed and nervous, particularly because the 87th Division had not done well and one colonel had been replaced for failure to prevent trenchfoot. This colonel afterward proved to be a splendid fighter.

At that time I believed the situation was much more favorable than it had been, and contemplated placing the III Corps behind the 35th Division to exploit any success we might get during the break-through, because, while Millikin was untried in battle, he was at least not fatigued.

I seriously contemplated making Eddy take a short rest, and would have done so had I not feared that the effect of a leave on him might be worse than that of staying at the front.

General Allen, Chief of Staff of the Twelfth Army Group, called on the night of December 16 to have the 10th Armored Division attached to the VIII Corps of the First Army in order to repulse a rather strong German attack. This was the first official notice we had of the, to us, anticipated German assault, later called the Bulge. As the loss of this division would seriously affect the chances of my breaking through at Saarlautern, I protested very strongly, saying that we had paid a high price for that sector so far, and that to move the 10th Armored to the north would be playing into the hands of the Germans. General Bradley admitted my logic, but said that the situation was such that it could not be discussed over the telephone.

On the seventeenth, information about the German attack became more definite. Quite a number of single enemy units were located on a wide front, but no large body of troops could yet be found. The night of the seventeenth there was considerable movement among the Germans in front of the XX Corps. This might have been a feint to cover the attack on the VIII Corps of the First Army, or the attack on the VIII Corps might be a feint to cover an attack on our XX Corps. I rather believed that the attack on the VIII Corps was the real thing.

The situation on the Third Army front was not bad in case the Germans attacked. The 5th Division was relieving the 95th, and the 80th was moving in to the XII Corps line in order to be sure we reached the Siegfried Line by the nineteenth. The only place the Germans could really have hurt the Third Army was in the Saar-Moselle Triangle where Colonel Polk with his reinforced 3d Cavalry, about four thousand men, was holding about a thirty-mile front.

I had General Millikin in and talked over with him the possible use of the III Corps in an attack to the north in case the Germans continued the attack on the VIII Corps of the First Army. I also directed Eddy to get the 4th Armored engaged, because I felt that, if we did not, it too might be moved to the north by higher authority. The fact that I did this shows how little I appreciated the seriousness of the enemy attack on that date.

At 1030 on the eighteenth, Bradley called me and asked me to come to Luxembourg with my G-2, G-3, and G-4 for a conference. He stated that he was going to suggest something which I would not like. When we arrived, he showed me that the German penetration was much greater than we had thought and asked what I could do. I told him I could halt the attack of the 4th Armored and concentrate it near Longwy, starting that midnight. I also said that the 80th Division could be removed from the line and start for Luxembourg in the morning, and that the 26th Division, though it had four thousand green replacements from Headquarters' units, could be alerted to move in twenty-four hours. That night about 2300, Bradley called and asked me to meet him and Eisenhower at Verdun at 1100 on the morning of the nineteenth, which was the next day. I immediately called a Staff meeting for 0800 on the nineteenth, with all members of the General Staff, and General Weyland and his Staff, to be present.

I started the meeting by saying that plans had been changed, and, while we were all accustomed to rapid movement, we would now have to prove that we could operate even faster. We then made a rough plan of operation based on the assumption that I could use the VIII Corps, First Army (Middleton), and the III Corps, Third Army (Millikin), on any two of three possible axes. From the left, the axes of attack were in order of priority as follows: From the general vicinity of Diekirch, due north; from the general vicinity of Arlon, on Bastogne, which was still held by our troops; and, finally, from the general vicinity of Neufchâteau, against the left nose of the enemy salient.

When it is considered that Harkins, Codman, and I left for Verdun at 0915 and that between 0800 and that hour we had had a Staff meeting, planned three possible lines of attack, and made a simple code in which I could telephone General Gay which two of the three lines we were to use, it is evident that war is not so difficult as people think.

We reached Verdun at 1045. Eisenhower, Bradley, Devers, Air Marshal Tedder, and a large number of Staff officers were present. General Strong, SHAEF G-2, gave a picture of the situation which was far from happy. Eisenhower stated that he wished me to get to Luxembourg and take command of the battle, and asked when I could do it. I said that afternoon, December 19. He also stated that he would like me to make a strong attack with at least six divisions.

I told him I would make a strong attack with three divisions, namely, the 4th Armored, and the 26th and 80th Infantry Divisions, by the twenty-second, but that I could not attack with more than that until some days later, and that, if I waited, I would lose surprise.

When I said I could attack on the twenty-second, it created a ripple of excitement. Some people thought I was boasting and others seemed to be pleased.

At that time I figured that I was to have the VIII Corps (First Army) with the 101st Airborne (commanded by Major General M. D. Taylor), the 28th Infantry Division and part of the 9th Armored Division; the III Corps with the 26th and 80th Infantry Divisions and 4th Armored Division; the XII Corps with the 5th and 4th Infantry Divisions and 10th Armored Division; and the XX Corps with the 90th and 95th Infantry Divisions and 6th Armored Division. The 87th Infantry Division and the infantry regiments of the 42d Division, which we also had at that time, would go to the Seventh Army.

After it was determined that the Third Army should attack, a conference was held between Eisenhower, Devers, and Bradley as to the shift of front. It was finally decided that the Seventh Army would take over part of the Third Army front and assume a static role from somewhere south of Saarlautern to the far end of their present line, the Rhine River. Pending the arrival of a division to relieve it, we were not to be allowed to move our 6th Armored.

Air Marshal Tedder urged me to get rid of the XX Corps so I would have only one offensive front. I stuck to the XX Corps, because I wanted to have it for a rest area. As it turned out some months later, the retention of the XX Corps was probably the luckiest thing I ever did, because through it I had a chance to take Trier and, having taken Trier, the final attack through the Palatinate was made possible.

As soon as these various decisions were made, I telephoned Gay to start the 26th Division and the 4th Armored on Arlon via Longwy, and the 80th Division on Luxembourg via Thionville. The 4th Armored had actually pulled out the previous night, December 18. The 80th started next morning, the nineteenth, and the 26th started on receiving orders.

If we take the casualty report as of December 21, which marked the termination of the fighting in the Saar battle, and subtract from that the casualty report as of November 8, we will see that the fighting in the Saar was bloody and difficult. We will also get a datum plane from which to judge the cost of the Battle of the Bulge, which was now about to start.

The casualty report as of December 21 was:

Third Army		*Enemy*	
Killed	10,264	Killed	63,800
Wounded	49,703	Wounded	180,200
Missing	9,149	Prisoners of war	140,000
Total	69,116	Total	384,000
Non-battle casualties	49,844		
Grand Total	118,960		

Less total casualties
(battle and non-
battle) as of
November 8   64,956

Total casualties for
   period November
   8 to December
   21 inclusive 53,904

Matériel losses as of December 21 were:

Third Army		Enemy	
Light tanks	198	Medium tanks	946
Medium tanks	507	Panther or	
Guns	116	Tiger tanks	485
		Guns	2216

4

THE BASTOGNE-ST. VITH CAMPAIGN—"THE BULGE"

19 December to 28 January 1945

On December 19, 1944, General Eisenhower called a conference at Verdun to deal with the Von Rundstedt break-through, known as "The Bulge." As early as the twelfth of December, General Patton had speculated on the possibility of a German offensive on his north flank in the First Army area, and plans to meet such an effort were studied. What happened during these days and those ensuing is best recorded in his notes on the campaign.

The Bulge was an exhausting operation, filled with grim fighting, unimaginable situations, precise timing and movement and a superhuman effort on the part of the American soldier. By January 28, the battle of the Bulge ended and American troops were once more well established on the German border, ready to strike at the heart of the Reich without respite. A new all-out offensive began on January 29. (See Map, page 190.)

During the period, General Montgomery took over command of the American First Army north of the German break-through. He countered the German offensive with a First Army push to the south, joining the Third Army in the vicinity of Houffalize. Both the Twenty-First and Twelfth Army Groups then joined in pushing the enemy back to the east and to the Siegfried Line. The Sixth Army Group, having assumed the defensive in order to free the Third Army troops for an offensive, took over a portion of the Third Army lines and set up de-

fensive positions in the Vosges Mountains. There was nothing new in Italy.

In the Phillippines, General MacArthur landed on Luzon and, at the end of the period, was in the outskirts of Manila.

The Russians, sweeping westward, took Warsaw, Cracow, Lodz, and were within ninety miles of Berlin.

The Air Force continued to blast Germany, while the Navy commanded all the seas.

P. D. H.

The Bulge

I spent the night of the nineteenth with the XX Corps in Thionville, and telephoned from there to have the 5th Division pulled out of action and started on Luxembourg. The next morning, I arrived at Bradley's Headquarters in Luxembourg and found that he had, without notifying me, detached Combat Command "B" (Brigadier General H. E. Dager) of the 4th Armored Division from Arlon to a position southwest of Bastogne and had halted the 80th Division in Luxembourg. Since the combat command had not been engaged, I withdrew it to Arlon and had the 80th Division resume its march to the vicinity of Mersch.

While Bradley and I were talking over the plans for a combined operation with the First and Third Armies, Eisenhower called up and informed Bradley that Montgomery was to have operational command of the First and Ninth United States Armies, owing to the fact that telephonic communications between Bradley and these armies were difficult. As a matter of fact, this was not entirely true, and it appeared to me at the time that Bradley was being sidetracked, either because of lack of confidence in him, or as the only way Eisenhower could prevent Montgomery from "regrouping."

Speaking of Montgomery's lack of speed reminds me of something Sergeant Meeks said to me when we first started, and Montgomery was holding valorously at Caen while we were carrying the ball. Sergeant Meeks remarked that, "'Fore God, General, if General Montgomery don't get a move on himself, those British soldiers are going to have grass and limpets growing on their left foot from standing in the water."

In any case, General Bradley took what was practically a demotion in a most soldierly manner, nor did he at any time during the subsequent campaign inject himself into the operations of the Third Army, as he might well have done, since that was the only unit he had to command. On the other hand, I always informed him of what I was going to do, and profited by consultations with him and his Staff.

From Luxembourg I drove to Arlon and saw Middleton, Millikin, Gaffey, and Paul, and got from Middleton a first-hand picture of what was going on. The VIII Corps was fighting very well, but had nothing but remnants with which to fight, except in the case of the 101st Airborne Division[1] in Bastogne. In Bastogne also was a combat command of the 9th Armored,[2] one of the 10th Armored,[2] the 705th Tank Destroyer Battalion, and some colored artillery and colored Quartermaster units. In contrast to some of the colored artillery, the colored Quartermaster men provided themselves with rifles and fought very well.

After leaving this meeting, I visited the Headquarters of the 9th and 10th Armored Divisions and the 4th and 80th Infantry Divisions (all northeast of Luxembourg) and directed General Morris,[3] who commanded the 10th Armored Division, to take temporary command of the two combat commands of his division present, and the one combat command of the 9th Armored Division in his vicinity, and also of the 4th Infantry Division, pend-

[1] The 101st Airborne Division, commanded by Brigadier General A. C. McAuliffe. Major General M. D. Taylor was in the United States at this time.

[2] The 705th Tank Destroyer Battalion, commanded by Lieutenant Colonel Clifford Templeton; Combat Command "B," 10th Armored Division, Colonel W. L. Roberts, Commanding; Combat Command "R," 9th Armored Division, Colonel J. H. Gilbreath, Commanding.

[3] In order to co-ordinate activities of the Third Army in the area northeast of Luxembourg, General Patton put all units in that vicinity initially under the command of Major General Morris.

ing the arrival of General Eddy's XII Corps from the south. I told General Leonard, commanding the 9th Armored Division, to move his Headquarters to join the VIII Corps and assume command of the two combat commands of the 9th Armored Division and the one of the 10th Armored Division in Bastogne. In my opinion, splitting up the 10th and 9th Armored Divisions in the VIII Corps had been a mistake; however, the situation at the time may have rendered it necessary. I also did a lot of telephoning to get up self-propelled tank destroyer battalions, divisional tank battalions, hospitals, ammunition, bridging materials, etc., and I directed the two armored divisions and the 4th Infantry Division to cannibalize their anti-tank gun units and turn them into riflemen, because all three divisions were excessively short.

At the end of this rather hectic day, my driver, Sergeant Mims, said to me, "General, the Government is wasting a lot of money hiring a whole General Staff. You and me has run the Third Army all day and done a better job than they do." Actually the remarkable movement of the Third Army from the Saar to the Bulge was wholly due to the superior efficiency of the Third Army Staff, particularly General Gay, General Muller, Colonel Nixon, and Colonel E. Busch, Quartermaster of the Third Army. Those who desire to inform themselves on how an army should be moved should study this operation as set forth in meticulous detail in the "After Action Operations Report" of the Third Army. The setup at nightfall of the twentieth of December was as follows: The VIII, Corps (Middleton), now Third Army, on the left consisted of the 101st Airborne with attachments, the 28th Infantry Division less about two regiments, the 9th Armored, and certain corps artillery units; the III Corps (Millikin) had the 26th and 80th Infantry and 4th Armored Division; the XII Corps (Eddy) had at that particular moment in Luxembourg the 4th Infantry Division, the 5th Infantry Division, the 10th Armored Division, currently commanded by Morris pending Eddy's arrival; the XX Corps (Walker) had the 90th, 95th, and 6th Armored. However, the 6th Armored was not free to leave its location near Saarguemines until it had been relieved by elements of the Seventh Army. The 35th Division was moving on Metz, where it was to pick up replacements and be attached to either the XII or VIII

Corps as circumstances indicated. The time of attack for the III Corps was definitely set at 0400, December 22.

On the twenty-first, I received quite a few telephone calls from various higher echelons, expressing solicitude as to my ability to attack successfully with only three divisions. I maintained my contention that it is better to attack with a small force at once, and attain surprise, than it is to wait and lose it. At that time, I was sure that by the twenty-third or twenty-fourth, I could get up General Eddy's Corps and have him attack with the 5th Infantry and 10th Armored Divisions, and possibly the 4th Infantry Division, although the latter was very short of men and battle-weary. I felt sure, and stated at the time, that the First Army could attack the northern flank of the Bulge on the twenty-third if it wanted to. I feared that the enemy might start a spoiling attack[1] south from the vicinity of Echternach against the 4th Division and, had he known the situation, he would undoubtedly have done this, but, as always, the German communications system was very bad, and I doubt that at this time he knew the Third Army was moving.

The Corps Staffs of the III, XII, and XX met me at Luxembourg. The VIII Corps was too far away and could not attend the meeting. As usual on the verge of action, everyone felt full of doubt except myself. It has always been my unfortunate role to be the ray of sunshine and the backslapper before action, both for those under me and also those over me. I can say with perfect candor that, at that time, I had no doubt as to the success of the operation, even when, at 1700, December 21, the 4th Infantry Division reported a violent attack, which later turned out to be nothing. My chief feeling at that time was that I wished it was one day later, because, when we are attacking, the enemy has to parry, while, when we are defending or preparing to attack, he can attack us. During the night Millikin asked to delay the hour of attack till 0600 December 22.

The III Corps jumped off at that hour, 0600, and in spite of considerable resistance and a great deal of trouble

---

[1] Spoiling attack: An old name given to an attack to cause a diversion or apprehension.

from blown roads and bridges, advanced for an average of seven miles. This was less than I had hoped, but I realized that it is always difficult to get an attack rolling, and I further felt that the enemy would probably not react for an additional thirty-six hours, by which time I hoped we would be moving.

The 10th Infantry Regiment (Colonel Robert P. Bell) of the 5th Infantry Division did a remarkable thing by attacking in the direction of Echternach at noon on the day of its arrival, after moving about seventy-five miles from Saarlautern. It fortunately ran into two German battalions just preparing to make an attack on the 4th Infantry Division, and destroyed them. At Arlon I met eight enlisted men and one officer who had been at Wiltz when the Germans attacked, and had walked out on the nineteenth of December. They had come straight across the southern portion of the German-occupied territory and seen only seven Germans. This led me to believe that the density of the German attack was less than reported.

Owing to weather conditions in England, we had been unable to resupply Bastogne by air on the twenty-second, but made arrangements to do so on the night of December 22-23. At this time it became evident that the XII Corps could not attack north of the Sauer River until we had driven the enemy east of that river and had replaced the 4th Infantry Division, which was exhausted and sixteen hundred men short, with a new infantry division—probably the 90th. The 6th Armored Division from the XX Corps was to join the XII Corps, while the 4th Infantry and 10th Armored Divisions would join the XX Corps. There was a possibility at this time that the 11th Armored, which was alleged to be closing in the vicinity of Reims in SHAEF Reserve, might be turned loose. The amount of corps and army artillery supporting the attack of the Third Army was quite impressive, consisting as it did of 88 battalions or 1056 guns of 105 mm. caliber or bigger.

On the twenty-second, Bastogne received a violent attack from the northeast which the 101st Airborne repulsed. It was possibly the first reaction to our attack.

From captured orders we learned that the Germans had intended to move west beyond Arlon and then turn south and attack the city of Luxembourg from the west.

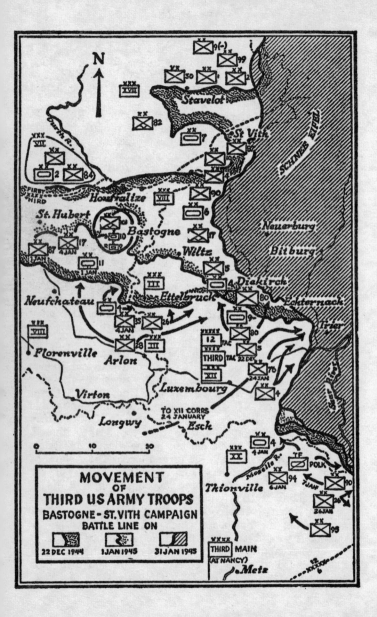

MOVEMENT
OF
THIRD US ARMY TROOPS
BASTOGNE - ST. VITH CAMPAIGN
BATTLE LINE ON

22 DEC 1944   1 JAN 1945   31 JAN 1945

Since this possibility still existed, it became necessary to consider the left flank of the army. The XII Corps, using all of the 5th and part of the 4th Infantry Divisions, made a limited-objective attack to drive the enemy east of the Sauer River, while the XX Corps made another limited-objective attack in the direction of Saarburg as a diversion. The weather had turned fine and we had seven groups of fighter-bombers doing a splendid job, also some planes from the 9th Air Force which bombed and destroyed bridges in the vicinity of Saarburg. On the other hand, it was necessary to move Combat Command "R" of the 4th Armored Division (Colonel Wendell Blanchard) from the right flank to the left flank of the III Corps in order to attempt a break-through to Bastogne. This movement left a huge gap between the 26th Infantry and the 4th Armored Division, which we filled up with the 6th Cavalry Group under Colonel E. M. Fickett. The advances for the day were not impressive, varying from two to five miles.

The day of the twenty-fourth was rather discouraging. All along the line we received violent counter-attacks, one of which forced Combat Command "B" of the 4th Armored Division back several miles, with the loss of a number of tanks. This was probably my fault, because I had insisted on a day and night attack. Such an attack is all right for the first night of battle and possibly the second night, but after that the men become tired. Furthermore, unless you have very bright moonlight and clear going, armored battle at night is of dubious value. I remember being surprised at the time at how long it took me to learn war. I should have known this before.

The 101st Airborne had got some supplies by air drop and had not been attacked during daylight, probably because the enemy was afraid of our fighter-bombers.

The XII Corps, attacking on the front Diekirch to Echternach to secure the Sauer River line, had progressed practically to the river, except in the vicinity of Echternach. Prisoners taken that day stated that they had not received any regular rations for some three to five days. We also intercepted a radio message from the German 5th Para Division (General Major Ludwig Hellman), fighting against the 26th Infantry Division, that they could not hold out much longer without help and needed bazookas and ammunition. On the front of the XX Corps nothing happened.

Casualties as of December 22:

Third Army		Enemy	
Killed	10,432	Killed	66,800
Wounded	50,824	Wounded	186,200
Missing	10,826	Prisoners of war	140,200
Total	72,082	Total	393,200
Non-battle casualties	50,241		
Grand Total	122,323		

Matériel Losses			
Light tanks	198	Medium tanks	946
Medium tanks	507	Panther and Tiger tanks	485
Guns	116	Guns	2216

It was my belief at that time, which subsequent events proved incorrect, that this attack had been planned and was being run by the German General Staff for the purpose of regaining the initiative. However, it was evident that they were already behind schedule, so I believed then that we might possibly surround and destroy them. There was the worrisome thought, though, that in 1940 they had attacked as at present and then swung southwest through Saarbrücken and Thionville to Metz, and of course they might repeat this. We had no idea what the German resources were and unquestionably overestimated them, although I was probably less guilty in this respect than most others.

Christmas dawned clear and cold; lovely weather for killing Germans, although the thought seemed somewhat at variance with the spirit of the day. I left early in the morning with the purpose of visiting all the divisions in combat, and succeeded in seeing two combat commands of the 4th Armored, the 26th, the 80th, the 5th, and elements of the 4th Infantry and 10th Armored Divisions.

It is to the great credit of the Quartermaster Corps that on this Christmas Day every soldier had turkey; those in the front had turkey sandwiches and the rest, hot turkey. I know of no army in the world except the American which could have done such a thing. The men were surprisingly cheerful.

While we were with Combat Command "A" (Brigadier General H. L. Earnest) of the 4th Armored, two German airplanes strafed and bombed us, but without success. This was the only time in the fighting in Germany or France that I was actually picked out on the road and attacked by German Air.

As a whole, the day was not too successful. We continued to advance, but we had not relieved Bastogne. Owing to weather conditions, Bastogne had not been re-supplied from the air. The only bright spot was that the 5th Infantry Division had driven the enemy back to the Sauer River in its front, and killed quite a few when they tried to escape across the river.

Arrangements had been made for the 6th Armored to relieve the 10th Armored north of Luxembourg, and for the 35th Division, which had been in Metz since the night of the twenty-third, to move up and join the III Corps on the morning of the twenty-sixth, taking its place between the 26th and the 80th Divisions. The 80th Division would then join the XII Corps.

Late that night we had a quiet Christmas dinner at General Bradley's mess. Afterward Bradley and I had a long talk, during which he told me that Montgomery stated that the First Army could not attack for three months, and that the only attacks that could be made would be made by me, but that I was too weak. Hence, we should have to fall back to the line of the Saar—Vosges, or even to the Moselle, to gain enough divisions to permit me to continue the attack. We both considered this a disgusting idea, which would, we felt, have tremendous political implications and probably doom to death or slavery all the French inhabitants of Alsace and Lorraine, whom such a move would abandon to the Germans.[1]

---

[1] On this matter, General Patton called for an opinion from his Staff. Their answer is embodied in the following letter:

26 December, 1944

MEMORANDUM:
FOR: The Army Commander

1. It is our belief that the Third Army should continue the offensive and carry the fight to the enemy, and destroy him

without delay. The following factors are bases for this recommendation:

a. That all the known German striking power in the west is now concentrated in a well-defined area.

b. Other enemy offensives, as far as can be estimated, at this time, would be of limited objective, and, unless armor has been moved from other fronts, it would lack the thrust and speed of armor.

c. At present the Third Army composes seven (7) strong infantry divisions and three (3) armored divisions. These forces are supported by 108 battalions of artillery. In addition, four potential divisions exist (94th, 87th, 17th AB, and 11th Armored). This would later be augmented by the 28th Infantry and the 9th Armored, plus the 101st Airborne when refitted. The Third Army service installations are exceptionally well situated at the present time to support continuation of the attack. Our stores in these installations are being improved daily. Our rail net in this area is excellent. The present supply situation within the Army is good. It has been geared to support the attack and if the Communications Zone can continue to put supplies within reach of Army, we can continue. Presently we have a strong Signal Communication Network, well placed and in operation.

d. Allied troops appear to be available to extend the north flank to the Meuse; thus, by using this river as an obstacle and with the troops enumerated above, Third Army can seal off the south flank of the German salient. It is suggested here that the present holding force on the Meuse River in the Third Army zone of responsibility move to the Semois River and there establish a containing line.

e. Third Army's continued attack is a constant threat to communications within the salient. A general withdrawal permits the enemy to effect reconstruction of forces, later permitting him the initiative. Time is his strategic objective now.

f. Our air effort will have a well-defined area of operations for a major effort in a restricted area such as the area indicated above. The Air is now based on fields capable of supporting the present offensive. They are wealthy in pilots and planes and have more than they have had at any other time during the operation.

g. The American (soldier and public) psychology must be considered. Although it cannot be evaluated, it would probably be seriously affected by a voluntary withdrawal. The American soldier has tried with all of his skill and heart to gain the ground now in our hands. To give it up might be catastrophic both from a psychologic and a military point of view. Third Army troops know and unstand the attack. They do not know or understand the retreat or general withdrawal.

Until 1400 on the twenty-sixth, the situation looked bad. We had been unable to break through to Bastogne and had received continuous counter-attacks. The 5th Infantry Division had, however, closed up on the Sauer River and the night of December 25-26 we had used the new proximity fuse on a number of Germans near Echternach and actually killed seven hundred of them.

The Combat Command (Colonel T. L. Harrold) of the 9th Armored Division, working with the XII Corps, was sent to join the 4th Armored in the III Corps, to extend still further the left of that unit. Also, a fragment of the 28th Infantry Division, which had come into the lines of the XII Corps, was sent to the VIII Corps. The 35th Division started to move into the line prepared to attack on the twenty-seventh, while two-thirds of the 6th Armored Division had closed north of Luxembourg. I believed then that this movement of the 6th Armored Division was premature. I should have waited longer and would then have found that it was better to engage it on the left flank, because the corridor north from Diekirch, which was my favorite line of attack, was supposed to be too narrow for armor. From later observation I think this was a mistake and that armor could have gone up the corridor. One never knows.

At 1400 on December 26, General Gaffey called me

---

2. It is the consensus of opinion that the present Saar positions can be held. A withdrawal on the extreme flank from along the Rhine River to the Saar-Vosges Mountain line would perhaps at most yield two American divisions. Initially these two divisions could support an attack to clear out the present triangle now held by the enemy in the XX Corps zone between the Saar and Moselle Rivers. This, in itself, would cause the enemy some concern. Giving up the Vosges area would yield little to the enemy from a supply, air, or strategic point of view. Withdrawal to the Moselle is not considered advantageous in any way.

CONCLUSIONS:

   a. That the main defensive line on the Meuse River between the flanks of the First and Third United States Armies extend to that river.

   b. Continue the offensive operation now undertaken by Third United States Army.

PAUL D. HARKINS   H. G. MADDOX   OSCAR W. KOCH
   Colonel, G.S.C.   Brig. Gen., G.S.C.   Colonel, G.S.C.
   Deputy Chief of Staff   G-3   G-2

and asked if I would authorize his taking a big risk with
Combat Command "R" under Colonel Blanchard for a
break-through to Bastogne. I told him to go ahead. At
1845 they had made contact and Bastogne was liberated,
but the corridor was only three hundred yards wide. During a German air raid on the night of the twenty-sixth, one
hundred German prisoners rushed our guards. Many
were shot; none escaped.

At this time I was doing my utmost through General
Bradley to secure one or all of the 11th Armored, 17th
Airborne, and 87th Infantry Divisions, which were sitting
around Reims in SHAEF Reserve. I felt that, with our
entry into Bastogne, the German was licked, and that it
was not necessary to hold a reserve, but to attack with
everything we had.

On the morning of the twenty-seventh, Bradley went
to see Eisenhower and Montgomery. Bradley and I were
very hopeful that Eisenhower would put him back in
command of the First and Ninth Armies, because we felt
Montgomery would never attack. I also asked him to suggest that the 11th Armored and 17th Airborne be moved
from Reims to a switch position along the Semois River,
from which location they could cover the left flank of the
Third Army and be just as well placed to protect the rest
of the American forces as they were on the line of the
Meuse.

After a meeting with Middleton and Millikin at Arlon, it was decided that the III Corps should keep operational control of the VIII Corps troops in Bastogne until
the situation clarified. We also planned an attack with one
armored division reinforced by an infantry combat team
on Houffalize on the thirtieth, and an attack with one
armored division and two infantry divisions on St. Vith on
the thirty-first. For the operation the VIII Corps was to
resume command of the 101st Airborne and attached
troops, and cover the left flank. I felt at that time if I
could get three more divisions the situation would end
very promptly.

On Bradley's return, he and I discussed, and actually
planned, with General Anderson[1] of the 8th Air Force, an

---

[1]Brigadier General, later Major General, O. A. Anderson,
Deputy Commander for Operations Headquarters, 8th Air Force.

attack across the Sauer River at Echternach up the corridor to Bonn. We proposed an air blitz to be preceded by an attack on Saarburg by the XX Corps in order to pull the enemy to the south. The possibilities of such an attack were very alluring, but in order to make it a success, at least three more divisions were necessary; that is, three more in addition to the 11th Armored and 87th Infantry which Bradley had succeeded in getting released to me. Troops were not available, so the show fell through.

I sent General Grow and Colonel Harkins to Bastogne to arrange to move the 6th Armored Division to that vicinity, under cover of darkness, for use in our projected attack on St. Vith, so they would come in as a complete surprise. The 11th Armored and 87th Infantry were to close southwest of Bastogne at 2400 on the twenty-ninth and to attack in the direction of Houffalize in the morning, passing through the left elements of the 101st Airborne. The situation on the front of the XII and XX Corps remained static.

On the thirtieth, the 11th Armored and 87th Infantry jumped off, the 87th on the left. They immediately ran into the flank of a large German counter-attack, consisting of the 130th Panzer Lehr Division and 26th Volksgrenadier Division. This meeting engagement upset both attacks, but was very fortuitous, so far as we were concerned, because had we not hit the flank of the Germans, they might have again closed the corridor into Bastogne. All the generals concerned in this particular attack were in favor of my postponing it twenty-four hours; had I done so, it would have permitted the Germans to drive home their attack.

This same day the Germans also put in a two-division attack, consisting of the 1st SS (Brigadier E. Wisch, SS Oberst Mohmke) and 167th Regulars (General Lieutenant Höcker) from the northeast against the 35th and 26th, and a third attack against the northern face of Bastogne. This was probably the biggest co-ordinated counterattack that troops under my command have ever experienced. We were successful at all points.

On this day four Germans in one of our peeps, dressed in American uniforms, were killed, and another group of seventeen, also in American uniforms, were reported by the 35th Division as follows: "One sentinel, reinforced, saw seventeen Germans in American uniforms. Fifteen were killed and two died suddenly."

I drove to Bastogne through the corridor, passing quite close to the Germans. Luckily they were not firing. On reaching the town, I decorated with the Distinguished Service Cross Brigadier General McAuliffe, who commanded the 101st during the fight, and Lieutenant Colonel S. A. Chappuis, who commanded the 502d Airborne Infantry. We then drove around so the soldiers could see us, and they were quite delighted. On the twenty-fifth, the Germans had sent a white flag demanding that McAuliffe surrender, to which he replied with the famous word, "Nuts."

On the thirty-first, the Germans made seventeen counterattacks against us, all of which were repulsed. We failed to gain much ground except that the 6th Armored Division, attacking by surprise along the road to St. Vith, advanced four kilometers.

There had been rumors for a number of days that Germans, flying captured P-47's, were strafing our troops. Of course, such rumors were very bad. Generals Spaatz, Doolittle, and Vandenberg came in, and we discussed ways and means of stopping the rumors, and finally decided that for the first of the year no P-47 would fly in the area of either XII or XX Corps, so that if any attacks came they would be definitely recognized as German planes. We succeeded also in getting the 17th Airborne turned over to

P-47

the Third Army in exchange for the 28th Infantry Division.

The following Order expresses briefly and to the best of my ability the occurrences of 1944:

GENERAL ORDERS   1 January, 1945
NUMBER 1

TO THE OFFICERS AND MEN OF THE THIRD ARMY
AND
TO OUR COMRADES OF THE XIX TACTICAL AIR COMMAND

From the bloody corridor at Avranches, to Brest, thence across France to the Saar, over the Saar into Germany, and now on to Bastogne, your record has been one of continuous victory. Not only have you invariably defeated a cunning and ruthless enemy, but also you have overcome by your indomitable fortitude every aspect of terrain and weather. Neither heat nor dust nor floods nor snow have stayed your progress. The speed and brilliancy of your achievements are unsurpassed in military history.

Recently I had the honor of receiving at the hands of the Twelfth Army Group Commander, Lieutenant General Omar N. Bradley, a second Oak Leaf Cluster to the DSM. This award was bestowed on me, not for what I have done, but because of what you have achieved. From the bottom of my heart I thank you.

My New Year wish and sure conviction for you is that, under the protection of Almighty God and the inspired leadership of our President and the High Command, you will continue your victorious course to the end that tyranny and vice shall be eliminated, our dead comrades avenged, and peace restored to a war-weary world.

In closing, I can find no fitter expression for my feelings than to apply to you the immortal words spoken by General Scott at Chapultepec when he said: "Brave rifles, veterans, you have been baptized in fire and blood and have come out steel."

G. S. PATTON, JR.,
Lieut. General, U. S. Army,
Commanding

Around the first of the year, the Germans began bombarding Luxembourg city with a peculiar weapon.[1] At first we thought it was a rocket, then a long-distance shell, and several rumors were started as to what it consisted of, until recently when the gun which fired it was captured. The projectile was about six feet long and four inches in diameter, but it had a forward collar six inches in diameter, and on the rear, an inverted cone with long trailing fins. The initial powder charge expanded the cone, producing a gas lock, and the missile started forward through an unrifled tube one hundred and ninety-five feet long, with about twenty-five joints bolted together with flanges. At every fourth section there were two short tubes coming in at an angle of forty-five degrees, each containing a booster charge. When the projectile left the muzzle, the forward collar fell off, and it was stabilized through the fins. Its probable range was thirty-five miles. The bursting charge was very small, but one unfortunate shot struck a hotel just as the Commanding Officer of Headquarters Company, Third Army, Captain John Clementi, stepped out, and killed him.

Our progress on New Year's Day was not outstanding, except in the case of the 6th Armored Division, which did fairly well; we had nothing to worry about. All the troops in the Third Army were exactly where they were supposed to be, so that if they lost, they would lose due to better fighting qualities on the part of the enemy,

---

[1] The German H.D.P. (Hochdruckpumpe, or high pressure pump). General Patton's figure of 195 feet for the length of the tube may have been conservative, as installations have since been found having tube lengths from 189 to 394 feet. This is explained by the fact that there are provided flanged sections of fifteen-centimeter tubing, three meters in length, for assembly of the weapons. The boosters are designed to be fitted to the tube at any of the joints.

St Vith

FIRST
THIRD
Houffalize

St. Hubert

87   101   Bastogne

Neufchateau

VIII   35   XV   80   Diekirch
                                        Echternach

Florenville   4   THIRD   5   Trier

Arlon   XII

Longwy   Luxemburg

Esch.   Merzig

Longuyon

Thionville   80

5
Saarbrucken
35   95

Metz   6   26

80

Pont-a-Mousson   4

N

Saarbourg

Nancy

THIRD U.S. ARMY
SWITCH OF MAJOR ELEMENTS

BATTLE LINE ON

22 DEC

10   0   10   20   30

and not through any mistakes which I had made in deploying the soldiers.

The 11th Armored Division fought fairly well in its opening gambit, but lost an unnecessarily large number of tanks. I did not believe that the command of that division was what it should have been. Later, under a new commander, this became a very fine division.

At midnight on the night of December 31, all guns in the Third Army fired rapid fire for twenty minutes on the Germans as a New Year's greeting. When the firing ceased, our forward observers stated they could hear the Germans screaming in the woods.

On the second, I learned more about the action of the 11th Armored and found that it was quite bad, and that General Middleton personally had had to intervene to get it straightened out. We planned to put the 17th Airborne through the 11th Armored, except that one battalion of tanks would have to support the 17th Airborne, because that division had no organic tanks. One of the chief defects of an airborne division is the fact that it never has anything it needs after it lands—no tanks, no adequate artillery, no transportation.

The 6th Armored Division still continued to do well. The XV Corps of the Seventh Army on our right got a heavy attack, but since all the units identified against it were those we had chased across the mud flats from the Moselle to the Saar, I did not at that time consider these attacks serious. Finally, after a long wait, the VII Corps of the First Army started in to attack in the direction of Houffalize with the 2d and 3d Armored Divisions[1] and the 83d and 84th Divisions.[2] The Germans, I thought, would not react to this attack for several days, but could see no reason for changing the then current disposition of the Third Army. I had had one of my few hunches on the night of January 2-3 that the Germans would attack. I was wrong. The 6th Armored made two miles during the third, while the 87th Division on the left gained a little.

The 11th Armored held an enemy counter-attack on

---

[1] The 2d and 3d Armored Divisions, commanded at this time by Major General E. N. Harmon and Major General Maurice Rose, respectively.

[2] Commanded by Major General Robert C. Macon and Brigadier General A. R. Bolling respectively.

its left center. Owing to the bad condition of the roads and the failure on the part of Com Z to move the 17th Airborne Division as rapidly as they had promised, it was not able to attack on the third, but was prepared to attack in conjunction with the 101st Airborne on the morning of the fourth.

We were delighted to see a SHAEF directive that the Twelfth Army Group would resume control of the First Army as soon as the First and Third Armies made contact at Houffalize. The desire to get to Houffalize was thus one of the important motives for our next few days of fighting. At this time Montgomery had the nerve to get someone in America to suggest that General Eisenhower was overworked and needed a Deputy Ground Force Commander for all troops in Europe and that he, Montgomery, was God's gift to war in this respect.

The 17th Airborne, in its attack on the morning of the fourth, got a very bloody nose, and reported a loss of forty per cent in one battalion. Whenever one gets such a report, it indicates that people do not know anything of war. A casualty report of more than ten per cent is seldom true, unless people have run away or surrendered.

I found Miley, Commander of the 17th Airborne, in Bastogne. While there we had considerable shelling, including airbursts. The flashes of our own guns and those of the enemy in the gathering darkness against the white snowfields were very beautiful, but not too reassuring. In my diary I made this statement of the afternoon of January 4, and it is significant, as it is the only time I ever made such a statement: "We can still lose this war."

I have stated earlier in these letters that Bradley did not in any way interfere with the combat of the Third Army. In one case, while he did not order, he did strongly suggest, that, instead of attacking north of Diekirch and cutting the enemy off at the waist, we should put in a new division southeast of Bastogne so as to insure the integrity of the corridor. I let myself be overpersuaded by him in this connection and assume full responsibility for the error of subsequently engaging the 90th Division too far west. Had I put the 90th Division in north of Diekirch, I am sure we would have bagged more Germans and just as cheaply.

In order to use the 90th Division of the XX Corps to

attack through the 26th Division and clean the Germans out of the pocket southeast of Bastogne, it was necessary to procure the services of the 94th Division. I proposed that when the 94th arrived, it would go to the XX Corps and the 90th would then go to the III. As soon as the 26th Infantry Division had been passed through by the 90th, it would then move to the XX Corps to relieve the 94th, which would then go to the XII Corps, so that we could have the new divisions to attack north from Diekirch. This was sort of a grand right and left, but was the shortest way of getting a division in. It is significant to notice the ease with which the Third Army Staff was able to move troops. To them it made no difference whether the division made one or three moves, provided they had a little notice. The operation was delayed a few days because SHAEF would not release the final Regimental Combat Team (one-third of the fighting strength of a division) of the 94th until the 28th Division had closed at Reims.

On the sixth, I had General Millikin, III Corps, and Van Fleet, who commanded the 90th Division, in with my Staff to work out details for the attack of the 90th through the 26th and along the ridge road to the northwest, south of Wiltz. One combat team of the 26th was to attack on each side of the 90th, while the 3d Combat Team was to relieve the right Combat Team of the 35th and attack north. The combat team of the 35th as released would then help the 6th Armored Division in an attack southeast to make a juncture with the 90th Division on the high ground.

We planned to support this attack with the fire of more than a thousand guns of 105 mm. caliber or larger. This fire was in two directions, about half the guns firing along the axis of movement of the 90th and the other half firing at right angles to it, so that we would get the advantage of dispersion in range both ways. I was very proud of this idea because it was my own. Furthermore, the guns firing at right angles would put their overs into the ridge northeast of the Wiltz River.

In order to deceive the Germans as to the movement of the 90th Division, we used a Signal Corps Deception Group at the former Command Post of the 90th, which kept up the radio traffic. Subsequently captured documents showed that this deception worked. The 90th Division did a very clever piece of work in registering in their guns. As they came in they registered, and a similar set of guns from the 26th Division ceased firing. In this way we believe that the enemy was kept wholly in the dark about the arrival of a new unit. Of course, the 26th Division covered the front so that no prisoners from the 90th could be captured. The fact that we received only three counter-attacks, and they light ones, led us to believe that the enemy was withdrawing.

The left regiment of the 80th Division, attacking through the 26th, captured the high ground in the vicinity of Dahl. This took the pressure off the right of the 26th and facilitated later movements of the 80th Division in a northerly direction. The attack by the 80th was very successful and cheap, for we succeeded in getting five enemy tanks and some self-propelled guns at the cost of two of our divisional tanks.

General Eddy became worried about an attack south from Diekirch. I did not agree with him, but took the only reserve I had, which was a company of towed tank destroyers, previously used for prisoner of war escort duty, and sent them to the XII Corps. I also had the G-3's of the 4th Armored (Lieutenant Colonel J. B. Sullivan) and 10th Armored (Lieutenant Colonel J. A. McChristian) make reconnaissance in the vicinity of the XII Corps so that they could deploy their units rapidly.

Colonel Conklin, the Army Engineer, inspected the road blocks and mines in front of the XII Corps. This was the only time in my service that I used road blocks and mines.

There was considerable effort on the part of Higher Headquarters to have us attack Houffalize on the morning of the eighth. However, as we were not told about it until about 0900, I postponed the attack until the next day.

In driving to Arlon, the Headquarters of the III Corps, to arrange this attack, I passed through the last combat team of the 90th Division moving up for battle. These men had been in trucks for a great many hours with the temperature at six degrees below zero, and were thoroughly chilled. On the opposite side of the road was an endless file of ambulances bringing men back—wounded men; yet, when the soldiers of the 90th Division saw me, they stood up and cheered. It was the most moving experience of my life, and the knowledge of what the ambulances contained made it still more poignant. On the way up, I met Gaffey and signaled him to follow me.

The plan for the attack on the ninth of January was as follows: From left to right in the VIII Corps, the 87th, the 17th Airborne, 101st Airborne, 4th Armored; III Corps, 6th Armored, 35th Infantry, 90th and 26th Infantry; and in the XII Corps the 80th Division; in all, nine divisions. Armored, 35th Infantry, 90th and 26th Infantry; and in the XII Corps the 80th Division; in all, nine divisions. Late that evening, Middleton called me to say he felt the 87th and 17th, which had had a pretty bad time the day before, should not attack until the tenth, and the same was true for the 4th Armored. I told him the attack on the ninth would go forward as planned.

We got continued rumors all this day, and in increasing emphasis, of a German counter-attack at Saarbrücken. The chief reason for these rumors was the fact that it was what the Germans should have done, as the road from Saarbrücken leads through St. Avold directly to Thionville, Metz, and Nancy. St. Avold was therefore very important and, in the area of the XX Corps, had the same relative value that Bastogne had in the area of the Bulge. In view of the persistence of these rumors, I called Walker of the XX Corps and told him to prepare delaying positions, and also obtained the final combat team of the 94th Division to close on Thionville.

The opening attack of the 90th almost ended tragically for General Van Fleet. As he was watching the leading battalion go in, German mortar fire fell around him and the men on either side of him were killed.

All the arrangements for this attack were made by word of mouth and in very short order, although they were complicated because the guns of General Gaffey's division, the 4th Armored, which was now attached to the VIII Corps, had been backing the 35th Division of the III Corps, and we had to arrange to let them back this division during the initial phases of this fight, and then follow the 4th Armored into its new assembly position.

In spite of our high hopes, the attack did not make more than about three kilometers, except that Combat

Command "B" of the 4th, attacking in conjunction with part of the 101st Airborne, got as far as the woods west of Noville.

It will be remembered that on January 8, I was urged by high authority to attack. At 1030, on the tenth, two days later, I received a direct order to pull out an armored division and put it in reserve south of the city of Luxembourg as a possible counter-measure to the supposedly impending break-through. These two instances, for which Bradley was not personally responsible, indicate the inadvisability of commanding from too far back.

On receipt of the order, I took General Bradley with me to Arlon, where we discussed with the Corps Commanders which division could be pulled out. The only possible one was the 4th Armored, which at that time had but one combat command engaged. The two Corps Commanders, myself, and the Commanding Officers of the 4th Armored, 6th Armored, and 101st Airborne, met at the Headquarters of the latter division at Bastogne, and, to the accompaniment of quite a heavy enemy concentration, perfected the arrangement for the withdrawal of the 4th Armored and the reuniting of the 6th Armored with the 101st Division. This is another case illustrating the extreme facility with which command can be exercised, provided commanders are willing to get close enough to the front to know and see what is going on. The order to start the 4th Armored was received at 1030. Two combat commands of the 4th Armored started via Arlon on Luxembourg before dark. The counterattack they were destined to repel did not come off.

On the way back to Headquarters, I visited the 35th, 90th, and 26th Divisions to explain to them that, while the attack on the left must cease, they were to continue. This was quite satisfactory, as they had made fairly good progress this date. On reaching Headquarters, I found a new rumor, dreamed up by Higher Headquarters, that the enemy was about to attack us across the river just north of Trier. It seemed to me then, and subsequent investigation has proved me correct, that it was impossible for the enemy to make any such counter-attack. He had no troops available—in fact, his attacks at that time were on a shoestring.

We lost several carloads of ammunition, reported as

three hundred tons, but probably one hundred tons, as a result of a freight train running into an ammunition train south of Arlon.

On the eleventh of January, it became quite evident that the end of the Bastogne operation was in sight. Anticipating this, I had had a study made of the river lines and road nets in the XX Corps area and drove to Thionville to see General Walker and talk over this study with him. It seemed to me that the enemy could cross the Saar River in three places; first, in the vicinity of Saarburg where he had some bridging and ferrying sites intact. However, the road net was cramped and I did not think he would take the chance. The next possible point of crossing was at Saarlautern through our bridgeheads. This I did not believe probable, first, because he would have to take the western half of the town, which we occupied, and, second, because the bridge was mined by us, and if he started to attack, we would blow it. Finally, Saarbrücken: and this was the place where I would have attacked had I been the Germans. In the town there were seven good bridges, and they had, on the west bank, a bridgehead of from seven to ten miles. The road net to Thionville, and thence to Nancy, was excellent. However, St. Avold was the critical point, and General Walker was perfectly aware of this fact and had made arrangements to defend it. He had also arranged to blow the crossing over the Nied River so as to canalize any German attack.

His and my personal solution at the time was to attack Saarbrücken with what we had. In the light of present knowledge, it would have been the ideal thing to do, and would probably have broken the German line completely and much earlier than it actually was broken.

Due to SHAEF's worry about the impending German counter-attack, the position of the vicinity of the XX Corps was strengthened. In addition to the 94th and 95th Divisions and the 10th Armored Division, which were at that time in the XX Corps, the 4th Armored Division in the Third Army Reserve could be used, and the 8th and 9th Armored Divisions were both closing, the one in the vicinity of Pont-à-Mousson and the other near Metz. The last two, however, were in SHAEF Reserve.

The final attack for the VIII and III Corps to take Houffalize was planned for the thirteenth. On the twelfth,

General Gay visited the corps to co-ordinate their attack plan and also to get a battalion of 155 mm. howitzers, which the XII Corps had loaned to the VIII, returned to the XII.

General Bradley told me the plans for the use of the Army Group. He wanted the First Army to attack east on Cologne, while the Third Army maintained pressure and really held a defensive flank from somewhere in the vicinity of St. Vith to the junction with the Seventh Army. This plan had the advantage of utilizing the existing breach in the Siegfried Line west of Cologne, which had been made by the First Army in November, and also of using the shortest route. Personally I was opposed to it, as it prevented me from attacking, and I believed that the XX Corps supported by the III or XII could attack straight east through Saarlautern with better chance of rupturing the German Army and capturing the Saar Valley. I still adhered to my theory, that in order to keep the Germans from attacking, we had to attack.

The attack on Houffalize started on the thirteenth, but the progress was not as rapid as we had hoped. However, the mental attitude of the men was excellent. Heretofore they had been somewhat dubious; now they were chasing a sinking fox and babbling for the kill.

On the fourteenth, Generals Somervell, Campbell,[1] Lee, and Plank[2] visited me, and we had considerable discussion on equipment. I definitely recommended the cessation of the construction of tank destroyers and the replacing of the tank destroyer battalion in an infantry division by a tank battalion. I also reiterated my request for two co-axial machine guns in each tank.

On the fifteenth, orders were issued for the XII Corps to start its attack north through Diekirch on the morning of the eighteenth. For this attack I assigned the 4th Armored Division, the 87th Infantry Division, together with the 80th, 4th, and 5th Infantry Divisions to the XII Corps. The weather still remained hideously cold.

I drove to visit the troops attacking Houffalize. At one point we came across a German machine-gunner

---

[1] Major General L. H. Campbell, Jr., Chief of Ordnance, U.S. Army.

[2] Brigadier General E. G. Plank, Commanding General, Advanced Section Communication Zone.

who had been killed and apparently instantly frozen, as he was in a half-sitting position with his arms extended, holding a loaded belt of ammunition. At another point I saw a lot of black objects sticking out of the snow, and on investigating, found they were the toes of dead men. Another phenomenon resulting from the quick-freezing of the men killed in battle is that they turn a sort of claret color—a nasty sight.

At 0905 on the sixteenth, the 41st Cavalry Squadron (Captain Herbert Foye) of the 11th Armored Division, covering our left flank, made contact with the 41st Armored Infantry Regiment (Colonel, later Brigadier General, S. R. Hinds) in the 2d Armored Division at Houffalize. This restored Bradley to the command of the Twelfth Army Group.

In the evening we received a directive to send the 10th Armored Division to the Sixth Army Group to aid in the liquidation of the so-called Colmar Pocket.

On the seventeenth, I personally congratulated Millikin and Middleton on the successful termination of the Bulge. Although we had not driven the Germans back to the line from which they started, we had on that date begun this final operation.

General Hughes was with me and we visited the 6th Armored, the 90th and 26th Infantry Divisions, and told them that, though we knew they were tired, it was necessary for them to continue to fight. I decorated General Van Fleet and two of his officers with the Distinguished Service Cross. I also saw the 120 mm. German mortar which the 90th Division used in lieu of the cannon in their cannon company. It was a very excellent and light weapon.

The VIII and III Corps were given orders to resume their offensive along the axis Bastogne—St. Vith on the twenty-first.

The XII Corps attack across the Sure River jumped off at 0330 on the morning of the eighteenth without an artillery preparation, and secured a complete tactical surprise.

General Eddy and I visited the 4th and 5th Infantry Divisions. The 4th Division was somewhat apathetic and General Eddy had to direct the division commander to get across the river himself and also see that his battalion commanders did. The 5th Division was in fine spirits. We visited an Observation Post from which we could look down on the Germans about six hundred feet below us in the river valley. Our men had on snow suits, some captured and some which General Eddy had had made in Luxembourg.

We had to dispatch the 101st Airborne, an AA unit, and some tank destroyer units to the Sixth Army Group, for an attack which had started by someone saying they could reduce the Colmar Pocket with one division, and ended up by requiring about five additional units.

Walker called up to know if he could make a serious attack in the Saar—Moselle Triangle with the 94th Division and a combat team of the 8th Armored. He got the green light.

The delay in the attack of the VIII and III Corps until the twenty-first might possibly bring a few extra troops formerly facing those two corps into combat with the XII Corps. However, the XII Corps was fresher and had a shorter distance to go.

On the nineteenth, the condition of the roads, due to sleet and ice, was so bad we could not move either the 101st or the 76th Division.

The 94th Division ran into elements of the 11th Panzer Division (General Lieutenant Weitershein) on this date.

In spite of terrible weather on the twentieth, the XII Corps advanced several kilometers, while the 95th Division at Saarlautern met the counter-attack of four hundred Germans and repulsed it—partly due to the German's own efforts. Because their counter-attack jumped off too soon, they were caught in their own barrage and then in ours. Only forty prisoners were taken. General Schmidt of the 76th Division reported one of his combat teams would close in the VIII Corps that day.

On the twenty-first, the XII Corps was practically on its initial objective and caught a large German concentration at the bridge near Vianden, where they had good artillery observation, and kept it under continuous artillery fire, using proximity fuse.

While visiting the VIII Corps on this date, I ran across two instructive incidents. In one place, elements of the 17th Airborne Division were stuck on a slippery hill, and yet the officers did not have enough sense to have the men dismount and push the trucks. When this was done, the sticking completely ended. The other was that the ice and sleet had made the Germans' and also the Americans' mines inoperative, as they filled with ice right under the spider so that no pressure was sufficient to detonate the mine. It was evident that we would have many casualties when the thaw came, as troops would use the roads, which were apparently demined; and suddenly find a mine that had become operative. We used detectors to the maximum.

General Van Fleet was Commander of a Corps then forming in England and later commanded the III Corps when General Millikin got into trouble at the Remagen Bridge in March. After canvassing the available brigadiers in the Third Army, we picked General Earnest to take Van Fleet's place with the 90th Division. However, that same evening General Eisenhower ordered me to take Major General L. W. Rooks as temporary commander of the division in order that he might familiarize himself with conditions at the front, prior to being placed on Staff duty under General Eisenhower.

The attack of the VIII and III Corps continued satisfactorily with nothing but weather and small-arms fire stopping them. The VIII Corps was practically pinched out[1] by the twenty-second. The 80th Division, XII Corps, was progressing very satisfactorily north of the Wiltz River, so I told General Eddy not to halt on his final objective, but to continue north, and, if necessary, use elements of the 4th Armored Division to cover his right flank.

I called General Bradley on this date, January 22, and urged that all armies attack whether they were fatigued and had losses or not, as I was sure, in view of the Russian offensive,[2] that that was the time to strike. It was.

At 1530, General Weyland called up and said there was a great deal of German armor moving in several

---

[1] Pinched out: The converging attacks of other units made it impossible for VIII Corps units to operate. Therefore, it was considered the VIII Corps was pinched out.

[2] The Russians were advancing through East Prussia, had captured Tannenberg and Lodz and were within twenty-five miles of Breslau and 165 miles from Berlin.

directions north of Diekirch; that, in fact, his pilots reported it the biggest concentration they had seen since the Falaise Gap, and that all his groups were attacking.[1]

On the twenty-third, everything was going well except that one battalion of the 94th Division lost forty men killed and wounded and four hundred missing in action. I directed General Walker to investigate.

In spite of strong remonstrances by General Bradley and myself, SHAEF ordered the 35th Division, less one combat team, which was in action with the 6th Armored, to join the Sixth Army Group. The 35th had been in actual combat with the enemy every day except five since the sixth of July, and I had only just succeeded in getting it out of the line.

The VI Corps of the Seventh Army was driven back a few miles.

The plan for the continuation of the Twelfth Army Group attack envisioned two corps of the First Army attacking the Siegfried Line north of the VIII Corps (Third Army with this corps), attacking parallel with them. The III, XII, and XX Corps were to hold defensively. If this plan failed to get results, it would possibly be necessary for Bradley to give Montgomery twelve divisions, so we were all very anxious to succeed.

When the question of attacking with a corps along my northern flank in conjunction with the attack of the First Army was broached, I thought of putting General Walker there, as he was less fatigued than the other Corps Commanders and also because I considered him a very aggressive soldier. However, after considering the fact that Middleton had already fought over this ground and, further, was in command of the northern VIII Corps, I determined to let him continue in that command and carry out the attack, for although he was tired, I knew him to be a very accomplished leader.

The plan for building his corps up to strength was complicated and worked out as follows: The 76th Division, a new division, in the VIII Corps was to relieve the 87th Division in the XII Corps; the 87th then going to

---

[1] On this day the XIX TAC flew seven hundred sorties and destroyed two thousand enemy vehicles, to date their best day of the war.

Middleton. The 17th Airborne Division of the III Corps
was to relieve the 26th Division in the III Corps, and the
26th Division, in turn, would join the XX Corps and relieve the 95th Division, which would go to Middleton.
The 90th Division of the III Corps and the 4th Division of
the XII Corps would also go to Middleton. Therefore, he
would have the 11th Armored and four infantry divisions,
which made a very powerful attack. These plans were arranged at my house at dinner with the Corps Commanders
on the night of the twenty-third.

On the twenty-fourth, General Hodges came to lunch
with Bradley and myself. After lunch the staffs of the
First and Third Armies had a discussion of boundaries between the armies. We arranged a very satisfactory boundary. Just as everyone was happy, General Whitely,[1] G-3
at SHAEF, called up and told General Bradley that he
wished to withdraw a Corps Headquarters from the
Twelfth Army Group to help the Sixth Army Group. This
was the only time, to my knowledge, that Bradley lost his
temper. He told Whitely that if he wanted to destroy the
whole operation he could do so and be damned, and take
not only one Corps Headquarters but all the corps and
divisions. General Bull, Whitely's assistant, then came on
the wire and Bradley repeated his statement, adding that
much more than a tactical operation was involved in that
the prestige of the American Army was at stake. We were
all extremely pleased with his attitude and told him so.
General Hodges said he would be able to jump off on
Sunday, the twenty-eighth, so I immediately decided to
jump off on Saturday, the twenty-seventh.

Bradley, Hodges, and I were unanimous that wasting
troops on the Colmar Pocket was a very foolish thing,
and, furthermore, it was the third time in our knowledge
that such a diversion of effort had been made. We were
personally determined to carry out our attack, no matter
how much we were reduced.[2]

At that time I was convinced that the Germans were
pulling out, probably as far as the Rhine. It is interesting

---

[1] Major General J. F. M. Whitely, British Deputy G-3, for
SHAEF.

[2] For further details of this gallant fight read Audie Murphy's
To Hell and Back, another infantry action volume in the Bantam
War Book Series.

to note that, in the reports of German officers which I have since read, that is what the German High Command wanted to do, but Hitler would not let them.

On the twenty-fifth of January, Codman, Stiller, and I visited the 4th, 5th, and 80th Infantry Divisions. We also took a look at Diekirch, Eittelbrück, and Wiltz. All of them had been very well "liberated." In freezing weather, and at this time the weather was always below freezing, the destruction of the doors and windows from bombardment resulted in the freezing and breaking of the water systems so that none of the large houses were habitable, since neither the sewer nor heating arrangements would work.

On this date also all the units of the VIII, III, and XII Army Corps, except the left regiment of the 80th Division, were on their final objective, namely, the hill mass east of the Diekirch—St. Vith road. The 76th and 87th Infantry Divisions were effecting their change of place.

The attack of the XII Corps in the operation was exceptionally good, being well planned, rapidly executed, and cheap.

On the twenty-fourth, the 5th Infantry Division found elements of five German divisions in one group of one hundred prisoners, while on the same date the 6th Armored Division, in a group of one hundred and fifty prisoners, found elements of ten German divisions. This indicated a bad state of disorganization among the Germans. Unfortunately, we did not realize how bad it was at that time. All during this period Higher Headquarters were very pessimistic and kept warning us not to have a reverse. This was a bad attitude.

By dark on the twenty-sixth, it was evident that all the shifts in troops would be accomplished on time and that the attack could start on the twenty-eighth. Had anyone proposed such a troop movement at Leavenworth, people would have gone crazy, but here it was being done. However, the difference between this operation and a problem at Leavenworth was that here we had an old and experienced staff of extremely capable men, while at Leavenworth one could have nothing but students more or less bemused with formulas.

On the twenty-eighth, I visited Middleton at Bastogne and found him very offensive-minded. His plan for the attack was to begin with the 87th on the left, the 90th on the right, followed respectively by the 95th and 4th Infantry. After a certain advance, the 90th Infantry was to form a defensive flank to the right and the 4th was to pass through it and do the same farther to the east. The 95th was to pass through the 87th when the latter became tired and would continue the attack along the axis of the corps. It was not necessary to form a defensive flank on the left because the First Army was guarding us there. The 11th Armored was to close in behind the 90th and be prepared for exploitation.

I stopped at Martelange, Headquarters of the III Corps, and told them to prepare to widen the base of the salient south of the 90th Division; that is, to cross through the hole made by the 90th and then attack southeast. To do this effectively, I had to get another division for the III Corps, which at that time had only the 17th Airborne, one combat team of the 35th Infantry, and the 6th Armored Division.

When I got to Headquarters, Eddy was there with a proposition to attack north and join up with the 4th Infantry Division. I was very much pleased with the idea and told him to go ahead with it. We also secured from the First Army a road running west from Houffalize. The road net in the area of the VIII Corps was extremely bad and was to get much worse.

On the twenty-eighth, we decided not to attack until the twenty-ninth, so, as usual before a battle, the twenty-eighth was a nerve-racking day. However, the replacement system was working better than it had ever done before and we were practically up to strength. All the transfer of divisions had been completed in spite of snow, ice, and sleet.

The situation as to truck maintenance was pretty bad because of the heavy toll taken of trucks by the glassy roads, and also because between the nineteenth of December and the sixteenth of January we had moved seventeen divisions an average distance of one hundred miles. Added to this, we were now moving eight divisions about the same distance. The ice, which stuck to the running gear of the trucks and froze the drivers, resulted in considerable laxity as to first echelon maintenance. Also, we were very short of Ornance personnel to do this type of maintenance.

So ended the campaign of the Bulge which had cost us 50,630 men.

During this operation the Third Army moved farther and faster and engaged more divisions in less time than any other army in the history of the United States—possibly in the history of the world. The results attained were made possible only by the superlative quality of American officers, American men, and American equipment. No country can stand against such an army.

Casualties for January 29 were:

Third Army		Enemy	
Killed	14,879	Killed	96,500
Wounded	71,009	Wounded	269,000
Missing	14,054	Prisoners of war	163,000
Total	99,942	Total	528,500
Non-battle casualties	73,011		
Grand Total	172,953		

Matériel Losses

Light tanks	270	Medium tanks	1268
Medium tanks	771	Panther and Tiger tanks	711
Guns	144	Guns	2526

THE EIFEL TO THE RHINE AND THE CAPTURE OF TRIER
29 January to 12 March, 1945

On the twenty-ninth of January, 1945, the thirteen divisions of the four corps of the Third Army were abreast the Moselle, Sauer, and Our Rivers, ready to crack the Siegfried Line from Saarlautern, north to St. Vith.

The VIII Corps opened the new offensive on this date, followed by the III Corps immediately to its south. The XII Corps jumped forward on the sixth and seventh of February, the XX Corps on the nineteenth.

By the end of the month, all corps had breached the Siegfried Line, famous "monument to the stupidity of man," and, for the Germans, March came in as anything but a lamb. The fury of the attack never ceased; Trier fell on the second of March to the XX Corps; on the fifth the 4th Armored Division broke loose, to reach the Rhine on the eighth. On the thirteenth, the Third Army controlled the Moselle from the Saar River to Coblentz, and the Rhine from Coblentz north to Andernach.

The Eifel, impossible of fast going according to the prophets, had been dominated in twelve days. Trier, key city of the Saar Triangle, fell to the XX Corps. (See Map, page 221.)

During this time nothing new happened on the Twenty-First Army Group front. In the Sixth Army Group, American and French troops cleared the Colmar Pocket and again advanced to the Rhine. The Russians reached the Baltic between Stettin and Danzig, and were *within forty miles of Berlin on the Oder River. There was nothing new in Italy. The First American Army broke through the Siegfried Line, secured a bridgehead over the Rhine at Remagen, and pushed three divisions across.*

In the Pacific, Iwo Jima was giving trouble.

P.H.D.

Many Rivers and Passive Defense

The VIII Corps jumped off as per schedule, January 29, one battalion of the 4th Infantry Division getting over the Our River. The 90th Division was to cross the same river that night farther to the north. The 87th Division, which, owing to the configuration of the ground, was farther from the river, was closing up to start its attack.

I had General Eddy in to discuss his forthcoming attack north against Bitburg. We both realized that this would be with inadequate strength, but we still had hopes that it would work.

Since my plan envisaged the XX Corps being relieved in the Saar Triangle by the Seventh Army, I had Walker come up and discuss with Eddy and myself how he would take over the right portion of the XII Corps zone when the attack started. It was thought at this time that the XX Corps would be relieved as soon as Colmar was taken.

We also got information that the 35th Division was going to the Ninth Army instead of coming back to us. It will be remembered we had loaned it to the Seventh Army. This division was one of the oldest in the Third Army and had always done well.

From a sentimental and morale standpoint it is unquestionably a mistake to move divisions from one army corps to the next. Similarly, it is a greater mistake to move army corps from one army to the next. However, our ability to do those two things was probably responsible for a great deal of our success.

At this period, January—February, 1945, the supply situation, as well as the replacement situation, was the best it had ever been.

On the thirtieth, I drove to Bastogne, where I picked up General Middleton, and we went to St. Vith. This town was the most completely destroyed I had seen since the First World War. The British, the Americans, and the Germans were all responsible for its destruction.

On the way we passed the scene of the tank battle during the initial German break-through. I counted over a hundred American armored fighting vehicles along the road, and, as a result, issued an order, subsequently carried out, that every tank should be examined and the direction, caliber, and type of hit which put it out made of record, so that we would have data from which to construct a better tank. These data are now in the hands of the Ordnance Department.

St. Vith had been so completely destroyed that it was impossible to move through the town, so the VIII Corps had to build a road around it. So long as the ground remained frozen, as it was at that time, the by-pass was excellent. Later it became impassable. However, by then the Engineers had cut a road through the obliterated center of the town.

On the way back we visited the 87th Division, which had done well, and on its northern flank had gained seven miles. The 4th Infantry Division, which we visited next, had not gone so far. Every precaution had been taken with both these divisions to prevent frozen and trench feet. At the time I was very fearful that we would have a great many of these cases on account of crossing the wet ground and rivers. As a matter of fact, the incidence of non-battle casualties went up only very slightly during all this period of extremely bad weather.

American soldiers are most ingenious. When they could not capture a town to sleep in, they would roll three large snowballs or snow rolls, place one on each side and the third on the windward end, and, lining them with pine-tree branches, they slept in groups of three or four. How human beings could endure this continuous fighting at sub-zero temperatures is still beyond my comprehension.

The 90th Division which we visited last had, as usual, done well and was on its objective.

The other three corps were still holding defensively and reorganizing.

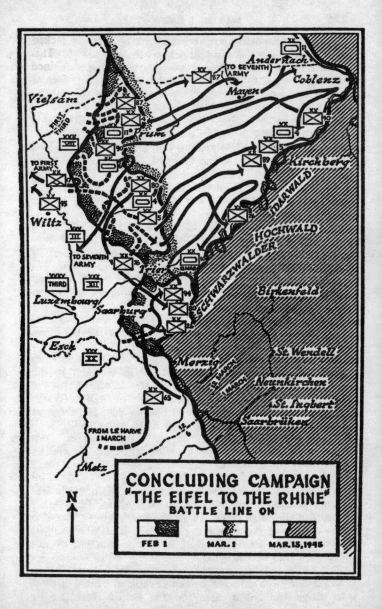

CONCLUDING CAMPAIGN
"THE EIFEL TO THE RHINE"
BATTLE LINE ON

FEB 1   MAR. 1   MAR. 13, 1945

Eddy proposed starting his attack on Bitburg on the sixth. I told him he must attack on the fourth. He complained very bitterly that I never appreciated time and space factors. I told him that, had I done so with him or any other corps commander, we would still be west of the Seine River.

After talking with Eddy, I called the Twelfth Army Group to see if I could get the 9th Armored Division and an infantry division to relieve the 17th Airborne, which was low in strength. When General Allen called back, he not only told me I could get nothing, but could not make any move until I got further orders. As a result of this, I had to tell Eddy to stop his plans for attacking on the fourth of February.

I drove to Thionville, had lunch with the XX Corps, and then visited the 94th Division, where I talked very plainly to the Division Commander because the non-battle casualties in that division were the highest in the Army, as were also the prisoners of war the division had lost. I had all the officers, and as many non-commissioned officers and privates as possible, assembled, and repeated my statements to them, telling them frankly that they had lost too many prisoners and must correct the poor impression the division had given.

On returning to Headquarters, I had a message from Bradley that we were to lose the 95th Division to the Ninth Army. As usual I kicked, but was informed that the order came from the Combined Chiefs of Staff in Washington. He also told me to be at Spa, in Belgium, the next day for an Army conference relative to a new attack.

On the second of February, Colonel Harkins, Codman, and I drove to Spa via Bastogne and Houffalize. The latter town was very completely removed, even more so than St. Vith.

Spa is a watering-place which, in 1918, was Hindenburg's Headquarters; the Headquarters of our First Army occupied the same room. From the windows of this office one could see the lake around which the Kaiser walked while waiting for Hindenburg to decide whether or not the war could be continued.

At the meeting we were informed that General Eisenhower had been directed by the Combined Chiefs of Staff to assign the Ninth Army to the British Twenty-First

Army Group, all under Montgomery. Could this be an attempt on the part of General Marshall to secure the services of the fourteen British divisions which had been doing very little for some time?

The purpose of the attack was alleged to be the securing of a large stretch of the Rhine River, so that, in the event of Germany collapsing, we could get across quickly.

I believed at the time that, since the British attack could not start until the tenth of February, the attack of the First and Third Armies then under way would go farther and faster. As a sop to our pride, we were told that we could continue to attack until the tenth and thereafter, providing casualties and ammunition expenditure were not excessive.

I heard also that the Sixth Army Group would not take over the Moselle—Saar Triangle. As a matter of fact, one of the luckiest things that ever happened to me was the failure of the Sixth Army Group to do this, because through the retention of the Moselle—Saar Triangle, the Third Army was subsequently able to capture Trier and start the attack through the Palatinate. At the time, however, I was very bitter. This is another example of the many I have encountered in life where great disappointments have proved to be the road to future successes.

We were all much upset because we felt it ignoble for the American armies to finish the war on the defensive. Another point which made us angry was the information that SHAEF was collecting a theatre reserve. This seemed like locking the barn door after the horse was stolen. Certainly at this period of the war no reserve was needed—simply violent attacks everywhere with everything.

On the third, I had all corps commanders in to discuss how we could continue the attack. General Middleton stated that, while he was reluctant to lose the 95th Division to the Ninth Army, he still believed he could attack with the three infantry divisions he had left, particularly in view of the fact that the road conditions in his area were so bad that the maintenance of the 95th Division was becoming a serious problem. In view of this, Eddy could still make his Bitburg attack, so I told him to jump off on the night of February 6-7.

All that happened as a result of the Spa conference was the loss of two days in the time of starting the attack. My plans were based on the assumption that the Germans were not in a position to make a serious counterattack. This proved to be correct.

I attempted also, without success, to secure the 9th or 10th Armored Division in order to permit the XX Corps to clean up the Saar—Moselle Triangle.

On the fourth, I visited the hospitals and found a surprisingly small number of wounded, but did run on to three self-inflicted wounds: two shot through the left foot and one through the left hand. It is my experience that any time a soldier is shot through either of these extremities there is a high probability that the wound is self-inflicted. I got out an order that, from then on, soldiers so wounded would be tried, first for carelessness, and then for self-inflicted wounds. It is almost impossible to convict a man for self-inflicted wounds, but it is easy to convict him for carelessness, for which he can get up to six months. After the soldiers had thought this over for about two months, they began to get their friends to shoot them; however, since the friends were frequently inaccurate and took off too many toes, the practice was never highly developed.

As I was trying to keep the impending Bitburg offensive a secret so it would not be stopped from above, I was quite perturbed when I received a telephone call directing me to report to General Eisenhower at Bastogne. When I got there, I was relieved to find it was simply a photographic mission, so to speak. It was rather amusing, though perhaps not flattering, to note that General Eisenhower never mentioned the Bastogne offensive, although this was the first time I had seen him since the nineteenth of December, when he seemed much pleased to have me at the critical point.

This meeting was momentous in one respect, namely, that of relieving a corps commander. General Bradley stated that Middleton should go back to the First Army, as he had come from it. I stated that I preferred to keep Middleton rather than Millikin, because, while Millikin had done a good job in the Bastogne offensive, he was inexperienced as compared to Middleton. General Eisenhower told me I could keep Middleton. All during the meeting I kept thinking about Nelson the night before the attack on Calvi in Corsica, when he had discovered the French were twice as numerous as he thought they were, but failed to report it to his chief for fear the attack would be called off.

On the way back from Bastogne, I drove to the Trois Vierges, the new Command Post of the VIII Corps. Their attack was going better than had been expected. The 4th Division was only three kilometers from Prum. This was the night that the 11th Armored Division was supposed to attack past the 4th Infantry to take the high ground east of the river, and failed to do so.

I awoke at 0300 on the morning of the sixth with the complete plan for a break-through by the VIII and XII Corps in my head, and the conviction that, when this break-through took place, we could use two, and possibly three, armored divisions for a re-enacting of the Brest Peninsula campaign. Whether these tactical thoughts of mine are the result of inspiration or insomnia, I have never been able to determine, but nearly every tactical idea I have ever had has come into my head full-born, much after the manner of Minerva from the head of Jupiter.

General Eddy came in, full of confidence as to the success of his opening attack.

The 5th Division jumped off on the morning of the seventh at 0100 and crossed the Sauer River. Due to the rapid current and flood conditions, there were a great many boat casualties and probably more than sixty men drowned.

One combat team of the 76th Division (417th, commanded by Colonel George E. Bruner), attacking on the right of the 5th Infantry Division, did a better job than the 5th in getting across the river because they did not realize how dangerous it was. After they got across, they did very little for about three days—probably recovering from the shock of their own heroism.

The 80th Division, attacking west of Wallensdorf, which is west of the junction of the Our and Sauer Rivers, had less difficulty and succeeded in getting two battalions across. In this case an artillery preparation of thirty minutes was used and the attack took place just at dawn.

The crossing of the three divisions over these rivers

was a magnificent feat of arms. The rivers were in flood to such an extent that the barbed wire along the Siegfried Line, which abutted on the rivers, was under water, and, when the men disembarked from the boats, they were caught in it. The whole hillside was covered with German pillboxes and barbed wire. A civilian observer told me afterward that he did not see how human beings could be brave enough to succeed in such an attack. Actually the audacity of the attack and the strength of the position materially aided in our success. However, weather conditions made progress at the time seem unnecessarily slow and both Eddy and I were considerably perturbed.

The remaining Corps (XX) of the Army did nothing of importance on this day.

In the afternoon I visited the section of the Moselle River covered by the 2d Cavalry Group under Colonel Hank Reed (Charles H. Reed) and was very much pleased with the methods he had used on this line. We succeeded in getting up on the bank and could look right down into the German positions at a surprisingly short range. In fact, not being used to such immediate proximity to the enemy, I was worried. However, no one fired at us.

The situation on the eighth had not improved. We still did not have a single bridge over either the Our or the Sauer River and the attack was very sticky. I made an unsuccessful attempt to delay the withdrawal of the 17th Airborne Division. I believe that a good deal of my success and a great deal of my unpopularity is due to the fact that I fought every order to take troops away from me, and frequently succeeded in holding on to them or in getting others to replace them.

The situation in the VIII Corps got so bad that Middleton suggested stopping the attack, but I told him to go ahead and take Prum, then I would try to supply him along the so-called "Skyline Drive."[1] This was under direct fire by the Germans, but I believed we could use it at night. We subsequently did.

General Muller (G-4) was making herculean efforts to get the railway running in the vicinity of St. Vith. We had to replace the 17th Airborne Division in the III Corps

---

[1] National Route 16—running north from Diekirch to St. Vith.

with two untried engineer battalions, so I visited Millikin to see how he was going to handle the situation, and found his solution entirely satisfactory.

On the ninth, I drove via Wiltz to the Trois Vierges to see Middleton. The road situation beggared description, but Middleton, with his usual tenacity, was doing his damnedest to get things moving.

General Keyes[1] arrived for a few days' leave. He had been fighting continuously since the tenth of July, 1943, so when he got a leave, instead of going to a quiet sector to rest, he came to visit me to see more war.

On the tenth, Bradley called up to ask me how soon I could go on the defensive. I told him I was the oldest leader in age and in combat experience in the United States Army in Europe, and that if I had to go on the defensive I would ask to be relieved. He stated I owed too much to the troops and would have to stay on. I replied that a great deal was owed to me, and unless I could continue attacking I would have to be relieved. I further suggested that it would be a good thing if some of his Staff visited the front to find out how the other half lived. Bradley himself came up a great deal, but his Staff did not. He referred to Montgomery's attack, using the Ninth Army, as the biggest mistake SHAEF had yet made. I was not sure it was the biggest, because I had always felt that that was made when General Eisenhower turned the First Army north to help Montgomery, toward the end of August, and, as a result, the supplies to the Third Army stopped.

On the eleventh, the situation in the VIII Corps got so bad that General Weyland arranged to drop supplies to the 87th and 4th Infantry Divisions by air when and if it became necessary.

Also, the two engineer battalions which were guarding the old III Corps front (the III Corps had gone to the First Army at that date) were withdrawn, so I told Middleton, who had taken over that portion of the front, that, if necessary, he was to dismount elements of the 6th Ar-

---

[1]Lieutenant General Geoffrey Keyes was Deputy Commander under General Patton in the Western Task Force and Seventh Army. He commanded a provisional corps in Sicily and left the Seventh Army to command the II Corps in Italy. He later commanded the Fifth, Seventh, and Third Armies.

mored Division and use them as infantry, but that he must hold the bridge over the Our River which that division had just secured.

The XII Corps, on the other hand, finally got bridges across the Our and Sauer Rivers and was making good progress.

On the twelfth, General Keyes and I drove to the VIII Corps via Arlon, Bastogne, and Wiltz, passing through the forest which we had attacked so heavily with artillery during the Bastogne operation. The effect of the use of proximity fuse on the forest was very remarkable. You could see the exact angle of impact of all the projectiles, which had burst about thirty feet above the highest treetops. After bursting, they cut the trees at an angle of about forty degrees down near the ground. However, it seemed to me then, and was later brought out by a talk with General Grow, that, in heavy woods, the proximity fuse is not efficient, as the timber absorbs the fragments. For such woods the delayed-action fuse, which bursts only on hitting heavy trees close to the ground, is preferable. One continues to learn about war by practicing war.

We also passed hundreds of dead horses from German artillery and transport teams, and a great many human bodies. There were several Royal Tiger Tanks along the road which seemed to have been abandoned by their crews and blown up. We inspected several of these.

The road from Trois Vierges to St. Vith was actually impassable to vehicles, but everybody in the VIII Corps not actually fighting was engaged in corduroying it. This was done by laying stringers lenthwise along the road about four feet apart, then spiking cross-pieces on them. The engineers did a remarkable job, as they always did.

The weather was so bad that I gave General Eddy permission to stop the attack, which immediately induced him to attack more vigorously. Such is the nature of man.

During the whole of the Bastogne operation, I spent five or six hours almost every day in an open car and had practically no trouble. I never had a cold, and my face, though sometimes slightly blistered, did not hurt me much nor did I wear very heavy clothes. I did, however, have a blanket around my legs, which was exceedingly valuable in keeping me from freezing. Codman and Stiller, who sat in the back seat, suffered a great deal more than I did.

On the thirteenth, the Troop Carrier Command (commanded by Major General P. L. Williams) dropped ammunition and supplies from eighty-three planes to the 4th and 87th Divisions.

Eddy and I crossed the Sauer River in the area of the 5th Division, and then drove along the northeastern bank in a peep, which we found on the far side. I think this is the origin of the story of my swimming the river. We crossed on a partly submerged assault bridge under a smoke screen, so, when we arrived on the far side, an excited soldier could believe that we had swum. Neither of us did. However, crossing the assault bridge in the smoke, where we could not see more than a foot ahead and there were no guard rails, was a very interesting operation. The men were glad to see us.

There were quite a number of pillboxes on the far side of the river. One, I remember, was camouflaged like a barn, and a wooden barn at that. When you opened the door through which the hay was supposed to be put, you came to a concrete wall nine feet thick with an 88 mm. gun sticking out. Another was completely built inside an old house, the outer walls of which were knocked down when it became necessary for the pillbox to go into action. The amazing thing about all these defenses is that they produced no results.

During the course of these operations, the 90th Division alone put out one hundred and twenty pillboxes in about forty-eight hours, with the loss of less than one hundred and twenty men. This feat was accomplished by careful reconnaissance, then smothering the embrasures with machine-gun and rifle fire, and using dynamite charges against the back door, or else by using self-propelled 155 mm. guns at short range. At three hundred yards the 155 shell will remove a pillbox for every round fired.

In the initial assault across the Sauer, we had guns on our bank firing at the enemy pillboxes across the river at ranges of from four hundred to six hundred yards. Without their assistance, the crossing would probably have been less successful.

Captain Krass, a noted German counter-attack artist and head of what was called Krass's Circus, walked in and

155 mm. Self-propelled Gun

surrendered to one of our divisions. He gave his name and said he had done his best to make himself well known to the Americans. When asked why he surrendered, he said he had done all a man could do, had received all the medals for valor issued by the German Army, and was not a fool. Therefore, he proposed to live so he could teach after the war—presumably how to fight the next one.

On the fourteenth, the Troop Carrier Command made a second drop with 103 plane-loads of supplies for the 4th and 87th Infantry Divisions. For the next few days things were fairly slow.

On the nineteenth, I wrote General Bradley a letter saying that all the United States troops except the Third Army were doing nothing at all, and that while I was still attacking, I could do better with more divisions. I asked

for from one to three additional. I believe this is the only
letter I ever wrote for the record, but I felt very keenly at
that time that history would criticize us for not having
been more energetic.

At 1130 on the nineteenth, Walker called up to say
he felt the situation was ripe for a break-through in the
Saar Triangle, provided he could get an armored division.
Bradley was away, so I called General Bull and succeeded
in getting the 10th Armored, but with a string tied to it—
namely, "Only for this operation."

It always made me mad to have to beg for opportunities to win battles.

On the twentieth, the 10th Armored Division joined
the XX Corps and started to attack north on the west
(left) of the 94th Division. This attack was well done and
the divisions were closing in on Saarburg by dark. The
10th Armored had fought in this area in November, so
knew the ground and conditions.

Joined by Eddy, I visited the front of the XII Corps
and came to a bridge over the Sauer River with the sign:
"General Patton's Bridge—Built by the Mighty Midgets."
The story behind this was that the last time I had gone
along the river line, the bridge was under construction, and
I made a remark that I had never seen so many little
men doing such a big job. The "midgets" actually were
Company "F" of the 1303d General Service Engineer
Regiment (commanded by Captain Walford T. Gradison).

Leaving Eddy, I drove up the "Skyline Drive" with
General Middleton and we inspected his roads. He had
done a remarkable job in keeping them going, and as soon
as the railroad reached St. Vith, the situation would be
safe, for then he could abandon the road in his rear
area and use only the railway, thus saving all his Engineers
for work at the front. Furthermore, he would be in Germany, where the roads are much better than in Belgium
or Luxembourg. As a matter of fact, the roads in the
two latter countries are extremely poor—probably because
they are not built to carry heavy traffic in winter, and the
local inhabitants state that in winter all heavy traffic is
barred from the roads by law.

After looking over the road, we visited the 6th Armored, the 90th and the 4th Infantry Divisions. General
Grow, of the 6th Armored, was not well, so I told him to

pull out for a couple of days and let his second in command (Brigadier General George W. Read, Jr.) run the show.

On the twenty-first, General Bradley came to Third Army Headquarters to give us the general plan for future operations, which was as follows: The Twenty-First Army Group and Ninth United States Army were to attack beginning on the twenty-third. When they reached the Rhine, they were to attempt to get a bridgehead. While this was going on, the First Army was to protect the right of the Ninth, and the Third was to stay put—at least in theory. When the Twenty-First Army Group had reached the river, the First Army was to start on Cologne with its left corps. When Cologne was invested, but not necessarily taken, the III and V Corps—that is, the middle and right corps of the First Army—were to attack successively while the Third Army was to drive from the direction of Prum on Coblentz. This phase of the operation was to end when the Allied Armies were bellied up against the Rhine from Cologne to Coblentz.

In the next phase, the First Army was to sit tight along the river, while the Third Army attacked up the old Frankfurt corridor, starting the attack from Saarlautern and either Saarguemines or Saarburg, depending on circumstances.

I asked definitely whether or not I could make a rush at Coblentz prior to the investment of Cologne, and was told that if the opportunity presented itself, I might do so.

On the twenty-second, I decorated a number of nurses with Bronze stars and also Lieutenant James H. Fields of the 4th Armored Division with the Medal of Honor. I told Gaffey I did not want Lieutenant Fields sent to the front any more, because it has been my unfortunate observation that whenever a man gets the Medal of Honor or even the Distinguished Service Cross, he usually attempts to outdo himself and gets killed, whereas, in order to produce a virile race, such men should be kept alive.

From this formation I drove to Remich and met Generals Walker and Morris. I found that Morris had let his bridge train get lost, and therefore was not across at Saarburg, and that, at a late hour in the afternoon when I met him, he was being held up by small-arms fire from the far side of the river. I told him he would have to get the bridge in at once, fire or no fire. General Walker went to Saarburg to put some life into the operation.

The VIII Corps was advancing well and promised to be on the Prum River on the twenty-third.

On that date, the situation in the triangle was very annoying, but due to SHAEF and not to the Germans. The idea of the SHAEF Reserve was very unfortunate, for whenever we succeeded in getting any men from it, we had to put another division back into it. This despite the fact that the three divisions of armor which I had were all properly placed for the attack, and two of them were actually engaged. The best I could do was secure a further respite of forty-eight hours before I would have to send something to replace the 10th Armored Division.

Bradley called and said we would get two new infantry divisions, provided we could send two old divisions to rest. Both the 80th and 90th needed a rest, so this was not difficult—particularly as we did not have to move them out of the Third Army area.

The twenty-fourth of February was noteworthy for the fact that, on this date, non-battle casualties of 13,976 for the operation since January exceeded the battle casualties of 12,296. This was the first time in the history of the Third Army that the non-battle exceeded the battle casualties. It was not due to a great increase in the number of non-battle, but to a marked decrease in the number of battle casualties. The proportion between the two types of casualty is a good index of the efficiency of a division, provided you remember what the normal non-battle rate usually is.

On the twenty-fifth, I had in for lunch Middleton, Walker, and Gaffey (who was Acting Corps Commander of the XII Corps, as Eddy was on sick leave). General Bradley called and asked if he and Allen could come down also. I coached the three Corps Commanders and General Weyland on persuading Bradley to let us continue the use of the 10th Armored Division for the purpose of taking Trier. Weyland in particular was most eloquent. I am sure Bradley agreed with us, but felt he had to carry out orders. However, we persuaded him to let us continue the attack until dark on the twenty-seventh, provided General Eisenhower would let me call the 90th Division, which was actually not fighting, a reserve division for the purpose of abiding by the rule. Had we been refused permission to continue this attack, the whole history of the war might have been changed, because the capture of Trier was one of the turning points.

I again got Bradley's assent to attempt a breakthrough east of the Prum River, if and when an opportunity offered. Both Bradley and Allen were much pleased, I am sure, in fact Allen so stated, to be among a group of people who were eager to fight.

The sequence of events leading up to the capture of Trier is of interest, because it violates the normal conception of how generals plan. The initial attack on the Saar—Moselle Triangle had been started by the XX Corps for the purpose of breaking in the 94th Division to battle. Then, on the nineteenth, Walker, who had a very good sense of timing, called to say that, with the assistance of an armored division, he thought he could clear out the triangle. As will be remembered, I borrowed the 10th Armored Division, and things went moderately well until we had forced the crossing at Saarburg. It then occurred to both Walker and me that we had never intended simply to take Saarburg, but had had our eyes fixed on Trier, so we continued.

On the twenty-sixth, the XX Corps was not doing much, as it had been violently attacked east of the Saar and north of Zerf by the German 2d Mountain Division (commanded by General Major Degen), and at that time it looked as if we should have to turn east to remove this division. On the other hand, the XII Corps was doing very well, with the 4th Armored, which was on its left at the Kyll River in the vicinity of Bitburg, while the 5th and 76th Divisions were at or approaching the Kyll. Knowing this, I conceived the idea of moving the 4th Armored south behind the 5th and 76th Infantry Divisions and attacking Trier from the north. General Gaffey, temporarily in command of the XII Corps, pointed out the difficulty, from a logistical standpoint, of moving the 4th Armored, and suggested using the 76th Division, which was on the right, reinforced by the tank battalion of the 80th Division, which was then resting.

The lesson to be gained from this is that successful

generals make plans to fit circumstances, but do not try to create circumstances to fit plans.

The mention of Bitburg reminds me of an incident I saw there, which is very illustrative of the Germans. I entered the town from the south while fighting was still going on along the northern edge, which was not too far distant, as Bitburg is a small place. In spite of the fact that shells were falling with considerable regularity, I saw five Germans, three women and two men, re-roofing a house. They were not even waiting for Lend-Lease, as would be the case in several other countries I could mention.

On the twenty-seventh, the 10th Armored Division advanced eight kilometers north from Zerf and was, therefore, halfway to Trier. The enemy had brought up the 2d Mountain Division the day previously, but had made a mistake in the direction of attack of the 10th Armored. He apparently thought the 10th Armored was to attack southeast from Zerf to get behind the Siegfried Line, so he put in his counter-attack from that direction. Actually the 10th Armored turned north toward Pellingen, but did expose its right rear to attack.

I called Bradley at dark, as I had promised, to tell him that I was not yet in Trier, but was within eight kilometers of it, and asked if I could keep on. He said to keep on until he was ordered by higher authority to stop me, and added that he would keep away from the telephone.

On the twenty-eighth, the 10th Armored was still out of Trier, but was doing better, having reached country in which it could attack with multiple columns. Heretofore it had been necessary to attack in a single column, which, for an armored division, is always difficult.

A visit to General Morris on this date proved rather convincingly that our telephone lines were tapped. Before starting, Codman telephoned and got the name of the town where we were to meet General Morris. When we reached the crossroads near there, an MP met us and stated that the General was in another town, to which he led us. While we were there, the first town received a heavy artillery concentration at the exact time we were supposed to be in it.

Saarburg, the Headquarters of the 94th Division, was the home of John the Blind, King of Bohemia and Duke of Luxembourg, who was killed at the Battle of Crécy in 1346. His crest of three feathers is that now used by the Prince of Wales. He was the founder of the Order of the Red Lion of Luxembourg and of the White Lion of Bohemia—both of which decorations I subsequently received.

On the way home General Malony took me to see what he thought might be a medieval château. It turned out to be a modern winery with some very bad wine. While we were looking it over, a shell came about as close to our heads as it could without hitting us.

I suppose the near-miss put our minds on religion. In any event, driving back from this place, one of the officers with me was quite emphatic about his religious ancestry, and finally, to prove his sanctity, said, "By God, General, my people have been Catholics for more than three thousand years." I remarked, "What, B.C. Catholics?" and he said, "Yes, sir." I have told this story many times and few people have laughed.

On the first of March, I flew to Bastogne and talked over with General Middleton the proposed plans for his next operation. His idea was to use the 11th Armored Division on the third in order to punch a hole to the Kyll River through the German 5th Paratroop Division. When they reached the river, the crossing was to be effected by the 4th Division following immediately behind the 11th Armored. The rest of his corps was doing well.

In the XII Corps all units were on the line of the Kyll River and the 76th Division alone had picked up one thousand prisoners.

At 1415, Walker called up to say the 10th Armored Division was in Trier and had captured a bridge over the Moselle intact. The capture of this bridge was due to the heroic act of Lieutenant Colonel J. J. Richardson, deceased. He was riding in the leading vehicle of his battalion of armored infantry when he saw the wires leading to the demolition charges at the far end of the bridge. Jumping out of the vehicle, he raced across the bridge under heavy fire and cut the wires. The acid test of battle brings out the pure metal.

I called Generals Smith and Bradley and told them Trier was ours. Both seemed very pleased.

On March 2, Walker and I were discussing plans for the reduction of the so-called Mettalach Salient south of Saarburg as soon as the 26th Infantry Division, which had rested, had relieved the 94th Division, which was tired. As we were talking, it suddenly occurred to me that a more telling operation would be to cross the Moselle at Schweich with the 10th Armored Division, reinforce it by a regimental combat team of the 76th Infantry Division and move on Wittlich. Walker started working on the plan at once.

Eddy and I crossed the Saar at Echternach and drove to Bitburg, visiting the 76th, 5th, and 80th Infantry Divisions and the 4th Armored Division. The trip was very interesting for two reasons. First, it showed the tremendous difficulties overcome by the 76th Division in forcing the Siegfried Line at this point, and second, the utter futility of fixed defenses.

From one point on the road along which the 76th Division had successfully advanced, fifteen pillboxes were visible in addition to dragons' teeth and anti-tank ditches. Yet this relatively green division went through them. We visited the command pillbox for the sector. It consisted of a three-story submerged barracks with toilets, shower baths, a hospital, laundry, kitchen, storerooms, and every conceivable convenience plus an enormous telephone installation. Electricity and heat were produced by a pair of identical diesel engines with generators. Yet the whole offensive capacity of this installation consisted of two machine guns and a 60 mm. mortar operating from steel cupolas which worked up and down by means of hydraulic lifts. The 60 mm. mortar was peculiar in that it was operated by remote control. As in all cases, this particular pillbox was taken by a dynamite charge against the back door. We found marks on the cupolas, which were ten inches thick, where our 90 mm. shells, fired at a range of two hundred yards, had simply bounced.

Pacifists would do well to study the Siegfried and Maginot Lines, remembering that these defenses were forced; that Troy fell; that the walls of Hadrian succumbed; that the Great Wall of China was futile; and that, by the same token, the mighty seas which are alleged to defend us can also be circumvented by a resolute and ingenious opponent. In war, the only sure defense is offense, and the efficiency of offense depends on the warlike souls of those conducting it.

On March 3, Gay delivered the order in person to the Commanding General of the 10th Armored Division to cross the Moselle, and, attacking in conjunction with one combat team of the 76th Division, to get a crossing over the Kyll River and continue east parallel to the Moselle. The rest of the XX Corps mopped up rear areas. The XII Corps, 5th Division, forced a bridgehead across the Kyll River for the purpose of breaking loose the 4th Armored. In the VIII Corps, the 11th Armored Division attacked six hours late, through the 4th Infantry Division and ran into considerable resistance.

General Bradley was of the opinion that the Third Army was getting too much spread out, and would not be in a position to make what he called a "power drive" on Coblentz. He was assured that, owing to the road net, no power drive bigger than two divisions could be made, and that those drives were under way: in the VIII Corps the 11th and 90th; in the XII Corps the 4th Armored and 5th Divisions; in the XX Corps the 10th Armored and part of the 76th Division. The 65th Division joined the Third Army in the area of the XX Corps and the 26th Division relieved the 94th Division.

On this date, March 4, the Ninth Army and the First Army were along the line of the Rhine River. During the preceding thirty days the prisoners taken by the Third Army had averaged one thousand per day, and the total number of prisoners taken since the start of the operation on January 29 exceeded the total number of battle casualties inflicted on the Third Army for the same period.

In the XII Corps, the 5th Infantry Division had forced its bridgehead over the Kyll and in the XX Corps the 10th Armored Division forced a crossing over the Kyll River farther south and moved east, north of the Moselle.

On March 5, the 4th Armored Division of the XII Corps started its break for the Rhine with an advance of sixteen kilometers, and in spite of rain and mud, reached the vicinity of the town of Daun.

At 1000 on the sixth, I called Bradley and told him for the first time that the XII Corps was on its way to the Rhine, and urged that the right of the First Army be ordered to get a move on so as not to delay the left of the 87th Division on the left of the Third Army.

During the course of the day, the 4th Armored overran and captured the Commanding General of the German 53d Army Corps (commanded by General Kau von Rothkirch and General Lieutenant Botsch).

In the VIII Corps, on our north flank, three bridges, one for the 4th Infantry, one for the 11th Armored, and one for the 90th Division, were placed over the Kyll.

Prince Felix of Luxembourg, escorted by General Gay, visited the front and inspected the 10th Armored Division and also the city of Trier. As a result of this trip, General Gay believed that the area north of the Rhine in the zone of the Third Army was almost cleaned up, and that we should make plans for an attack to the southeast in the Palatinate. He recommended that the attack of the 10th Armored be discontinued, as it would eventually be pinched out by the continued attack of the XII Corps, and he thought it could be used more profitably elsewhere.

On March 7, at 1700, the 4th Armored Division reached the Rhine River. The 11th Armored Division, which began to do better on this day, pushed forward to the vicinity of Kyllberg. The attack of the 10th Armored Division was ordered stopped.

On this day we processed through the cages and photographed the two hundred thousandth German prisoner. When we sent this to Public Relations, Twelfth Army Group, they would not publish the picture, because, as the man had a sign on him stating he was the two hundred thousandth prisoner of war, they said he was being degraded, which was contrary to the Geneva Convention.

On the eighth, on orders from above, we lost the 6th Armored Division to the Sixth Army Group.

We had a Staff conference at which all the Staff, including General Weyland, was present, to determine the future plan of action of the Third Army and XIX Tacti-

cal Air Command. The scheme then devised, and later
executed, was as follows: To attack with two corps with
the purpose of seizing bridgeheads over the Rhine River
in the vicinity of Mainz, Oppenheim, and Worms. The
XX Corps, consisting of the 94th, 26th, and 80th Infantry
Divisions and the 10th Armored Division, later reinforced
by the 65th Infantry and the 12th Armored, was to attack
from Trier—Saarburg in the direction of Kaiserslautern.
The XII Corps, consisting of the 4th Armored, the 5th,
76th, 90th, and 89th Infantry Divisions,[1] was to attack
south across the Moselle River southeast of Mayen, heading initially on Bingen and Bad Kreuznach, with the purpose of cutting off the recrossing of the Rhine by the
enemy and securing a crossing for us somewhere between
Mainz and Worms. The VIII Corps, with the 87th and
4th Infantry and 11th Armored, was to continue mopping
up north of the Moselle and west of the Rhine, with the
distinct understanding that if we could secure a crossing
over the Rhine, it was to be exploited.

General Bradley stated he would prefer us not to attack south, over the Moselle, unless we secured a bridge
intact.

The First Army seemed to be doing very well at the
Remagen bridgehead. We were quite happy over it, but
just a little envious.

On the ninth, I joined Generals Bradley, Hodges,
Doolittle, Simpson, and some others to receive the French
Legion of Honor, Grand Officer grade, and Croix de
Guerre with Palm. Before the ceremony, Bradley and I
arranged to have the boundary of the Third Army moved
to the south, so as to give us Saarlautern as a place to
cross over the Saar River. I then ordered Gay, over the
telephone, to have the 80th Division join the XX Corps
and the 90th Division join the XII Corps. We all felt it
was essential that the First and Third Armies should get
themselves so involved that Montgomery's plan to use
most of the divisions on the western front, British and
American, under his command, for an attack on the Ruhr
plains, could not come off, and the First and Third Armies
be left out on a limb.

There was some talk of trying to co-ordinate the

---

[1] Commanded by Major General T. D. Finley.

plans of attack of the Third and Seventh Armies, but since the Seventh Army could not jump off until the fifteenth, I determined to attack as soon as I could, as I felt that time was more valuable than co-ordination. In fact, it is my opinion that co-ordination is a very much-misused word and its accomplishment is difficult.

The tenth and eleventh were very slow days, as everybody was getting set for the next operation. However, it gave us time to assemble the Corps Commanders. Fortunately, General Patch, Seventh Army, was also present at the meeting, so everyone knew what was going to happen, and Patch agreed to let Walker (my south corps) co-ordinate with Haislip, commanding his north corps. Patch was always extremely easy to work with.

This was the day that I received my set of Third Army table silver, which I had ordered through General Littlejohn,[1] and paid for personally.

Walker was unable to get off on the twelfth, but promised to jump at 0300 on the thirteenth. The XII Corps was ready to jump shortly after midnight on the fourteenth.

Littlejohn and I spent a long time discussing and inspecting uniforms. We finally came to the conclusion that the best uniform for war is combat shoes properly made, with the flesh side out, heavy woolen trousers cut not to exceed eighteen inches at the bottom, a woolen shirt, a helmet or helmet liner, and, for winter, a modified trench-coat with a liner and gloves. The shirt and trousers make the most useful, most uniform, and the best-looking outfit which our soldiers possess, and by giving them two weights of shirt and possibly one weight of trousers (heavy), we would have a simple and effective uniform which nobody could easily deface.

A general who had been relieved came in at his own request and tried to explain why he was no good. I offered him a lesser command in another division, but he told me he needed forty-eight hours to consider it. I did not tell him so, but I realized that any man who could not make up his mind in less than forty-eight hours was not fit to command troops in battle.

---

[1] Major General Robert M. Littlejohn, Chief Quartermaster for General Eisenhower.

Here ended the campaign which will probably be referred to in history as that of the Eifel. It had been a long, hard fight with many river crossings, much bad weather, and a great deal of good luck. As of this date, March 12, the casualty balance stood as follows:

Third Army		*Enemy*	
Killed	18,529	Killed	116,000
Wounded	87,566	Wounded	321,800
Missing	15,328	Prisoners of war	216,500
Total	121,423	Total	654,300
Non-battle casualties	93,801		
Grand Total	215,224		
Less total as of January 29	172,953		
Cost of Eifel Campaign	42,217		

Matériel Losses

Light tanks	284	Medium tanks	1369
Medium tanks	837	Panther and Tiger tanks	805
Guns	158	Guns	2811

6

THE CAPTURE OF COBLENTZ AND THE PALATINE CAMPAIGN
13 March to 21 March, 1945

The Third Army's Campaign was considered by many, including the Germans, to be one of the greatest campaigns of the entire war.

In ten days, twelve of its divisions catapulted south across the Moselle, each trying to outdo the other, racing through the rear areas of German troops still facing the American Seventh Army in the Siegfried Line farther south, surrounding or destroying two German armies, and capturing over sixty thousand prisoners and ten thousand square miles of territory with minimum losses.

On March 22, eight divisions, set for the kill, were on the Rhine, south of Coblentz. Four armored divisions, followed by supporting infantry units, thundered over the Honsbrouck Mountains, "impassable to armor." The Germans were confused, bewildered, and helpless. The enemy was a beaten mass of men, women, and children, interspersed with die-hard Nazis. The war had been won west of the Rhine, as General Patton had predicted almost a year before. The Third Army was in a position to cross the Rhine at Mainz, Worms, and Oppenheim. (See Map, pages 244–245.)

In the Sixth Army Group, the offensive to the Rhine continued, and the enemy withdrew on the north flank, offering stiff resistance in the Siegfried Line.

On other fronts, Panay capitulated to MacArthur, Mandalay still held out in Burma, and the fighting progressed slowly in Italy.

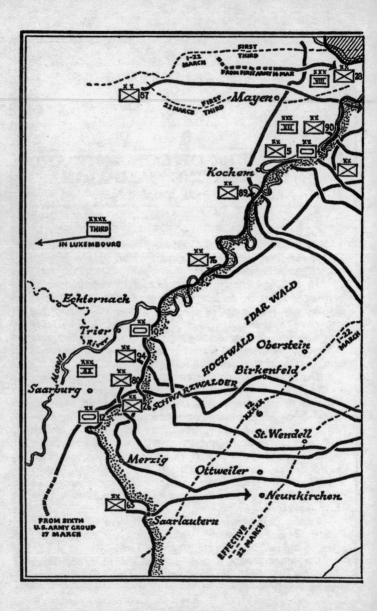

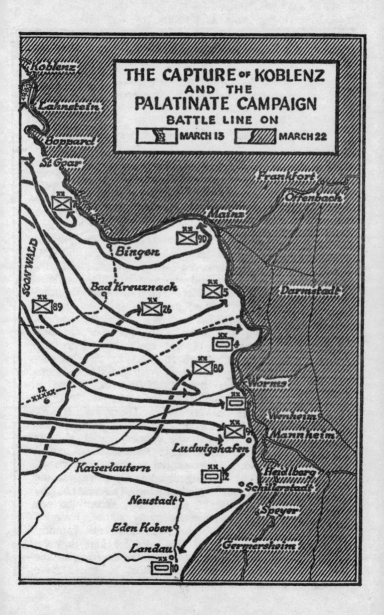

THE CAPTURE OF KOBLENZ
AND THE
PALATINATE CAMPAIGN
BATTLE LINE ON
MARCH 13   MARCH 22

Koblenz
Lahnstein
Boppard
St Goar
Frankfort
Offenbach
Mainz
90
Bingen
Bad Kreuznach
5
Darmstadt
89
26
4
80
Worms
6
10
Wenheim
9
Mannheim
Ludwigshafen
Kaiserlautern
12
Heidelberg
Schillerstadt
Neustadt
Speyer
Eden Koben
Landau
Germersheim
10

SOONWALD

The air forces continued pounding Germany, concentrating their heavy raids on Berlin.

P.D.H.

The Beginning of the End

The attack of the XX Corps jumped off on time, March 13, but was not fast, owing to particularly bad terrain in front of both the 94th and 26th Infantry Divisions. The XII Corps was ready to jump off in the vicinity of Treis at 0200 on the morning of the fourteenth. When the XII Corps attacked, with the 5th Infantry Division on the right and the 90th on the left, it built four bridges across the Moselle before noon, and by the end of the day had fourteen battalions on the southern side of the river. Here a case of extremely good luck, or Divine intervention, occurred, because, on the afternoon of the twelfth, at least half of the 2d German Mountain Division was opposite the place of crossing, but apparently they were fooled by the attack of the XX Corps and moved down to meet it, thereby permitting the XII Corps to cross over, practically unopposed. This illustrates the desirability of having a divergence of timing in an attack.

I drove to Trier via Wasservillig. The Roman legions marching on Trier from Luxembourg used this same road, and one could almost smell the coppery sweat and see the low dust clouds where those stark fighters moved forward into battle. As a memorial to their great deeds, the least demolished building standing in Trier was the gateway to the Roman amphitheater. The rest of the middle of the city, and all the bridges, except the one we captured intact, were pretty badly ruined. I visited the 10th Armored, the 80th, 94th, and 26th Infantry Divisions. I was anxious at this time for fear that the Seventh Army, which jumped off on the morning of the fifteenth, would beat me into Mainz. It would have helped my self-confidence if I could have read the future.

On the fifteenth, I flew to Mayen and saw General Eddy of the XII Corps and General Middleton of the VIII Corps. When I told Middleton I would have to take everything away from him except the 87th Division, but would give him the 76th as soon as possible, he made no kick at all, but came back with a brilliant suggestion for the immediate capture of Coblentz with the 87th. He was one of the easiest Corps Commanders to do business with I have ever known, and also one of the most efficient.

The rest of the Army did not do very well except on the front of the 80th and 94th Infantry Divisions, where gains up to six miles were secured.

Flying back to Headquarters, I made detours to get pictures of Vianden and Clairvaux, both of which are excellent châteaux of different types—one the river fort, the other the rock fort.

At 1100 on the sixteenth, Bradley called up to say that General Eisenhower was probably over my town in an airplane, since he had been unable to land at Bradley's. I hurried to the field and met him shortly after two o'clock. He was accompanied by General Smith. We went at once to the Map Room, and both were quite enthusiastic and complimentary, Smith stating that I could borrow any division I needed after the success I had had with the 10th Armored. In the afternoon we had a guard of honor for Smith, which I believe was the first one he had ever had.

Then General Eisenhower and I took two peeps and drove to Trier, visiting the Command Post of Combat Command "A" of the 10th Armored Division, where we met General Morris and the Assistant Division Commander, General Piburn. Elements of the 10th Armored and the 90th Divisions both reached the Nahe River and secured bridges. The 11th Armored Division joined the XII Corps and assembled in the vicinity of Boullay, preparatory to crossing behind the 89th Division. The 87th Division crossed the Moselle northeast of the 90th and got into the outskirts of Coblentz, while the 28th Division, temporarily loaned to me by the First Army, joined the VIII Corps and took over the river front south of the First Army to Coblentz exclusive.

General Eisenhower told Smith to have the 12th Armored Division from the Seventh Army released to my Army and join the XX Corps, moving on the morning of the seventeenth.

On the seventeenth, General Eisenhower attended the morning briefing and was most complimentary. He stated that we, as veterans, did not realize our own greatness and were not cocky enough, and told us to be sure that other people realized how good the Americans were. As an example, he said that the newspapers referred to the enemy fighting on the front of the 4th Armored Division as done by weak numbers of Germans, but failed to give credit to the 4th Armored for its rapidity of movement, which prevented large numbers of Germans from getting ahead of it.

We flew to Lunéville to see Generals Patch and Devers. There was some idea that Patch and I should occupy the same Command Post, but after we explained that we had perfect telephone communication and that our points of interest were widely separated, the thing was not pushed.

On returning to Luxembourg, I had a press conference and brought out the points mentioned by General Eisenhower. I stated also that three divisions of Marines in the Pacific were getting great credit by reporting their tremendous losses, while twelve or thirteen divisions in our Army were getting no credit because we did not have tremendous losses. I asked the newspapers to fix it up, then gave them the score sheet (the American casualty list, actual, compared to the estimated German casualty list) of the Third Army and told them to publish it.

The question of our tanks versus German tanks came up, and I answered that by saying that, in the course of the fighting so far, we had got two German tanks for every one we lost. I stated also that all of our equipment, clothing, etc., was superior to anything the Allies or the Germans had.

Thinking over the criticism of the tanks as a result of the discussion with the war correspondents, I wrote a letter to General Handy restating what I had told the correspondents. This letter was given wide publicity and had considerable effect in stopping the foolish criticism, which was not only untrue, but was also having a bad effect on the morale of our soldiers.[1]

Walker called up around 1800 with a request to relieve one of his division commanders. I told him if he could name a better one, he could relieve him, but he could not. I then called Eddy and gave him hell because the 11th Armored had not got anywhere. In order to make it a perfect day, I called Middleton and told him that at least he had not been cussed out, and congratulated him on his great feat in capturing Coblentz.

The eighteenth was not a particularly good or bad day. The 4th Armored was held up by a vicious counter-attack by two Grenadier regiments of the 2d Panzer Division (commanded by General Lieutenant von Lutt-witz and General Major von Lauchert). The remaining units of the VIII, XII, and XX Corps did well, but not brilliantly.

---

[1] The story that spread throughout America about our tanks being inferior to German tanks finally reached the soldiers on the front lines and caused some apprehension among them.

Taking two individual tanks and comparing them on a point by point basis—gun, muzzle velocity, armor protection, etc.—perhaps gives a shade to the German tank if you compared their "top" heavies to ours at that time. If the two tanks met on a village street and were to fight it out, everything else being equal the American tank would probably have suffered. However, this was not General Patton's idea of how tanks should be used in battle. His idea was never to use tanks in a tank-to-tank fight, but to break them through the enemy lines and let them run amuck in the rear areas.

General Patton, knowing how such rumors were apt to affect adversely the morale of the troops, tried to explode the rumor before its unfortunate results took effect. The General probably knew tanks as well as any other American soldier. He had studied them intensely from their inception in World War I. He pointed out the advantage of mobility, lack of mechanical failures, power turrets, gyro stabilizers, and total numbers, in all of which we held the upper hand over the enemy. He showed where we were and with what, compared to where the enemy had retreated to and what he had left.

The results were self-evident, and General Patton's faith in the American soldier, coupled with the soldier's ingenuity, guts, and fighting ability when in an American tank, did a lot to spike the nasty rumor that was likely to affect, not only American fighting morale at the front, but also the morale of the workers at home, who were striving so hard to produce nothing but the best.

On the nineteenth, the situation was much better. The VIII Corps had completed the cleaning-up of Coblentz. In the XII Corps the 4th Armored was six miles from Worms and ten miles from Mainz. The 90th and 5th Infantry Divisions were across the Nahe River. Part of the 11th Armored Division was at Neisenheim and in contact with the 12th Armored of the XX Corps, which was at Lauterecken. The 10th and part of the 12th Armored were both about twelve miles from Kaiserslautern, with the 80th and 94th right on their tails.

It was my opinion then that, if the war ceased at that moment, troops under my command would have had the best and most successful campaign in history. I am still of that opinion.

Hodges and Bradley came in in the afternoon and things looked gloomy, for if we could not secure a crossing over the Rhine, we would probably lose ten divisions to the Ninth Army under Montgomery, and have to go on the defensive. If, however, we could get across before the British attack, we could carry the ball. Hodges and I determined that he would cross at Remagen and I in the vicinity of Mainz, and make an initial meeting at Geissen. From there he would take the autobahn road and roads to the west, while I would get the roads east and advance through Kassel and Hanau.

On the twentieth, the operations were going particularly well. In the XII Corps, a task force of the 90th Division was approaching the Rhine and closing in south of Mainz, which would cut off all the available escape routes as far south as that town. Combat Command "A" of the 4th Armored (commanded by Colonel H. A. Sears) was nine miles northeast of Kaiserslautern, while Combat Command "B" (commanded by Colonel C. W. Abrams) of the same division was by-passing the town, the occupation of which was left to the 80th Division.

I made arrangements with Patch for a new boundary, hitting the Rhine south of Worms and giving the Seventh Army Kaiserslautern, when and if they got there. I told Patch that when I got to Kaiserslautern, I intended to turn at least one armored division and one infantry division south for the purpose of making contact with his VI Corps,[1] thereby completely surrounding the remaining Germans, and that, as soon as this was accomplished, I would clear out of his area.

On the nineteenth, our total losses, both battle and nonbattle, were eight hundred, while we captured approximately twelve thousand Germans in addition to those we had killed.

It was amusing at the time, and it is even more amusing to remember now, the difficulty I had in securing permission to take Trier, and in getting permission to get the 4th Armored Division cut loose for the Rhine. In fact, it was necessary to use certain chicanery in order to secure permission to cross the Moselle in a southerly direction.[2]

While I was with Patch, he jokingly said, "George, I forgot to congratulate you for being the last man to reach the Rhine." I replied, "Let me congratulate you on being the first man to leave it," referring to the time when his VI Corps (commanded by Major General E. H. Brooks) had been ordered back, after having gained the Rhine.

On the twenty-first, the operations in the Palatinate were practically ended, because in the XII Corps the 90th Division had reached Mainz, and was attacking the town with two regiments. The 4th Armored was at Worms and the 11th Armored was south of Worms. In the XX Corps, the 12th Armored was closing in on Mannerheim and the 10th Armored had turned south from

---

[1]Commanded by Major General E. H. Brooks.

[2]True to General Bradley's desires that the Palatinate Campaign could not start unless the Third Army secured a bridge over the Moselle intact, the XII Corps rushed reconnaissance elements to the river in an effort to get one. The leading elements arrived in the vicinity of Treis and saw one of the bridges across the river still standing. It immediately radioed back, "Bridge at Treis intact. Continuing on mission." This message was relayed from Division to Corps to Army to Group. The campaign was on; the troops moved on the Moselle. The message was the last received from the vehicle that sent it. As it proceeded to and started to cross the bridge, the bridge blew up, taking vehicle and crew along with it. It was too late to stop the attack when the news came that the bridge was no more. It did not take long to build temporary bridges of our own and the war was on again. This was the fourth time that the Third Army had crossed the Moselle.

Neustadt on Landau. The 80th Division had cleared Kaiserslautern, while the 94th and 26th Divisions were both closing in that direction in spite of some confusion caused by the 6th Armored, from the Seventh Army, crossing the line of march of the 26th Division.

I consulted with Eddy at Simmeren. It was evident that the Germans thought we were crossing at Mainz, and had placed two regiments in the town with orders to hold till the last. We, therefore, decided to put a smoke screen on the river at Mainz to give the impression that we were to cross there, and to make the crossing at Oppenheim. This was a particularly fortunate place to cross, because on our side there was a barge harbor which could be entered through the town without being seen from either side of the river. Our assault boats could be launched in this barge harbor without the enemy's knowledge and slip into the river quietly. Eddy had selected this point many months before.

However, I believe I was guilty of a great mistake in not making a river crossing north of the confluence of the Main River with the Rhine; that is, north of Mainz. My reason for not doing it was the fear of being held on the high ground north of the juncture of the two rivers. On the other hand, had I crossed there, the crossing of the Main River at Frankfurt, and at its mouth, would have been avoided. This was one of the few times when I took what seemed to be good precautions and which were, in effect, too good.

In any event, we determined to cross the Rhine on the night of the twenty-second with the 5th Infantry Division. I gave a plan to Eddy, which might have been quite picturesque, of using some two hundred L-4 planes to carry one rifleman per plane across the river. By the use of these planes we would have taken two hundred men across every thirty minutes. The idea was that of Brigadier General E. T. Williams, Chief Artillery Officer of the Army, and an extremely good one.[1]

After things had been arranged with Eddy, we flew

---

[1] The assembled Cub planes were nicknamed the Third Army Troop Carrier Command. In view of the situation, General Patton's idea was to get as many men as possible across the Rhine in the shortest possible time. At this particular time he believed the strength was in the greatest numbers.

to Mainz and saw General Middleton of the VIII Corps, and made arrangements for him to force a crossing in the gorge of the Rhine in the vicinity of Boppard, or else near Lorch, with the idea of moving initially on Mastatten, which was a good crossroad, and gave the option of moving either northeast on Limburg or of coming south to facilitate the Mainz crossing from the east bank.

The matter of getting bridge matériel for these river crossings was extremely difficult and was only made possible by superhuman efforts on the part of General Conklin, Army Engineer, and also by the Navy Detachment[1] which co-operated with us.

At this time the question of rations became quite acute, and we took steps to save everywhere we could.

The twenty-first terminates the campaign of the Palatinate, but before leaving it I believe it well to point out that our attack across the Rhine at Oppenheim was made without halting—that is, we simply changed the direction of the 5th and 90th Divisions from south to east, while continuing south with the remainder of the two corps. This deluded the Germans into the belief that we were not making a serious attempt to cross. I felt that the way to get across the Rhine was by a *coup de main*. The execution of this *coup* was magnificently planned by General Eddy and gloriously executed by General Irwin.

Casualties as of March 21 were:

Third Army		*Enemy*	
Killed	19,281	Killed	123,800
Wounded	91,081	Wounded	337,300
Missing	15,556	Prisoners of war	282,900[2]
Total	125,918	Total	744,000

[1] Navy Detachment (Naval Unit N-2) consisting of twelve LCVP's and their crews were attached to the Third Army. They had practiced at Toul especially for the crossing of the Rhine. They were moved forward in time to be launched in the water and operating at 0730 on the twenty-third of March. This unit greatly expedited the crossing.

[2] The prisoner of war total as of 13 March was 220,000, so during the Palatinate Campaign 62,900 German prisoners were captured.

Non-battle
casualties 96,593
Grand total 222,511
Less total as of
March 13 216,106
Cost of Palatinate
Campaign 6,405

On March 23, I published General Order Number 70 covering the operations for the period January 29 to March 22. Since this order expressed my ideas of the Palatinate Campaign, it is inserted here:

GENERAL ORDER   23 March, 1945
  NUMBER 70

TO THE OFFICERS AND MEN OF THE THIRD ARMY

AND

TO OUR COMRADES OF THE XIX TACTICAL AIR COMMAND

In the period from January 29 to March 22, 1945, you have wrested 6484 square miles of territory from the enemy. You have taken 3072 cities, towns, and villages, including among the former: Trier, Coblentz, Bingen, Worms, Mainz, Kaiserslautern, and Ludwigshafen.

You have captured 140,112 enemy soldiers, and have killed or wounded an additional 99,000, thereby eliminating practically all of the German 7th and 1st Armies. History records no greater achievement in so limited a time.

This great campaign was only made possible by your disciplined valor, unswerving devotion to duty, doubled with the unparalleled audacity and speed of your advance on the ground; while from the air, the peerless fighter-bombers kept up a relentless round-the-clock attack upon the disorganized enemy.

The world rings with your praises; better still, General Marshall, General Eisenhower, and

General Bradley have all personally commended you. The highest honor I have ever attained is that of having my name coupled with yours in these great events.

Please accept my heartfelt admiration and thanks for what you have done, and remember that your assault crossing over the Rhine at 2200 hours last night assures you of even greater glory to come.

G. S. PATTON, JR.
Lieutenant General, U.S. Army,
Commanding

7

FORCING THE RHINE, FRANKFURT-AM-MAIN AND ACROSS THE MULDE
22 March to 21 April, 1945

At this period of the war, speed was of the essence. Capture of terrain was more important than the mopping-up of a beaten enemy. Total disruption of the enemy's interior was in order. Only confused and bewildered enemy organizations were left; fighting everywhere was by remnants.

Sensing this, General Patton ordered the first assault crossing of the Rhine to be made by the XII Corps on the night of March 22-23.

Behind advanced elements of the Third Army, already along the Rhine from Coblentz to Speyer, was a mass of confused Germans, and also some confused Americans. Everyone was heading east, Americans advancing, Germans retreating, and some of the advancing Third Army units reached the Rhine ahead of the Germans retreating before the Seventh Army. As these American divisions hit the Rhine, they came to a bottleneck. As the Germans hit it, they became prisoners.

At 2200 on the night of March 22, the 5th Infantry Division of the XII Corps rowed across the Rhine on schedule. There was no artillery preparation, no air blitz, no dropping of paratroops. The crossing was made so quietly and efficiently that it surprised not only the enemy but our own troops as well.

For the ensuing month, though some casual pockets

of resistance had to be forced, the war, for the most part, became a road march. In fact, at one time on the autobahn, north of Frankfurt, two armored and two infantry divisions, using both sides of the road, were moving north abreast, toward Kassel, while in the center of the same road tens of thousands of German prisoners were moving south without guard.

German reserves were overrun, rear installations crushed or ignored, and the civilian population bewildered. Nazi atrocities came to light and cries of the phantom "redoubt" went up.

By the end of a month, the advanced elements of the Third Army had overrun the district of Saxe, Coburg, and Gotha, were on the outskirts of Chemnitz, and beyond Nuremberg. The Mulde had been crossed when orders from above indicated a new direction of attack —not to the east, but to the southeast, through Bavaria, along the Czechoslovakian border. (See Map, pages 282–283.)

Except in Italy, on all other fronts the situation was fluid. All the Allied Armies on the Western Front were across the Rhine. The Twenty-First Army Group was on the Elbe River in the north; the First, farther south, reached the outskirts of Dresden. Nuremberg fell to the Seventh Army. The Russians took Vienna and Danzig. The air forces continued their strikes in support of the ground troops on all fronts.

The Commander-in-Chief, President Franklin Delano Roosevelt, died on April 12.

P.D.H.

"The Rhine, the Rhine, the German Rhine"

On March 22, the 10th and 11th Armored Divisions, one with the XII and the other with the XX Corps, had relieved the 4th Armored Division in the vicinity of Worms. Elements of the 12th Armored Division, in the XX Corps, were moving on Ludwigshaven, while the 10th Armored Division had got a combat command at Landau. Finally, one combat command of the 12th was moving on the town of Speyer. When it reached Speyer, all the German exits over the Rhine, in my area, were cut off.

On the twenty-second, we reached our height, up to that time, in prisoners taken in one day—eleven thousand.

General Weyland, Colonel Codman, and I drove from Saarburg via St. Wendel to Kaiserslautern, and from there through the woods, for about twenty kilometers, in the direction of Neustadt. Here we witnessed one of the greatest scenes of destruction I have ever contemplated. A German column entering the road from the northwest, and consisting mainly of animal transport and guns, was struck on the right flank by a company of medium tanks of the 10th Armored Division. The Germans were moving up a rather steep canyon with a precipitous cliff on their left, while the tanks came in between them and the mountain. For more than two miles horses and vehicles were pushed over the cliff. You could see the marks of the tank treads on the flanks and shoulders of the horses, and see the powder marks on the men and horses where they had been shot at point-blank range. In spite of my pride in the achievement of the 10th Armored, I was sorry for the poor creatures.

When we got back to Headquarters about dark, we found that elements of the 10th Armored had made contact with elements of the VI Corps of the Seventh Army in the vicinity of a town called Schwanim, thus completely pocketing the German troops. I also got a telegram from Grow, now commanding the Fifteenth Army, saying, "Congratulations on surrounding three armies, one of them American."

On the night of the twenty-second the Fifth Infantry Division, jumping off at 2230, crossed the Rhine and made its twenty-third successful river crossing at Oppenheim; it got six battalions across before daylight with a total loss of twenty-eight men killed and wounded.

In connection with this crossing, a somewhat amusing incident is alleged to have happened. The Twenty-

First Army Group was supposed to cross the Rhine on March 24, and, in order to be ready for this earth-shaking event, Mr. Churchill wrote a speech congratulating Field Marshal Montgomery on the first assault crossing over the Rhine in modern history. This speech was recorded and, through some error on the part of the British Broadcasting Company, was broadcast, in spite of the fact that the Third Army had been across for some thirty-six hours.

Owing to the fact that the 10th Armored Division was so deep in the Seventh Army area, I swapped it for the 6th Armored Division, which was on the left of the Seventh Army, by mutual agreement between General Patch and myself.

On March 24, Codman, Stiller, General Eddy, and I crossed the Rhine at Oppenheim, stopping to spit in the river. When we got to the far side, I also deliberately stubbed my toe and fell, picking up a handful of German soil, in emulation of Scipio Africanus and William the Conqueror, who both stumbled and both made a joke of it, saying, "I see in my hands the soil of Africa" or ". . . the soil of England." I saw in my hands the soil of Germany.

We then flew to the Headquarters of the VIII Corps to see about the crossing at Boppard, which took place the night of the twenty-fourth, and the crossing of the 76th Division at St. Goar on the next night, the twenty-fifth.

It was rather prophetic, I thought, that we should cross at St. Goar, near the legendary site of the Lorelei—one of the sacred spots of German mythology.

The Rhine crossing was going very well for the XII Corps. All the 5th Infantry, two regiments of the 90th, and most of the 4th Armored were across, and arrangements were made for the 6th Armored to start crossing on the morning of the twenty-fifth. In the meantime, the XX Corps was assembling in the vicinity of Mainz, where we had decided to construct a railway bridge, because the railway net was such that this was of necessity on our main supply line.

The plan for the ensuing operation envisaged sending one combat team of the 76th Division south along the Rhine, so as to take the high ground covering the crossing opposite Mainz; to have the 5th Division cross the Main River in the vicinity of Mainz, and the 80th Division cross the Rhine north of the confluence of the Rhine and Main, while the rest of the XII Corps crossed the Main east of Frankfurt, with an initial rendezvous point at Giessen where the VIII Corps was also headed. I told each Corps Commander that I expected him to get there first, so as to produce a proper feeling of rivalry.

At this time I had an idea of creating a completely armored corps of three armored divisions, supported by one motorized combat team from an infantry division, putting them all under Walker and making a rush for Kassel or Weimar, depending on circumstances.

On the twenty-fifth, the 87th Division succeeded in making its crossing and had two regiments over the river by daylight, in spite of the fact that all the historical studies we had ever read on the crossing asserted that, between Bingen and Coblentz, the Rhine was impassable. Here again we took advantage of a theory of our own, that the impossible place is usually the least well defended.

We had quite a heavy German air attack on our bridge sites—at least two hundred sorties—but, thanks to our anti-aircraft guns and to the XIX Tactical Air Command, the bridge was not hit, although one raft was struck and sunk.

On March 26, I crossed the Rhine with Codman and directed Eddy to send an expedition across the Main River to Hammelburg. There were two purposes in this expedition: first, to impress the Germans with the idea that we were moving due east, whereas we intended to move due north, and second, to release some nine hundred American prisoners of war who were at Hammelburg. I intended to send one combat command of the 4th Armored, but, unfortunately, was talked out of it by Eddy and Hoge, commanding the 4th Armored Division, so I compromised by sending one armored company and one company of armored infantry.

I learned that Colonel John Hines, son of my old friend Major General John L. Hines, had been struck in the face with a solid 88 and had both eyes taken out while leading his tanks in the attack on the airfield south of Frankfurt. After he was wounded, he took the radio telephone, called the Division Commander, gave an exact statement of the situation and ended up by saying, "And also, General, you had better send someone to take my place, as I am wounded."[1] For this super-

---

[1] From a letter from Colonel John L. Hines, Jr., to Mrs. Patton:
"My combat command, C.C. 'A' of the 6th Armored Division, had crossed the Rhine and passed through the 5th Infantry Division on the left of our C.C. 'B.' Our mission was to clear the angle between the Main and Rhine rivers and attack the bridges into Frankfurt and Frankfurt itself. We had pushed through some very difficult wooded and swampy terrain and after a brisk fight had taken the village of Morfelden. My advance guard of my right combat team, the 9th Armored Infantry Battalion (reinforced) under Lieutenant Colonel Britton, was pushing on through scattered woods against heavy infantry and machine-gun opposition to clear the airport. The airport we knew had a large concentration of 88 and 105 anti-aircraft artillery and we were receiving heavy fire from them. Also we were receiving some 150 millimeter artillery, probably from Frankfurt. I had left Morfelden in my tank and gone on with the advanced troops to push through the airport as rapidly as possible and get to the bridges in hopes of capturing one or more intact. When I reached our road junction near the autobahn, very heavy artillery caught our advanced reconnaissance, setting several vehicles on fire. This artillery was moving down the road near the road junction where I was and was about two hundred yards away. I moved about two hundred yards off to the flank across country to avoid this concentration. I remember we flushed some German infantry in foxholes who came past us to surrender. I was standing in the turret of my tank talking on the radio telephone. The tank had been swung around so that its tail end was toward Frankfurt. I had been talking first to my other task force to ascertain its progress, and then I was either talking to or trying to contact Colonel Britton and looking over the rear of my tank toward Frankfurt when a shell which I did not hear coming hit the deck of my tank and the side of the turret. I had my left hand on the hatch and was facing the shell. I remember seeing the explosion and trying to pull down the hatch with my left hand only to find that I had lost the fingers of it. I remember dropping down into the tank and finding that I was choking from bone and shrapnel fragments in my throat and scooping them out with the fingers of my right hand. I then remember trying to call to report our situation and to have someone take my place, but I am confused as to whom I called or what I said. General Grow told me later that I had called and said substantially what General Patton quoted. I was then taken to the rear in my tank and I remember later talking to General Grow somewhere down the line. I have a confused recollection of not being able to say anything and of trying to, but he says I actually did talk to him and asked him to get me back to the Division as soon as possible. . . ."

heroic act he was given an Oak Leaf Cluster to the Distinguished Service Cross which he had won during the Saar Campaign. He was a very great soldier and should not die. General Grow was upset by the loss of Hines; in fact, so upset that he didn't do anything for a day afterward and had to be prodded to take Frankfurt.

Later, I met General Walker at the rear echelon of the XII Corps and we completed arrangements for the 80th Division to cross the Main with one column and the Rhine with another.

On reaching Headquarters, I discovered that a task force of the 9th Armored Division, First Army, had broken loose to the south, and Bradley asked me if I wished it to come to Wiesbaden, which I was about to attack. I immediately assented and then flew to Bad Kreuznach to see Colonel Hines. When I got there, he was on the operating table and unconscious. It was a very painful sight.

On the twenty-seventh, we moved the Command Post to Oberstein and occupied the barracks of the former 107th German Infantry Regiment (Colonel Gronaw commanding). Here we captured a tremendous carved eagle which we sent to the United States Military Academy as a gift from the Third Army.

On the twenty-eighth, considerable complication arose from the fact that the 80th Division had completed its crossings of the Rhine and the Main without much difficulty and was headed on Wiesbaden, as was the combat team of the 76th and also the task force from the 9th Armored Division. It looked for a while as if each of the three would shoot into the other two. Eventually we got the 9th Armored and the 76th stopped and returned to their proper places.

Colonel E. M. Fickett, commanding the 6th Cavalry Regiment, with a task force from the VIII Corps, crossed the autobahn and kept on east, doing a very splendid job, while the 4th Armored advanced more than two-thirds of the way to Giessen. The 6th Armored had also forced its way across the Main River into the heart of Frankfurt, and was moving north.

On the other hand, we were very much disturbed because we could get no information at all as to what had happened to the task force sent east from the 4th Armored Division.

While talking to Bradley about the boundaries between the Third and First Armies, I made the suggestion that, after we took Kassel, for which we were then heading, we should turn east into the Dresden—Leipsig Triangle. This idea was partly the result of my own study of the map and partly from conversation with General Giraud of the French Army. Bradley was quite sympathetic, and at the time we made plans for this operation.

Giraud stated that members of his family—his wife and two daughters-in-law, I think—were prisoners somewhere in the vicinity of Weimar. I suggested that his Aide accompany the 4th Armored Division, which at the time seemed most likely to get there first. The Girauds were eventually rescued, as well as a Belgian princess, who had some very interesting stories to tell about what she referred to as a *lager* for important women north of Berlin. She said that in this *lager* there were some four thousand German women whose husbands occupied important positions and that they were, in effect, hostages. Apparently they were fairly well fed, but the Germans executed a large number of young girls where she could see it from her window. These executions apparently took place every night, so she lost considerable sleep. We considered her story quite an exaggeration.

On the twenty-ninth, the 70th Infantry Division (Major General A. J. Barnett) and the 13th Armored (Major General J. B. Wogan) were attached to the Third Army, but had to be held in SHAEF Reserve west of the Rhine. This eased the situation in the rear a good deal, and we put the 70th along the Rhine from Coblentz to Oppenheim. We also got the use of all four cavalry groups assigned to the Third Army, as heretofore we had been required to hold one in reserve. Bradley asked that I leave one infantry division in an assembly area for Army Reserve somewhere in the vicinity of Frankfurt or Wiesbaden. We selected the 5th Infantry Division for this role.

For the rest things were going very well. The 4th and 6th Armored Divisions had made substantial ad-

vances, although the 11th Armored Division, which had
turned east, was held up beyond Hanau. The northern
division of the VIII corps was also slowed down, owing
to the fact that the First Army had made a boundary
of its own without reference to the boundary prescribed
by the Twelfth Army Group, with the result that the
right boundary of the First Army cut across the line of
advance of the 87th Division. This was eventually
straightened out.

On the thirtieth, the German radio announced that
the American armored division attacking Hammelburg
had been captured and destroyed.[1]

We received instructions to move as rapidly as
possible to the line of the Werra—Wesser Rivers, and
after that to move east on the Elbe River. It was suggested by Higher Headquarters that we make this move
slowly. However, we pointed out that the only way to
avoid casualties was to move fast.

The 6th Armored Division, supported by elements
of the 80th and 65th Infantry Divisions, reached a point
twelve miles southwest of Kassel.

On March 31, I flew to Headquarters of the XII
Corps east of Frankfurt and explained that, after passing
the Werra—Wesser Rivers, this corps would confine itself to advancing approximately fifteen miles a day. I
had intended to fly to the XX Corps to explain the
same thing to them, but Walker arrived at XII Corps
Headquarters and we completed the arrangements there.

I then drove to the airfield for the purpose of taking
off for the VIII Corps, when General Sibert, G-2 of the
Twelfth Army Group, landed and signaled me to stop.
He had a plan for the capture of the German communication center in the vicinity of Gotha, Erfurt,
Weimar, and Ohrdruf, which, when he explained it to
me, seemed full of promise. I telephoned from the airfield to hold Walker at XII Corps Headquarters until
Sibert and I got there. Unfortunately, Walker had left,
but they caught him, and he arrived back at Headquarters
about the same time Sibert and I did. We then explained

---

[1]The actual composition of the task force was one company
of tanks and one company of armored infantry, 11 officers and
282 men.

the idea of the rapid advance on the Weimar Quadrilateral—Eddy on the right, Walker on the left. I told them they would have the greatest chance in history to make names for themselves, and to get moving. I gave Walker permission to by-pass Kassel in order to accelerate the operation.

Then I flew to the Command Post of the VII Corps, just west of Limburg. The Limburg airfield was taking on gasoline from the Troop Carrier Command at the rate of sixty planes an hour. Had it not been for the Air Transport Command, we would have run out of gasoline again. Each plane carried 115 five-gallon cans.

Before leaving Headquarters, Gay had agreed with me to telephone the boundary between the VIII Corps and the XX and XII Corps, as we proposed to put the VIII Corps in the middle. Middleton had just received the boundaries and was satisfied with them. However, in view of the impending attack on the Weimar Quadrilateral, and the possibility of a German counterattack from the vicinity of Hanau, I told him not to start his operation, because, in the position he then occupied near Limburg, he was ideally situated to stop any attempt on the part of the Germans through Hanau.

Flying home, Codman and I followed the gorge of the Rhine and took photographs from the air of the two crossings, made in the gorge, by the VIII Corps.

At 1830, Bradley called to state that General Eisenhower was somewhat perturbed about the risk we were taking in our proposed rush on Weimar, but after we discussed it, I got permission to continue the attack.

I made arrangements to reconstitute the two companies of the 4th Armored Division, which we now definitely knew had been captured. After forcing a crossing over the Main east of Frankfurt, in which the Captain in command was slightly wounded, they continued the attack and reached the outskirts of Hammelburg. There they ran into elements of three German divisions which, as we hoped, had been drawn by their attack. While some of the tanks and some of the armored infantry engaged these divisions, other tanks went to the prison camp, some six miles to the north, and released the prisoners. These tanks, accompanied by some twelve hundred prisoners, rejoined the rest of the force in the vicinity of Hammelburg and started back over the road they had taken. The following report was made by my Aide, Major Stiller, who was with them but not in command. He suggested that, instead of returning over the road already used, the column strike north. The officer in charge declined that advice and the column stopped to refuel. While engaged in this refueling, they were attacked by three regiments of German infantry from three different directions, and scattered. When the confusion had cleared, Major Stiller, the Captain in command of the force, and five enlisted men continued to fight until they had used up all their ammunition and had their vehicles destroyed, when they surrendered.

On the first of April, two years from the day Jenson[1] was killed, we were not going so fast, due primarily to road blocks or demolitions. However, the 4th Armored Division was six kilometers west of Eisenach, while the north column of the 11th Armored Division, also in the XII Corps, was in Oberfeld. We received a message from the Twelfth Army Group that, if we could not get Weimar by the night of the first, we had better stop and wait until the First and Ninth Armies came abreast of us. However, we persuaded them to let us continue until 1700 hours on the second.

On the second of April, the VIII Corps began to move in, as planned, between the XX on the north and the XII on the south, and to take over the 4th Armored Division. The 80th Division of the XX Corps resumed the attack on Kassel and had a rather rough time of it, but whenever we turned the 80th Division on anything, we always knew that the objective would be attained.

It was reported, on this date, that a certain number of German troops, later discovered to be members of the 2d Mountain Division, had escaped from the hills northeast of Frankfurt, and, cutting across the rear of the XII Corps, had captured a hospital column, killed one officer and two enlisted men, and also captured an ammunition dump. The first reports, which came in at

---

[1]Major Richard N. Jenson, General Patton's Aide, killed by an air bomb in Tunisia.

night, gave a most horrible account of atrocities, including the murder of all members of the hospital, the raping of all nurses, and the destruction of the ammunition dump. This is simply another illustration of my opinion that the report of no incident which happens after dark should be treated too seriously. They are always overstated.

In this particular case an officer and two enlisted men were killed in the first fighting. Thereafter, the Germans, while helping themselves to the trucks and ambulances, which they used for their own transportation, in no way molested the doctors, nurses, or enlisted personnel of the hospital. Furthermore, when they reached the ammunition dump, which was defended by some dusky soldiers who ran away, they did not take the trouble to ignite it, but hurried on in an attempt to get clear. We rounded them up next day with the 71st Infantry Division, the 10th Infantry Regiment (Colonel R. P. Bell) of the 5th Infantry Division, and the Reconnaissance Battalion (Lieutenant Colonel M. W. Frame) of the 13th Armored, which had been released to us that day. In all some eight hundred prisoners were taken and probably five hundred killed, as the soldiers were still under the impression that atrocities had been committed.

The total casualties for the whole army on this day amounted to 190 men killed, wounded, and missing, which is the most eloquent statement of the weakness of the opposition.

The Werra River proved more of an obstacle than we had anticipated, as it practically stopped both the 6th and 4th Armored Divisions and slowed up the 11th Armored. Also the 6th Armored Division, on this day, received very heavy German air attacks while attempting to bridge the river.

On the third, we moved the Command Post to a German barracks on the northern exit from Frankfurt. Codman and I drove there from Oberstein. The valley leading to Mainz is very reminiscent of the Kaw Valley in Kansas. The roads were in extremely good condition, and all the German civilians were out, working violently to clean up their towns. The city of Mainz itself was very badly bashed in. I would estimate that at that time at least two-thirds of it was in ruins. All the bridges over the Rhine were blown up by the Germans, but fortunately the railway bridge, which collapsed north of Oppenheim, made a complete barrier, so that the Germans could not float either barges or mines down to destroy our bridges north of the railway bridge.

On the way we stopped at Bad Kreuznach to see Colonel Hines, but he had been evacuated about two hours before our arrival.[1]

We did see a number of recaptured prisoners of war, who were in fairly good shape considering where they had been. In this particular group there were at least six enlisted SIW's (self-inflicted wounded), including one officer, the only one I had ever seen. I gave them my usual speech, which ran something like this:

"Did you get the man who shot you?"

"No, sir. I done it myself."

"Oh, you did! What time did it happen, in the daytime?"

"No, sir, it was at night."

"Did you suffer much?"

"No, sir, my buddy fixed me up right away."

"Do you know what you are?"

"No, sir, I don't."

I would then say, "Now, all of you other soldiers listen," and would use about three lines of choice profanity and state that, by wounding himself, he not only showed he was a coward, but also added to the labor and risk of the brave men who did not use this means of getting out of battle. I gave the officer a special treatment.

On arriving at the new Headquarters, we discovered that the 4th Armored Division was in the vicinity of Gotha, and Combat Command "B" of the 11th (commanded by Colonel W. W. Yale) was twelve kilometers southwest of Ohrdruf. We also had a definite order from Higher Headquarters that, on reaching the line Meiningen—Ohrdruf—Gotha—Mühlhausen, we were to stop and await the arrival of the First and Ninth Armies.

On April 4, we were given new boundaries between ourselves and the First and Seventh Armies, also the new

---

[1] Colonel Hines recovered, but lost the sight of both eyes.

halt line running through Meiningen—Gotha—Suhl—Langersalz-Mühlhausen. After reaching this line, we were ordered not to advance more than a few miles a day until the First and Ninth Armies could close up. This would require a long period of time, because two of the four corps of the First Army and one corps of the Ninth were still engaged in cleaning up the Germans trapped in the Ruhr Pocket. We had loaned the 5th Infantry Division and 13th Armored to Hodges to help.

Fortunately, General Patch of the Seventh Army was present when we got the boundaries and the halt line.

I then visited the Headquarters of the three corps. In the XX Corps the 6th Armored Division had taken Mühlhausen, and the 80th Division had removed the final resistance in Kassel and also most of the town. There they captured a German general and four hundred men. This general stated that he believed that Germany would still win. His ideas seemed at variance with his action in surrendering. Furthermore, he was the first German general who had stated he thought Germany would win. All the others said Germany was defeated, but that they continued the battle because they were ordered to.

In the VIII Corps I saw twenty-nine World War I German standards which that unit had captured. These were later sent to the Adjutant General in Washington.

That evening two lieutenants, who had been liberated from Hammelburg and made their way across country to our lines, paid me a visit.[1]

Late that evening, Patch called up to say that three other officers from Hammelburg had reached his Headquarters and told him Colonel Waters had been badly wounded. Patch said he would do everything in his power to capture the camp on the fifth.

On the fifth, the 4th Armored Division had definite control of the cities of Gotha, Ohrdruf, and Mühlberg. I was very happy, because General Gay was finally promoted to Major General, and General Williams, Army

---

[1] These two lieutenants reported that General Patton's son-in-law, Colonel J. K. Waters, was a prisoner in the camp at Hammelburg and had been shot during the mêlée at the camp when the American troops arrived.

Artillery Officer, and General Conklin, Army Engineer, also received their first stars.

We had the Corps Commanders in for lunch for the purpose of arranging boundaries. Whenever boundaries are arranged, there is always a bitter fight between all concerned over the question of roads, so I decided to let the three settle this themselves, which they eventually succeeded in doing after a long and acrimonious debate. I felt, and the Corps Commanders, I think, agreed with me, that there was nothing in front of the Third Army which it, or any of its three corps, could not easily overcome. We were, therefore, opposed to stopping, but, in order to occupy the new boundaries as prescribed by higher authority, we practically had to stop, or at least slow down, in order to perform, for the first time in the history of the Third Army, the act of regrouping. Even while doing this, however, we pushed along several miles each day, so as to prevent the enemy from digging in.

On the sixth, I decorated Private Harold A. Garman, of the 5th Infantry Division, with the Medal of Honor. Garman was an attached medico in one of the battalions that forced the crossing over the Sauer River. During the action, a boat with three walking and one prone wounded, paddled by two engineers, started back and was caught by German machine-gun fire in the middle of the river. The engineers, and one of the walking wounded, jumped overboard and swam for shore. The other two wounded jumped overboard, but were too weak to swim and clung to the boat while the litter case lay prone. The boat, still under a hail of bullets, drifted toward the German shore. Private Garman swam out and pushed the boat to our side. I asked him why he did it, and he looked surprised and said, "Well, someone had to."

After the ceremony I went, via Limburg, to Ehrenbreitstein to be present at the ceremony of rehoisting the American colors, which we had taken down twenty-six years before, when the 4th Infantry Division started home at the termination of our occupation of the Rhineland. Mr. McCloy, the Assistant Secretary of War, was present.

The 13th Armored Division started to close as Army

Reserve in the rear area of the XX Corps. Late in the evening, Patch telephoned that the 14th Armored Division (commanded by Major General A. C. Smith) had recaptured Hammelburg and that only about seventy American prisoners remained, among whom was Colonel Waters, critically wounded.

Elmer Davis of the OWI and General McClure[1] came to dinner. Also Colonel Darby of the Rangers, whom I had twice decorated with the Distinguished Service Cross, once in Tunisia and once in Sicily. He was later killed.

The good news of the day arrived when, at 1705, General Eddy called up to say that the 90th Division of his corps had captured the German gold reserve at Merkers, justifying General Sibert's guess as to the location of a German Headquarters. I had been burned on so many rumors that I told Eddy not to mention the capture of the gold until we had definitely identified it.

On the seventh, Bradley asked me if I could lend the 13th Armored Division to the First Army for the purpose of cleaning out the pocket between it and the Ninth Army. It was during this operation that General Wogan, the Division Commander, was seriously wounded. In order to replace the 13th Armored Division, I transferred the 4th Armored from the VIII Corps to the XX, leaving the VIII Corps temporarily without an armored division, but this was not too disadvantageous, as the country in its zone of action was not suitable for armor.

A Quartermaster detachment of the Third Army had the signal, and, as far as I know, solitary distinction of capturing a German lieutenant general, General Hahm, commanding the 82nd German Corps, together with a colonel, a major, a lieutenant, and seven privates. They were apparently fed up with fighting and simply waited until American troops passed. The colored soldiers capturing them were the most elated soldiers I have ever seen.

At 1500, Eddy called to say that he had entered the gold reserve vault and found the equivalent of a

---

[1]Brigadier General R. A. McClure, Chief Psychological Warfare Division, SHAEF.

billion dollars in paper marks, but that the gold, if it existed, was behind a steel door. This I ordered him to blow up. He stated also that he had two members of the Reichsbank in custody.

On this day the four hundred thousandth prisoner captured by the Third Army was processed through the cages and photographed.

Late in the evening, quite a fight developed in the VIII Corps, when some two thousand Germans were caught between the 89th and 87th Divisions. At the same time the XX Corps was attacked on its northern flank, and repulsed the attack by using the 76th Division and one combat command of the 6th Armored.

General Giraud's Aide came in at suppertime with the Giraud family, which he had found at the town of Friedrichroda. I kept them all night and flew them to Metz in the morning, as it was quicker and safer than sending them by car.

On the eighth, Mr. McCloy, accompanied by General Craig[1] of the Air Force, arrved and attended our morning briefing. The Secretary was extremely complimentary. He was anxious to get to the front to see some of the fighting, but owing to the distances involved and the fact that the roads were quite infested with small German groups, who shot up our isolated convoys, I at last dissuaded him. On the seventh, Colonel R. S. Allen, Assistant G-2, Third Army, had been seriously wounded, one man killed, and three others captured out of a total of seven while driving in the vicinity of Gotha. Mr. McCloy and I discussed what, to me, was the seemingly barbaric bombardment of the centers of cities. The Secretary stated that he had talked to Devers and Patch and they both agreed with me that it was a useless and sadistic form of war.

The Chief of Staff of the 90th Division let out the news of the capture of the gold, which, as previously stated, I was trying to conceal. In addition to the paper money previously reported, Eddy had found, on blowing the door, some 4500 gold bricks weighing thirty-five

---

[1]Major General H. A. Craig, Assistant Chief Air Staff for Operations, Headquarters, AAF, Washington, D.C.

pounds apiece and alleged to be worth $57,600,000. I immediately telephoned General Bradley that, owing to the amount of the seizure and the fact that it had been made public, I believed it was now a political rather than a military question and requested that G-4 from SHAEF be asked to send somebody to take it over.

Mr. McCloy, at his own request, visited Colonel Waters in the hospital, and we also examined a number of wards and the operating rooms. He was extremely complimentary in his remarks concerning the efficiency with which things were run. After the Secretary left, I returned to the hospital and pinned the Silver Star and Oak Leaf Cluster on Waters. He did not know that he had been awarded either decoration, having not lived, in an historical sense, for more than two years, since his capture in Tunisia.[1]

All three corps which I visited in the afternoon were ready to resume the limited offensive to attain Grid Line 20.[2] In the case of the XX Corps, I told them that if, on reaching the grid line, they could get Erfurt, a little to the east, to go ahead, taking it by envelopment from the south in order to dish up any high ranking Germans who attempted to pull out to the so-called "Redoubt"—the existence of which I then personally discounted. The VIII Corps, with the 89th Division on the north and 87th on the south, moved on the same grid line with orders to take Arnstadt. The XII Corps was already in advance of the grid line, but I believed it would probably be held up except on its right, where it was directed to take Eisfeld and Coburg.

On the tenth, the objective set the day before had been attained, and we moved the Army Headquarters from Frankfurt to Hersfeld, driving over the autobahn. When we first encountered the autobahns, we looked forward to them as of great military value, but after some experience it was evident that, as immediate routes of attack, the secondary roads were better, owing to the fact that the autobahns overpass the secondary roads and

[1] Colonel Waters was captured in February, 1943.
[2] A limiting line on the map upon which adjacent units were to co-ordinate prior to advancing.

these points are easily destroyed by demolition. In fact, we captured a German colonel who was quite proud of himself because he said that through the use of five hundred-kilo aviation bombs he had certainly delayed the Third Army two days; which was probably true. After an autobahn had been in our possession for three days, it was extremely valuable, because by that time the Engineers had repaired the damage. They became very clever at this, as they did at all other military tasks. To show the extent to which the Germans went in demolition, Codman and I once passed fourteen demolitions in twenty kilometers.

On the way to the new Command Post at Hersfeld, we stopped at Wiesbaden and had lunch with General Bradley. The new Command Post had apparently been an armored training center, or a Quartermaster training center. It was very well situated and had an excellent mess hall and kitchen for the enlisted men's mess; also a number of sheds, one completely full of spare parts for horse-drawn escort wagons.

During the long drive to Hersfeld, I noticed evidence of great carelessness in leaving gasoline cans along the road, so issued an order that the Assistant Quartermaster General of the Third Army was personally to drive along the road, followed by two trucks, and pick up all the cans he found.

I also found that practically every enlisted member of the Medical Corps had captured a civilian automobile or motorcycle, with the result that we were wasting gasoline at a magnificent rate and also cluttering up the road with transportation which would later be needed by the German civilians to rebuild the country. We therefore issued orders for the sequestration of these vehicles.

Another thing I noticed was the fact that the Army was going to hell on uniform. During the extremely cold weather it had been permissible, and even necessary, to permit certain variations, but with the approach of summer I got out another uniform order.

When we reached the new Command Post at Hersfeld, there was considerable excitement over a rumor that the Germans were going to land a small glider-borne expedition for the purpose of killing me. I never put much faith in this rumor, but did take my carbine to my truck[1] every night when I went to bed.

General Eisenhower and General Bradley arrived at our Cub landing field at 0900 on April 12, and we at once set out to see General Eddy and Colonel Bernard D. Bernstein[2] at the salt mine in Merkers. They were accompanied by several German officials, whom we took with us in the elevator and descended twenty-one hundred feet. The mine, usually described as a salt mine, does

---

[1]While in the field and when at home in Army Headquarters, General Patton lived and worked in two truck trailers.

His parlor, bedroom, and bath was a converted Ordnance Trailer, entered from the rear after climbing a steep set of steps. The steps were corrugated iron and were a great hazard to Willie, the General's dog. After Willie had lost several of his toenails in the corrugations, it became necessary to cover the steps with boards.

Inside, there was a desk with side drawers, electric light, two telephones, and other necessary office fixtures. The General had a small map-board, which he referred to seldom, if ever. He did not keep the situation posted in his living trailer, as it was posted in his office trailer. There was a small closet for clothes, a small washstand and cabinet for toilet articles, and a built-in bed at the far end of the trailer. A radio was installed in an upper panel inside the truck, which the General used frequently in listening to broadcasts. He never used radio in talking to his commanders. Even during the most rapid advances, the Signal Corps usually kept up with wire communications. Once in a while it was necessary to use radio telephone, but this was handled over the regular telephone system installed in the truck. One of the two telephones —incidentally it had a green receiver—was a direct line to General Bradley and General Eisenhower. This particular telephone had a device supposed to scramble the words as they passed over the wire and come out as spoken on the other end. Most of the General's oaths were used at this device. It seemed he could never get it in phase and complained that it scrambled his own words before he uttered them.

All the electrical devices were run by a mobile generator that furnished electricity for the Headquarters group.

The office trailer was a long, moving-van type of truck, fitted inside with a desk, map-boards, and telephone. It was located in camp close to the General's living trailer and was used frequently for conferences.

The General preferred to use the two trailers for living and work, and it was not until the winter set in that he moved inside. When spring came in 1945, while moving through Germany, he favored his truck-house for sleeping and used it even though his office was in a building and his meals served indoors.

[2]From Finance Section, SHAEF.

not produce table salt, but some sort of chemical which looks very much like asbestos. It is a tremendous affair, having five hundred and eighty kilometers of tunnels. These are from thirty to fifty feet high and about the same width.

In addition to the paper money and gold bricks, there was a great deal of French, American, and British gold currency; also a number of suitcases filled with jewelry, such as silver and gold cigarette cases, wrist-watch cases, spoons, forks, vases, gold-filled teeth, false teeth, etc. These suitcases were in no way labeled, and apparently simply contained valuable metal gleaned by bandit methods. General Eisenhower said jokingly that he was very much chagrined not to find a box full of diamonds. We found no precious stones in this particular hideout. We examined a few of the alleged art treasures. The ones I saw were worth, in my opinion, about $2.50, and were of the type normally seen in bars in America.

From the mine we drove to Eisfeld, Headquarters of the XII Corps, where we were joined by General Weyland. After lunch we flew, accompanied by a mythical air support which did not materialize because it got lost, to the Headquarters of the XX Corps at Gotha, where we met both Middleton and Walker. At Walker's suggestion, we drove to Ohrdruf and visited the first horror camp any of us had ever seen. It was the most appalling sight imaginable. A man who said he was one of the former inmates acted as impresario and showed us first the gallows, where men were hanged for attempting to escape. The drop board was about two feet from the ground, and the cord used was piano wire which had an adjustment so that when the man dropped, his toes would just reach the ground and it would take about fifteen minutes for him to choke to death, since the fall was not sufficient to break his neck. The next two men to die had to kick the board out from under him. It was stated by some of the Germans present that the generals who were executed after the Hitler bomb incident were hanged in this manner.

Our guide then took us to the whipping table, which was about the height of the average man's crotch. The feet were placed in stocks on the ground and the man was pulled over the table, which was slightly hollowed, and held by two guards, while he was beaten across the back and loins. The stick which they said had been used, and which had some blood on it, was bigger than the handle of a pick. Our guide claimed that he himself had received twenty-five blows with this tool. It later developed that he was not a prisoner at all, but one of the executioners. General Eisenhower must have suspected it, because he asked the man very pointedly how he could be so fat. He was found dead next morning, killed by some of the inmates.

Just beyond the whipping table there was a pile of forty bodies, more or less naked. All of these had been shot in the back of the head at short range, and the blood was still cooling on the ground.

In a shed near-by was a pile of forty completely naked bodies in the last stages of emaciation. These bodies were lightly sprinkled with lime—not, apparently, for the purpose of destroying them, but to reduce the smell. As a reducer of smell, lime is a very inefficient medium. The total capacity of the shed looked to me to be about two hundred bodies. It was stated that bodies were left until the shed was full and then they were taken out and buried. The inmates said some three thousand people had been buried from this shed since January 1, 1945.

When our troops began to draw near, the Germans thought it expedient to remove the evidence of their crimes. They therefore used the inmates to exhume the recently buried bodies and to build a sort of mammoth griddle of 60 cm. railway tracks laid on a brick foundation. The bodies were piled on this and they attempted to burn them. The attempt was a bad failure. Actually, one could not help but think of some gigantic cannibalistic barbecue. In the pit itself were arms and legs and portions of bodies sticking out of the green water which partially filled it.

General Walker and General Middleton had wisely decided to have as many soldiers as possible visit the scene. This gave me the idea of having the inhabitants themselves visit the camp. I suggested this to Walker, and found that he had already had the mayor and his wife take a look at it. On going home those two committed suicide. We later used the same system in having

the inhabitants of Weimar go through the even larger
slave camp (Buchenwald) north of that town.

From here we drove to the 80th Division, where
General McBride described the new technique he had
devised. It consisted in firing a couple of projectiles containing proclamations to the effect that, unless the town
in question surrendered by a certain hour, it would be
given a treatment, and that if it intended to surrender,
the burgomaster was to come out with a white flag and
be responsible that no German troops were in the town.
While the proclamation was sinking in, a few flights of
the XIX Tactical Air Command fighter-bombers flew
overhead and, toward the end of the period, got lower
and lower. When the time had elapsed, if no action had
been taken by the Germans, the fighter-bombers were
informed by the air-support party and dropped their
eggs. Synchronized with this, an artillery concentration
hit the town. As a result of this method, a great many
towns surrendered without difficulty.

We developed later a system known as the "Third
Army War Memorial Project" by which we always fired
a few salvos into every town we approached, before
even asking for surrender. The object of this was to let
the inhabitants have something to show to future generations of Germans by way of proof that the Third Army
had passed that way.

I went to bed rather late and noticed that I had
failed to wind my watch, which was run down, so turned
on the radio to get a time signal. Just as I turned it on,
the announcer reported the death of President Roosevelt.
I immediately informed General Eisenhower and General
Bradley, and we had quite a discussion as to what
might happen. It seemed very unfortunate to us that at
so critical a period in our history we should have to
change horses. Actually, subsequent events demonstrated
that it made no difference at all.

On the thirteenth, Bradley asked me to leave the
65th Infantry Division in its present position until the
following Sunday in order to facilitate certain operations
being undertaken by the First Army.

I visited Colonel Allen in the hospital, as he had
been recaptured when we took Weimar. His right arm
had been shot off just below the elbow. He gave me

some very interesting information. The surgeon who operated on him used the last ether in his possession to put Allen under, but it was insufficient and toward the end he gave him brandy and some sort of chloral drug. Allen said he saw at least eighty Germans operated on without any anaesthetic at all except chloral and cognac; there were no sanitary arrangements, no soap nor water, and the doctors and nurses were literally wading in blood. Many of the men were dragged into the operating room by the hand, as there was a shortage of stretchers. The surgeon who operated on him was an Austrian, and, during the few days Allen was in the hospital, repeatedly gave false information as to his state of health, because the Germans, having discovered that he was a colonel, were very anxious to get him to Army Headquarters for interrogation. The surgeon finally told Allen that if the worse came to worst he would help him to escape and keep him hidden in the hills until we came up. Allen was a very sporting character and the only request he had was that he be left on duty at Army Headquarters, which request was granted. He did an extremely good job until the end of the war.

On April 14, the XX and XII Corps, due to the armor which assisted them, were on the stop line running along the Mulde River from our northern boundary near Hochlitz to the vicinity of Zwickau, thence through Plauen and Hof, then generally parallel to and east of the autobahn to Bayreuth.

Lieutenant Graves[1] and I flew to Mainz to be present by invitation of General Plank, of Com Z, at the opening of the railway bridge over the Rhine, which had been built by my friend and former classmate, Colonel Frank Hulen. Hulen, it seemed, was much depressed because he had built the bridge in nine days, twenty hours, and fifteen minutes, which, according to him, was some twelve hours longer than Caesar had taken to build a similar bridge. We pointed out to him that Caesar did not build a railway bridge. After appropriate ceremonies I was asked to cut the red tape, in lieu of a red ribbon, to open the bridge, and was

---

[1]Later Captain F. P. Graves, Jr., Aide to General Patton.

handed a pair of scissors. However, my romantic instinct prompted me to ask for a bayonet with which I cut the tape. We then got on a flatcar and drove across the bridge in the first train to pass over it. Personally I was much more worried for fear the bridge would fall down than I usually am in a fight. On returning, Hulen showed us some of the equipment he had made for the purpose of building the bridge. One item was a huge crane capable of lifting a whole bay at once, which, I believe, he called a "Moby Dick."

On returning to Headquarters, I found that General Gay, Colonels Pfann[1] and Codman had visited another slave camp north of Weimar, Buchenwald, which was apparently much worse than the one at Ohrdruf. I immediately called General Eisenhower and suggested he send senior representatives of the press and photographers to get the horrid details. General Eisenhower not only did this, but also got Congressmen to come over. This was the camp where we paraded some fifteen hundred citizens of Weimar to give them a firsthand knowledge of the infamy of their own government. In honesty, I believe that most of them were ignorant of much that had gone on there.

I was unable to get any information as to what was to happen after I got on the stop line, except that I was told that, in the opinion of the Twelfth Army Group, I did not have sufficient supplies to go farther, in spite of the fact that I knew perfectly well I had.

I was informed by higher headquarters that a correspondent named Driscoll,[2] with the Third Army, had written an article stating that the Third Army was held up by the First Army. Apparently people are getting touchy. In briefing correspondents once a week I always refused to answer questions about other armies or to discuss them in any way, as I felt the Third Army could stand on its own feet and needed to make no excuses to anyone. I had Major Quirk[3] in and issued instructions

---

[1] Lieutenant Colonel G. R. Pfann, Secretary, General Staff, Third Army.

[2] Joseph Driscoll, *New York Herald Tribune*, President of American War Correspondents' Association.

[3] Later Lieutenant Colonel J. T. Quirk, Public Relations Officer, Third Army.

that no article making a comparison of the relative merits of the various armies shall ever go out.

On April 15, the three corps (XII, XX, VIII) were practically on the stop line and I flew to Weimar and visited what I then thought was going to be my next Command Post. It was the home of the former local *Gauleiter,* who had been responsible for the slave labor and all the general nastiness in that vicinity. Here General Walker presented me with a toy boat for a grandson, and I took it without hesitation, for it had unquestionably been stolen from someone else by this German bandit.

I then visited, in company with General Walker, the Weimar slave camp, Buchenwald. This camp was in the vicinity of a factory largely engaged in the construction of parts for the V-1 bomb and of artillery caissons, and is a monument to the accurate bombing of our air force, because they completely eliminated the factory without putting a single bomb in the camp, which was contiguous.

In addition to the workers in the factory, a large number of political prisoners were assembled at this camp and fed eight hundred calories a day, with the result that they died at the rate of about one hundred each night. I walked through two buildings, each with four tiers of bunks on a side. The bunks were at right angles to the gangway and were built so that they sloped slightly toward the front, and so that the fecal matter and other refuse left by the prisoners trickled down under their chins onto the floor, which was at least three inches deep in filth when I went through. Strange to say, the smell was not particularly bad; it was rather more musty than putrid.

The inmates looked like feebly animated mummies and seemed to be of the same level of intelligence. If a sufficient number did not die of starvation or if, for other reasons, it was desirable to remove them without waiting for nature to take its course, they were dropped down a chute into a room which had a number of hooks like those on which one hangs meat in a butcher shop, about eight feet from the floor. Each of these hooks had a cord of clothesline thickness with a grommet at each end. One grommet was passed through the other

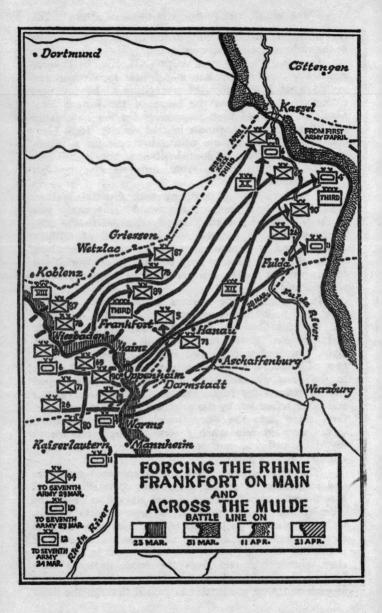

FORCING THE RHINE
FRANKFORT ON MAIN
AND
ACROSS THE MULDE
BATTLE LINE ON
23 MAR.   51 MAR.   11 APR.   21 APR.

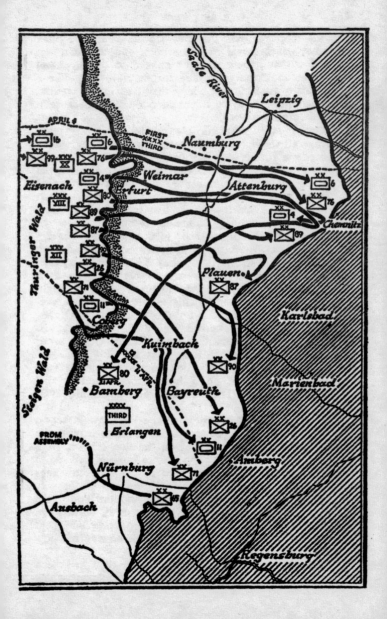

and the loop put over the slave's head, while the other grommet was fastened over the hook and the man was allowed to hang there until he choked to death, except that if he took too long they had a club, very like a large potato masher, with which they beat out his brains. This club must have been considerably used because it was splintered on one side.

One of the most horrible points about this place was that all these executions were carried on by slaves. There was a further devilish arrangement of making the various groups select those who had to die. Each racial group had a certain number of men who represented it. These men had to select those from their group who would be killed locally, or sent to camps like Ohrdruf, which were termed "elimination camps."

In this camp there was a number of allegedly eminent physicians whose professional rectitude had been so completely destroyed that they had been persuaded to perform some very abominable experiments on their fellow inmates. One case was reported in which eight hundred slaves had been inoculated with anti-typhus vaccine and then inoculated with the typhus bug. Of the eight hundred, some seven hundred died, and the experiment was considered unsatisfactory. Colonel Odom asked some of these doctors if there was anything he could do for them. One said yes, that he was making a very interesting experiment on a human brain and needed some carbon black. The human brain, apparently, was still alive.

From the execution room in the Buchenwald set-up there was an elevator, hand operated, which carried the corpses to an incinerator plant on the floor above. Here there were six furnaces. The corpse was placed on a loading tray similar to those used in the 155 mm. guns and, at the command "Ram home!" the end of the tray hit against the stopper on the door and the body shot forward into the oven, where it was shortly burned up. The slave in charge of this took great pride and kept rubbing his hand on the floor and then showing me how clean it was.

When I got home, I found that Bradley had been trying to talk to me on the scrambler telephone, which

was out of order, so Gay had told him in the clear that I would see him in the morning.

One of the interesting things to be seen in flying over Germany is the large number of swimming pools. Practically every little town has one. I think it must have been in line with their health movement.

It was also noteworthy that, whereas in France all the main electric power lines were completely destroyed, after we crossed into Germany proper, and particularly after we got east of the Rhine, the main power lines were not destroyed or, if so, were demolished at only one or two points.

On April 16, in company with Colonel Harkins, I flew to Wiesbaden, where I met General Bradley, and later Hodges and his G-3, and we got the new plan, which was, in effect, a change of direction to the south for the purpose of attacking the so-called "Redoubt." In order to effect this change, the VIII Corps remained in place and reverted to the First Army, at the same time broadening its front both to the north and to the south. We selected the VIII Corps because it was quicker for it to expand both ways than it would have been to put in another corps, which would have to expand twice as far on one side. The expansion to the south was as far as Hof; and on the north to the former boundary of the XX Corps. To do this we turned over the 76th Division of the XX Corps to the VIII Corps, and also the 4th and 6th Armored Divisions.

The XX Corps Headquarters and artillery, and the 80th Division, were pulled out and came to the south, with their left boundary on the right boundary of the XII Corps in the area which had been heretofore occupied by the XV Corps of the Seventh Army. They picked up the 71st Division from the XII Corps, which also side-slipped to the right, and an additional division from the rear was to come up eventually. (*See Map, pages 282–283.*)

In addition to this, we got the III Corps under General Van Fleet, with elements of that corps and other troops from the Ruhr Pocket. The III Corps was to take over the general frontage heretofore occupied by the XXI Corps (Major General F. W. Milburn) of the Seventh Army.

We also picked up the three armored divisions in addition to the 11th; namely, the 13th (Major General John Millikin), which had seen action, and the 16th (Brigadier General J. L. Pierce) and 20th (Major General Orlando Ward)—both virgin divisions. I was glad to get them, as I felt we should get these green troops into battle, after all the training they had had, before the war ended.

The Third Army was to attack in a southeasterly direction parallel to the Czechoslovakian border, with the Danube River splitting the zone between the XII Corps on the north and the XX Corps in the middle. The Seventh Army was to attack straight south, and the First and Ninth Armies were to remain on the defensive.

On the way back, we flew over von Rundstedt's Headquarters at the town of Ziegenburg, sixteen kilometers west of Bad Nauheim, which had been bombed by our fighter-bombers just before we crossed the Rhine. The effect produced by these bombings was remarkably good. I am continually amazed at the efficiency of the fighter-bombers, particularly their ability to pick out isolated motor transport and hit it.

We had the four Corps Commanders in and explained the new set-up. They were all perfectly confident of their ability to side-slip, change direction, and do whatever was necessary. General Weyland, who was always present when any decision was made in the Third Army, was equally confident of his ability to support any activities in which we might become engaged. Middleton, as usual, was the perfect soldier and suggested that he consult with General Hodges and find out what front line the latter desired him to take, and also the time at which the transfer between armies should be effected. At lunch, after the meeting, I sat next to General Eddy and was somewhat alarmed at his apparent lack of life, because usually he was extremely talkative and cheerful.

Late in the afternoon, General Williams, myself, Colonel Codman, Colonel Odom, and Lieutenant Graves flew to Paris, where I had a long talk in the hospital with Colonel Waters, whom I found much improved. I saw him again on the morning of the eighteenth before flying back.

At breakfast that morning, General Hughes and I

were each reading a copy of *The Stars and Stripes*. I was looking at the right-hand column describing the activities of the Third Army when Hughes reached across and pointed to the center column in which it stated I had just been made a full General. While I was, of course, glad to get the rank, the fact that I was not in the initial group and was therefore an "also ran" removed some of the pleasure. When the initial list of names came out, Sergeant Meeks, who heard it over the radio, came to my room and said, "Good God, General, they are making all the troop clerks." Codman secured for me the last set of four stars in Paris and I dispatched my three-star set to General Keyes, who was promoted to Lieutenant General in the same list.

On the nineteenth, we had some radio commentators and some experts from the Secretary of War's Office. The latter were quite interesting.

General Canine, Chief of Staff of the XII Corps, called up with the depressing information that General Eddy was in such a physical state that he would have to be relieved from command and sent home. He had been a very fine Corps Commander and I hated to see him go. Also, he had been with me almost since the initial landing in Africa and had probably commanded larger units of combat troops longer than any other general. I was prevented from going to see him that day because General Bradley sent for me to go to Wiesbaden for a conference with General Eisenhower, so I told Canine to carry on in General Eddy's name and I would get a new Corps Commander when I saw Generals Eisenhower and Bradley. The names I suggested were Gaffey, Harmon, and Irwin.[1] It was decided that neither Gaffey nor Harmon could be spared at the moment, so the choice was between Irwin, my candidate, and Wyche, whom General Eisenhower suggested. I believe he suggested Wyche, not only because Wyche was senior, but also because Irwin was a classmate of his, and Eisenhower leaned over backward from promoting a classmate. I eventually secured the selection of Irwin on the ground that he had had more combat experience,

---

[1] Major General S. LeRoy Irwin, Commanding General, 5th Infantry Division.

since he had not only fought continuously on the Continent, but had also been through the Tunisian Campaign.

General Eisenhower stated that he was anxious for us to start in the direction of Linz as soon as possible, but that, owing to the failure of the British to make sufficient progress, it might be necessary for him to send a corps up there. He said he did not wish to get overextended until the situation in the north cleared up, and therefore I was to get ready to go, but was not to go until I received permission.

C-47

On the twentieth, we sent the Army C-47 to General Eddy's Headquarters for the purpose of flying him to Paris, and I flew there in a Cub to tell him good-bye. His trouble was such high blood pressure that it was considered practically fatal..[1]

After seeing Eddy off with great regret, I flew to the Headquarters of the XX Corps at Schloss Weissenstein. This was the most magnificent and most hideous building I had ever seen. It was built around 1700 and is full of murals and gigantic plaster statues of overfed females.

[1]He was operated on in the United States and entirely recovered.

There is also a collection of really great paintings. In one room, the inlay in the parquet floor is silver. Another room is all solid gold enamel. General Walker had an uncanny capacity for choosing excellent Command Posts for himself. The stable at this château was built in a semicircle directly across from the main door. The saddle room, where apparently people congregated while getting ready to take off, had some excellent murals, and was more luxurious and better furnished than many drawing rooms at home. The stables were also remarkably modern and in a good state of repair. There were over twenty box stalls. Apparently the Weissensteins had been a hunting family.

From here we flew to the Headquarters of the III Corps at Reidfeld. Just before we got there, I noticed some tracers coming by the right side of our plane which, at the same instant, dove for the ground, very nearly colliding with a plane which looked like a Spitfire. This plane made a second pass, again firing and missing. By this time I was sure we were being attacked and decided that, since there was nothing else to do, I would try to get a picture of the assailant, but was so nervous I forgot to take the cover off the lens, so the picture was a blank. On the third pass, our attacker came in so fast and we were so close to the ground that he was unable to pull out of his dive and crashed, to our great satisfaction. While Codman and I were engaged in hedge-hopping to avoid this belligerent gentleman, four other planes were circling over us, but did not engage in the attack.

The XV Corps of the Seventh Army, which had sideslipped from its area to that of the XXI Corps, Seventh Army, was having considerable difficulty in clearing the front of our III Corps, which had come in behind it. I told the III Corps to infiltrate forward through the XV so that it could be on the starting line and ready to take off on Sunday, the twenty-third.

General Millikin, who had formerly commanded the III Corps and had now been given the 13th Armored Division, spent the night. His attitude was excellent, and I promised to talk to his division at the earliest opportunity.

The country between Nuremberg and Hersfeld was

some of the most beautiful I had ever flown over. We passed several farms which were undoubtedly horse farms, as they had exercise tracks behind the stables.

While at the XX Corps Headquarters I presented General Walker with my three-star pins, as he had also been promoted on the list with me.

On the twenty-first, the Third Army lost its Surgeon, Brigadier General Thomas D. Hurley, and nearly lost its Ordinance Officer, Colonel Nixon, with stomach complaints. Hurley had to go home and Nixon had to be operated on, and would probably have died had not Colonel Odom visited him and ascertained his precarious state of health.

So ended the Rhine Campaign which had cost us 17,961 casualties.

Casualties reported as of April 21 were:

Third Army		Enemy	
Killed	21,098	Killed	138,700
Wounded	97,163	Wounded	369,700
Missing	16,393	Prisoners of war	545,800
Total	134,654	Total	1,054,200
Non-battle casualties	106,440		
Grand total	241,094		

Matériel Losses

Light tanks	298	Medium tanks	1492
Medium tanks	934	Panther or Tiger tanks	857
Guns	174	Guns	3324

8

CROSSING THE DANUBE AND ENTERING CZECHOSLOVAKIA AND AUSTRIA

April 22 marked the beginning of the end. General Patton had landed the first American troops in Africa on November 8, 1942, and his Third Army ended the main fighting in Europe on May 9, 1945. (See Map, pages 300–301.)

He conducted American troops through three years of successful operations against the enemy. He never issued a defensive order. His theory—attack, attack, attack, and, when in doubt, attack again—shortened the war by never giving the enemy a chance to organize or reorganize enough to make a concerted attack against him.

The termination of hostilities and the stop line imposed by higher authority halted the Third Army on May 9. They had gone farther, captured more prisoners, crossed more rivers, liberated more friendly territory and captured more enemy territory, than any army ever before in American history.

At the end of the campaign, the Third Army switched its attack to the southeast, cleared Bavaria, cleaned out the "Ghost of the Redoubt," entered Czechoslovakia, crossed the Alps, and joined the Russians in Austria, east of Linz.

Farther north, the British and Americans joined hands with the Russians on the Elbe River and in Berlin. The Seventh American and French First Armies cleared the Alps in their zone and joined with the American Fifth Army in Italy.

In the Pacific, Rangoon fell to the British, and all effort went to establishing bases for an invasion of Japan proper.

The air forces and the Navy pounded the enemy on all fronts.

P.D.H.

The Last Round-up

By April 22, it was obvious to me that the end of the war was very close, but there were still those who insisted that a great German concentration existed to the south in the so-called "Redoubt."

We shifted our Command Post from Hersfeld to Erlangen. Codman and I drove there in the rain and sleet and, while passing over the top of the mountains at an altitude of four thousand feet, ran into a little snow. From Bamberg to Erlangen the traffic situation was extremely bad, owing to the fact that we had only one-way bridges, and that no officers except General Maddox and myself had enough initiative to get out and straighten out the messes.

Erlangen is a university town built at the time of the Huguenot persecutions. I was surprised to discover that mansard roofs dated from that period, as for some reason I thought they originated in 1870.

The 11th Armored Division, the 71st and the 65th Divisions did very well. I made arrangements with General Bradley to keep the 70th Division in the vicinity of Frankfurt on occupation duty, and to increase its strength with replacements, who were not being used owing to our low casualties. Actually, this division, for a time, was almost a division and a half.

On the twenty-third, I drove to Headquarters of the XII and XX Corps. The autobahn from Erlangen to Bayreuth, Headquarters of the XII Corps, was a very beautiful drive, as was the cross-country drive from Bayreuth to Bamberg, although, from a military standpoint, the latter road was crooked and difficult.

When I returned to Headquarters, General Patch called up and asked me to swap the 14th Armored for the 20th Armored. The 14th Armored was still fighting in the vicinity of Munich and in the zone of the III Corps, while the 20th Armored was in the vicinity of Wurzburg and could be more readily put into the zone of the Seventh Army. I agreed at once.

On the twenty-fourth, I addressed the officers and men of Milliken's 13th Armored Division as requested.

The 3d Cavalry Regiment reached the Danube in the vicinity of Regensburg at 0400 on the morning of the twenty-third. The III Corps, under the great leadership of Van Fleet, started moving out rapidly, and it was amusing to find that the 14th Armored Division, which, prior to the arrival of Van Fleet, had been conducting a protracted, though unsuccessful, war with the 17th SS Panzer Grenadier Division (SS Oberführer Bochmann), suddenly drove them from its front.

April 25 was quite an interesting day. We learned that the five thousand enemy soldiers, who had got in touch with the 26th Division the previous afternoon and stated their desire to surrender, were White Russians who had been fighting for the Germans against the Russians. The question then arose as to whether they were prisoners of war or allies. We finally got a decision that they were prisoners of war, and they were and still are. In my opinion, they are in a very bad fix, because if the Russians ever get them they will unquestionably be eliminated.

The XIX Tactical Air Command reported large numbers of troops, race unknown, moving upstream on both sides of the Danube, and that they contained some armor with a great deal of horse transport and guns. Whether they were Russians, or Germans fleeing before the Russians, we were unable to decide, but figured that, by a vigorous advance, we would eventually solve the problem.

At noon Bradley called up suggesting that the First Army extend to the south and take over the line of the Czechoslovakian frontier to a point close to the juncture of that frontier with the Austrian border, moving there by successive corps as the situation to the north cleared up. This was very satisfactory to us, as we had a very long open flank along the frontier.

The 14th Armored reached the Altmuhl River about the center of the III Corps sector, while the leading regiment of the 86th Division, same corps, reached the river on the right of the corps boundary at Eichstätt. Van Fleet assured me he would get across that river and be on the Danube by night. He was a very willing worker and a great soldier.

We had been having continuous rumors from air reconnaissance of a movement up the Danube Valley on both sides of the river, and felt that the 11th Armored Division, which had crossed the Naade River and progressed eight kilometers southeast of it, would possibly be the first to run into these troops. Combat Command "A" (commanded by Brigadier General W. A. Holbrook, Jr.) and Combat Command "B" (commanded by Colonel W. W. Yale) were then six miles south of Regensburg, where they had had quite a fight, but, after breaking the crust there, the rest of the advance was simply a road march.

The battle casualties of the Third Army for the two preceding days had not exceeded a hundred on either day, and the non-battle casualties were equally low.

Considering that at this time the Third Army had fourteen divisions in action and an equivalent number of corps and army troops, one gets an idea of how cheap the fighting was. As a rough measure, if you multiply the number of divisions by thirty thousand, you come very close to the total number of troops present; this includes division, corps, and army troops.

On the twenty-sixth, at Schwabach, I decorated Van Fleet with the Distinguished Service Medal and then visited the 99th Division and the 14th Armored. Neither Van Fleet nor I was particularly impressed with the activities at the Headquarters of these two units.

The 86th Division of the III Corps had reached Ingoldstadt and was fighting just outside the town.

Returning to Headquarters, I found that both the 65th and 71st Divisions of the XX Corps had crossed the Danube, one east and one west of Regensburg. They encountered moderate resistance without artillery fire, and were proceeding rapidly on their mission.

In the XII Corps, the 11th Armored Division was six miles from the Austrian border. One battalion of the 90th Division was closing in on Cham to cover the pass through that town in the rear of the 11th Armored Division, as we had a constant rumor that the 11th German Panzer Division was about to attack through this pass.

A German officer came into the 26th Division and informed General Paul that there were five barges anchored on the Danube in the immediate vicinity, which, if bombed or shelled by us, would cause the death of all human beings within a radius of thirty kilometers. Paul told him to put guards on the barges and wait until we arrived, which was done. He also took precautions to warn our air force not to do any promiscuous bombing of barges on the river. Actually, the barges contained poison gas.

This reminded me of a story I had just heard from a captured German. It seems that two hundred SS troops, all of whom had been Hitler Youth, were given a special course of instruction in bombing and navigation. They were told they were to use a new type of lead-dust bomb, which we interpreted to mean an atomic bomb, for the purpose of destroying all human life in Germany. On hearing this happy plan, eighty of the boys refused to participate and were eliminated—or so the others were told. The remaining boys were taken to a high point to see an experiment. An airplane flew low over an area and dropped a bomb, which produced something which looked to them like great air waves. Later the boys were blindfolded and driven for an hour in trucks, and then their eyes were unbandaged and they were told to examine the ground. The area to which they were taken had been covered with snow, but whatever had gone off had melted the snow, pulverized the small rocks, cracked the big ones, and removed all trees. However, they stated that the waves were apparently of a visual nature, as anything behind a big hill was unhurt. The same prisoner stated that, in the vicinity of Salzburg, there was an underground hangar containing one hundred and eighty airplanes, each of which was provided with one of these bombs.

Two points in the story seemed dubious. General Doolittle pointed out to me, for example, that the airplane dropping such a thing would not fly low; also, the prisoner seemed too intelligent. Later, when we got to Salzburg, we could find no indication of the underground hangar or the one hundred and eighty airplanes.

This was the first day I had visited the center of Nuremberg, which was really an appalling sight. The old walled city, which had been so beautiful, was completely destroyed—I think the most completely of anything we had so far seen. All of this could not be attributed to the Air Corps, because it had been necessary for the XV Corps, Seventh Army, to put on quite an artillery bombardment in order to persuade the Germans to leave.

On the twenty-seventh, Codman and I flew to the Headquarters of the XX Corps at Pittersberg and had the ceremony of pinning three stars on General Walker. He had been reluctant to put the stars on until he heard that the Senate had confirmed him. I teased him, saying he must have had a bad conscience. Personally I have always worn my new rank as soon as I have heard it has been forwarded to the President.

Accompanied by Walker, we drove to a point east of Regensburg and then across the Danube River on a treadway bridge. The Danube is not particularly impressive. Near the bridge, however, were several barges loaded with the knocked-down parts of a submarine.

Later, we flew to the Headquarters of the XII Corps and talked to General Irwin. The 11th Armored Division had crossed the Austrian border and the 90th and 26th Divisions were closing up. Irwin was still somewhat worried about his long open flank, which had not been completely covered when the V Corps[1] of the First Army came in under Bradley's plan. I authorized Irwin to let the 11th Armored lay up a couple of days for maintenance, as it had been out of action only four days in the last thirty.

---

[1] The V Corps was commanded by Major General Clarence R. Huebner.

In the III Corps, the 86th and 99th Divisions were successfully over the Danube and the 14th Armored was crossing the river.

There was very evidently a race on between the III and XX Corps, both of which were commanded by efficient and pushful officers.

The XII Corps could not be in the race, owing to the fact that the road conditions in its area were so bad that it could advance only in column of divisions, and then with difficulty.

The 5th Infantry Division was again released to us under the command of General "Burfey" Brown.[1] We promised that we might eventually trade the 97th, a green division, for it when the 5th had passed to the front.

Generals Spaatz, Doolittle, and Vandenberg came to lunch and I had a guard of honor for Spaatz and Vandenberg, as neither of them had been saluted since they were promoted.

The British Broadcasting Company came out with the statement that Himmler had sent a proposition to the United States and Great Britain for an unconditional surrender, but had been told that there was nothing doing unless Russia was also considered.

On the twenty-ninth, Lieutenant Graves and I flew to Viechtach, fifteen miles southeast of Cham, but were unable to land, so had to fly back to Cham and then drive to the aforementioned town, which was the Headquarters of the XII Corps. This corps was pushing on Linz, and I suggested they turn off to the right sufficiently to capture, or threaten to capture, Passau, with a view to getting control of, or causing the Germans to blow up, the bridges over the Inn and Danube Rivers, which meet at this point. Either solution would have been satisfactory, as the chief purpose of securing the bridges was to prevent the Germans from moving troops up the south bank of the Danube with a view to putting them in the "Redoubt" area.

We then flew to the XX Corps at Regensburg, where we found General Walker ensconced in the palace of the Princes of Thurn and Taxis. This is a most ornate building occupying four sides of a city square

---

[1] Major General A. E. Brown.

and containing a theater, a library, an armory, and three churches, to say nothing of a park and picnic area. I subsequently lived in the palace, so should not criticize Walker for occupying it. In fact, he showed good judgment. The Princes of Thurn and Taxis acquired the Bavarian mail monopoly some three hundred years ago and invented the postage stamp. As a result of their forethought the family is still very rich.

The bag of prisoners for the twenty-ninth amounted to twenty-eight thousand.

The month ended with the situation of the Third Army not greatly changed, except that the 26th Division was almost in Passau and the 11th Armored was closing on Linz. We secured from General Bradley the 4th Armored Division in a swap for the 16th, which had not yet been in action. The idea was to use the 4th Armored and the 5th Infantry Divisions to attack southwest up the valley of the Traun River on Salzburg, in conjunction with the attack from the northwest by the XX and III Corps. In this part of the war, terrain was more important than the enemy, and the route from Linz to Salzburg up the river was better than the roads being used by the other two corps. Had we secured Passau in time, the 4th Armored and 5th Infantry could have moved up from there, because, in addition to the route from Linz to Salzburg, there was also another one up the southern bank of the Inn River from Passau which could be utilized, provided we were successful in capturing the bridges at that town; so the plan gave me, in effect, two strings to my bow.

We learned that, on the twenty-ninth, the XIX Tactical Air Command had had some very good shooting on an armored concentration north of Cham, which later turned out to be armored elements of the 11th Panzer Division.

As an indication that everybody thought the war was over, I was directed to make a two-minute recording of a speech to be given on VE-Day.

On May 1, General Lee and his Aide, Major H. D. Rothrock, Colonel Codman, and I flew from the airfield at Nuremberg in some Cubs to Headquarters of the III Corps at Mainburg. We then drove to the Isar River, where the 86th Division was effecting a crossing at

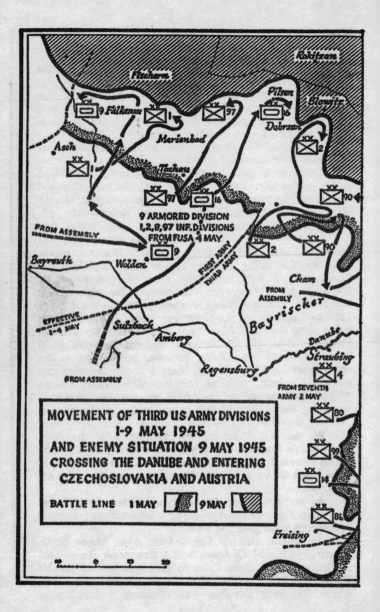

MOVEMENT OF THIRD US ARMY DIVISIONS
1-9 MAY 1945
AND ENEMY SITUATION 9 MAY 1945
CROSSING THE DANUBE AND ENTERING
CZECHOSLOVAKIA AND AUSTRIA

BATTLE LINE   1 MAY   9 MAY

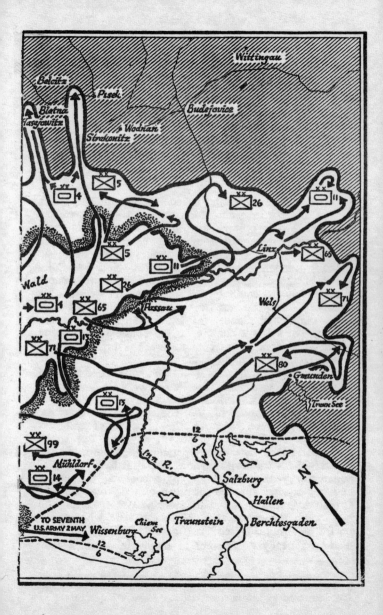

Freising, and then downstream toward Moosberg. On the way we came to the 14th Armored Division which was crossing, and I noticed that all the tanks were covered with sandbags. This was very stupid. In the first place, it made the soldiers think the tanks could be hurt; in the second place, it overloaded the machinery; and in the third place, it provided no additional protection. I ordered their removal at once.

While we were at this bridge, an International Red Cross man and his alleged wife tried to get over with the troops—also a group of drunken Englishmen. Neither party succeeded.

We then drove to the Allied Prisoner of War Camp at Moosberg, where some thirty thousand Allied prisoners of war, mostly officers, had been confined and were still awaiting repatriation by air. The camp was commanded by an RAF Group Captain with whom I had dined in London in 1942. The executive officer was Colonel P. R. Goode, U.S.A., whose illness during the march from Poland to southern Germany was the reason that Colonel Waters did not try to escape. Waters felt that, if he abandoned Goode, the latter would probably die. No one knew I was coming, so the considerable ovation which greeted me was spontaneous. The prisoners were well disciplined and quite clean.

I went through several of the living quarters, and also the cooking shacks, in which latter were some most ingenious cooking devices, mostly invented and constructed by members of the United States Army Air Force. They were based on the principle of a blacksmith's forge and burned practically anything, during the course of which incendiary operation they produced the densest and most evil-smelling smoke I have ever encountered. With the aid of these cookers, the ample and well-selected supplies furnished by the American Red Cross[1] were heated and made more palatable. During the last month the prisoners at Moosberg were wholly supported by American Red Cross packages, as the Germans made practically no attempt to supply food which they

---

[1] These supplies were bought by the Army, packed by volunteer Red Cross workers, shipped by the American Red Cross vessels, and distributed by the International Red Cross.

themselves did not possess. To their credit be it stated that they did not tamper with the packages.

From here we drove to Landshut, where the 99th Division was crossing the Isar River. It was at Landshut in the château on the south side of the river that Colonel Codman spent quite a long period of confinement during the First World War, and from which he subsequently escaped. I took a picture of the château and also one of Charley with the château in the background.

During the trip, we passed a German candy and cooky factory, where, on the previous day, General Van Fleet had found a mob of German civilians looting. Had it not been for the prompt and personal action of General Van Fleet and his driver, the valuable store of sugar, chocolate, and flour stored in the factory would probably have been utterly destroyed. As it was, we walked through passageways where sugar and chocolate lay on the floor higher than my shoetops. Apparently the desire for rationed food made the normally quiescent German completely crazy.

When I got back to Headquarters, I discovered there was a movement on foot to turn over the reduction of the "Redoubt" to the Seventh Army. It occurred to me that, if we could secure a crossing over the Inn River at Wasserburg, so as to retain control of the road from Wasserburg to Altenmarkt and Salzburg, we would pinch out the embryonic ambitions of the Seventh Army.

I called Van Fleet on the telephone and asked him to do his damnedest to get the crossing at Wasserburg and also to get other units across the Inn in his sector. He made a task force and forced the crossing at Wasserburg before daylight, which was one of the most handsome and fastest operations of the war.

On the second, we were to move our Command Post from Erlangen to Regensburg, or Ratisbon, where Napoleon fought the famous battle and inspired the poem beginning: "You know, we French took Ratisbon, about a mile away, On a little mound Napoleon stood," etc. Apparently army commanders did not get as relatively near the front in those days as they do now.

Personally, I was unable to leave the Command Post until 1330, as I had to wait to find out from General Bradley whether or not we would continue the attack

on the "Redoubt" or turn it over to the Seventh Army.
At 1330 he gave me a new boundary, which answered
the question; the Seventh Army got the decision. This
boundary was as follows: the old boundary Third Army
and III Corps northwest of Freising; thence in a general
easterly direction to Mühldorf; thence along the Inn
River to the junction of the Inn and the Salzach Rivers;
thence to Strasswalchen; thence generally parallel to the
Enns River to where it joins the Danube at Mauthausen,
ten kilometers east of Linz. The Russians were on the
other side of this river. North of the Danube, the
temporary boundary between the United States and the
Russians was the railway running north from the point
where the Enns River enters the Danube. The result of
this boundary was practically to pinch out the III Corps
and also to give us a definite stop line.

Being of a hopeful nature, I told the III Corps to
hold on at Wasserburg, and also to get any other intact
crossings over the Inn River which they could find.

The Seventh Army asked us to take the 4th Infantry
Division (Major General H. W. Blakeley) from them
in exchange for our 86th Division at Wasserburg. Since
there was no help for it, we agreed. However, we succeeded in getting the 23d Reconnaissance Squadron (commanded by Lieutenant Colonel R. C. Adkinson) of the
16th Armored Division, which had been with the 86th,
pulled back, and also two companies of the 14th Armored Division which had been operating with the 86th.

I called the III Corps and told them what had
happened, but to keep going in the small zone which
was still open to them.

I had the idea of letting the XII Corps utilize the
crossing made at Passau by the 65th Division of the
XX Corps and move rapidly on Linz by the road
Scharding—Linz. However, General Gay and General
Maddox, dissuaded me, as they judged, more rightly than
I did, the small amount of opposition in front of the
XX Corps. I believe they also sensed, even at that time,
the possibility of changing direction to the northeast with
the XII Corps. There had been throughout the operation
a strange fatality about the times the Third Army moved
its Command Posts. Practically every time we moved

them, we got a change in direction or a change in mission.

On May 3 we heard over the radio of the unconditional surrender of the German troops in Italy.

Both the 65th Infantry Division of the XX Corps and the 11th Armored of the XII Corps continued crossing the rivers which had been holding them up, and advanced rapidly on Linz. I decided to send the 4th Infantry Division to Nuremberg on line of communication duty and, in the event of an operation in Czechoslovakia, to give the III Corps a division from either the XII or XX Corps.

We next visited the XX Corps Headquarters, which we found situated in a rather nice country house, with an excellent collection of old firearms. Apparently the ancestors of the owner had been proprietary colonels of an infantry regiment.

Driving back to Third Army Headquarters, we passed a large number of Hungarians who looked extremely well fed, and were moving happily along with only one of our soldiers for about a thousand prisoners.

We were very nearly killed by a bull-cart, which came out of a side street so that the pole missed us only by about an inch. The American soldier is absolutely incapable of enforcing the rule that civilians stay off the roads during active operations. His goodness of heart is a credit to him, but I am sure it has cost us many casualties. In war, time is vital, and bull-carts cause waste of time and therefore death.

If I were to fight another war, I would make it an inflexible rule that no civilian vehicle, horse, cow, or motor-drawn, appear on any axial road, and I would enforce this by shooting the animals and destroying the vehicles. I did this in Sicily and was criticized by an ignorant press, who considered it very brutal to kick a few donkeys off bridges, and ignored the fact that by so doing we took Palermo in one day and at very low cost. Again, during the Saar battle, through the co-operation of the local authorities, we kept all the axial roads, including those in the city of Nancy, cleared for our use.

On May 4, the 11th Armored passed the north-

and-south line through Linz and therefore was about to run into the Russians. On the initiative of General Irwin, the 90th Division, the 5th Division, and the 2d Cavalry Group (commanded by Colonel C. H. Reed) all secured crossings over the mountains into Czechoslovakia, so that, in case we had to attack Prague, we would at least be through the passes before anything hit us.

The V Corps, First Army, under General Huebner, was transferred to the Third Army. This gave us the biggest army we had yet had; namely, eighteen divisions, or slightly more than 540,000 men.

My old-time friend of 1912 at Saumur, the French five-star General Jean Houdemon, called to see me on the fourth. A cavalry officer in World War I, he later became an aviator and fought for France in World War II, until, as he said, "le vieux Pétain m'a renvoyé."[1] At that time he was sixty-four, and the senior flier in the French Army. He then retired to his home at Pont-à-Mousson, where he acted as mayor and maintained a hospital in his house during the German occupation. Under pretext of negotiating some sort of armistice for the evacuation of his sick, he and his daughter, Catherine, an *infirmière,* crossed the Moselle under fire and came to my Headquarters. As a young cavalry officer on maneuvers, he had learned all the fords at this point of the Moselle, and his real purpose was to indicate them to me. Unfortunately, I was absent, and the officer who saw him did not realize that he was acting in good faith and ordered him back across the river with a parting shot at his boat for luck. He insisted, however, on leaving a note for me with a chart of the fords and the information that the medieval château of Mousson, on a steep hill behind the town, was an important German Observation Post. His chart of the fords was the one we later used in crossing the Moselle. Two days after this visit to my Headquarters, the Germans evacuated him and we had quite a search trying to locate him and for a long time thought him dead. He was a very fine man and most interesting in his conversation. I later had him flown to Paris, which he enjoyed, as he had

---

[1] "The old Pétain sent me back."

been chief of the southern portion of the French Air Force prior to the fall of France. His daughter received the Croix de Guerre for her work in the war, which included the heroic rescue from the Moselle of two wounded American soldiers.

At 1930, General Bradley called up and said the green light was open for the attack on Czechoslovakia, and wanted to know when I could put it into effect. I told him next morning. He was somewhat incredulous, but, as we were pretty well used to each other, he believed me.

I immediately called the V Corps and told them to get going with the 1st (then commanded by Major General Clift Andrus) and the 2d Infantry Divisions[1] and the 16th Armored. I also told the XII Corps to attack as planned. General Gay, who has a sixth sense, had already alerted the 16th Armored in the afternoon, because he felt that something was going to happen. We were very anxious to get the 16th into a fight before the war stopped, and they were very anxious to get there.

---

[1] On May 5, 1945, the V Corps (Major General C. R. Huebner) was assigned to the Third Army.

General Huebner was sitting down to dinner, about seven-thirty, when his G-3 came in with orders assigning his corps to the Third Army. General Huebner remarked, "Well, I'll give us just about twelve hours before General Patton calls up and tells us to attack something." The soup was still hot when the Chief of Staff of the corps was called from the table to the phone. He came back with a grin on his face, saying, "General, it's General Patton. He wants to talk to you." The conversation went something like this:

"Hello, Huebner?"

"Hello, General. How are you?"

"Fine. Where in hell have you been since Sicily–"

"Oh, we've been around making a nusiance of ourselves."

"I'm sure glad you're back with me again."

"Glad to be back, General."

"I want you to attack Pilsen in the morning."

"Yes, sir."

"Can you do it?"

"Yes, sir."

"Fine, move fast now. We haven't got much time left in this war. I'll be up to see you. Good-bye."

General Huebner returned to his table and said, "Well, I missed that one. Instead of twelve hours, it was twelve minutes. We attack Pilsen at daybreak."

Both corps jumped off between 0800 and 1000 on the morning of the fifth, the V Corps with the 97th and 2d Infantry Divisions and part of the 16th Armored. The 1st Division was to join in the attack starting on the sixth, also a portion of the 9th Armored Division.

I had instructions from Bradley, which I passed on to the corps, that we were not to advance beyond a northwest-southeast line through Pilsen in large force, but could and should reconnoiter vigorously toward Prague.

The XII Corps jumped off with the 90th and 5th Divisions and also captured Linz with the 11th Armored and 26th Divisions, which were then released for action to the north by the 65th Infantry Division of the XX Corps.

I remember that, during this offensive, I was talking to General Paul, commanding the 26th, and he reminded me that when his division had gone in green on October 7, I had told him that his soldiers were a group of amateurs about to play in a professional league, and it behooved them to bestir themselves in order to compete with the pros. He said those remarks applied equally well to his final attack on Linz, because, owing to casualties and attrition, the division was largely filled with un-battlewise soldiers. However, there is a great difference between an old division, irrespective of the individuals composing it, and a new division. War develops a soul in a fighting unit, and while there may not be many of the old men left, it takes very little yeast to leaven a lump of dough. I suppose I might be funny and say it takes very few veterans to leaven a division of doughboys.

It is an unfortunate fact that few commanders, and no politicians, realize the individuality of units and the necessity of playing on human emotion. Speaking of this reminds me that this same Paul once told me, with perfect sincerity, that the greatest moment of his life had been at the Battle of the Bulge when I put my arm around him and said, "How is my little fighting son of a bitch today?" He said that this remark inspired not only him, but every man in the division, and it is highly probable that it did.

Huebner told me that when and if I met any Rus-

sians, I must be prepared for mutual exchange of
medals, flags, and personal equipment, and that for that
reason I had better not wear my good pistol nor my
expensive watch, as I would certainly not get the equivalent from the Russians in a swapping match. I immediately called General Bradley and asked what
authority I had to present medals. We arranged that we
would give medals approximately as follows: a division
could give six Legions of Merit of the lowest grade,
and six Bronze Stars to the Russian division with which
it made contact. In the corps, we could give nine
Legions of Merit and three Bronze Stars to the opposite
corps. In this case, half of the Legions of Merit were
of the officer grade. In the Army, we could give twelve
Legions of Merit of assorted grades, including the third,
or commander, grade, and piece out with a few Bronze
Stars if desirable. We immediately set to work and secured
the requisite number of medals.

In view of the radio reports that the Czechoslovakian
citizens had taken Prague, I was very anxious to go on
and assist them, and asked Bradley for authority to do
so, but this was denied. As a matter of fact, however,
reconnaissance elements of the Third Army were in the
vicinity of Prague, and by that act marked the farthest
progress to the east of any western army. Also, the Third
Army had the distinguished privilege of being the last
western army to maintain the offensive.

On the sixth it was definitely established that we
were not to pass beyond the stop line running through
Pilsen for greater distances than required by security
reconnaissance—up to about five miles. I was very much
chagrined, because I felt, and I still feel, that we should
have gone on to the Moldau River and, if the Russians
didn't like it, let them go to hell. I did not find out until
weeks afterward the reasons, which were sound, which
implemented General Eisenhower's decision to order us
to stop where he did.

We were also directed to stop our advance southeast in the Danube Valley and to stand fast where we
were until the Russians made contact with us. As of
1100, the leading Combat Command of the 16th Armored Division (commanded by Colonel C. H. Noble)

entered Pilsen. We moved the III Corps to the vicinity of Nuremberg to start occupying Bavaria under the so-called Eclipse Plan.[1]

It was also reported to us that one hundred thousand White Russians were attempting to surrender. These people were certainly in a bad fix and had a number of women and children with them. The soldiers were treated as prisoners of war, the women and children as displaced persons.

On the seventh, we knew the war would end at midnight on the night of May 8-9. Bradley sent a Russian colonel general through the V Corps to go to Prague and inform the German Army Group Commander there, General Sthoerner, of the rules for the surrender.

General Gay had the forethought to direct the Chief Surgeon of the Third Army personally to inspect Moosberg and to be sure that the Allied prisoners of war were getting proper medical attention and ample food.

Judge Patterson, the Under-Secretary of War, spent the night of May 6-7 with us and on the seventh we flew to the XX Corps, utilizing two Cubs. During this day we crossed the Enns River and also the Isar and at one point saw at least one hundred undestroyed locomotives on a side track.

On arrival at General Walker's Headquarters, we found that the XX Corps had captured intact, at an adjacent château, the whole of the Imperial Spanish Riding Academy which had left Vienna on the approach of the Russians. This Academy had been running in Vienna since the time of Charles V of Spain.

Originally the gyrations taught the horses were of military importance. That is, the courbette, or half-rear, was for the purpose of letting the horse come down at the same time that the sword was swung, so as to give the latter more force; the volte, or demi-volte, was for the purpose of avoiding attack; while the leap into the air, striking out fore and aft with the feet, was for the purpose of extricating the rider from too close contact with the enemy, and so on. With the passing years and changes in the art of war, the purpose of this form of

---

[1] The code name of the plan for the occupation of Germany.

equitation was forgotten, and the movements were taught as of value in themselves. In other words, people began, as in many other arts, to glorify the means rather than the end which the means were supposed to produce.

After lunch, General Walker arranged for us to witness one of the exhibitions, which was extremely interesting and magnificently performed. However, it struck me as rather strange that, in the midst of a world at war, some twenty young and middle-aged men in great physical condition, together with about thirty grooms, had spent their entire time teaching a group of horses to wiggle their butts and raise their feet in consonance with certain signals from the heels and reins. Much as I like horses, this seemed to me wasted energy. On the other hand, it is probably wrong to permit any highly developed art, no matter how fatuous, to perish from the earth—and which arts are fatuous depends on the point of view. To me the high-schooling of horses is certainly more interesting than either painting or music.

After leaving the XX Corps, the Under-Secretary and I flew over Linz, which was much more destroyed than I had thought. We then landed at the Headquarters of the XII Corps, where we were met by General Irwin. From there we flew back to Headquarters, arriving at 2000 o'clock.

The Under-Secretary has a most remarkable memory for names, and could tell the officers to whom he was introduced where he had last seen them. He is also exceptionally well informed on history, particularly that of the Civil War, so we had a very enjoyable talk together. He is the only member of the Government, so far as I know, who possesses the Distinguished Service Cross, which he won in the infantry in World War I.

After he left on the eighth, Bradley and Allen came to lunch and we discussed a number of points which we wished to determine about the zones we would occupy. However, owing to the fact that SHAEF had as yet not come to a decision, it was impossible to do more than surmise what was going to happen.

At the regular briefing on the morning of the eighth, I spoke to the officers stating that this was the last briefing we would have in Europe, emphasizing the word

"Europe." I think most of them realized I was hoping to have some more briefings in Asia, but "The best-laid plans of mice and men," etc. I then thanked each member of the Staff for what he had done and assured them that no one man can conduct an army, but that the success of any army depends on the harmonious working of its staff and the magnificent fighting ability of the combat officers and enlisted men. Without this teamwork, war cannot be successfully fought.

The eighth of May marked exactly two and one-half years since we had landed in Africa. During all that time until midnight of May 8-9, we had been in practically continuous battle, and, when not in battle, had been under the strain of continuous criticism, which I believe is harder to bear.

At 1130 I said good-bye to the war correspondents after having a final briefing with them, during which one of them said, "General, why didn't we take Prague?" I said, "I can tell you exactly why," whereupon they all got out their notebooks and looked expectant. I said, "Because we were ordered not to," which produced a laugh, even though they were disappointed. Afterward I signed a great many short snorter notes and posed for innumerable photographs with them. By and large the correspondents with the Third Army did a splendid and loyal job and succeeded in getting to the people at home an excellent and intimate picture of war as we fought it.[1]

I received a very fine letter of congratulation from

---

[1] Little or nothing is known or has ever been said of the Third Army's duplication of Hannibal's feat—crossing the Alps.

At war's end, when the situation in Jugoslavia was not clear, the Third Army was ordered to move five divisions into the Fifth Army and British Area, south of the Alps, north of Trieste. Without so much as a wink of an eyelash, the 3d United States Cavalry Group moved out. In twelve hours, it had crossed the Alps and was thoroughly mixed up with British troops in northern Italy. General Clark, who had not been informed of such a movement, made haste to congratulate General Patton on the alacrity and boldness of his movement; however, he lost no time in informing General Eisenhower that additional troops were not needed. General Clark requested that the troops be withdrawn—for administrative reasons.

They were—with the same zest and determination as aforementioned.

the Secretary of War, Mr. Stimson, which reads as follows:

> I congratulate you and your heroic soldiers of the Third Army. I commend you for the dashing and spectacular victories which have played a great part in bringing about this glorious day. The exploits of the Third Army have been in the highest traditions of the armies that have defended America throughout its history. You and your gallant forces well deserve the nation's homage.

This letter, I think, very fittingly marks the termination of the war, and, I fear, my last one.

I can say this, that throughout the campaign in Europe I know of no error I made except that of failing to send a Combat Command to take Hammelburg. Otherwise, my operations were, to me, strictly satisfactory. In every case, practically throughout the campaign, I was under wraps from the Higher Command. This may have been a good thing, as perhaps I am too impetuous. However, I do not believe I was, and feel that had I been permitted to go all out, the war would have ended sooner and more lives would have been saved. Particularly I think this statement applies to the time when, in the early days of September, we were halted, owing to the desire, or necessity, on the part of General Eisenhower in backing Montgomery's move to the north. At that time there was no question of doubt but that we could have gone through and on across the Rhine within ten days. This would have saved a great many thousand men.

As the Church says, "Here endeth the Second Lesson.")

The final casualty report, that of May 8, 1945, follows:

Third Army		Enemy	
Killed	21,441	Killed	144,500
Wounded	99,224	Wounded	386,200
Missing	16,200	Prisoners of War	956,000[1]
Total	136,865	Total	1,486,700
Non-battle casualties	111,562		
Grand Total	248,427		

Matériel Losses

Light tanks	308	Medium tanks	1529
Medium tanks	949	Panther and Tiger tanks	858
Guns	175	Guns	3454

---

[1]The prisoners of war scored above were those taken in actual battle prior to midnight of May 8-9. Subsequent to that date the taking of prisoners was not a sporting event, so I have not recorded it, although the numbers went into the millions. *Author's note.*

PART THREE
RETROSPECT

1

REFLECTIONS AND SUGGESTIONS

Probably there is nothing original in what I shall now put down, because war is an ancient subject and I, an ancient man, have studied and practiced it for over forty years. So, what appears to me as original thought may be simply subconscious memories.

I

CONCERNING THE SOLDIER

The soldier is the Army. No army is better than its soldiers. The soldier is also a citizen. In fact, the highest obligation and privilege of citizenship is that of bearing arms for one's country. Hence it is a proud privilege to be a soldier—a good soldier. Anyone, in any walk of life, who is content with mediocrity is untrue to himself and to American tradition. To be a good soldier a man must have discipline, self-respect, pride in his unit and in his country, a high sense of duty and obligation to his comrades and to his superiors, and self-confidence born of demonstrated ability.

There has been, and is now, a great deal of talk about discipline; but few people, in or out of the Army, know what it is or why it is necessary.

When a man enters the Army, he leaves home, usually for the first time, and also he leaves behind him the inhibitions resulting from his respect for the opinion of his parents and his friends; which inhibitions, unknown to himself, have largely guided his existence. When he joins a unit and lacks this corrective influence, he is apt to slip in morals, in neatness, and in energy. Administrative discipline must replace the absent inhibitions.

All human beings have an innate resistance to obedience. Discipline removes this resistance and, by constant repetition, makes obedience habitual and subconscious. Where would an undisciplined football team get? The players react subconsciously to the signals. They must, because the split second required for thought would give the enemy the jump.

Battle is much more exigent than football. No sane man is unafraid in battle, but discipline produces in him a form of vicarious courage which, with his manhood, makes for victory. Self-respect grows directly from discipline. The Army saying, "Who ever saw a dirty soldier with a medal?" is largely true. Pride, in turn, stems from self-respect and from the knowledge that the soldier is an American. The sense of duty and obligation to his comrades and superiors comes from a knowledge of reciprocal obligation, and from the sharing of the same way of life. Self-confidence, the greatest military virtue, results from the demonstrated ability derived from the acquisition of all the preceding qualities and from exercise in the use of weapons.

It is an unfortunate and, to me, tragic fact that, in our attempts to prevent war, we have taught our people to belittle the heroic qualities of the soldier. They do not realize that, as Shakespeare put it, the pursuit of "The bubble reputation even at the cannon's mouth" is not only a good military characteristic, but also very helpful to the young man when bullets and shells are whistling and cracking around him. Much more could be done if the women of America would praise their heroes, and if papers would publish the citations of soldiers in their home towns; and further, if foolish ideas of security did not make the citations so unrealistic. Perhaps the returning soldiers of this war may correct this very unfortunate situation.

One of Kipling's poems starts as follows:

When the 'arf-made recruity goes out to the East,
'E acts like a babe an' 'e drinks like a beast,

An' 'e wonders because 'e is frequent deceased
Ere 'e's fit for to serve as a soldier . . .[1]

All our soldiers do not drink like beasts. In fact, the lack of drinking in our Army is remarkable. However, many do act like babes. What follows is an attempt to make certain suggestions which have proved useful.

Do not dig slit trenches under trees if you can avoid it, because a shell passing overhead and striking the tree acts as an airburst and the fragments come straight down, so that your slit trench is useless to you, although it may be of some assistance to the Graves Registration people.

Slit trenches for gun crews must be in the close vicinity of the gun, else the men waste too much time getting from the trenches to the gun. Also they are just as apt to get killed while making the run as they would be if they stayed by the gun. Finally, a gun that is not firing is useless and its crew are disloyal to the soldiers in front of them, whom they are supposed to be supporting.

The trick expression, "Dig or die," is much overused and much misunderstood. Wars are not won by defensive tactics. Digging is primarily defensive. The only time it is proper for a soldier to dig is when he has reached his final objective in an attack, or when he is bivouacking under circumstances where he thinks he may be strafed from the air or is within artillery range of the enemy. Personally, I am opposed to digging under such circumstances, as the chance of getting killed while sleeping normally on the ground is quite remote, and the fatigue from digging innumerable slit trenches is avoided. Also, the psychological effect on the soldier is bad, because if he thinks he has to dig he must think the enemy is dangerous, which he usually is not.

"Hit the dirt" is another expression which has done much to increase our casualties. Frequently in fighting Germans, and probably other troops in the next war, we will find that they have resort to their knowledge of our custom of hitting the dirt. What they do is wait until

---

[1]*Barrack-Room Ballads,* "The Young British Soldier."

we have arrived at a predetermined spot on which they
have ranged rockets, mortars, or artillery and then they
put on a sudden and violent machine-gun fire—frequently straight up in the air. The soldier, obsessed with the
idea of hitting the dirt, lies down and waits supinely for
the arrival of the shells from the mortars, rockets, etc.
He usually does not have to wait long.

The only time it is proper for a soldier to drop is
when he is caught at short range—under three hundred
yards—by concentrated small-arms fire. But even then he
must not hit the dirt and stay supine. He must shoot fast
at the enemy, or in the direction of the enemy, because
it is as true now as when Farragut stated it in the Civil
War that "The best armor (and the best defense) is a
rapid and well-directed fire." It is a sad commentary on
our troops that frequently we get the report that such
and such a unit is pinned down under fire, and later
the same unit comes back.

When soldiers are caught in a barrage, either from
mortars, rockets, or artillery, the surest way to get out
of it is to go forward fast, because it is almost the invariable practice of the enemy to increase rather than
decrease his range.

In the days when the chief small-arms fire on the
battlefield was delivered by rifles, it may have been necessary to advance by rushing in order to build up the
firing line. Today, when the chief small-arms fire on the
battlefield and the majority of the neutralizing fire is delivered by machine guns, mortars, and artillery, there is
no advantage in advancing by rushes, because, until you
get within three hundred yards, small-arms fire has very
little effect, whereas when you lie down between rushes
you expose yourself to the effect of shrapnel. When you
get to three hundred yards, your own small-arms fire,
which is superior to anything now existing or which will
probably ever exist, will neutralize that of the enemy
small-arms fire, so that you do not have to advance by
rushes. I say this very feelingly because I have seen, on
many occasions in maneuvers and in battle, troops advancing by rushes when they were defiladed behind hills
and could have gone forward in limousines, had they
been available, with perfect impunity.

Marching Fire: The proper way to advance, particularly for troops armed with that magnificent weapon, the M-1 rifle, is to utilize marching fire and keep moving. This fire can be delivered from the shoulder, but it is just as effective if delivered with the butt of the rifle halfway between the belt and the armpit. One round should be fired every two or three paces. The whistle of the bullets, the scream of the ricochet, and the dust, twigs, and branches which are knocked from the ground and the trees have such an effect on the enemy that his small-arms fire becomes negligible.

Meanwhile, our troops in rear, using high-angle fire, should put out the enemy's mortars and artillery. As I have stated, even if we fail to put out the mortars and artillery, the most foolish thing possible is to stop under such fire. Keep walking forward. Furthermore, the fact that you are shooting adds to your self-confidence, because you feel that you are doing something, and are not sitting like a duck in a bathtub being shot at.

In marching fire all weapons must be used. The light machine guns can be used while walking—one man carrying the belt, the other man carrying the gun. The same is true of the Browning automatic rifle and, of course, of the M-1. The 60 mm. mortar, advanced by alternate sections, can do much in the same way. The 81 mm. usually should support from one position.

I think, if we should say that "Fire is the Queen

60 mm. Mortar

of Battles," we should avoid arm arguments and come nearer telling the truth. Battles are won by fire and by movement. The purpose of the movement is to get the fire in a more advantageous place to play on the enemy. This is from the rear or flank.

Every soldier should realize that casualties in battle are the result of two factors: first, effective enemy fire, and second, the time during which the soldier is exposed to that fire. The enemy's effectveness in fire is reduced by your fire or by night attacks. The time you are exposed is reduced by the rapidity of your advance.

Bravery and Courage: If we take the generally accepted definition of bravery as a quality which knows not fear, I have never seen a brave man. All men are frightened. The more intelligent they are, the more they are frightened. The courageous man is the man who forces himself, in spite of his fear, to carry on. Discipline, pride, self-respect, self-confidence, and the love of glory are attributes which will make a man courageous even when he is afraid.

The greatest weapon against the so-called "battle fatigue" is ridicule. If soldiers would realize that a large proportion of men allegedly suffering from battle fatigue are really using an easy way out, they would be less sympathetic. Any man who says he has battle fatigue is avoiding danger and forcing on those who have more hardihood than himself the obligation of meeting it. If soldiers would make fun of those who begin to show battle fatigue, they would prevent its spread, and also save the man who allows himself to malinger by this means from an after-life of humiliation and regret.

Trenchfoot: Soldiers must look after themselves, particularly in wet or cold weather. This applies particularly to "trenchfoot," which, with reasonable assistance by the Higher Command, can be largely prevented if the soldier will only take the trouble to massage his feet and put on dry socks. He is not responsible for the arrival of the dry socks, but, provided they do arrive, he is responsible for putting them on.

The same thing is true of venereal disease. Soldiers do not have to contract it if they will take the precautions which the military establishment provides. When they do contract it, they are disloyal to their comrades, because, while they are recovering, somebody else is doing their work.

II

SMALL UNIT TACTICS

Squads should seldom be split. However, if it is necessary to split a squad, be sure that the unit separated is at least capable of mutual support. This means that the unit separated from the squad should not be fewer than three men. The squad possesses in itself the weapons necessary for a base of fire and a maneuvering element. This should be its invariable method of attack, but the squad leader should not spend so much time thinking which way he is going to envelop that he suffers casualties which would have been avoided had he attacked at once.

In small operations, as in large, speed is the essential element of success. If the difference between the two possible flanks for envelopment is so small that it requires thought, the time wasted in thought is not well used. Remember that the life of the infantry squad depends on its capacity of fire. It must fire.

When a small unit disposes both 60 mm. and 81 mm. mortars in an attack, the 60 mm. mortars should fire on the front line of the resistance while the 81 mm. fire for depth and to hit the supports and heavy weapons.

Fighting in Woods: The best way for infantry to go through woods in the daytime is to advance in a skirmish line on a distant direct point, if such is available, or, more probably, on a compass bearing. The skirmish line should be at reduced interval, and should move straight forward through the wood, using marching fire. If this is done, it will be surprising how little resistance will be encountered, because, if the enemy attempts to fire through the woods, his rifles, which are always less effective than ours, will not penetrate through the trees, while ours will penetrate and so get him.

In fighting through European woods, which are intersected at right angles every thousand meters by lanes, do not walk down the lanes, and be careful how you cross them—cross them fast—because the enemy usually has them swept with machine guns.

81 mm. Mortar

Night Attack in Woods: It is not necessary or advisable to attack through woods at night. In the first place, the woods themselves give the cover which the darkness does in the open. In the second place, it is almost impossible to move through woods at night except in column on roads.

Tanks and Infantry: The question of whether infantry or tanks lead in attacking is determined by the character of the ground and of the enemy resistance. Whenever the ground permits tanks to advance rapidly, even the certainty of a loss from mine fields, they should lead. Through dense woods or against prepared positions or unlocated anti-tank guns, infantry leads, followed closely by the tanks, which act as close supporting artillery. But, irrespective of the foregoing, some tanks must accompany the infantry when they reach the objective. These tanks are for the purpose of removing enemy weapons which emerge after the passage of the leading tanks.

Pillboxes: Pillboxes are best attacked by the use of prearranged groups. A satisfactory group consists of two Browning automatic rifles, a bazooka, a light machine gun, two to four riflemen, and two men with the demolition charge. Sixty pounds of TNT is ample. Before

BAR

initiating an attack on a pillbox area, a reconnaissance should be made to determine which boxes are mutually supporting. Those in such a group must be attacked simultaneously. The best results are obtained by a silent night attack, which places the assault groups in position close to their respective pillboxes at dawn. The apertures are immediately taken under fire and silenced. When fire is achieved, the demolition charge, covered by riflemen and light machine guns, is placed against the door at the rear of the pillbox, the fuse is lit, and the men withdraw around the corner of the building. As soon as the charge is exploded, riflemen throw in grenades—preferably phosphorous. Any enemy emerging are killed or captured, according to the frame of mind of the enemy.

When circumstances prevent a night operation, similar but more expensive results are obtained by advancing close in the wake of an artillery concentration.

Another adjunct to the attack on pillboxes is a self-propelled 155 mm. gun where conditions permit its use. At short range the effects are very satisfactory.

Street Fighting: Street fighting is simply a variation of pillbox fighting. A similar group, but reinforced with more riflemen, is effective. The additional riflemen are split on opposite sides of the street so as to take under fire enemy personnel appearing in the upper stories on the side across from them. When a house offers resistance, the windows are silenced by fire as in the case of pill-boxes, and under cover of this immunity a bazooka crew fires one or two rounds at the corner of the house about three feet from the ground. When a hole has been made by this means, phosphorous or high-explosive grenades are thrown into the lower floor and cellar to discourage those operating there. The demolition essential in pillboxes is really not needed in street fighting.

In street fighting, it is very essential to avoid hurry-ing. One group, as above described, can usually clear a city block in twelve hours. When tanks are available, they replace the bazookas in blowing holes in the walls of the lower floor. However, they must be buttoned up to avoid grenades from the upper floors, and should be further protected by riflemen to keep the enemy from the win-dows. Self-propelled 155 mm. guns are extremely useful in cities against moderate masonry construction. One round with delayed fuse will breach all the houses on one side of a city block if fired at a very obtuse angle.

Two-Way Attack: Wherever possible, beginning with the squad, use a base of fire and a maneuvering element. The maneuvering element should be the larger of the two forces, and should start its attack well back from the point of contact of the base of fire. The maneuvering force must proceed sufficiently far beyond the hostile flank to attack from the rear. As soon as the enveloping attack, or, better, the rear attack, has progressed suffi-ciently to cause the enemy to react, the base of fire transforms itself into a direct attack along the original axis of advance.

River Crossings: In river crossings or assault land-ings, there is a high probability that the boats containing a company or even a platoon will not all land at the same point. Therefore, each boat should be organized on a boat-team basis and contain means for producing a base of fire and an encirclement. These boat teams should practice as such before embarking, and each boat team in the assault wave must be informed of the geographical feature to which the assault wave is supposed to penetrate. This geographical feature, preferably a road or railway, should be far enough from the water's edge to prevent small-arms fire bearing on the beach. No beachhead can be considered at all sure until it has advanced to a perimeter at least eight thousand yards from the beach and/ or occupies the controlling terrain features. In a night landing, desperate efforts must be made to gain this distance before daylight.

Hill Fighting: During fighting in hilly or rolling country, platoons get widely separated. The best practice is for the support and reserve squads of an attacking platoon to envelop on the uphill side. When you have once gained a ridge or a hogback, do not lose altitude.

Never attack along the bottom of a valley unless you have the heights on both sides in your possession. In all valleys there are geographical features which form obstacles to a direct advance, and subject those on the valley floor to observed fire from the heights.

Open Country: In open country with isolated groups of trees, avoid occupying the trees, because they will invariably be attacked by the enemy artillery and air. In this type of country, use dispersal in open fields. You may be able to use the woods as a decoy to draw enemy fire by the emplacement of bad camouflage along the edge, but do not get into the woods yourself.

By the same token, do not occupy as a Command Post the only house on a hill, as I have seen done, and do not put your Command Post, as I have also seen done, in the immediate vicinity of a monument located on the map, and which could be seen for several kilometers.

Large radio sets should not be in the immediate vicinity of a Command Post or of each other. They should be separated, camouflaged, and communicated with by telephone. Otherwise, the enemy air will home on them and get the Command Post.

Fire on Infested Areas: Owing to the pernicious traditions of our known distance rifle marksmanship, we are prone to hold our fire until we see targets. In battle these are seldom visible. When any group of soldiers is under small-arms fire, it is evident that the enemy can see them; therefore, men should be able to see the enemy, but seldom are. When this situation arises, they must fire at the portions of the hostile terrain which probably conceal enemy small-arms weapons. I know for a fact that such procedure invariably produces an effect and generally stops hostile fire. Always remember that it is much better to waste ammunition than lives. It takes at least eighteen years to produce a soldier, and only a few months to produce ammunition.

Surrender: Any soldier who surrenders with arms in his hands is not doing his duty to his country and is selling himself short, because the living conditions of the prisoner of war are extremely bad. Also the prisoner of war is apt to become the unintended victim of our own air and artillery bombardment.

If the enemy indicates a desire to surrender, make him come to you with his hands up. Don't advance toward him, and do not stop shooting until he does so surrender himself. When the enemy has surrendered, he must be treated in accordance with the rules of land warfare.

II

BATTLE TRICKS

Bridges: In river crossings, all bridges must be one way—toward the enemy—until the situation has steadied. Prior to that time, wounded and empty transportation come back in ferries.

In building an assault bridge over rapid water, put the anchor cable as high as possible—at least ten feet above the water. This will prevent the floats from submerging.

Mines and Barbed Wire: Do not use mines or wire on the defensive except in the form of booby traps, to give warning of enemy prowlers. Mining and wiring a position has a very bad effect on the morale of our troops. As a feint, however, mining and wiring may be useful. For example, we could put light wire in a dummy mine field across a section of the front over which we intend to attack and ostentatiously leave other sections of the front unwired; then, when the attack starts, we need not bother about the dummy mine field and the wire can be got rid of rapidly.

Methods of Attack: If, in a unit the size of a division, the attack is not going well four hours after it starts, it is necessary to make a careful personal reconnaissance and see if it may not be necessary to change the emphasis; because four hours of fighting should produce substantial effects. This does not mean that a man should be wobbly about continuing in the face of uncertain victory, but it does mean that, after four hours, one should know whether the thing is going to be a go or not, and if it is not, he should slow up his attack on the old line while implementing it in a new direction.

Frontal Attacks: Do not try a sneak frontal attack at night or in the daytime against a dug-in enemy who has been facing you for some time. He will have ultimate bands of fire arranged. Therefore, he must be pounded by air and guns before you attack. This does not apply to a pillbox line. If the enemy is occupying the pillboxes and not the trenches outside them, a sneak attack is quite all right with the purpose of getting the troops in the immediate vicinity of the pillboxes just at dawn. If the enemy is occupying trenches outside the pillboxes, he must be pounded consistently to make him take shelter in the pillboxes, where he is much less dangerous than outside.

Use of Telephone Wire: In all attacks, make the maximum use of wire lines and use every effort to keep it up with the advancing units. Radio, while theoretically efficient, is not so good as wire, and should be considered as a secondary means of communication. On one occasion we actually launched a tank attack by quite a large number of tanks at the end of seventeen miles of wire.

Place to Attack: Never attack where the enemy expects you to come. It is much better to go over difficult ground where you are not expected than it is over good ground where you are expected. This remark applies to units to include the division. For corps and larger units an exception is necessary, in that such units must take ground where roads and railways permit the establishment of lines of supply. These roads and railways will probably be defended. The point is that the division must secure them by attacking over hard ground and not by going up the railway or road.

Fire and Movement: The policy of holding the enemy by the nose with fire and kicking him in the pants with movement is just as true as when I wrote it, some twenty years ago, and at that time it had been true since the beginning of war. Any operation, reduced to its primary characteristics, consists in moving down the road until you bump into the enemy. It may be one road or it may be several roads. When you have bumped, hold him at the point of contact with fire about a third of your command. Move the rest in a wide envelopment so that you can attack him from his rear flank. The enveloping attack should start first. The initial nose attack starts to move forward only when the enemy has properly reacted to the enveloping attack. Then the direct attack can go in easily and fast.

Time Fire: Either proximity or normal time fire is very efficient as a means of covering a tank attack and will frequently prevent the enemy from manning his anti-tank guns. Tanks can move with perfect impunity under time fire provided by either 105 mm. or 155 mm. projectiles. Proximity fuses in woods are wasteful, because the projectile explodes above the top of the tallest trees and the fragments are absorbed in the woods before they get down to where they will have much effect on the enemy.

In shelling woods to produce casualties, use slight-delay fuses so that they will not burst until they hit a reasonable size limb or tree trunk.

Envelopments: Vertical or horizontal envelopment for tactical effect should not go too deep or be too large. The best results are attained when the envelopment arrives in or just back of the enemy's artillery positions. Here you disrupt his supply and signal communications and his guns, and are close enough to the troops advancing along the axis to be sure of making contact in a reasonable time.

Cemeteries: Do not place military cemeteries where they can be seen by replacements marching to the front. This has a very bad effect on morale, even if it adds to the pride of the Graves Registration Service.

Haste and Speed: There is a great difference between

these two words. Haste exists when troops are committed without proper reconnaissance, without the arrangement for proper supporting fire, and before every available man has been brought up. The result of such an attack will be to get the troops into action early, but to complete the action very slowly.

Speed is acquired by making the necessary reconnaissance, providing the proper artillery and other tactical support, including air support, bringing up every man, and then launching the attack with a predetermined plan so that the time under fire will be reduced to the minimum. At the battalion level four hours spent in preparation for an attack will probably insure the time under fire not exceeding thirty minutes. One hour spent in the preparation of an attack will almost certainly insure time under fire lasting many hours with bloody casualties.

Covering Detachments: Make the maximum use of mechanized and armored reconnaissance and covering detachments. In actual war, these merge into each other. In general, they should consist of a reconnaissance troop reinforced by at least a platoon of medium tanks with infantry riding on them.

Maximum Use of Vehicles: In a modern infantry division, if every available vehicle—tanks, armored cars, gun carriages, AA guns and trucks—is utilized, no soldier need, or should, walk until he actually enters battle. While the sight of a division moving under this system is abhorrent to the best instincts of a Frederickan soldier, it results in rapid advance with minimum fatigue. Units so mounted are dismounted by placing a sign, or even a guidon, on the side of the road indicating the dismounting point.

MISCELLANEOUS NOTES

During mobile operations it is better to use secondary roads for the axis of advance than primary roads. In the first place, the secondary roads are less apt to be thoroughly guarded, and, in the second place, there will be fewer demolitions on them. The primary roads must be repaired as promptly as possible behind the fighting front to secure efficient supply lines.

Obstacles and demolitions, unless defended, are of little value. It is not necessary to sit on a demolition or obstacle in order to defend it, because the enemy will place fire there. These points are best defended from a distance of several hundred yards for small arms and from normal artillery range for that arm.

Administrative discipline is the index of combat discipline. Any commander who is unwilling or unable to enforce administrative discipline will be incapable of enforcing combat discipline. An experienced officer can tell, by a very cursory administrative inspection of any unit, the caliber of its commanding officer.

The more senior the officer, the more time he has. Therefore, the senior should go forward to visit the junior rather than call the junior back to see him. The exception to this is when it is necessary to collect several commanders for the formulation of a co-ordinated plan. In that case, the juniors should report to the superior headquarters.

There is a very great danger in making retrograde movements at night, even when these movements are for a continuation of the tactical offensive, because troops not involved hear or see them and become worried to the extent of panic. If a unit must be withdrawn, see that all soldiers along the line of withdrawal are informed why it is taking place and when it will occur.

Hospitals should be set up in the open so that the enemy has no excuse for thinking them other than what they are. They must not be placed in the vicinity of dumps or air strips.

Never halt on the near side of a river or mountain range. Secure a bridgehead in both cases, because, even if you do not intend to exploit the crossing, the possession of a bridgehead on the far side cramps the enemy's style.

In an infantry or armored division, relief of the division or immediate replacements are vitally necessary as soon as seventy-five per cent of the riflemen have become casualties.

Always capture the highest terrain feature in your vicinity at once, and stay on it.

Prisoner of war guard companies, or an equivalent organization, should be as far forward as possible in action to take over prisoners of war, because troops heated with battle are not safe custodians. Any attempt to rob or loot prisoners of war by escorts must be strictly dealt with.

Whenever officers enter a prisoner of war cage, all prisoners of war must come to attention.

IV

COMMAND

Use of Codes: The decision as to whether to use clear or code radio or wire communications is very easily reached on the following basis: if the period of action is shorter than the period of reaction, use clear; otherwise use code. By this I mean that if you tell a combat team to attack at 1000 and your experience shows that the enemy cannot react to the information until 1100, use clear; and so on for higher units.

Judging Reports: When you receive reports of counterattacks, find out who sent them—that is, the size of the unit which sent them. A squad occupying a position will report an enemy section approaching it as a counter-attack, but such a counter-attack has no material effect on a division or a corps.

Night Attacks: Soldiers must be taught to move and fight at night. This is becoming more and more imperative, and it does not mean to make an approach march at night. It means to conduct lethal operations in the dark. To do this, previous and very accurate daylight reconnaissance is desirable and limited objective attacks are essential. In addition to the usual reserve following such an attack, a second reserve should be at hand to move up after daylight in case the enemy counter-attacks.

Timely Thoughts on Supply: Reasonable study and a consultation of the almanac will avoid situations in which, through lack of forethought, heavy clothing, etc., have not been ordered in time.

Similarly, a knowledge of the tactical situation will insure that gasoline and ammunition are asked for in time. The Combat Service and not the Supply Service is responsible for failure to get such things.

In wet weather it is vital that dry socks come up for

the soldiers daily with the rations. These socks should be wool, or an analogous thick material treated so it will not shrink.

With the advent of almost unlimited motor transport, it is foolish to load soldiers down with blankets, etc. This is particularly true in wet and cold weather. The answer is to see that light bedrolls go up to the ammunition distributing point prior to dark, where they are picked up by units and used during the night, rolled up by the men, and left to be picked up again by rear units. This sounds wasteful, because the bedrolls cannot be accounted for, but it is much cheaper than pneumonia.

The fighting soldier should carry nothing into battle except what he wears, his ammunition, his rations, and his toilet articles. When he goes back, he should get new uniform, new underclothes, new everything.

The two-bag system ("A" and "B") with which we began this war is utterly foolish, because by the time the "B" bags get up, many of their owners have become casualties.

In landing operations and river crossings where men lose their clothes or become very wet, assorted sizes of uniforms, complete with helmet, belt, shoes, underclothes, etc., should be provided for twenty per cent of the command and should arrive with the second echelon of the landing. This insures that those who have lost their clothing are immediately reequipped with a minimum of cluttering of the supply lines.

The chief purpose of the General and Special Staffs is to insure that the troops get what they want in time. In battle, troops get temperamental, and ask for things which they really do not need. However, where humanly possible, their requests, no matter how unreasonable, should be answered.

Supply and administrative units and installations are frequently neglected by combat commanders. It is very necessary to their morale and efficiency that each one be inspected by the senior general of the unit with which it is operating.

Length of Attack: Infantry troops can attack continuously for sixty hours. Frequently much time and suffering are saved if they will do so. Beyond sixty hours, it is rather a waste of time, as the men become too fatigued from lack of sleep.

Marching at Night: Marching at night in the proximity of the enemy is not economical. It is better to halt two hours before dark, see that the men are fed, their socks dried if the weather is wet, and the vehicles serviced and made ready for the next day. Then start before dawn. Except under very favorable circumstances of terrain, and where very thorough daylight reconnaissance has taken place, night attacks by armor are not economical.

Look Before Changing: In the old Navy of sail there was a custom that the new Officer of the Deck did not call for any change in the setting of the sails for one half hour—that is, for one bell after he took over. The same thing might well apply to commanders and staff officers who take over new jobs in war. They should wait at least a week before they make any radical changes, unless and except they are put in to correct a situation which is in a bad way.

Don't Delay: The best is the enemy of the good. By this I mean that a good plan violently executed *now* is better than a perfect plan next week. War is a very simple thing, and the determining characteristics are self-confidence, speed, and audacity. None of these things can ever be perfect, but they can be good.

Reports: In war nothing is ever as bad, or as good, as it is reported to Higher Headquarters. Any reports which emanate from a unit after dark—that is, where the knowledge has been obtained after dark—should be viewed with skepticism by the next higher unit. Reports by wounded men are always exaggerated and favor the enemy.

Identification: Legible unit signs in the clear are more valuable than dangerous, and they should be placed where they can be seen.

Sand-Table Exercises by staffs up to and including corps or army, even on the most rudimentary type of sand table, are extremely helpful prior to an attack.

General Officers: There are more tired division commanders then there are tired divisions. Tired officers are always pessimists. Remember this when evaluating reports. Generals must never show doubt, discouragement, or fatigue. Generals should adhere to one type of dress so that soldiers will recognize them. They must always be very neat.

In cold weather, General Officers must be careful not to appear to dress more warmly than the men.

Commanders and their staffs should visit units two echelons below their own, and their maps should be so kept. In other words, Corps Commanders or their staffs should visit Division and Regimental Command Posts; the Division Commander should visit Regimental and Battalion Command Posts; the visits above referred to are for command purposes. What might be called inspirational visits should go farther up. The more senior the officer who appears with a very small unit at the front, the better the effect on the troops. If some danger is involved in the visit, its value is enhanced.

When speaking to a junior about the enemy confronting him, always understate their strength. You do this because the person in contact with the enemy invariably overestimates their strength to himself, so, if you understate it, you probably hit the approximate fact, and also enhance your junior's self-confidence.

All officers, and particularly General Officers, must be vitally interested in everything that interests the soldier. Usually you will gain a great deal of knowledge by being interested, but, even if you do not, the fact that you appear interested has a very high morale influence on the soldier.

In my experience, all very successful commanders are prima donnas, and must be so treated. Some officers require urging, others require suggestions, very few have to be restrained.

A General Officer who will invariably assume the responsibility for failure, whether he deserves it or not, and invariably give the credit for success to others, whether they deserve it or not, will achieve outstanding success.

In any case, letters of commendation and General Orders presenting to the command the glory and magnitude of their achievements have a great influence on morale.

Corps and Army Commanders must make it a point to be physically seen by as many individuals of their command as possible—certainly by all combat soldiers. The best way to do this is to assemble the divisions, either as a whole or in separate pieces, and make a short talk.

When a unit leaves your command, if its performance at all justifies it, a letter of farewell and commendation to the unit should be sent.

During battle, it is very important to visit frequently hospitals containing newly wounded men. Before starting such an inspection, the officer in charge of the hospital should inform the inspecting General which wards contain men whose conduct does not merit compliments.

Generals and their principal staff officers should keep diaries.

Avoid the vicious habit of naming the next superior as the author of any adverse criticism while claiming all complimentary remarks for yourself.

Inspections: When a unit has been alerted for inspection, do not fail to inspect it and inspect it thoroughly. Further, do not keep it waiting. When soldiers have gone to the trouble of getting ready to be inspected, they deserve the compliment of a visit. Be sure to tell the unit commander publicly that his unit was good, if such is the case. If it is bad, tell him privately and in no uncertain terms. Be sure to speak to all enlisted men who have decorations, or who have been wounded, and ask how they got the decoration or how they were wounded.

Infantry and Armored Divisions: The chief difference between infantry divisions supplied with tanks and armored divisions is that, in the infantry division, the purpose of the tanks is to get the infantry forward. In the armored division, the function of the infantry is to break the tanks loose. In the infantry division, the tanks use their guns to facilitate the advance of the infantry. In the armored division, and tank uses its gun to break through to a range where it can use its machine guns. It is therefore of vast importance that two, instead of one, co-axial machine guns be placed in the mantle of all tanks.

Air-Ground Co-operation: The effectiveness of air-ground co-operation is still in its infancy. Air and ground commanders must be constantly on the alert to devise, and use, new methods of co-operation.

Fire Power: There can never be too many projectiles in a battle. Whether they are thrown by cannon, rockets, or recoilless devices is immaterial. The purpose of all these instruments is identical—namely, to deluge the enemy with fire. Nor is it necessary that these projectiles be discharged on the ground.

Issuing Orders: The best way to issue orders is by word of mouth from one general to the next. Failing this, telephone conversation which should be recorded at each end. However, in order to have a confirmatory memorandum of all oral orders given, a short written order should always be made out, not necessarily at the time of issuing the order, but it should reach the junior prior to his carrying out the order; so that, if he has forgotten anything, he will be reminded of it, and, further, in order that he may be aware that his senior has taken definite responsibility for the operation ordered orally.

It is my opinion that Army orders should not exceed a page and a half of typewritten text and it was my practice not to issue orders longer than this. Usually they can be done on one page, and the back of the page used for a sketch map.

Commanders must remember that the issuance of an order, or the devising of a plan, is only about 5 per cent of the responsibility of command. The other ninety-five per cent is to insure, by personal observation, or through the interposing of staff officers, that the order is carried out. Orders must be issued early enough to permit time to disseminate them.

Never tell people *how* to do things. Tell them *what* to do and they will surprise you with their ingenuity.

Avoid as you would perdition issuing cover-up orders, orders for the record. This simply shows lack of intestinal fortitude on the part of the officer signing the orders, and everyone who reads them realizes it at once.

In planning any operation, it is vital to remember, and constantly repeat to oneself, two things: "In war nothing is impossible, provided you use audacity," and "Do not take counsel of your fears." If these two principles are adhered to, with American troops victory is certain.

Maps: In my opinion the use of large-scale maps by senior officers is distinctly detrimental, because by the use of such maps they get themselves enmeshed in terrain conditions.

Putting it in general terms, Army and Corps Commanders are not so much interested in *how* to beat the enemy from a tactical standpoint as in where to beat him. The where is learned from a careful study of road, railway, and river maps. The question of the tactical means to be used by divisions in securing these points is, of necessity, studied from large-scale maps. However, the size of the map used does not continue to increase as the size of the using unit diminishes. At the level of the regiment, a map should be sufficiently large and accurate to assist the commander in selecting his Observation Posts and Command Post and his general line. For the rest, he should rely on personal reconnaissance on the ground. From the battalion down, the use of maps is of no value and is frequently fraught with great danger. I have never seen a good battalion commander direct his units from a map. I have seen many bad battalion commanders indulge in this pusillanimous method of command.

Staff Organization: The Headquarters of higher units —that is, Corps and Army—should be arranged by sections as follows: the Forward Echelon consisting of the Commanding General, Chief of Staff, Secretary of the General Staff, G-1, G-2, G-3, Engineers, Field Artillery, Anti-Aircraft, Signal, and Co-operating Air. Also subsections of the Provost Marshal, Special Troops, Headquarters Commandant, and liaison representatives from G-4, Ordnance, Medical, Quartermaster, and G-5 Sections. Where circumstances require, this Forward Echelon can be divisible into an advance Tactical Headquarters consisting of the Commanding General, Forward Echelon Chief of Staff, and a small operation section of G-2, G-3, Engineers, Field Artillery, and Signal. In this Advance Section it is desirable but not necessary to have a liaison group from G-4.

The Rear Echelon should be under the command of G-4 and contain G-5, Chemical Warfare, Finance, Medical, Quartermaster, Ordnance, Signal, Engineers, Adjutant General, Inspector General, Judge Advocate General, Special Services, and Chaplain.

Wherever circumstances permit, and accommodations warrant, all three echelons should be together. The Rear Echelon must be in one place and within easy driving distance, not to exceed three hours, of the Forward Echelon. Ample wire communications between the Forward and Rear Echelons must exist.

Headquarters Arrangements: All Headquarters, from Regiment up to Army, should be laid out on the same general plan so that any visitor who finds himself at the Message Center will know in which direction to go to find any section.

Trucks arranged for sleeping accommodations for General and Senior Staff Officers save much time and promote efficiency. In addition, in the Forward Echelon there should be three large office trailers—one for the Commanding General and Chief of Staff, one for the G's, and one for the Secretary of the General Staff and the clerks and stenographers, so that paper work and planning may be carried out during inclement weather.

A ruined building is better than a good tent for offices, dining room, and kitchen. In any staff office, or trailer, the telephone should be placed near the principal map, so that the officer consulting the map may talk over the telephone at the same time he scans the map. It is a strange commentary on human weaknesses that the Third Army, in occupying its twenty-third Command Post, placed the map and telephone on opposite sides of the room.

In my opinion, generals—or at least the Commanding General—should answer their own telephones in the daytime. This is not particularly wearisome because few people call a general, except in emergencies, and then they like to get him at once. At night the phone of the Commanding General should be answered by an Aide, who should have means of buzzing either the Commanding General or the Chief of Staff, depending on for whom the message is intended. It is very important that a stenographer or a stenographic reporting machine be constantly on duty, so that the Chief of Staff or the Commanding General will have a written transcript of any telephone messages. This is particularly important when they receive or issue orders by telephone. This record must show date, time, place, and the two speakers. Adherence to the foregoing will save many mistakes and prevent much acrimonious discussion.

In every type of Headquarters there are, during each

twenty-four-hour period, two peak loads. During these peak hours all officers and enlisted men should be present. During the slow periods, the maximum number of officers and enlisted men should be absent eating, sleeping, or exercising. Many officers have, to my knowledge, destroyed their future usefulness by being too conscientious at the beginning of a campaign and being always at their desk. This must not be done and they *must* take exercise.

A secretary for the General Staff, with a competent Deputy Chief of Staff, is a vital necessity to see that the subsections and sections of the General and Special Staffs do not get too independent and issue contradictory orders. The Deputy Chief of Staff is the bottleneck through which these orders must go.

At the Army, Corps, and Division level, the Forward Echelon of each staff should have a staff meeting, or briefing, daily, as early as the Headquarters under consideration can obtain the information for the day. In my opinion this time varies as follows: Division—one hour after dawn; Corps—two hours after dawn; Army—three hours after dawn.

One officer from each staff section of Corps and Army should go to the front daily and visit corresponding officers of the next lower echelon. However, he should also collect general information not normally applicable to his branch or section. Anything of vital moment obtained during his visit he will report to the Chief of Staff immediately on his return. If it is not vital, he will bring it up at the staff conference the next day. The Commanding General or the Chief of Staff must visit part of the front daily after the briefing.

The Commanding General, or the Chief of Staff of the Tactical Air Command operating with an army, should be present at all staff conferences and planning meetings. If this is not done, the maximum co-operation with this powerful arm will not be obtained. The A-3 must work with the G-3 and the A-2 with the G-2.

Staff officers of inharmonious disposition, irrespective of their ability, must be removed. A staff cannot function properly unless it is a united family.

Decorations: It is vital to good morale that decorations get out promptly and on an equitable basis. There should be in every Army and Corps Staff one member of

G-1 Section whose duty it is to prod divisions and attached lower units to get citations out. He should further see that they are properly written. When time permits, there should be a citation writers' school attended by officers from Corps, Army, and Division G-1 sections.

Casualty Reports: Similarly, there should be an administrative school attended by officers from Division, Corps, and Army, where special attention is given to Casualty Reports, etc. In order to know constantly the situation, two sets of Casualty Reports, both enemy and our own, must be kept. One is based on factual reports, the other on estimates. The one based on factual data usually lags from two to three weeks behind the estimated one. However, if properly made, the estimated report will be within two or three per cent of the factual report.

Equality of Punishments: The Judge Advocate and the Inspector General should make checks and see that the schedule of punishments accorded for analogous crimes in each unit below them is generally the same, so that a general level and equality of punishment will exist through the Army.

V

GENERAL

One of the great defects in our military establishment is the giving of weak sentences for military offenses. The purpose of military law is administrative rather than legal. As the French say, sentences are for the purpose of encouraging the others. I am convinced that, in justice to other men, soldiers who go to sleep on post, who go absent for an unreasonable time during combat, who shirk in battle, should be executed; and the Army Commanders or Corps Commanders should have the authority to approve the death sentence. It is utterly stupid to say that General Officers, as a result of whose orders thousand of gallant and brave men have been killed, are not capable of knowing how to remove the life of one miserable poltroon.

Uniforms: The purpose of the uniform is to provide the soldier with something he can wear which makes him look like other soldiers, and which is warm or cool according to circumstances. In my opinion, the proper uniform for the American soldier is the helmet with liner, and olive-drab wool shirt and trousers, the trousers cut reasonably narrow at the bottom, and combat boots. When weather becomes cool in the fall, the weight of the shirt and trousers can be increased up to twenty-six- or thirty-ounce cloth. At the same time, the soldier should be issued heavy underwear and socks (all wool) and a forty-eight-inch woolen muffler which he can wear around his neck, around his head at night, or around his stomach.

In zero or sub-zero weather the soldier should, in addition, be issued an overcoat of the trench-coat variety with a liner, but without a belt, and provided in front with a muff in which he can thrust his hands so that he can use his gun trigger without the necessity of removing his gloves.

Use of Sight: The peep-sight is not adapted to warfare, since it is inefficient in the dark, or in a bad light. I have met only three or four officers, out of hundreds questioned, who have ever seen a soldier set a sight in battle. Therefore, our rifles should be equipped with two open sights—one for a range of one hundred yards, one for a range of three hundred yards. This will insure that the soldier shoots low and will correct for the fact that in the excitement of battle he always takes too much front sight.

Gun Slings: The same officers whom I questioned on the sight informed me that they had never seen a gun sling used, except on two occasions by snipers, as an aid to firing. Therefore, the heavy and expensive leather gun sling should be dispensed with and a cloth sling, used solely for the purpose of carrying the piece, should be substituted.

Mortars: Infantry mortars should be provided with an illuminating device for night firing.

Red Cross Marking: Ambulances should be painted white all over, except for a large Red Cross on top, sides, back, and front.

Attached medical personnel with front-line units should have a tabard covering the whole chest and back as far as the belt. For combat this should be white with a large Red Cross back and front. When approaching combat and white would be too easily seen from the air, the reverse side of the tobard, olive-drab, with a small red cross, is worn.

Air Attacks: We know the effect of our attacks on the enemy's means of signal, rail, and road communication. We must therefore contemplate similar attacks upon our means of communication, and think how we can get on with those means limited or destroyed.

Where possible, it is best to request the Air to cut railways far from cities and to cut them at three points, because this entails great delay in getting to the center point from either direction. It also makes it necessary to move the repair crews over considerable distances, and forces them to work at points from which they can more easily be attacked from the air; because out in the country there are, as a general thing, no anti-aircraft guns.

After-Action Reports: As soon as an operation starts, a group composed of officers from G-2 and G-3 should start the compilation of the After-Action Report which should be organized on a calendar month basis, so that each month is a complete entity. At the termination of hostilities, the data thus secured can be re-edited on a campaign basis. This report must contain copies of orders, letters of instruction, maps, etc.

Guards on Trains: Railroad trains, carrying rations, or fuel, or other articles with a sales value on the black market, must be guarded, and any persons attempting pillage must be shot and the fact published.

Dead and Wounded Casualties: In order to evaluate properly the effectiveness of enemy fire, more information than that now obtainable on the subject of casualties is necessary. At the present time, we know only the number of casualties and the type of wounds of those reaching the hospitals, but even in their case, we do not know on what part of the battlefield they were wounded. We have no knowledge of how, or where, battle deaths occurred. In collecting wounded, a method should be prescribed which would show that a man was hit in the vicinity of such and such a point. The Graves Registration personnel should state what type of missile caused death. No medical experience is necessary. Anybody who has seen a few wounds can tell a small-arms wound from a fragmentation wound. This information should be made of record. The location of both types of casualties could be secured through the issue of sketch maps to Medical and Graves Registration personnel. The purpose in collecting the foregoing information is that, if we know what causes our casualties and where they occur, we can take steps to avoid them.

Overhead Cover: Owing to the certainty that, in the next war, the enemy will have proximity fuses, we must contemplate the necessity of providing all mechanized combat weapons, including artillery pieces, with overhead cover.

Replacements: When the current infantry division has lost four thousand men, its offensive value is zero, because ninety-two per cent of these four thousand men are riflemen and there are less than four thousand riflemen in a division. The same fact applies, with slightly less emphasis, to armored divisions. Therefore, every division must have a replacement battalion organic in the division. In an infantry division, this replacement battalion should contain fifteen per cent of the rifle strength of the division, and five per cent of all other, including company officers. There should be a company for each infantry regiment, and a company for all others.

A similar unit in an armored division should contain ten per cent of the rifle strength of the armored infantry, ten per cent of the personnel strength of the armored battalions, and five percent of all others, including company officers.

During a campaign, the returned wounded will occasionally produce a state where the strength of the replacement battalion is over the percentages recommended, but one or two days of battle will invariably correct this situation. It is vital to morale that men return to their old units without loss of rank.

American Ingenuity: The Americans, as a race, are the foremost mechanics in the world. America, as a nation, has the greatest ability for mass production of machines. It therefore behooves us to devise methods of war which exploit our inherent superiority. We must fight the war by machines on the ground, and in the air, to the maximum of our ability, particularly in view of the fact that the two races left which we may have to fight are both poor mechanics but have ample manpower. While we have amply manpower, it is too valuable to be thrown away.

Loyalty: There is a great deal of talk about loyalty from the bottom to the top. Loyalty from the top down is even more necessary and much less prevalent.

In terminating these remarks, it is sad to remember that, when anyone has fairly mastered the art of command, the necessity for that art usually expires—either through the termination of the war or through the advanced age of the commander.

2

EARNING MY PAY

The responsibilities of an officer are quite analogous to those of a policeman or a fireman. The better he performs his daily tasks, the less frequently does he have to take direct action.

Looking back over my rather lengthy military career, I am surprised at the few times when I have, so to speak, earned my pay. Perhaps, however, the fact that I have had to take drastic action so seldom indicates that, in the interim, I did my·duty.

The following episodes stand out in my mind as occasions on which my personal intervention had some value.

I

The Cadets of the Military Academy have, on a few occasions, taken upon themselves the dubious responsibility of being supercritical of officers through what is known as a "Silence." This act is performed when the officer whom they consider to be in error enters the Mess Hall. All Cadets come to attention and do not move or speak while he is there. I have always been opposed to such acts, as, to me, it is very close to mutiny.

On one occasion, when I happened to be in command of the Battalion and had marched it to lunch, the officer in charge entered, and I immediately saw that a "Silence" was about to be perpetrated. I felt that the Cadets were misinformed upon this officer and, in any case, I was against "Silence." I therefore called the Corps to attention and marched them home without lunch. The officer, who was somewhat young and inexperienced, criticized me for my action until I explained why I did it.

II

During the summer of 1914, I happened to be the only officer on duty at Fort Riley, Kansas, when one of the colored soldiers was accused of having raped a white girl in the neighboring town. It was rumored that the inhabitants intended to lynch this man. Naturally I am opposed to rape. However, I felt that it was my duty as an officer to see that the soldier of the United States Army was not lynched. I, therefore, informed the leading citizens that, if any such attempt were made, it would be over my dead body. As a result of my stand, the man was not lynched, and, later, was proven not guilty.

III

During the border troubles in 1916, I was on duty in charge of a patrol of twenty men at Hot Wells, Texas. My mission was to protect from attacks by the Villistas some forty miles of the Southern Pacific Railroad, over which Carranzista trains were operating. Hot Wells was the center of my sector. I sent a sergeant with half my command to the west and took the remainder to the east, having previously telephoned the Commanding Officer of the 13th Cavalry that I would take over to include a certain bridge. As we approached this bridge in the dark, the point came back and reported to me that he heard voices on the bridge speaking Spanish. I therefore presumed that the Villistas were mining the Bridge. It has always been my belief that a surprise attack is correct. I therefore formed my group in line and gave the command, "Raise pistols, Charge!" Just as we got under the very shadow of the bridge, we ran into a wire fence and had to stop. At the same time a number of rifles stuck over the top of the bridge. I challenged with much profanity, demanding who was there, and was greatly relieved when a voice replied, "Patrol, 13th Cavalry." They had missed the bridge where they were supposed to stop and were in my bailiwick.

This instance convinced me of the value of adhering to a plan.

IV

During the operations of the American Punitive Expedition in Mexico in 1916-17, General Pershing had his advance Command Post, consisting of himself, Major Ryan, and myself, with four soldiers, at a place called El Cobre. Late one evening General Pershing dictated an order to Major Ryan, which I was to carry to a squadron of the 13th Cavalry at Saca Grande. This message was to the effect that the squadron would proceed to the vicinity of a ranch called Providencia and search the mountains to the west. When he wrote the order, General Pershing was looking at the mountains to the west which I was morally certain he desired to have searched.

To deliver this message, it was necessary to drive for about an hour and a half in a broken-down Ford, using headlights, over roadless country full of Villistas. I then secured a horse and, after riding all night in very bad weather consisting of rain, sleet, hail, and snow, joined the squadron. When we arrived at Providencia, the Major assembled his captains and started to issue orders to search the mountains to the west of Providencia. Now, Providencia is in a valley with mountains on both sides, and General Pershing's Command Post was east of the mountains to the east of Providencia. I therefore told the Squadron Commander that he should search the mountains to the east. He showed me the written order and said, "Do you tell me to violate this written order?" I said, "I do." He made some uncomplimentary remarks concerning me, but stated that he would carry out the order. We searched all day without success, finally returning over the mountains to General Pershing's Command Post.

The Major sent for me and we rode to the Command Post, where the Major stated that: "This young so and so had caused him to fail in his mission." General Pershing said, "Whatever Lieutenant Patton ordered you were my orders." Then, turning to me, he said, "What orders did you give?" I stated what I had done, and he said, "You were perfectly correct."

At that time the difference between a Second Lieu-

tenant and a Major was much greater than the difference
between a Second Lieutenant and a full General today, so
that my act, in my opinion, took high moral courage and
built up my self-confidence, and was correct.

V

Shortly after the preceding incident, General Pershing sent me to deliver a message to General Howze.
The only information we had as to General Howze's
whereabouts was that he had passed through the Providencia Ranch. I reached the ranch with an automobile
just at dark, and chanced to meet there a pack train of
the 7th Cavalry. I secured two soldiers and three horses
from the packmaster and started to look for General
Howz. At that time it was still light enough to follow the
tracks of the squadron. When we had proceeded a short
distance, we met a patrol of the 10th Cavalry, who urged
me to go no farther because they assured me that the
woods were full of Villistas. However, I continued, and
finally came, near midnight, to a place where, at the top of
a divide, two canyons took off from the canyon I had
previously been traversing. It was necessary to make a
decision. Looking over the ground, I thought I saw a slight
reflection of fires in the clouds over the easternmost canyon. I therefore followed this canyon and met a patrol of
the 7th Cavalry under General Fechet, then Major, who
urged me to go no farther because the canyon was full of
Villistas, and he did not know whether or not General
Howze had gone down it, and rather believed he had not.
However, we continued and eventually found General
Howze.

While there was no real danger connected with this
operation, there were certainly a great many mental
hazards, all of which I have not recounted.

VI

Once, when I was an instructor at Fort Riley, I had
a bachelor party at my house for the members of the
Second Year Class. Naturally, there was considerable
hilarity, but no one behaved in a drunken or unseemly
manner. The next day the Commanding Officer, who
was hag-ridden by his wife, sent for me and stated he

had definite information that a certain lieutenant who had been my guest had been disgracefully drunk and he asked me to substantiate this statement. I told him that I declined to do it. He said, "You have only a month and a half to go before your tour of duty here is over, and if you do not answer me, I will relieve you at once and spoil your otherwise excellent record." I lied, stating that I was too drunk at the party to notice the condition of the other officers. No further action was taken by the Commanding Officer.

VII

In the summer of 1918, a group of soldiers of the 301st Tank Brigade, which I commanded, was having 37 mm. gun practice which I was observing. One defective round exploded in the muzzle, wounding two or three men. The next round exploded in the breech, blowing the head off the gunner. The men were reluctant to fire the next round, so it was incumbent on me, as the senior officer present, to do so—in fact, I fired three rounds without incident. This restored the confidence of the men in the weapon. I must admit that I have never in my life been more reluctant to pull a trigger.

VIII

During the Muese—Argonne Offensive, the tank crews of Captain Matt English's company of the 301st Brigade were digging a breach through the German trenches when we came under direct machine-gun fire at about three hundred yards. The men took shelter and stopped working, so, in order to restore confidence, Captain English and myself stood on top of the parapet. This persuaded the men to resume their digging. Strange to say, several of the men were hit, but neither of us was touched. After we got five tanks through the gap thus constructed, they advanced rapidly on the German machine guns, which ceased firing. I followed the tanks on foot, passing through about three hundred disorganized infantry on the reverse slope of a hill, which was under extremely heavy long-range machine-gun and artillery fire. It was very necessary that the infantry follow the tanks in order to exploit the break-through. I ordered them for-

ward, without result. I then called for volunteers, and six
men, including my orderly, Joseph Angelo, volunteered
to accompany me. We started forward, with the result
that the remaining troops did not continue their retrograde movement. During the course of this operation,
four of the volunteers were killed and I was wounded.
When more tanks came up, the infantry followed, and the
operation was a success. I received the Distinguished Service Cross for these two efforts.

IX

After I was wounded in the St. Mihiel operation, I
had quite a hemorrhage and lay in a shell hole some thirty
yards from the German lines for about an hour, during
which time we were continually fired on by machine guns
and mortars, but without result. Not having been wounded
before, I felt I was in a serious condition and, in fact,
thought I was going to die. However, I insisted, against
the advice of the doctor, on being taken to the Headquarters of the 35th Division, which I was at that time
supporting, in order to give an exact statement of the
affairs on the front as I then knew them before permitting
myself to be taken to the hospital. Actually, my wound
was not particularly serious, but again, the mental hazard,
which is as great as the physical hazard, played its part.

X

On the morning of November 9, 1942, I went to the
beach at Fedhala accompanied by Lieutenant Stiller, my
Aide. The situation we found was very bad. Boats were
coming in and not being pushed off after unloading.
There was shell fire, and French aviators were strafing
the beach. Although they missed it by a considerable distance whenever they strafed, our men would take cover
and delay unloading operations, and particularly the unloading of ammunition, which was vitally necessary, as
we were fighting a major engagement not more than fifteen hundred yards to the south.

By remaining on the beach and personally helping to
push off boats and by not taking shelter when the enemy
planes flew over, I believe I had considerable influence in

quieting the nerves of the troops and on making the initial landing a success. I stayed on that beach for nearly eighteen hours and was wet all over all of that time. People say that army commanders should not indulge in such practices. My theory is that an army commander does what is necessary to accomplish his mission, and that nearly eighty per cent of his mission is to arouse morale in his men.

XI

At 0230 on the morning of November 11, 1942, I was awakened by Colonel Harkins with the statement that a French officer had come down from Rabat with an order for the French at Casablanca to surrender. We gave this officer an escort to get him to Casablanca. Then the question arose as to whether or not I should call off the attack, which was to begin with an air bombardment at seven o'clock the same morning. Many excellent officers advised me to call off the attack. However, I was not content, because I believed that if we kept the pressure up, we would certainly force the French surrender, whereas if we showed a willingness to debate with them, they might not surrender, and since they outnumbered us two to one, time was vital. Therefore, I gave the order to continue the attack. Next morning, when we received at 0645 the surrender offer from Casablanca, we had a very bad eight minutes getting a radio message to the airplanes who were to bomb at 0700, and to the Navy who was to shell at 0716. There was less than a minute and a quarter to go when the airplanes acknowledged our signal.

XII

At 1330 on the afternoon of November 11, 1942, Admiral Michelier, the Supreme French Commander in West Africa, and General Noguès, the Resident General, came with their staffs to the Hotel Miramar at Fedhala to surrender. When I left Washington, I had been provided with two sets of surrender conditions, one more lenient than the other. I had, naturally, read them several times on the trip across, but owing to a lack of historical knowledge, did not realize until the French arrived that the conditions were drawn for Algiers, which is a French Department, whereas Morocco is a protectorate where the prestige of the French Army is the only thing holding the Arabs in check. In view of this fact it was evident to me that neither set of conditions was applicable.

The situation was further complicated by the fact that I was out of all communication with General Eisenhower and had no knowledge as to how the other attacks in Africa were progressing. I had to make a decision, and I had to maintain Morocco as a gateway for the Americans entering the continent of Africa. Morocco could not be used as a gateway if it were in the throes of an Arab uprising. Hence I had to maintain the prestige of the French Army.

I got up and said, in my not too good French, that I was a former student at the French Cavalry School, that I had served with the French for two years in World War I, and that I had great respect for and belief in the word of honor of a French officer, and that if the French officers present would give me their word of honor that they would not fire against American troops or American ships, they could retain their weapons, man their seacoast forts, and carry on in all respects as they had carried on previously—but under my orders.

I have never had reason to regret my decision. Had I done otherwise, I am convinced that at least sixty thousand American troops would have had to occupy Morocco; thereby preventing our using it to the maximum and reducing our already inadequate forces.

XIII

About 1000 o'clock on the night of March 5, 1943, General Walter B. Smith, Chief of Staff for General Eisenhower, phoned me to report by air to Maison Blanche Airfield at Algiers on the morning of the sixth, accompanied by an Acting Chief of Staff and two or three Staff officers prepared for extended field service. I could not take any of my regular General Staff officers because it was necessary for them to continue planning for the Sicilian operation.

I took my two Aides, Captain Jenson and Lieutenant Stiller, my orderly, Sergeant Meeks, General Gaffey from the 2d Armored Division as Acting Chief of Staff, Colonel Kent Lambert, my G-3 whom I replaced with Maddox, and Colonel Koch, my G-2. We arrived at Maison Blanche shortly after noon on March 6, where I was met by General Eisenhower and General Smith, who told me they were going to relieve General Fredendall and that I was to go to his Headquarters and assume command of the II Corps with a view to attacking on the fourteenth, the plans for said attack having already been made and approved. I asked what authority I had for relieving General Fredendall. General Eisenhower said he had talked to Fredendall on the telephone, and he then wrote in longhand, on a small piece of paper, a note to Fredendall telling him that he was to stay with me until I relieved him.

We flew from there to Constantine, where I spent the night and made the acquaintance of General Alexander, who commanded the Army Group to which the II Corps was attached. General Alexander told me that, after the tenth of March, the II Corps would be relieved from the British Command and treated as a separate Army, although retaining the title of a corps.

I flew to Tebessa in the early morning of the seventh and arrived at Headquarters of the II Corps about 0900 o'clock, and found most of the officers in bed. The situation was evidently very poor. Three of the four divisions had been roughly handled and had an inferiority complex. The other divisions had had very limited battle experience and had nothing but the valor of ignorance. There was no discipline, and every member of the General Staff was issuing direct orders to everyone, to the extent that the G-3 could issue an order to a division telling them to send a reinforced platoon to such and such a place.

Between the morning of the seventh and the late afternoon of the thirteenth, I personally talked to every battalion in the four divisions and restored discipline. This was a very difficult job—I think the most difficult I have ever undertaken. However, we were lucky in securing a complete victory in our first attack on Gafsa on the morning of the fourteenth. This corrected all the evils of lack of confidence, and from then on the II Corps fought in a magnificent manner.

XIV

During our operation in Tunisia, we were under very close tutelage by the British, and I had a British Brigadier General at my Headquarters. Sometime around the beginning of the second week of April, I was making desperate efforts to take the mountain called Djebel Berda. After supper on this particular evening, General Eddy, commanding the 9th Division, which was conducting the attack, came to my quarters, and in the presence of the English Brigadier stated that, while he would carry out my orders of continuing the attack, he felt that it was hopeless, owing to the fact that the infantry regiments engaged in it had already suffered twenty-six per cent casualties.

I was faced with the necessity of making a decision either to continue a hopeless attack or to lose face in front of the British and violate my own principles of war by agreeing to stop the attack. I felt that, under the circumstances, I was not justified in demanding further sacrifice. I therefore directed General Eddy to discontinue the attack. I think this was one of the most difficult decisions I ever had to make.

Fortunately, on the next day the 1st Division across the valley captured an Observation Post from which we could place a very effective artillery concentration on the part of the mountain we had been trying to storm. We put all the guns in the corps and the two divisions on the target and gave them, just at dawn, twenty-five rounds per gun of rapid fire with white phosphorus, with the idea of persuading the enemy that we were going to launch an attack and hoping he would man his trenches. After a wait of ten minutes, we put on a second twenty-five rounds per gun of high explosive. As a result of this operation, we took the position without casualty, except to the Germans.

XV

In the early morning of July 10, 1943, General Gay, Colonel Odom, Captain Stiller, and myself landed at Gela, Sicily. The landing beach was under fire, but most of the projectiles were hitting about twenty-five feet beyond the beach, in the water, where they did little harm. There was a great deal of confusion on the beach and nobody was working. I walked up and down the beach for some time, accompanied by my Staff, and we restored the confidence of the people there, particularly when we failed to take cover when the Germans flew along, strafing the beach.

Later we entered the town of Gela, and remained there for some time under very intense artillery and mortar fire. We could see, on our left, a brigade of Italian infantry attacking our very thin line consisting of two Ranger companies, and on our right, twelve tanks which had cut in and were not over four hundred yards from the beach.

It was necessary to drive along a road between these tanks and the 1st Division in order to find General Terry Allen. This was a somewhat hazardous operation, as we were driving between two armies engaged in quite a battle because the Germans had launched a counter-attack of some sixty tanks against us. However, we found General Allen and arranged plans for the continuation of the attack the next morning. This meeting was made vivid in my recollection by the fact that shells were hitting in our vicinity during the whole of the conference, which, as a result, was probably one of the shortest staff meetings in history. For this act I was given an Oak Leaf Cluster to my Distinguished Service Cross, which I feel I did not earn, as I was not doing more than my duty and the situation was not too hazardous, although on one occasion a shell lit within a very few feet of General Gay and myself, and on another occasion a bomb fell just across the road from us.

XVI

By the night of the thirteenth of July, 1943, I was of the opinion that the German counter-attack of the eleventh and twelfth was the last major counter-offensive of which they were capable. On this assumption I revised my plans for the remainder of the operation in Sicily. Had I taken counsel of my fears, or believed what the G-2's reported, the campaign could have been much longer and less successful.

The making of such a decision sounds easy, but is, in my opinion, quite difficult.

XVII

On the fourteenth of July, I received a telegram from General Alexander to the effect that I would take up a defensive position in the vicinity of Caltanissetta to cover the left rear of the British Eighth Army. To have adhered to this order would have been disloyal to the American Army. With the help of General Keyes, General Wedemeyer, and General Gay, I drafted an order for an enveloping attack, via Agrigento and Castelvetrano, on Palermo.

Accompanied by General Wedemeyer, I then flew to Africa and presented this order to General Alexander, stating that I was convinced that this was what he intended, and not that I should remain in a defensive attitude. I asked him to initial the order. He did so, but stated I should not attack Agrigento unless I could do it with a reconnaissance in force. I did it with a reconnaissance in force, using all the troops I had available—namely, the 3d Division, part of the 82d Airborne, two Ranger Battalions, and a task force of the 2d Armored. Had I failed, I would have been relieved. We took Palermo on the twenty-second.

XVIII

During the advance on Messina, along the north road in Sicily, we had made one successful amphibious turning operation and were in the act of executing a second one when, shortly after supper, General Keyes, who was with the 3d Division, telephoned me that General Bradley, commanding the II Corps of which the 3d Division was a unit, and General Truscott, commanding the 3d Division, were both convinced that this second amphibious operation was too dangerous and therefore requested authority to postpone it. I told General Keyes to tell them it would not be postponed and that I would be there at once.

I took General Gay with me, dropping him off at the beach where the amphibious troops were then taking off, with orders to see that they took off. I then went to the Headquarters of the 3d Division, which was under limited shell fire, and found General Truscott, a most dashing officer, suffering from such physical fatigue that he was convinced that the operation could not succeed. I directed him to carry it out, stating that if he succeeded he would get the full credit, and that if he failed, I would take the blame. I then called General Bradley on the telephone and told him the same thing. I stated to both of them that, having complete confidence in them, I was returning to my Headquarters, because if I stayed around I would fail to show confidence. I spent a very restless night, particularly as the enemy was shooting at us, but they failed to get a hit. Shortly after reveille, Colonel Harkins, who was duty officer, called up to say that the attack had been a complete success.

It is a very difficult thing to order two officers in whom you have great confidence to carry out an operation which neither of them thinks is possible.

XIX

During the attack on Troina, I drove to the Headquarters of General Bradley, who was conducting the attack, accompanied by General Lucas. Just before we got there, I saw a field hospital in a valley and stopped to inspect it. There were some three hundred and fifty badly wounded men in the hospital, all of whom were very heroic under their sufferings, and all of whom were interested in the success of the operation.

Just as I was leaving the hospital, I saw a soldier sitting on a box near the dressing station. I stopped and said to him, "What is the matter with you, boy?" He said, "Nothing; I just can't take it." I asked what he meant. He said, "I just can't take being shot at." I said, "You mean that you are malingering here?" He burst into tears and I immediately saw that he was an hysterical case. I, therefore, slapped him across the face with my glove and told him to get up, join his unit, and make a man of himself, which he did. Actually, at the time he was absent without leave.

I am convinced that my action in this case was entirely correct, and that, had other officers had the courage to do likewise, the shameful use of "battle fatigue" as an excuse for cowardice would have been infinitely reduced.

XX

On the twenty-eighth of July, 1944, General Bradley informed me that the Third Army would become operational at noon on August 1, but that in the interim I was to take over control of the VIII and XV Corps—this without becoming officially connected with the operations. On the afternoon of the twenty-ninth, south of Coutances, I found an armored division halted on the road while the Headquarters was having a map study as to the possibility of crossing the Sienne River with a view to advancing along the coast road toward Granville. Taking a glance at the map, I saw that the river was within a few miles, so went down and reconnoitered it. I found it was only about two feet deep and, so far as I could tell, defended by one machine gun which missed me by a good deal. Fortified with this information, I went back to the Commanding General and asked him why he didn't get across the river. He said he didn't know whether the tide was in or out, and that he understood the river was strongly defended. I told him in very strong language what I had just done and to get a move on himself, which he did. From that time on, this division was one of the boldest in the Third Army, but since this was its initiation to battle, it needed just that sort of a kick to get it started.

XXI

After supper on July 31, 1944, General Gaffey, Colonel Harkins, and I drove to the Headquarters of the VIII Corps. I told General Middleton, who was commanding the corps, that I was taking over in the morning. He said he was glad I had arrived because he had obtained his objective, which was the Selune River. I asked him if he was across and he said, "No." I told him that throughout history, many campaigns had been lost by stopping on the wrong side of a river, and directed him to go across at once. He said that the bridge below Avranches was out. While we were discussing ways and means of getting across, a telephone message came in that the bridge, while damaged, was usable—further, that the 4th Armored Division had captured a dam to the east of Avranches, across which troops could move. I directed that the VIII

Corps start across that night, which it did. This is no criticism of General Middleton, who is an outstanding soldier, but it shows that a little extra push at a critical moment is sometimes useful. Had we failed to secure a bridgehead that night, our whole operation would have been jeopardized.

XXII

The passage of the Third Army through the corridor at Avranches was an impossible operation. Two roads entered Avranches; only one left it over the bridge. We passed through this corridor two infantry and two armored divisions in less than twenty-four hours. There was no plan, because it was impossible to make a plan. I simply put the Corps and Division Commanders at critical points and sent units through as they arrived. It was a hazardous operation, because the troops were jammed head to tail for miles, but there was no other way of attaining the necessary speed. The operation was made successful by the driving power of the General Officers—particularly Middleton, Wood, Haislip, Gaffey, and Gay—by the superlative ability of the Staff of the Third Army to improvise under pressure, and by the help of God.

XXIII

During the course of the advance of the Third Army from Avranches to the Moselle, many instances occurred where it was necessary to use considerable persuasion to permit the uninterrupted progress of the Third Army, and naturally to assume considerable risk should the spectacular advance fail.

One of the more important hazards encountered was that of leaving the right flank of the Third Army completely open from St. Nazaire to a point near Troyes. This decision was based on my belief that the Germans, while they had ample force, did not have sufficient mobility to strike fast, and that the ever-efficient XIX Tactical Air Command would spot any force large enough to hurt us and be able to hold it down long enough to permit the greatly superior mobility of the American troops to intervene. The soundness of the decision was indicated by the result.

XXIV

About the fifth of September, it became apparent that we would run out of gasoline. I directed the two corps, the XX and XII, to continue the advance until the tanks ran out of gas, and then to go on foot. This was actually done, and the bridgehead across the Moselle River was secured as a result. There was considerable resistance on the part of the Corps Commanders to what appeared to them an unnecessarily dangerous operation. Its success again proved that it was not dangerous.

XXV

On the thirtieth of September, 1944, I visited the Headquarters of the XII Corps at Nancy, and was informed that two combat teams of the 35th Division were being violently attacked on a hill east of the Moselle River. I had given orders that no ground would be given up and directed the Corps Commander to use his last remaining reserves, which consisted of part of the 6th Armored Division, to insure that the hill was held. Next day General Gaffey, the then Chief of Staff, was sent by me to see how things were going on. At 1400 he called up to state that orders had just been issued for two combat teams of the 35th Division to fall back. I told him to countermand the order and to have the Corps Commander and the Division Commanders of the 35th and 6th Armored Divisions present at the Command Post of the 6th Armored Division, where I would arrive by air at once.

On reaching this point, I found that all three commanders were somewhat overanxious and had contemplated and issued the orders for the withdrawal. I directed that these orders be countermanded at once and that the 6th Armored Division be put into action in the morning. It was objected that the 6th Armored Division was all we had left. I stated that it could do no good being left, that it was there to fight.

Next day the attack by the 6th Armored and the 35th Infantry was renewed with complete success, and over eight hundred dead Germans were counted in one field. The officers concerned were all of the highest caliber, but were all very fatigued, and, as I have stated before, fatigue produces pessimism.

XXVI

During the fighting west of the Moselle and west of Metz in October, General Walker, commanding the XX Corps, suggested that we attempt to take Fort Driant. The attack was started and, in spite of an initial success, it was evident that, if continued, it would prove unduly expensive. It was then necessary to go against my strongly held opinion that one should never fall back and order that the attack be suspended. This was done. It was a very difficult decision. As a result of this decision, we saved a great many lives and took Metz on November 25, with comparatively little loss.

XXVII

By November 1, the Third Army had secured enough gasoline, ammunition, and replacements to make it possible to renew the attack with a view to breaking the Siegfried Line and establishing the bridgehead over the Rhine River, in the vicinity of Mainz. The attack was to take place at 0430 on the morning of November 8. The weather was extremely bad and the flood condition of the river was appalling. At 2000 on the evening of the seventh, a corps and a division commander came to my house and stated that in their opinion they would be unable to attack in the morning. The moral effect of discontinuing an attack is very bad for the troops, and at such a late hour was almost physically impossible of accomplishment, due to difficulty of communications. I therefore asked the officers whom they recommended as their replacements in command of their respective units, because, I stated, I would keep on relieving until I got somebody who would lead the attack. They stated that if I felt that way they would continue the attack.

The attack next morning, in spite of atrocious weather, was entirely successful. Of course, it is pertinent to remember that Corps and Division Commanders suffer from greater physical fatigue and danger than does an Army Commander, and hence it is the duty of the Army Commander to supply the necessary punch when fatigue starts sapping the energy of the other officers.

XXVIII

On December 19, 1944, General Eisenhower had a meeting at Verdun with General Bradley, General Devers, and myself and the members of his Staff present. The decision was made for the Third Army to attack the southern flank of the Bulge. I was asked when I could make the attack. I stated that I could do so with three divisions on the morning of the twenty-third of December. I had made this estimate before going to Verdun, and had taken exactly eighteen minutes to make it. General Eisenhower stated that I should wait until I got at least six divisions. I told him that, in my opinion, a prompt attack with three was better than waiting for six—particularly when I did not know where I could get the other three. Actually the attack of the III Corps with the 80th, 26th, and 4th Armored Divisions jumped off on the morning of December 22, one day ahead of the time predicted.

In making this attack we were wholly ignorant of what was ahead of us, but were determined to strike through to Bastogne, which we did on the twenty-sixth. I am sure that this early attack was of material assistance in producing our victory.

XXIX

On the twenty-seventh of December, the 87th Infantry Division and the 11th Armored Division were supposed to join the VIII Corps in the vicinity of Neufchâteau by midnight of the twenty-eighth, to attack at 0900 on the morning of the twenty-ninth. Owing to road difficulties, these divisions did not reach the rendezvous point until near daylight on the twenty-ninth, and General Middleton requested a delay of one day in the attack. I demanded that he attack anyway that morning, because my sixth sense told me it was vital. The attack jumped off, and ran directly into the flank of a German counter-attack consisting of two and a half divisions. Had my divisions delayed one day, the German counter-attack might well have cut off the tenuous corridor we had been able to establish from Arlon to Bastogne.

XXX

All during the battle of the Bulge, I had been very anxious to start an attack north along the Ridge Road from Echternach. Finally, on February 6, the XII Corps forced a crossing over the Our and Sauer Rivers, using, from left to right, the 80th Division, the 5th Division, and one combat command of the 76th Division. In my opinion the audacity of this operation was its chief virtue, because, to look at it, no human being could possibly have envisaged a successful crossing. The credit goes to the XII Corps and to the divisions which made the crossings. The only claim I have is my insistence that it be made at the time it was made.

XXXI

On February 19, General Walker called me on the telephone and stated that he felt that if I could get an armored division from SHAEF Reserve he could, with it and the 94th Division, clear up the Saar Triangle and take Saarburg. I succeeded in getting the loan of the 10th Armored Division for that specific operation, which was a success in two days. Thereafter, by continued persuasion and with the assistance of General Bradley, who shut his eyes and ears to certain rumors, we were able to keep the 10th Armored Division and eventually take Trier. I believe this is the only time in history when it was necessary to beg, borrow, and even steal troops in order to win a victory. The taking of Trier was the key to the start of the Palatinate Campaign.

XXXII

In March, 1945, the First and Third Armies were supposed to attack in echelon from the left; that is, the First Army, and then the Third Army, with the idea of getting up to the Rhine from Coblentz to Cologne. I was told to wait until the First Army had closed on the Rhine. However, after we crossed the Kyll River, I started to break the 4th Armored Division loose and, fearing that I might be ordered to stop it, I sent in no reports for twenty-four hours until it was so committed it could not be ordered to halt. It reached the Rhine River without difficulty. Again, the danger was more apparent than real, but, personally, I am not sure that I deserve much credit for the decision except that it was a decision.

XXXIII

About the eighteenth of March, we became aware that if the Third Army did not secure a bridgehead over the Rhine prior to the crossing of the British on the left wing of the groups of armies, we might lose troops to them and have to resume a defensive role. This was not at all to our liking. Therefore, I told General Eddy that he must cross the Rhine before the twenty-third. The epic crossing of the Rhine by the 5th Division of the XII Corps was a magnificent feat of arms for which General Eddy, Corps Commander, and General Irwin, Division Commander, deserve all credit. My sole virtue was having the idea. As a matter of fact, Eddy got across twenty-four hours earlier than I thought he could.

XXXIV

THE PRESS CONFERENCE OF SEPTEMBER 22, 1945

This conference cost me the command of the Third Army, or rather, of a group of soldiers, mostly recruits, who then rejoiced in that historic name, but I was intentionally direct, because I believed that it was then time for people to know what was going on. My language was not particularly politic, but I have yet to find where politic language produces successful government.

The one thing which I could not say then, and cannot yet say, is that my chief interest in establishing order in Germany was to prevent Germany from going communistic. I am afraid that our foolish and utterly stupid policy in regard to Germany will certainly cause them to join the Russians and thereby insure a communistic state throughout Western Europe.

It is rather sad to me to think that my last opportunity for earning my pay has passed. At least, I have done my best as God gave me the chance.

Appendix A

OPERATION "TORCH"

Headquarters Western Task Force

Commanding General: Major George S. Patton, Jr.

Deputy Commanding General: Major General Geoffrey Keyes

Chief of Staff: Colonel Hobart R. Gay[1]

Deputy Chief of Staff: Lieutenant Colonel Paul D. Harkins[1]

G-1 (Personnel): Colonel Hugh Fitzgerald

G-2 (Intelligence): Colonel Percy Black

G-3 (Plans and Training): Colonel Kent C. Lambert

G-4 (Supply): Colonel Walter J. Muller[1]

Adjutant General: Colonel R. E. Cummings[1]

Artillery: Colonel J. J. B. Williams

Engineers: Colonel John Conklin[2]

Ordinance: Colonel Thomas H. Nixon[1]

Signal Officer: Colonel Elton H. Hammond[1]

Medical Officer: Colonel Albert Kenner

Northern Landing Force, Major General Lucien K. Truscott

    60th Infantry Regiment, 9th Infantry Division, Colonel F. J. de Rohan

    Armored Task Force from 2nd Armored Division, Colonel Harry H. Semmes[3]

    Supporting troops

---

[1]With General Patton throughout the war.

[2]Went to United States in 1943; returned with the Third Army.

[3]Wearer of three Distinguished Service Crosses; served with General Patton in two World Wars.

Central Landing Force, Major General Jonathan W. Anderson
    3d Infantry Division, General Anderson
    Armored Task Force from 2d Armored Division, Lieutenant Colonel Richard Nelson
    Supporting troops
Southern Landing Force, Major General Ernest A. Harmon, commanding 2d Armored Division

Appendix B

COMPOSITION OF II CORPS

The II Corps of Tunisia was composed of three Infantry and one Armored Division. The Corps was supported by the 13th Field Artillery Brigade and the available number of supporting units; such as, Signal, Ordnance, Medical, Engineers, etc.

CORPS COMPOSITION

Headquarters and Headquarters Company, II Corps:

1st Infantry Division:	Maj. Gen. Terry de la M. Allen
1st Armored Division:	Maj. Gen. Orlando Ward,
	Maj. Gen. Ernest A. Harmon
34th Infantry Division:	Maj. Gen. Charles W. Ryder
9th Infantry Division:	Maj. Gen. Manton C. Eddy
13th Field Artillery Brigade:	Brig. Gen. John A. Crane

Appendix C

OPERATION "HUSKY"

Headquarters and Headquarters Company, I Armored Corps, later redesignated as Headquarters and Headquarters Company, Seventh Army

Headquarters II Corps: Major General O. N. Bradley

Headquarters Provisional Corps (formed after the landing was made, and commanded by the Deputy Army Commander, Major General Keyes)

1st Infantry Division:	Major Gen. Terry de la M. Allen
45th Infantry Division:	Major Gen. Troy Middleton
3d Infantry Division:	Major Gen. Lucien K. Truscott
2d Armored Division:	Major Gen. Hugh A. Gaffey
9th Infantry Division:	Major Gen. Manton C. Eddy
82d Airborne Division:	Major Gen. Matthew Ridgeway
3 Ranger Battalions:	Colonel William Darby

The normal complement of supporting units

Appendix D

LETTERS OF INSTRUCTION

HEADQUARTERS
THIRD UNITED STATES ARMY
APO 9563   U.S. ARMY

6 March, 1944

SUBJECT: Letter of Instruction Number 1.
To   : Corps, Division, and Separate Unit
          Commanders

I. GENERAL

This letter will orient you, officers of the higher echelons, in the principles of command, combat procedure, and administration which obtain in this Army, and will guide you in the conduct of your several commands.

II. COMMAND

  a. Leadership

  (1) Full Duty

Each, in his appropriate sphere, will lead in person. Any commander who fails to obtain his objective, and who is not dead or severely wounded, has not done his full duty.

  (2) Visits to Front

The Commanding General or his Chief of Staff (never both at once) and one member of each of the General Staff sections, the Signal, Medical, Ordance, Engineer, and Quartermaster sections, should visit the front daily. To save duplication, the Chief of Staff will designate the sector each is to visit.

The function of these Staff officers is to observe, not to meddle. In addition to their own specialty, they must observe and report anything of military importance. Remember that praise is more valuable than blame. Remember, too, that your primary mission as a leader is to see with your own eyes and be seen by your troops while engaged in personal reconnaissance.

b. Execution

In carrying out a mission, the promulgation of the order represents not over ten per cent of your responsibility. The remaining ninety per cent consists in assuring by means of personal supervision on the ground, by yourself and your staff, proper and vigorous execution.

c. Staff Conferences

Daily, at the earliest possible moment that the G-2 and G-3 can get their maps posted, a Staff conference will be held, attended by the Commanding General, the Chief of Staff, and the heads of all General Staff sections, the Surgeon, the Signal Officer, the Ordnance Officer, the Engineer Officer, and other special Staff heads when called on. Also present will be the Staff officers described in paragraph II *a* (2) above, who visited the front on the previous day. Any person present with a statement to make will do so briefly. (*N.B.* If a Staff inspector saw anything during his visit to the front requiring immediate action, he would have reported the fact to the Chief of Staff immediately on his return.) The Commanding General then gives his intentions, and the Chief of Staff allocates the sectors for the day's Staff inspectors.

d. Rest Periods

Staff personnel, commissioned and enlisted, who do not rest, do not last. All sections must run a duty roster and enforce compliance. The intensity of Staff operations during battle is periodic. At the Army and Corps levels the busiest times are the periods from one to three hours after daylight, and from three to five hours after dark. In the lower echelons and in the administrative and supply Staffs, the time of the periods is different, but just as definite. When the need arises, everyone must work all the time, but these emergencies are not frequent: unfatigued men last longer and work harder at high pressure.

e. Location of Command Posts

The farther forward the Command Posts are located, the less time is wasted in driving to and from the front. The ideal situation would be for the Army Command Post to be within one half hour's drive in a C & R car of the Division Command Post. The driving time to the front from the Command Post of the lower units should be correspondingly shorter.

Much time and wire is saved if Command Posts of higher units are at or near one of the Command Posts of the next lower echelon.

All Command Posts of a Division and higher units must have at least two echelons; the forward one—and that is the one referred to in this paragraph (e)—should be kept as small and mobile as possible with the minimum amount of radio traffic.

III. COMBAT PROCEDURE

a. Maps

We are too prone to believe that we acquire merit solely through the study of maps in the safe seclusion of a Command Post. This is an error.

Maps are necessary in order to see the whole panorama of battle and to permit intelligent planning.

Further—and this is very important—a study of the map will indicate where critical situations exist or are apt to develop, and so indicate where the Commander should be. In the higher echelons, a layered map of the whole theater to a reasonable scale, showing roads, railways, streams, and towns is more useful than a large-

scale map cluttered up with ground forms and a
multiplicity of non-essential information.

b. Plans

Plans must be simple and flexible. Actually
they only form a datum plane from which you
build as necessity directs or opportunity offers.
They should be made by the people who are going to execute them.

c. Reconnaissance

You can never have too much reconnaissance.
Use every means available before, during, and after battle. Reports must be facts, not opinions;
negative as well as positive. Do not believe inter-
cepts blindly; cross-check—sometimes messages
are sent out to be intercepted.

Information is like eggs: the fresher the
better.

d. Orders

(1) Formal Orders

Formal orders will be preceded by letters of instruction and by personal conferences. In this way the whole purpose of the
operation will be made clear, together with
the mission to be accomplished by each major
unit. So that, if during combat communication breaks down, each Commander can and
must so act as to obtain the general objective.
The order itself will be short, accompanied
by a sketch—it tells what to do, not how.
It is really a memorandum and an assumption of responsibility by the issuing Commander.

(2) Fragmentary Orders

After the initial order, you will seldom
get another formal order, but you will get
many fragmentary orders, in writing, or orally, by phone or personally.

Take down all oral orders and repeat
them back. Have your juniors do the same to
you.

Keep a diary with all orders and messages and the resulting action pasted in it in
sequence.

Keep your own orders short; get them out in time; issue them personally by voice when you can. In battle it is always easier for the senior to go up than for the junior to come back for the issuance of orders.

A division should have twelve hours, and, better, eighteen hours, between the physical receipt of the order at Division Headquarters and the time it is to be executed.

(3) Warning Orders

Warning orders are vital and must be issued in time. This requirement applies not only to combat units but also to the Surgeon, the Signal Officer, the Quartermaster, the Ordnance Officer, and the Engineer Officer, who must get warning orders promptly. They, too, have plans to make and units to move. If they do not function, you do not fight.

Orders, formal or otherwise, concerning units further down than the next echelon of command, are highly prejudicial.

(4) Keep Troops Informed

Use every means before and after combats to tell the troops what they are going to do and what they have done.

IV. ADMINISTRATION

   a. *Supply*

      (1) General

The onus of supply rests equally on the giver and the taker.

Forward units must anticipate needs and ask for supplies in time. They must stand ready to use all their means to help move supplies.

The supply services must get the things asked for to the right place at the right time. They must do more: by reconnaissance they will anticipate demands and start the supplies up before they are called for.

The DESPERATE DETERMINATION to succeed is just as vital as it is to supply the firing line.

(2) Replacements

Replacements are *spare parts*—supplies. They must be asked for in time by the front line, and the need for them must be anticipated in the rear. An educated guess is just as accurate and far faster than compiled errors. During lulls, you can balance the account. Keep your combat units full. A company without riflemen is just as useless as a tank without gasoline.

(3) Hospitals

Evacuation or field hospitals must be kept close to the front.

Visit the wounded personally.

b. Decorations

Decorations are for the purpose of raising the fighting value of troops; therefore they must be awarded promptly. Have a definite officer on your staff educated in writing citations and see that they get through.

c. Discipline

There is only one kind of discipline—PERFECT DISCIPLINE. If you do not enforce and maintain discipline, you are potential murderers. You must set the example.

V. RUMORS

Reports based on information secured through reconnaissance conducted after dark should be viewed with skepticism. The same thing applies to reports from walking wounded and stragglers. These latter seek to justify themselves by painting alarming pictures.

It is risky and usually impossible to move reserves during darkness on every call for help. Units cannot be wholly destroyed in a night attack. They must stick. Launch your counter-attack after daylight and subsequent to adequate reconnaissance and see that it is coordinated.

VI. CONDITION

High physical condition is vital to victory.

There are more tired corps and division commanders than there are tired corps and divisions. Fatigue makes cowards of us all. Men in condition do not tire.

VII. COURAGE

DO NOT TAKE COUNSEL OF YOUR FEARS.

/s/ G. S. PATTON, JR.
G. S. PATTON, JR.
Lt. General U.S. Army, Commanding

CONFIDENTIAL

HEADQUARTERS
THIRD UNITED STATES ARMY
APO 403   U.S. ARMY

3 April, 1944

SUBJECT: Letter of Instruction Number 2.
TO   : Corps, Division, and Separate Unit Commanders.

I. GENERAL

1. This letter stresses those tactical and administrative usages which combat experience has taught myself and the officers who have served under me to consider vital.

2. You will not simply mimeograph this and call it a day. You are responsible that these usages become habitual in your command.

II. DISCIPLINE

1. There is only one sort of discipline—PERFECT DISCIPLINE. Men cannot have good battle discipline and poor administrative discipline.

2. Discipline is based on pride in the profession of arms, on meticulous attention to details, and on mutual respect and confidence. Discipline must be a habit so engrained that it is stronger than the excitement of battle or the fear of death.

3. The history of our invariably victorious armies demonstrates that we are the best soldiers in the world. This should make your men proud. This should make you

proud. This should imbue your units with unconquerable self-confidence and pride in demonstrated ability.

4. Discipline can only be obtained when all officers are so imbued with the sense of their awful obligation to their men and to their country that they cannot tolerate negligence. Officers who fail to correct errors or to praise excellence are valueless in peace and dangerous misfits in war.

5. Officers must assert themselves by example and by voice. They must be pre-eminent in courage, deportment, and dress.

6. One of the primary purposes of discipline is to produce alertness. A man who is so lethargic that he fails to salute will fall an easy victim to the enemy.

7. Combat experience has proven that ceremonies, such as formal guard mounts, formal retreat formations, and regular and supervised reveille formations, are a great help, and, in some cases, essential, to prepare men and officers for battle, to give them that perfect discipline, that smartness of appearance, that alertness without which battles cannot be won.

8. In the Third Army, when troops are not in the actual combat zone nor engaged in tactical exercises, or range firing, etc., Corps and separate Division Commanders will see:

> *a.* That regular reveille formation be held, in attendance at which there will be a minimum of one officer per company, or similar unit, and in addition thereto, when practicable, a minimum of one field officer per regiment or separate battalion.
>
> *b.* That it shall be customary for all organizations to hold formal retreat under arms. Attendance, in addition to the prescribed enlisted men, shall be all officers of company grade. In the case of regiments and separate battalions, a minimum of one field officer.
>
> *c.* That in the case where music is available and it is practicable from a billeting standpoint, frequent regimental and battalion retreat parades and similar ceremonies will be held.
>
> *d.* That unit and organizational guard shall be performed strictly in accordance with FM 26-5.

When music is available, formal guard mounts will be held frequently.

e. That officers in formation wear uniform analogous to that worn by the enlisted men, and that all officers participate in all drills and marches at all times with their organizations or units. This includes marching to and from training areas and ranges.

9. Officers are always on duty and their duty extends to every individual, junior to themselves, in the U.S. Army—not only to members of their own organization.

10. Americans, with arms in their hands, are fools as well as cowards to surrender. If they fight on, they will conquer.

11. Cases of misbehavior before the enemy will be brought before General Court Martial and tried under the 75th Article of War. It has been my experience that many Courts Martial are prone to view this most heinous offense, for which the punishment of death may be inflicted, in too lenient a manner. They should realize that the lives of troops are saved by punishment of the initial offenders. Cowardice is a disease and must be checked before it becomes epidemic.

III. TACTICAL USAGES
1. *General*
a. Combat Principles

(1) There is no approved solution to any tactical situation.

(2) There is only one tactical principle which is not subject to change. It is: "To so use the means at hand to inflict the maximum amount of wounds, death, and destruction on the enemy in the minimum time."

(3) In battle, casualties vary directly with the time you are exposed to effective fire. Your own fire reduces the effectiveness and volume of the enemy's fire, while rapidity of attack shortens the time of exposure. A pint of sweat will save a gallon of blood!

(4) Battles are won by frightening the enemy.

Fear is induced by inflicting death and wounds on him. Death and wounds are produced by fire. Fire from the rear is more deadly and three times more effective than fire from the front, but to get fire behind the enemy, you must hold him by frontal fire and move rapidly around his flank. Frontal attacks against prepared positions should be avoided if possible.

(5) "Catch the enemy by the nose with fire and kick him in the pants with fire emplaced through movement."

(6) Hit hard soon; that is, with two battalions up in a regiment, or two divisions up in a corps, or two corps up in an army—the idea being to develop your maximum force at once before the enemy can develop his.

(7) You can never be too strong. Get every man and gun you can secure, provided it does not unduly delay your attack. The German is the champion digger.

(8) The larger the force and the more violence you use in the attack, whether it be men, tanks, or ammunition, the smaller will be your proportional losses.

(9) Never yield ground. It is cheaper to hold what you have than to retake what you have lost. Never move troops to the rear for a rest or to re-form at night, and in the daytime only where absolutely necessary. Such moves may produce a panic.

(10) Our mortars and our artillery are superb weapons when they are firing. When silent, they are junk—see that they keep firing!

b. Tactical Rules in Particular Subjects

(1) Use roads to march on; fields to fight on. In France we will find roads mined or demolished in many places, certainly when we approach the enemy. When that happens, get off the roads and keep moving.

But when the roads are available for use, you save time and effort by staying on them until shot off.

(2) Troops should not deploy into line until forced to do so by enemy fire.

(3) When you are advancing in broken country against possible tank attacks and using the leapfrog method described in my Sicilian notes, be sure to keep the antiguns well up.

(4) In mountain country secure the heights. This is best done by daylight reconnaissance followed by night attack of a platoon reinforced at dawn twilight.

(5) In forcing a pass secure the heights first. There are always trails leading to the rear of hills. Remember that inviting avenues of approach are invariably defended, and an advance by such lanes, without securing the heights covering them, is suicidal.

(6) The effect of mines is largely mental. Not over ten percent of our casualties come from them. When they are encountered, they must be passed through or around. There are not enough mines in the world to cover the whole country. It is cheaper to make a detour than to search; however, the Engineers should start clearing the straight road while the advance elements continue via the detour. See that all types of troops have mine detectors and know how to use them. You *must*—repeat—*must* get through!

(7) Never permit a unit to dig in until the final objective is reached; then dig, wire, and mine.

(8) Slit trenches in artillery will be placed within ten yards of the guns. They will not be placed under trees, as those induce air bursts. Camouflage nets must be rigged so that when they catch fire they can be immediately pulled off.

(9) Take plenty of time to set up an attack.

It takes at least two hours to prepare an infantry battalion to execute a properly co-ordinated attack. Shoving them in too soon produces useless losses.

(10) In battle, small forces—platoons, companies, and even battalions—can do one of three things, go forward, halt, or run. If they halt or run, they will be an even easier target. Therefore, they must go forward. When caught under fire, particularly of artillery, advance out of it; never retreat from it. Artillery very seldom shortens its range.

(11) Security detachments must get out farther, and must stay out at night. One radio car, well off the road, or where it can see the road, or where a member of the crew can observe the road from close quarters, can send information which will be vital.

(12) We are too slow in putting out minefields and in wiring positions for all-around defense. More training time should be devoted to mine-laying and mine-removal.

(13) A battalion of 4.2 chemical mortars, when available, should be attached to an infantry division. An infantry regiment in combat should have a 4.2 chemical company attached.

c. General Training

(1) More emphasis will be placed on the hardening of men and officers. All soldiers and officers should be able to run a mile with combat pack in ten minutes and march eight miles in two hours. When soldiers are in actual contact with the enemy, it is almost impossible to maintain physical condition, but if the physical condition is high before they gain contact, it will not fall off sufficiently during contact to be detrimental.

(2) Much time is wasted in mounting and dismounting mortars and machine guns. Standing gun drill will be practiced so

that the operation will be automatic and can be accomplished in the dark. The ladder method of ranging with mortars is recommended.

(3) Our ability to fight at night, as opposed to moving into position at night for a dawn attack, is pitiably bad. We must learn to execute the attack in the dark.

(4) Sharpen axes, pickaxes, and shovels now, and keep them sharp.

(5) Battles are fought by platoons and squads. Place emphasis on small unit combat instruction so that it is conducted with the same precision as close-order drill. A good solution applied with vigor *now* is better than a perfect solution ten minutes later.

(6) In instruction from the squad to the regiment, sand tables should be used, and the officer or non-com being instructed should give the actual orders he will give in combat. Sand tables need not be complicated. A piece of ground in the lee of a building is just as good and much simpler.

(7) Officers and men must know their equipment. They must train with the equipment they intend to use in battle. Equipment must be in the best operational condition when taken to the Theater of Operations.

d. Guides for Officers

(1) Officers must possess self-confidence and the confidence of their men. Two of the best ways of producing this is meticulously conducted close-order drill, conducted by officers, and platoon marches of forty-eight to sixty hours, during which the platoon is wholly on its own.

(2) In the first actions, new troops must receive aggressive leadership by all grades, including general officers, who must be seen in the front line during action.

(3) The Adjutant General or Secretary to

General Staff must keep for the immediate information of the Commanding General a list showing casualties, matériel losses, prisoners of war, captured matériel, and replacements of both men and matériel received. Two lists are necessary. The first one based on rumor, the second corrected by data. The first one will be found surprisingly close to the second one.

(4) Note the time of your requests for, and the time of arrival of, all artillery and air support missions called for. If support fails to arrive, so note.

(5) There is a universal failure to repeat oral orders back. This failure is certain to result in grave errors.

(6) Messages and orders must use concise military verbiage.

(7) Push wire communications to the limit. A wire phone is worth three radios for both speed and security.

(8) Battalion and company commanders fail to use runners and walkie-talkie radios. They frequently fail to have runners with or near them.

(9) Military police at road junctions must have a map or diagram showing the points to which various roads lead and the units to be found on them.

(10) Don't place large radio sets near CP's if the CP is to be in position more than six hours. If radios must be used for longer periods, put them well away, scatter them, and use remote control.

e. Prisoners

German prisoners over forty talk more easily than the younger ones. They must be examined separately and not returned to the cage where the young ones are. Prisoners other than German usually talk freely and inaccurately. They, too, should be examined out of the hearing of, and later separated from the young Nazis.

f. **Needless Firing**

The needless firing of artillery will be checked by the senior artillery officer.

g. **Needless Requirements**

There is a tendency for the chain of command to overload junior officers by excessive requirements in the way of training and reports. You will alleviate this burden by eliminating non-essential demands.

2. *Infantry*

a. Infantry must move in order to close with the enemy. It must shoot in order to move. When physical targets are not visible, the fire of all infantry weapons must search the area occupied by enemy. Use marching fire. It reduces the accuracy of his fire and increases our confidence. Shoot short. Ricochets make nastier sounds and wounds. To halt under fire is folly. To halt under fire and not fire back is suicide. Move forward out of fire. Officers must set the example.

b. The heavy weapons set the pace. In the battallion the heavy weapons company paces the battalion. In the regiment the cannon company paces the regiment, but it is the function of the rifles and the light machine guns to see that the heavy weapons have a chance to move. In other words, the rifles and machine guns move the heavy weapons in to do the killing.

c. Mortars use great quantities of ammunition. The 81-mm. will fire 800 rounds and a 60-mm. 500 rounds in 24 hours. To provide this ammunition, transportation of all kinds must be utilized, and infantry riflemen in the vicinity of the mortars should each carry one round which they can dump at a predestined spot on going into the fire fight. When not on the move, all mortars, machine guns, and anti-tank guns of the infantry must be emplaced to fire.

d. Anti-tank guns should be placed where they cannot see or be seen beyond their lethal anti-tank range unless they are being used in the role of light artillery.

e. Few men are killed by the bayonet; many are scared by it. Bayonets should be fixed when the fire fight starts. Bayonets must be sharpened by the individual soldier. The German hates the bayonet and is inferior to our men with it. Our men should know this.

f. The M-1 rifle is the most deadly rifle in the world. If you cannot see the enemy, you can at least shoot at the place where he is apt to be.

g. Flat trajectory fire against machine guns must be delivered near and parallel to the axis of enemy fire. This pins him down until the grenadiers with bomb and bayonet can kill him from behind.

h. Fire distribution is practically non-existent in our Army, with the result that those portions of the enemy who are visible receive all the fire, while those portions who are not visible fire on our men with perfect impunity. This defect will be corrected.

i. The infantry battalion is the smallest unit which can be sent on a separate mission. When so used, it is always desirable to reinforce it with artillery, anti-tank guns, AA guns, and, if possible, tanks and engineers.

j. Armored infantry should not attack mounted. It should use its vehicles to deploy mounted and also to assemble from deployed formation.

k. Night attacks mean attacks during darkness or by moonlight. On moonless nights the attacks should start 2½ hours before dawn twilight; on moonlight nights, with the moon. Night attacks must be preceded by careful day reconnaissance and ample warning. Limited objectives must be sought and must be easily recognizable in the dark. Attack formation is in column or in line of columns. Distances and intervals are reduced. Depth is necessary.

l. Supporting fires must be arranged, first, to attack the enemy after our infantry has been discovered, second, to destroy counter-attacks at dawn. Assaulting columns are preceded by a security detachment which in turn is preceded by a patrol. The security detachment and patrol are absorbed when contact is made. In addition to the assaulting columns, a reserve should be available for exploitation after daylight. Countersign and challenge and identification marks on sleeve or helmet are necessary. Offensive grenades should be used. When discovered, open rapid fire and make as much noise as possible, while rushing in to use the bayonet.

m. The defense will consist of mutually supporting small groups arranged in depth and completely wired in. Mines will be placed.

n. All infantry officers must be able to observe and direct artillery fire.

3. *Artillery*

a. Sixty-five to seventy-five per cent of all artillery targets are provided by forward observers. The same percentage of tactical information originates with these observers, but much of the information of both characters the observers get comes from the infantry. Therefore, the forward observer must be in intimate association with the infantry. He must be under the control of the artillery liaison officer with the battalion. Artillery officers with infantry do not return to their batteries at night.

b. As soon as a position is captured, the forward observer must report through the liaison officer which of the possible channels of hostile counter-attack he is in a position to cover with observed fire. This information must go to the infantry battalion commander.

c. Observers must be able to operate both by day and night. Use any caliber of gun at any time to hit any target of opportunity. For this reason forward observers of large calibers must be up.

d. Artillery observers on their own initiative will bring fire on enemy weapons firing on our infantry. Infantry officers are equally responsible to call for such fire.

  e. Machine guns giving local protection to artillery must be sufficiently far out to prevent small-arms fire bothering the firing battery.

  f. Construct dummy batteries. In choosing sites for them, avoid places where fire directed at them will adversely affect other arms.

  g. Tank attacks can be stopped by artillery concentration of white phosphorus and high explosive.

  h. Artillery will be emplaced as far forward as possible and will move forward at every opportunity.

4. *Armor*

  a. The primary mission of armored units is the attacking of infantry and artillery. The enemy's rear is the happy hunting ground for armor. Use every means to get it there.

  b. The tactical and technical training of our armored units is correct. Added emphasis should be put on tank crew training with a view to hitting the enemy first.

  c. Against counter-attacks, the offensive use of armor striking the flank is decisive. Hence a deep penetration by infantry, whose rear is protected by armor, is feasible and safe.

  d. There is no such thing as "tank country" in a restrictive sense. Some types of country are better than others, but tanks have and can operate anywhere.

  e. The integrity of armored divisions should be preserved through the use of GHQ tank battalions for special, close supporting missions with infantry. On such missions, the tanks should advance by bounds, from cover to cover in rear of the infantry. They will only be exposed when the situation demands their intervention. In such cases they will attack in close association with the infantry.

5. *Reconnaissance*

  a. Reconnaissance, particularly on the part of the infantry, must be stressed, especially at night. It is necessary to secure information every night through the capture of prisoners and the observation of hostile actions. Good men must lead those patrols. Mechanized observation units should not be employed for security except in cases of dire emergency.

b. Junior officers of reconnaissance units must .be very inquisitive. Their reports must be accurate and factual. Negative information is as important as positive information. Information must be transmitted in the clear by radio and at once. The location of the unit giving the information should, where possible, be in a modified code. The enemy should be located by a magnetic azimuth and range from the point of observation. All members of a reconnaissance unit should know what they are trying to do. The results of all reconnaissance obtained in front of one division must be transmitted to adjacent units.

c. Reconnaissance must not lose contact. At night, when not in contact, listening posts should be at least six miles in front of our lines. Day reconnaissance must be pushed until contact is made. The use of light tanks in night reconnaissance usually induces the enemy to fire and display his position.

IV. AA AND ANTI-TANKS
    1. *AA*
       a. At least one, preferably self-propelled, AA weapon should be attached to each company or battery of artillery, infantry, or tanks. There should be two at Headquarters from the Division up. The 155 and larger guns should have at least two AA mounts per battery. Owing to our air superiority, AA should never open fire until attacked. AA is also good for anti-tank.
    2. *Anti-Tanks*
       a. Towed anti-tank guns should be well to the front and located to cover likely avenues of enemy tank approach. They must be emplaced so that they cannot see or be seen beyond their lethal anti-tank range. Self-propelled anti-tank weapons should be held in reserve to intervene

against enemy armored attacks. They should locate routes to and firing positions from probable sites of future activities. All anti-tank guns should be trained to fire as artillery and be provided with a large proportion of high-explosive shell.

V. Maintenance

1. Weapons will be kept in perfect order.

2. Preventive maintenance will be enforced. Particular attention should be given to tire pressure, lubrication, battery, voltage, water in radiators. Vehicles will be serviced and made operational before their crews rest. Vehicles will be marked in accordance with paragraph 6-14, A-R 850-5.

VI. Care of Men

1. Officers are responsible, not only for the conduct of their men in battle, but also for their health and contentment when not fighting. An officer must be the last man to take shelter from fire, and the first to move forward. Similarly, he must be the last man to look after his own comfort at the close of a march. He must see that his men are cared for. The officer must constantly interest himself in the rations of the men. He should know his men so well that any sign of sickness or nervous strain will be apparent to him, and he can take such action as may be necessary.

2. He must look after his men's feet, see that they have properly fitting shoes in good condition. That their socks fit—loose or tight socks make sore feet. He must anticipate change of weather and see that proper clothing and footgear is asked for and obtained.

3. Field and evacuation hospitals must be kept as close to the front as enemy fire permits. The shorter a haul of a wounded man to the hospital, the better his chances of recovery.

4. Hospitals should be placed in the open and clearly marked. Do not permit liaison planes or groups of vehicles to park near them. Such action gives the enemy an excuse for attacking.

5. The successful soldier wins his battles cheaply so far as his own casualties are concerned, but he must

remember that violent attacks, although costly at the time, save lives in the end. He must remember that replacements need special attention and see that they get acclimatized to their new units as quickly and harmoniously as possible.

/s/   G. S. PATTON, JR.
G. S. PATTON, JR.
Lt. General U.S. Army, Commanding

SECRET

HEADQUARTERS THIRD UNITED STATES ARMY
APO 403

25 September, 1944

SUBJECT: Letter of Instruction Number 4

To   : Corps Commanders and the Commanding General XIX Tactical Air Command

1. The acute supply situation confronting us has caused the Supreme Commander to direct that, until further orders, the Third Army, with its supporting troops, and those elements of the Ninth Army placed in the line, will assume the defensive.

2. It is evident that the successful accomplishment of this mission will require particular concentration upon two points:

   a. First, this change in attitude on our part must be completely concealed from the enemy, who, should he learn of it, would certainly move troops from our front to oppose other Allied Armies.

   b. Second, we must be in possession of a suitable line of departure so that we can move rapidly when the Supreme Commander directs us to resume the offensive.

3. In order to carry out the requirements of paragraph 2a, above, we will not dig in, wire, or mine, but will utilize a thin outpost zone backed at suitable places by powerful mobile reserves. We will further insure that all possible avenues of tank attacks are registered in by all batteries—Division, Corps, and Armies—whose guns can bear. Under the supervision of the Army Artillery Officer these zones of concentration will be numbered from north

to south and recorded on a uniform map to be distributed to the units concerned, so that fire may instantly be opened in any zone. Further, a copy of this map will be placed in the possession of the Commanding General of the XIX Tactical Air Command so that he may co-ordinate the concentration of planes upon any critical area in the most expeditious manner. Counter-attacks by our mobile reserves should be planned and executed to secure a double envelopment of the hostile effort with the purpose of not only defeating it but destroying it.

4. To insure our possessing a suitable line of departure for the future offensive, we shall secure the dotted line shown on the attached overlay by means of limited operations in consonance with our reduced scale of supply. To provide the necessary means for such limited operations, the utmost parsimony will be used in the expenditure of gasoline and ammunition consistent with the economy of the lives of our troops.

5. Wherever circumstances admit, troops not in the immediate presence of the enemy will be billeted. As soon as the troops so billeted have rested and been equipped, they will be given constant practice in offensive tactics.

6. The defensive instructions contained in this letter will not be circulated below the grade of General Officer.

7. In closing, I desire to again compliment all of you on the magnificent dash and skill which you have shown in the operation to date. We only await the signal to resume our career of conquest.

/s/ G. S. PATTON, JR.
G. S. PATTON, JR.
Lt. General U.S. Army Commanding

Appendix E

COMPOSITION OF AN ARMY

The composition of an Army is not clear to many people, and it may be of interest to many to give a brief résumé of its composition during a campaign.

An Army's aggregate total of men varies from one hundred thousand to three hundred thousand, depending upon the number of corps and divisions assigned to it. (These figures do not include supporting air units.) First, it must fight. Second, it must eat. Third, it must be capable of rapid movement. And last, but not least, it must be equipped with all essentials necessary to the accomplishment of its mission. In reality, an Army provides most of the necessities of life found in a community of equal size.

The Army Headquarters is made up of a Headquarters Company and some special troops to provide its own housekeeping, protection, and administration. Usually, three or four Corps Headquarters, similarly organized and equipped though much smaller, are assigned to an Army. In the Corps, there are infantry and armored divisions which do the fighting, and many supporting troops, which help them to accomplish their missions. The supporting troops are made up of fighting units; such as Cavalry, Artillery, Engineers, Anti-Aircraft Artillery, Tank Destroyer, and Chemical Warfare Units.

There are Military Police Units to enforce law and order and Medical Units to take care of the sick and wounded and to supervise the general health of the command. The Quartermaster handles the general supplies, such as gas, food, clothing, and so forth. The Transportation Corps hauls these supplies. Signal Units provide all types of communication, and the Engineers have many types of units which enable them to do anything from fighting the enemy and fires to building railroad bridges over rivers. Civil Affairs Detachments handle the civilian population in liberated and captured towns, and Special Service Units provide entertainment for all the troops. Several miscellaneous detachments, such as Secret Intelligence Units, Finance Units, Prisoner of War Interpreters, and the like, finish off the list.

Most of the units are complete with Transportation and Cooking Detachments. If not, they are assigned or attached to other units which have facilities to provide for them.

Appendix F

ROSTER OF PRINCIPAL STAFF OFFICERS

HEADQUARTERS THIRD U.S. ARMY

Chiefs of Staff: Major General Hugh J. Gaffey, April to December, 1944
Major General H. R. Gay, December, 1944, to end of war
Deputy Chief of Staff: Colonel Paul D. Harkins
Secretary, General Staff: Lieutenant Colonel G. R. Pfann
G-1: Colonel F. S. Matthews
G-2: Colonel O. W. Koch
G-2 Air: Colonel H. M. Forde
G-3: Brigadier General H. G. Maddox
G-4: Brigadier General W. J. Muller
G-5: Colonel N. W. Campanole; Colonel R. L. Dalferes
Adjutant General: Colonel R. E. Cummings
Anti-Aircraft: Colonel F. R. Chamberlain, Jr.; Colonel T. F. Gallagher
Artillery: Brigadier General E. T. Williams
Chaplain: Colonel T. H. O'Neill
CWS: Colonel E. C. Wallington
Engineers: Brigadier General J. F. Conklin
Finance: Colonel G. B. Milliken
Headquarters Commandant: Colonel R. C. Bratton
Inspector General: Colonel C. C. Park
JAG: Colonel C. E. Cheever
Medical Section: Brigadier General T. D. Hurley; Colonel T. J. Hartford
Ordnance: Colonel T. H. Nixon

Provost Marshal: Colonel J. C. MacDonald; Colonel P. C.
  Clayton
PRO: Lieutenant Colonel K. A. Hunter; Lieutenant
  Colonel J. T. Quirk
QM: Colonel Everett Busch
Signal: Colonel E. F. Hammond
SSO: Colonel K. E. Van Buskirk
Tank Destroyer: Brigadier General H. L. Earnest; Colonel
  L. C. Berry

XIX TACTICAL AIR COMMAND

Commander: Brigadier General O. P. Weyland
Chief of Staff: Colonel R. Q. Browne

Appendix G

CORPS THAT SERVED WITH THIRD ARMY
1 August, 1944, to 9 May, 1945

INCLUDING COMMANDERS AND CHIEFS OF STAFFS

VIII Corps: 1 August, 1944, to 5 September, 1944
21 December, 1944, to 22 April, 1945
Commander: Major General Troy H. Middleton
Chief of Staff. Brigadier General C. H. Searcy

XV Corps: 1 August, 1944, to 24 August, 1944
29 August, 1944, to 29 September, 1944
Commander: Lieutenant General Wade H. Haislip
Chief of Staff: Brigadier General Pearson Menoher

XII Corps: 1 August, 1944, to 9 May, 1945
Commanders: Major General Gilbert R. Cook
1 August, 1944, to 17 August, 1944
Major General Manton S. Eddy
17 August, 1944, to 20 April, 1945
Major General S. LeRoy Irwin
20 April, 1945, to 9 May, 1945
Chief of Staff: Brigadier General R. J. Canine

XX Corps: 1 August, 1944, to 9 May, 1945
Commander: Lieutenant General Walton H.
Walker
Chief of Staff: Brigadier General W. A.
Collier

III Corps: 31 October, 1944, to 11 February, 1945
18 April, 1945, to 9 May, 1945
Commanders: Major General John Millikin
31 October, 1944, to 11
February, 1945
Major General James A. Van
Fleet
18 April, 1945, to 9 May,
1945
Chief of Staff: Colonel James H. Phillips

V Corps: 6 May, 1945, to 9 May, 1945
Commander: Major General Clarence R.
Huebner
Chief of Staff: Colonel S. B. Mason

Appendix H

DIVISIONS THAT SERVED WITH THIRD ARMY
1 August, 1944 to 9 May 1945

INCLUDING COMMANDERS AND ASSISTANT DIVISION
COMMANDERS

DIVISION	COMMANDER	ASST. DIV. COMMANDER
1st Inf.	Maj. Gen. Clift Andrus	Brig. Gen. G. A. Taylor
2d Inf.	Maj. Gen. W. M. Robertson	Brig. Gen. J. A. Van Fleet
	Maj. Gen. R. O. Barton	Brig. Gen. J. H. Stokes, Jr.
4th Inf.	Maj. Gen. H. W. Blakeley	Brig. Gen. J. S. Rodwell
5th Inf.	Maj. Gen. S. Leroy Irwin	
	Maj. Gen. A. E. Brown	Brig. Gen. A. D. Warnock
8th Inf.	Maj. Gen. D. A. Stroh	Brig. Gen. C. D. W. Canham
26th Inf.	Maj. Gen. W. S. Paul	Brig. Gen. H. N. Hartness
28th Inf.	Maj. Gen. N. D. Cota	Brig. Gen. G. A. Davis
29th Inf.	Maj. Gen. C. H. Gerhardt	Brig. Gen. L. H. Watson
35th Inf.	Maj. Gen. P. W. Baade	Brig. Gen. E. B. Sebree
		Brig. Gen. B. B. Miltonberger
42d Inf.	Maj. Gen. H. J. Collins	Brig. Gen. H. Linden
65th Inf.	Maj. Gen. S. E. Reinhart	Brig. Gen. J. E. Copeland
69th Inf.	Maj. Gen. E. F. Rheinhardt	Brig. Gen. L. H. Gibbons
70th Inf.	Maj. Gen. A. J. Barnett	Brig. Gen. T. W. Herren
71st Inf.	Maj. Gen. W. G. Wyman	Brig. Gen. O. S. Rolfe
76th Inf.	Maj. Gen. W. R. Schmidt	Brig. Gen. F. A. Woolfley
79th Inf.	Maj. Gen. I. T. Wyche	Brig. Gen. F. U. Greer
		Brig. Gen. J. S. Winn, Jr.
80th Inf.	Maj. Gen. H. L. McBride	Brig. Gen. O. Summers
		Brig. Gen. G. W. Smythe
83d Inf.	Maj. Gen. R. C. Macon	Brig. Gen. C. B. Ferenbaugh
86th Inf.	Maj. Gen. H. M. Melasky	Brig. Gen. G. V. W. Pope
87th Inf.	Maj. Gen. F. L. Culin, Jr.	Brig. Gen. J. L. McKee
89th Inf.	Maj. Gen. T. D. Finley	Brig. Gen. J. N. Robinson
90th Inf.	Maj. Gen. R. S. McLain	Brig. Gen. W. G. Weaver
	Maj Gen. J. A. Van Fleet	Brig. Gen. J. M. Tully
	Maj. Gen. H. L. Earnest	

DIVISION	COMMANDER	ASST. DIV. COMMANDER
94th Inf.	Maj. Gen. H. J. Malony	Brig. Gen. H. B. Cheadle
95th Inf.	Maj. Gen. H. L. Twaddle	Brig. Gen. Don C. Faith
97th Inf.	Brig. Gen. M. B. Halsey	Brig. Gen. F. H. Partridge
99th Inf.	Maj. Gen. W. E. Lauer	Brig. Gen. H. T. Mayberry
4th Armored	Maj. Gen. J. S. Wood	Brig. Gen. W. L. Roberts
	Maj. Gen. H. J. Gaffey	
	Maj. Gen. W. H. Hoge	
5th Armored	Maj. Gen. L. E. Oliver	
6th Armored	Maj. Gen. R. W. Grow	Brig. Gen. G. W. Reed, Jr.
7th Armored	Maj. Gen. L. M. Silvester	
	Maj. Gen. R. W. Hasbrouck	
8th Armored	Maj. Gen. J. M. Devine	
9th Armored	Maj. Gen. J. W. Leonard	
10th Armored	Maj. Gen. W. H. H. Morris, Jr.	
11th Armored	Brig. Gen. C. S. Kilburn	
	Maj. Gen. H. E Dager	
12th Armored	Maj Gen. R. R. Allen	
13th Armored	Maj. Gen. J. B. Wogan	
	Maj. Gen. John Millikin	
14th Armored	Maj. Gen. A. C. Smith	
16th Armored	Brig. Gen. J. L. Pierce	
20th Armored	Maj. Gen. Orlando Ward	
17th Airborne	Maj. Gen. W. M. Miley	Brig. Gen. J. L. Whitelaw
101st Airborne	Maj. Gen. M. D. Taylor	Brig. Gen. G. L. Higgins
2d French Armored	Maj. Gen. LeClerc	

QUANTITY PURCHASES